PRAGMATISM, NATION, AND RACE

PRAGMATISM, NATION, AND RACE

Community in the Age of Empire

EDITED BY

Chad Kautzer

AND

Eduardo Mendieta

Indiana University Press

BLOOMINGTON AND INDIANAPOLIS

This book is a publication of

Indiana University Press
601 North Morton Street
Bloomington, IN 47404-3797 USA

http://iupress.indiana.edu

Telephone orders   800-842-6796
Fax orders   812-855-7931
Orders by e-mail   iuporder@indiana.edu

Manufactured in the United States of America

Library of Congress Cataloging-in-Publication Data

Pragmatism, nation, and race : community in the age of empire / edited by
    Chad Kautzer and Eduardo Mendieta.
        p. cm. — (American philosophy)
    Includes bibliographical references and index.
    ISBN 978-0-253-35311-5 (cloth : alk. paper)
    ISBN 978-0-253-22078-3 (pbk. : alk. paper) 1. Pragmatism. 2. Philosophy, American—20th
century. 3. United States—Social conditions—20th century. I. Kautzer, Chad. II. Mendieta,
Eduardo.
B944.P72.P735 2009
144'.30973—dc22

                                                                                    2008052937

1 2 3 4 5   14 13 12 11 10 09

Dedicated to Richard Rorty (1931–2007)

"The cost of empire is not properly tabulated in the dead and maimed, or in the wasted resources, but rather in the loss of our vitality as citizens. We have increasingly ceased to participate in the process of self-government. We have become ever more frustrated and fatalistic, and hence concerned with individual gratification. Finally, we deny any responsibility; and, as part of that ultimate abdication of our birthright, indignantly deny that the United States is or ever was an empire. But that is to deny our own history. We have transformed our imperial way of life from a culture that we built and benefited from into an abstract self-evident Law of Nature that we must now re-examine in light of its costs and consequences. It is, we shrug, simply the way of the world. Empire is freedom. Empire is liberty. Empire is security. We may well be doomed by our acceptance of the imperial dogma that democracy is dependent upon a surplus of space and resources. Our only chance is to talk straight to ourselves and to flinch."

William Appleman Williams, *Empire as a Way of Life*

CONTENTS

PART TWO

The Racial Nation

ACKNOWLEDGMENTS

This book would not have been possible without the support and encouragement of Kelly Oliver. While Kelly was Chair of the Philosophy Department at Stony Brook University, she provided the seed money to host the conference at which many of these papers were originally presented. We also want to thank Ann Kaplan, Director of the Humanities Institute, for her support and encouragement, and José Medina for his many insightful comments on the original manuscript. Dee Mortensen, our editor at Indiana University Press, took this project under her wing and raised it to its present quality. We are particularly grateful for her wisdom as well as that of John Stuhr, which guided us through many hurdles and editorial challenges.

Contributors who participated in the Stony Brook conference have been particularly gracious. They generously accepted the invitation to come and join us at Stony Brook without monetary reward and have been patient throughout the manuscript's long journey to publication. The papers by Jim Bohman, Max Pensky, and Mitch Aboulafia were originally presented at a panel at the annual meeting of the Society for Phenomenological and Existential Philosophy. They were expanded for inclusion in the book together with original essays by Shannon Sullivan and Robert B.

Westbrook. We are profoundly grateful to all of them for their trust and solicitude.

We also want to acknowledge Robert Brandom for granting us permission to reprint his essay on Louis Menand's *The Metaphysical Club*, and Cornel West, who granted Eduardo Mendieta the time to conduct a long interview, originally intended for this book. Chad Kautzer would also like to thank Manuel Schottmüller, Farnaz Shahshahani Far, Daniel Loick, and particularly Jenny Weyel for their friendship and hospitality during his stays in Frankfurt and Berlin, where much work on this volume was completed with generous financial support from the *Deutsche Akademische Austauschdienst* (DAAD) and the Max Kade Foundation.

Finally, a special thanks goes to Richard Rorty, who as always was very generous with his time. He gave the plenary lecture at the Stony Brook conference but also joined us for its entirety, eating with the graduate students and participating in the friendly banter that followed each paper. The paper he presented, and here included, went through several revisions, evidence that he was deeply worried about the subject matter of what was to be one of his last lectures. We are very saddened that he did not see this volume in print before his untimely death.

PRAGMATISM, NATION, AND RACE

Introduction:
Community in the Age of Empire

Chad Kautzer and Eduardo Mendieta

The recent revival of American pragmatism has, for the most part, been a retrieval wary of elision, involving a return not only to figures like George Herbert Mead, William James, Charles Sanders Peirce, and John Dewey, but to previously neglected pragmatists like W.E.B. Du Bois and Alain Locke, who placed the color line on the front line of democratic struggles. This retrieval could thus be seen as the beginning of a *reconstruction* of American pragmatism that seeks to fulfill the radical democratic promise of American Reconstruction. Yet not long into this process, the attacks of 9/11 pierced the social imaginary, rejuvenating American imperialism and its logic of racial supremacy and gentrification. A creative rethinking of the pragmatist tradition, intended to meet this new challenge to the democratic project (in both its actualities and potentialities), has thus become more urgent and more challenging as political hope becomes increasingly tempered and philosophical vision more circumscribed.

This anthology seeks to engage the relationship among the historical context, intellectual milieu, rational unfolding, and meta-narratives that gravitated around and framed both the emergence and resurgence of pragmatism. Our contributors investigate the political-philosophical status of community, democracy, and cosmopolitanism as well as the enduring legacy of racism and nationalism in American philosophy and cultural identity. The diversity of theoretical orientations brought to bear in this volume—from American Philosophy, Critical Theory, and Race Theory to American Studies, African American and Diaspora Studies, and Post-

Colonial Theory—provide a uniquely rich and informative engagement with several ongoing debates concerning the limits of solidarity and the possibility of cosmopolitanism, the role that race and ethnicity should play in American culture and identity, the problems implicit in the status of the United States as republic and empire, and whether early pragmatism's conciliatory, experimental disposition inevitably led to the Unionist compromise and subsequent oppressive ideologies after the Civil War. While the book has organized these debates around three thematic rubrics that guide the contributions and dialogue, each part inevitably overlaps with the others, producing a continuous and coherent, albeit polyphonic, dialogue throughout.

One possible way of talking about the emergence of pragmatism in the United States could be to refer simultaneously to the Civil War and the transformation of the United States into a fledging empire. The Civil War was and remains one of the most central events in the history of the United States. It stands on the same level as the Declaration of Independence and the revolutionary war at the end of the eighteenth century. In fact, the Civil War was a second founding of the nation. One may even argue that the Civil War provided the opportunity to establish the nation on a different foundation than the founding fathers had. Slavery was abolished, states unified, and the power of the Constitution as the supreme law of the land was reasserted. Above all, the creed of fundamental human equality was reaffirmed and given a more precise meaning. The Constitution was amended to reflect these expansive notions of human equality. The Civil War was the crucible in which a new constitution, and a new understanding of the Declaration of Independence, was forged. Louis Menand has suggested in his important intellectual history of pragmatism, *The Metaphysical Club,* that the Civil War conditioned the ways pragmatists thought about reason, belief, progress, and trust in the human ability to abolish forms of human cruelty and tyranny.[1]

Less than a decade later, the wounds of the Civil War not yet healed—and in fact, festering with the burning cross of racial supremacy—the United States began to renege on its commitment to racial equality. What the Civil War accomplished was to be overshadowed by the black codes of the post-Reconstruction period and almost rendered obsolete by the legal sanctions of Jim Crow offered by the Supreme Court's decision *Plessy v. Ferguson* (1896). At the same time that racial privilege and segregation are legalized and legislated, the United States is engaging in a process of imperial affirmation through the Caribbean and the Pacific Ocean. The Spanish-American War of 1898 will give way to U.S. colonial outposts from the Philippines and Guam to Cuba. Hawaii will be annexed for the same reason that Panama will become a geopolitical and geostrategic asset that the United States will covet and seek to control. What Max Boot has disingenuously called the "Little Wars" of the United States during the end of the nineteenth and the beginning of the twentieth century were both imperial and racial enterprises. A vast amount of scholarship has documented both the imperial trust and the overt racial tone of these enterprises. And even if the American literature produced during these decades did not, as Walter Benn Michaels has claimed, address imperialism directly, it did register its consequences as well as its opposition to them.[2]

Pragmatism as a form of social criticism as well as a form of philosophical analysis was pursued and developed in the shadow of these momentous historical events and processes. Indeed, one may boldly assert that if one cannot discuss Socrates without the Peloponnesian Wars, Hegel without Napoleon, Heidegger without Hitler, and Levinas without Auschwitz, one surely cannot discuss Charles Sanders Peirce, Josiah Royce, G. H. Mead, William James, and John Dewey without reference to both the Civil War and the emergence of the United States as an imperial power that will come of age during World War II. John Dewey himself noted in his essay "The Development of American Pragmatism": "They [the ideas that form pragmatism] do not aim to glorify the energy and love of action which the new conditions of American life exaggerated. They do not reflect the excessive mercantilism of American life. Without doubt all these traits of the environment have not been without a certain influence on American philosophical thought; *our philosophy would not be national or spontaneous if it were not subject to this influence.*"[3]

This is not to suggest that pragmatism can or should be reduced solely to these historical factors. The aim is rather to raise a fundamentally pragmatist question: If both the imperial project and the resistance to it shaped and colored American pragmatism, what are the practical consequences when we relate pragmatism to imperialism? Could we not associate pragmatism's experimentalism and futurism with the kind of entitlement granted by an imperialist mode of existence and experience? Is not imperialism a type of radical futurity that advocates the elimination of all barriers to what it claims it brings in its wake: progress, civilization, rights, and democracy? What is the relationship between Jackson Turner's announcing the closing of the American frontier in the 1890s and the end of a period in American history? For Turner, to claim and enclose the Western frontier defined what Dewey calls the glorification of "energy and the love of action" that American life so exaggerates. But this type of thinking may be excessive, for it smacks of conservatism and a visceral reaction to anything that celebrates innovation and the possibility of change. Indeed, the issue may not be about *what* future is possible, but about the *how* it is made possible.

That empire is one way to birth the future, and democracy another, is surely one of the background assumptions that critics of empire had in mind when they asked: Nation or empire? Democracy or empire? Republic or empire? Alternatively, it could be argued that we should perhaps stop talking about empire so long as we still have a democratically elected government. What use, as Dewey and Rorty ask, is there in talking about the national dilemma: empire or republic? Does attributing the label empire to the United States lead to quietism or to activism, to pessimism or optimism, to self-loathing or to a sense of incompleteness? What are the practical consequences to using these labels in the present context, in which neither international nor national public opinion serves as a constraint to the use of U.S. force in what some argue are unequivocal imperialist ways and for imperialist goals?

A narrative such as we have just described above is certainly only one of the possible ways to talk about pragmatism, as Richard Rorty himself has noted when he distinguished among four types of genres in the historiography of philosophy. For Rorty, the historiography of philosophy can benefit generously from an analysis of the historical milieu in which a particular figure or figures thought. These narratives, however, must be complemented by rational and historical reconstructions, *geistesgeschicht-lichen* meta-narratives, and indispensable, if suspect, doxographical accounts. Thus, one could also talk about pragmatism in terms of its relentless preoccupation with questions of truth, meaning, evidence, experience, fallibility, and language.

It should go without saying that pragmatism is perhaps a very recent name for very old forms of dealing with these seemingly insurmountable philosophical problems. Yet whether we approach pragmatism from the standpoint of either rational or historical reconstruction, we cannot neglect the centrality of the concept of *community* within this tradition. For pragmatism will inspect all of the central philosophemes on its ledger through the prism of community. For Peirce, community refers to a semiotic community—or community of communication, as Karl-Otto Apel will rename it—and a community of investigation. For Royce, community refers to the community of memory, or anamnestic community. For Mead, the community is a community of significant others, without whom there is no possibility of communication or moral consciousness. For Dewey, community refers to a public and a democratic community. In the work of neo-Pragmatists like Nancy Fraser, Richard Bernstein, Cornel West, and Richard Rorty, community is also a pivotal concept. For Fraser, community refers to the community of both recognition and redistribution in such a way that this community is both symbolic and material. For Bernstein, community is the practical context of interpretation as well as the horizon of normative expectations that allows for the rational adjudication of conflicting and competing claims. For West, community refers to the prophetic community, a combination of Royce's community of memory and Dewey's democratic community. For Rorty, community refers to the hermeneutical horizon from which we depart and to which we return when we seek to diminish cruelty by educating our moral imaginations through compelling narratives.

Community, in short, is the key word for pragmatism, just as dialectic is for Hegelianism, *differance* is for deconstruction, and *dispositif* is for Foucauldian genealogy. What has not been sufficiently underscored is that for pragmatism community was also an ideal, not just an analytical devise. Nor has it been sufficiently recognized that as an ideal, community in pragmatist thought served as a cipher for a critique of all that the United States was becoming as pragmatism itself developed into a distinctly U.S. philosophical tradition. For Mead and the Chicago pragmatists, as well as for Dewey and later for Fraser, Bernstein, West, and Rorty, community is the foundation for a critique of racism, class stratification, and imperialism.

The concept of community is both normative and descriptive. It also serves as a point of reference to other important questions that orient pragmatist thinking. Paul Kennedy noted with reference to nations in the context of globalization that they are both too small and too big. They are too big to address the needs of local communities, that is, communities with unique traditions and self-images. They are too small to deal with the problems that besiege all nations, and within them, their communities: global warming, migrations, unemployment, violence, new forms of communication, and fluctuations in global financial markets, to name just a few. The concept of community in pragmatist thinking suffers from a similar lack of size specification. One could ask of Dewey: Is community greater or smaller than a public? Is this public made up of all citizens, all voting citizens, all informed citizens, and all citizens that vote and those that can't because of Jim Crow, or punitive disenfranchisement as it is practiced today? Does the prophetic community in West include or exclude all those who are unabashed secularists? Does the community of redistribution in Fraser include so-called illegal aliens, and if so, does her notion of community stand above that of a community of citizens? What is the relationship between a moral community, in the broadest sense possible, and another community, which is internal to this, and whose identity is partly formed by the injury caused by larger community? Community has remained under-specified.

Here, however, we want to juxtapose empire and community so that we can begin to triangulate the limits of community but also the kinds of community that emerge or are forged, given either acquiescence or resistance to empire. If moral consciousness and civic engagement are enabled by community, what kinds of moral and political engagement are called for by an imperial ethos? Or conversely, as William Appleman Williams put it, if empire is a way of life, what kind of ethos does it instigate in our communities?[4]

Still another way to talk about pragmatism would be to talk about its re-emergence during the last few decades of the twentieth century. One way to describe those last two decades could be to say that with the fall of the Soviet Union, the one factor checking U.S. imperialism was removed. The floodgates were opened, and the imperial ambitions of the United States became brutally overt. Another way to describe those last decades of the twentieth century, but now from the perspective of philosophy, would be to describe the thawing of the so-called Continental-Analytic divide. Arguably, pragmatism was overshadowed by the emergence after World War II of analytic philosophy as the dominant form of doing philosophy. John McCumber's pioneering work on American philosophy during the Cold War argued that the rise of analytic philosophy to dominance had a lot to do with the silencing of philosophical dissent on the one hand, and the domestication of philosophy into a docile servant of techno-scientific university on the other.[5]

McCumber's provocative thesis notwithstanding, the re-emergence of pragmatism can be explained in terms of the internal development of these seemingly disparate forms of doing philosophy. If Analytic philosophy took its point of departure in the work of Frege, Wittgenstein, Russell, and Ayer, and Continental philosophy in the work of Hegel, Marx, Freud, Husserl, Heidegger, Sartre, and Derrida, there were philosophers already in the 1960s questioning the alleged incommensurability of Wittgenstein and Heidegger, Russell and Sartre. This was facilitated and instigated by pragmatism, or neo-pragmatism, most notably in the works of Richard Bernstein and Richard Rorty. But they were not alone: Ernst Tugendhat, Umberto Eco, Jacques Derrida, Karl-Otto Apel, Von Kempski, Jürgen Habermas, Hans Joas, Axel Honneth, and a host of other European philosophers began to take U.S. pragmatism very seriously. That was so once again because pragmatism was now seen, along with Marxism, existentialism, and phenomenology, as a legitimate and formidable response to the demise of the Hegelian edifice, as was first argued by Karl Löwith and later echoed by figures like Bernstein and Rorty.

Alternatively, the re-emergence of pragmatism can be explained in terms of the linguistic turn of philosophy, putatively heralded by Peirce,

Wittgenstein, and Heidegger. If philosophy was to abandon its Cartesian and Kantian solipsism and monologism, and take up its problems from the standpoint of language, then a pragmatist turn was ideal. For pragmatism, after all, had from its inception given a privileged role to language in its philosophizing. Indeed, it was Charles Sanders Peirce who first attempted a semiotic or linguistic transformation of Kantianism, and it was G. H. Mead who first gave an account of moral consciousness in terms of a linguistic model rather than in an epistemological construal of subjectivity. The linguistic turn of modern philosophy, in other words, came to be understood as both uncircumventable and already inchoate in the thinking of nineteenth- and early twentieth-century pragmatist philosophers. Some may want to argue a stronger version of this claim, namely, that the linguistic turn of twentieth-century philosophy was anticipated and catalyzed by the work of Charles Sanders Peirce and Josiah Royce long before Wittgenstein and Heidegger.

Again, such internal developments of philosophy, explainable in terms of conceptual and rational reconstruction, are indispensable but not sufficient. If philosophy is its time comprehended in thought, as Rorty frequently invokes, echoing Hegel, then we must return our gaze to the question of the historical milieu in which such resurgence and revival of pragmatism takes place. Undoubtedly, the end of the Cold War is central in this story, just as the Cold War was part of the story of the eclipse of pragmatism during the 1950s, 60s, and 70s. The new generation of pragmatists, the neo-pragmatists, came of age during another series of convulsive and momentous events in the history of the United States: the civil rights movement, a movement that sought to reclaim the ideals and institutions gained by and then lost after the Civil War; the women's movement, which affirmed the commitment to radical egalitarianism of the U.S. society; and then the student and youth movements of the late 1960s, which affirmed the Emersonian and Whitmanian romanticism of youth and inexhaustible renewal. All of these movements put on the agenda questions about the limits of community, the possibility of reconstructing community, the duties and rights of community, and finally, the relationship between community and empire.

In Part I of this volume, "Transformative Communities and Enlarged Loyalties," we have gathered together essays by Robert Brandom, David Kim, Max Pensky, Mitchell Aboulafia, and James Bohman. In the first two essays, a pragmatist methodology and vision of democracy is situated in the domestic context of conflict resolution and racial exclusion after the Civil War (Brandom), and the construction of American identity and community in the international context of U.S. racial imperialism (Kim).

The emergence of pragmatism is, for Brandom, the announcement of a second (pragmatist) enlightenment, which embraces experiential contingency and ontological fallibilism, and shifts its center of gravity from epistemology to semantics. In the context of a critique of Menand's *The Metaphysical Club*, Brandom employs this methodological understanding of pragmatism to assess the actual race politics of the early pragmatists and Menand's impressive genealogical analysis of them as well as his thesis that the Unionist compromise was a logical outcome of pragmatist thought. Brandom contests this logical entailment and the "structural irony" of Menand's ultimately unpragmatic, retrospective approach. As for the early pragmatists, Brandom argues in chapter 1 that their suspicion of ontological justifications of authority and naturalized conceptual categories made them well suited to see the "various ways in which the concept of race as embodied in ground-level practical politics (personal and institutional, as well as national) owed more to culture and social prejudice than to biology and adaptive fitness—to see it as a complex, inherently questionable product of contingent cultural significance and given biological fact." That said, excepting Dewey, "they did not rise to the occasion."

Kim, however, argues that Brandom does not go far enough, challenging his exception of Dewey, and walking us step-by-step through the development of an "Asia-hermeneutic" engendered by the influential experience of a racialized U.S. imperialism, particularly evident in Dewey's frontier thesis. Through a "metaphysics of the frontier," it is argued that Dewey inoculated himself with a notion of American innocence both domestically and internationally, inhibiting him from theorizing the human suffering, structural racism, and military imperialism that made possible post-Reconstruction American expansionism. Such an understanding of Dewey presents us with a greater challenge than more traditional criticisms of Dewey's "neglect" of race, for here race is viewed as a generative structural absence, a productive silence or quietism that fostered an intellectual atmosphere conducive for the Unionist compromise and U.S. imperial ambitions. Indeed, it is a motivating and even necessary challenge, for the very relevance of Deweyan pragmatism to a contemporary critique of, and engagement with, American racial imperialism is in question. "With the twentieth century behind us and still more racism and imperialism ahead of us," Kim writes in chapter 2, "we must expand the pressing issue that Brandom has raised and see that pragmatism's compromises have been far more disastrous than he or Menand have noted." Together, Brandom and Kim's investigations provide challenges as well as resources for a reconstructed pragmatism that can incorporate a conflicted past and reconceive the contours of democratic community.

The following three essays by Pensky, Aboulafia, and Bohman continue this investigation, elucidating the normative claims that memory has on community through a predominantly Meadean perspective and from the standpoint of two entwined problems. First, what are the boundaries of community, or rather, how are the boundaries of community drawn? Communities may be so broad as to overlap with nation, and so narrow as to be limited to one's family or ethnicity. Surely, community in either sense was not what pragmatists had in mind. Second, communities have a synchronic dimension: they exist now and they are amorphous but describable, if only with a broad Wittgensteinian brush, but they also have a diachronic dimension—they exist in a temporal continuum. What is the status of the temporality of communities in their normativity? Or to ask the question in a more pedestrian fashion: What normative consequences result from acknowledging that communities are also communities of solidarity and memory with the past, both its past and the past of other communities? If we use the language of Giles Gunn from his important book *Beyond Solidarity,* pragmatism was, from its inception, a philosophy that was both global and cosmopolitan.[6]

With Mead and Walter Benjamin, Pensky argues in his essay that the past is "incessantly novel"; and thus our relations to it, particularly through collective memory, are subject to reconstruction, transforming its significance and our identities. According to him, there are two understandings of collective memory that, although often conflated, should be distinguished. The first, largely descriptive social constructivist model, of which he gives David Kim's essay as an example, views the past as continually renegotiated by contemporary social and political practices, affording the possibility of disclosing, through reconceptualization, neglected experiences of past suffering and injustice. It is a critical memorial politics with normative intent. The second model is one of solidarity, which relies not on redescription but on the acknowledgement of unfulfilled obligations to the past, and which advocates contemporary practices to discharge such obligations through commemorative practices, new historiography, or restitution. While generally complementary, it seems possible that commitment to the solidarity model could constrain redescriptive practices of the social construction model, as opposition to Habermas's adherence to the solidarity model in the Historians' Debate of the 1980s demonstrates. Pensky argues, however, that we can find resources in Mead, particularly his concept of sociality, to understand and even reconcile this tension within an enlarged sense of community.

Aboulafia, however, questions whether Mead's cosmopolitanism can sufficiently address our responsibilities to past persons in the manner that Pensky suggests, particularly in the context of uninhibited nationalism and war. Noting a tension in Mead's social theory that seems to simultaneously contain a commitment to the universalism and reciprocity of discourse ethics, communitarian tendencies, and a theory of moral sentiments, Aboulafia asks which of these resources could help us to avoid the dehumanizing and objectifying tendencies of grand narratives and ideologies mobilized to engender conflict with the other. In general, Mead appears to offer up a dilemma: we are simultaneously presented with a universalism of abstract inclusiveness that potentially elides the particularity of human suffering, and a particularism of sympathetic identification that is potentially thwarted by our encounter with persons too different from ourselves. A solution, Aboulafia argues, is the cultivation of the habit of openness to novelty, which could mediate the universal and particular and keep us responsive to others' claims, past and present. Such a habit, together with the cumulative moral effect of experiencing ever more perspectives by becoming ever more cosmopolitan, is a valuable contribution toward actions that develop sympathy with the suffering and help us to avoid the generation of future conflict-related suffering.

Bohman incorporates several of the themes taken up by Pensky and Aboulafia in his effort to temporally expand his model of cosmopolitan deliberative democracy. We deliberate with, not just about, the past, argues Bohman, and thus we must attempt to decenter the prevalent presentist assumptions in public deliberation—just as we have already recognized the importance of the spatial decentering of deliberative publics—which preclude normative obligations to the past. To this end, he devises a Meadean approach to moral deliberation with past communities, with an eye to righting past wrongs within an expanded understanding of community (as Generalized Other) that is not temporally bound to present interlocutors. Temporal borders, like spatial ones, inhibit the recognition and fulfillment of obligations beyond one's present community and thus the self-understanding of democracies. "Any democracy that denies such obligations outside of its community does so at its own peril," concludes Bohman in chapter 5, "since to close its borders is very often accomplished at the price of its democracy within and peace without." All three essays attest to the way pragmatist thinking was and remains attuned to the problems raised by its times. Inasmuch as they address the role of memory in community, they are also major contributions to the specification and delimitation of the concept of community and bring American pragmatism into dialogue with the Frankfurt School tradition of critical theory.

In Part II, "The Racial Nation," we have gathered together essays by Lucius T. Outlaw Jr., Harvey Cormier, Tommie Shelby, and Shannon Sullivan that take up the question of race within the work of pragmatists such as Dewey, Du Bois, James, West, and Rorty as well as the *problématique* of the racialized origins of American democracy, pragmatist approaches to a black nationalist philosophy of culture, and the relation of prophetic pragmatism to the black church. The heterogeneity of approaches to the relationship between pragmatism and race in this section exhibits the richness of the tradition as well as the vexed relation between it and the persistent racism of contemporary American life.

Questions of black identity and culture were, of course, elided by early theorists of the American democratic experiment, argues Outlaw, most notably in Alexis de Tocqueville's *Democracy in America,* wherein the idea of American national identity was decidedly synonymous with white national identity. Black and Native American life in the early nineteenth century, while noted, was silenced by the social distance of an otherwise acute observer such as Tocqueville, who identified racial diversity as a threat to the stability of the democratic project and national identity. By identifying the white hermeneutic operative in Tocqueville's famous text, which is so influential in the construction of white America's self-understanding, Outlaw demystifies and rightly problematizes the powerful motif of American Providence and exceptionalism—a motif taken up within the American pragmatist tradition. While Tocqueville explicitly theorized national unity and character on a foundation of racial division, exclusion, and subjugation, Outlaw argues that Dewey implicitly drew from the same tainted well.

While Dewey is subject to probing, albeit often constructive, criticism on the place of race in American history and pragmatism throughout several essays in this anthology, Cormier advocates a positive reconstruction of William James's much neglected ideas on the subject. Indeed, it is argued that James put race at the center of his important discussion on the relation between the community, which he sometimes refers to as a "race," and the individual. James's musing on race are thus not only contextualized within the particularities of his criticisms of Herbert Spencer's racial determinism but also within a nineteenth-century understanding of race that is inextricably bound up with notions of community and nationhood, themselves constituted and continually subject to change, by free and innovative individuals. While James may not have dealt with the issue of race in terms palatable to us today, and while he did not take up race as a political problem, what he did say, concludes Cormier, was true and can productively contribute to debates about race in our time.

Shelby is concerned precisely with a contemporary pragmatic understanding of race—and, more specifically, with the coherence and usefulness of black cultural nationalism. In his essay he demonstrates the problems of a black nationalist doctrine—without denying specifically black forms of cultural life—in a world of overlapping cultural communities and globalization, where both historical origins and contemporary inter-actions defy the strictures of cultural authenticity. Rather than take up the specific doctrines of black nationalist advocates such as W. E. B. Du Bois, Alain Locke, Amiri Baraka, Harold Cruse, Maulana Karenga, Haki Mad-hubuti, or Molefi Asante, Shelby develops a kind of Weberian ideal type consisting of eight tenets that are then systematically subjected to scrutiny. Finding that each tenet exhibits both conceptual and normative diffi-culties, a pragmatic approach to more cosmopolitan cultural projects and black freedom struggles is advocated, particularly to those addressing so-cioeconomic inequality and unequal educational opportunities.

In the final essay of Part II, Sullivan takes up Richard Rorty's critique of Cornel West's prophet pragmatism, trying to reconcile how Rorty can take such a dismissive stance toward West but laud the prophetic pragma-tism of feminist philosophers such as Marilyn Frye. Is this asymmetrical position an instance of white privilege on Rorty's part? Sullivan argues that answering this question is more complicated than it might seem, for West's antiracist philosophy has a religious, particularly Christian, inflec-tion, and Rorty's "anemic" understanding of pragmatism dismisses reli-gion as a positive force or inspiration for political change. In particular, Sullivan argues that the supposed universalism of Rorty's public/private distinction conceals its inapplicability to the experiences of black slaves, their descendents, and the black church. In defense of West, Sullivan argues that religion can contribute to the kind of creative redescriptions and transformative possibilities that Rorty advocates without violating non-foundationalist pragmatic principles.

In Part III, "The Tragedy and Comedy of Empire," we have gathered together essays by Richard Rorty, Eduardo Mendieta, Robert Westbrook, and Cynthia Willett that discuss, both critically and positively, the rela-tionship among pragmatism, nationalism, empire, and war. The attacks of 9/11 have reinvigorated American chauvinism, while imperialism has ap-parently shaken off its publicly maligned past and rapidly gained credi-bility in an atmosphere of offended innocence. The labels of Republic and Superpower have given way to Empire and patriotism in the new "war on terror" has seemingly become a litmus test for determining membership in the American national identity.

Some neo-pragmatists, such as Richard Rorty, have condemned the messenger but provocatively condoned the message: U.S. interventionism and war in the name of democracy. Rorty argues in his essay that, like the Roman Republic, the U.S. is a corrupt plutocracy but a democratic repub-lic nonetheless. The reckless foreign policy of the Bush regime, he argues, is not an inevitable outcome of U.S. hegemony but rather a case of very bad luck; and those, such as Nikhil Pal Singh, who have embraced a "depressed and skeptical" view of the United States, must be challenged and confronted with a different narrative. The Emerson-Lincoln-Whitman-Dewey story of America that Rorty advocated in *Achieving our Country,* and that David Hollinger shares in his *Postethnic America,* is still the right one, now so more than ever.[7] Good leftist, pragmatist reformists must not only fight to achieve American ideals domestically, asserts Rorty, but attempt to spread them internationally. To be leftist is to be internationalist, and to be internationalist is to be interventionist: "There is a perfectly good leftist case for using the military power of democratic countries to conquer countries ruled by tyrants," argues Rorty in chapter 10, "and to replace them with democratic regimes."

Historically, however, war has functioned as much more than a mere means to foreign policy ends. In his essay, Mendieta argues that Josiah Royce and William James both sought to sublimate the domestic function of war—thought by Hegel and Steinmetz, for example, to contribute to the moral health of a nation through self-sacrifice and community solidarity —in very different, yet complementary ways. Mendieta demonstrates how Royce takes a two-pronged approach in his analysis of community, addressing both the inherent cosmopolitanism of loyalty and the structural nature of intercommunal conflict. According to Royce, it is a disastrous and reductive mistake to view the warrior spirit as engendering loyalty, as Steinmetz and others have done. Loyalty, for him, is the fulfillment of moral law, which is universal. Loyalty is indeed a *loyalty to loyalty,* insofar as loyalty entails the commitment to and furtherance of loyalty in others, a relation that cannot be circumscribed to particular groups and interests. Additionally, Royce identifies the structural danger that dyadic relations pose to communities. Developing a triadic understanding of communities of interpretation, he proposes institutional mechanisms, such as an international system of insurance, to embed triadic relations in the international sphere.

William James, again in response to Steinmetz's work, took a different route toward a similar goal. For James, the greatest enemy of nations dwells within them, and it is the civic virtue of those courageous individuals whose day-to-day struggles against parochial and antidemocratic forces embody a sublimation of the spiritual side of war that theorists like Steinmetz have primitively debased. In a timely critique of the "fear-regime," James argued that it is our fear of emancipation from fear that is our true enemy, not the fear of an external enemy. The struggle against this fear, which is the moral equivalent of war, is the civic virtue to be cultivated, recognized, and institutionalized. In his conclusion, Mendieta addresses the critique of the warrior spirit in contemporary neo-pragmatism, arguing that even those such as Rorty, who advocate U.S. interventionism, rightly recognize the internal antidemocratic threat that such external policies engender.

Pragmatism has not only developed an intimate relationship with the wars that have shaped the United States but has, to the dismay of many critics, seemingly contributed with great abandon and alacrity to their justification. Indeed, few could overlook the parallel between Rorty's call for a benevolent American empire and Dewey's support for U.S. entry into World War I. Not only did both become the subject of stinging criticism, but more importantly, both provoked the question of pragmatism's very relevance as a tool of social criticism and as a model for creative democracy—a question most poignantly and famously raised by Randolph Bourne in the case of Dewey. The imputation is that pragmatism's rejection of moral foundations and critique of all normative principles has made it into a philosophy of U.S. imperialism. Focusing in his essay on the recent debates about what has been called "the imperial presidency," Westbrook juxtaposes in chapter 12 the work of Richard Posner, whom he calls "the most powerful philosophical pragmatist in contemporary American life," with Bourne's earlier critique. Posner, a federal judge, has argued that the "constitution is not a suicide pact" that would tie the hands of the president or U.S. security agencies and thus offers a judicial justification for some of the anti-terrorist measures enacted by the Bush administration. In his analysis of Posner's debate with legal and activist scholar David Cole, Westbrook is sanguine enough to acknowledge that Posner offers genuinely pragmatist arguments and that Cole, who claims Posner to be unprincipled, does in fact argue like a pragmatist on the question of how to gauge the costs to civil liberties when constraining or abridging them for the sake of some incalculable and elusive security. Posner, argues Westbrook, is closer to the spirit of pragmatism than some would like to acknowledge; and in order to give warrant for this argument, Westbrook turns to the Bourne-Dewey exchange during World War I. In fact, Westbrook notes, it was Bourne and not Dewey who developed a pragmatist analysis and critique of U.S. entry into that war. In the end, Bourne and Posner exhibit what Westbrook takes to be central to both pragmatism and American democracy: its commitment to moral pluralism that argues in the mode of giving and taking reasons within a fractious but ecumenical public sphere. Not only is pragmatism not "unprincipled," but on the contrary, pragmatism exhibits the commitment to pluralism and the public use of reason within an open and democratic polity that is so distinctively American. As Westbrook writes, "Like it or not (and many still do not like it), pragmatism is a public philosophy well-suited to a fractious, quarrelsome people who nonetheless hope to remain politically one" (23).

In the final essay of Part III, Willet challenges interpretations of American imperialism such as those of Rorty, Michael Ignatieff, and John Lewis Gaddis that ascribe romantic and democratic themes of innocence to a long tradition of foreign policy dedicated to rather un-cosmopolitan U.S. economic and political interests. Such interests often result in subjugation, dispossession, systems of dependency, and the codification of racial hierarchies; while the moralizing rhetoric of U.S. exceptionalism is nothing new in the history of empires. Within this context, Willet examines the rise of postmodern consumerism after 9/11, in which self-sacrifice is marginalized by the call for hedonistic consumption, reflecting an economy of diminishing production but holding its own threat of feminization. The American antidote to such passivity has been the much more masculine, unrestrained image of the warrior-patriot, preemptively lashing out at will and hungry for power. Power, however, breeds hubris; and hubris has its own tragic trajectory, which Willet examines, drawing upon a long tradition of tragic-comic theorizing from Aristotle and Nietzsche to Martha Nussbaum and Toni Morrison. To repair the damage wrought by the imperial and tragic hubris, we would do well, concludes Willet, to turn to comic wisdom and a normative theory that supplants autonomy with a social eros as its normative axis, relying on the connectedness of friendship, community, and belonging that Morrison calls "home."

In the Appendix, we have an interview with Cornel West, conducted by Mendieta. Continuing Willet's discussion, West argues that the comic allows us to recognize our limitations, incongruities, and hypocrisies and still "smile through the darkness" that has made the future of a democratic politics more precarious today than at any time in recent memory. Throughout, West addresses many, if not most, of the themes discussed in all three parts of this volume, from the Unionist compromise, nationalism, the tensions between republicanism and imperialism, and patriotism, to black nationalism, the racial politics of incarceration, terrorism, American Christianity, and the future of the color line in American life. As always, West keeps a pragmatic eye on what have been the leitmotifs of his entire career: "the deepening of democracy and the dismantling of empire."

Notes

1. Louis Menand, *The Metaphysical Club: A Story of Ideas in America* (New York: Farrar, Straus, and Giroux, 2001).

2. Walter Benn Michaels, *Our America: Nativism, Modernism, and Pluralism* (Durham, N.C.: Duke University Press, 1995), 17.

3. John Dewey, *The Later Works 1925–1927* (Carbondale and Edwardsville: Southern Illinois University, 1988), 2:19; emphasis added.

4. William Appleman Williams, *Empire as a Way of Life: An Essay on the Causes and Character of America's Present Predicament, Along with a Few Thoughts about an Alternative* (New York: Oxford University Press, 1980).

5. John McCumber, *Time in the Ditch: American Philosophy and the McCarthy Era* (Evanston, Ill.: Northwestern University Press, 2001).

6. Giles Gunn, *Beyond Solidarity: Pragmatism and Difference in a Globalized World* (Chicago: University of Chicago Press, 2001).

7. Richard Rorty, *Achieving Our Country: Leftist Thought in Twentieth-Century America* (Cambridge, Mass.: Harvard University Press, 1999); David A. Hollinger, *Postethnic America: Beyond Multiculturalism,* rev. ed. (New York: Basic Books, 2000).

PART ONE

Transformative Communities and Enlarged Loyalties

ONE

When Philosophy Paints Its Blue on Gray: Irony and the Pragmatist Enlightenment

Robert Brandom

1. A Second Enlightenment

Classical American pragmatism can be viewed as a minor parochial philosophical movement that was theoretically derivative and practically and politically inconsequential. From this point of view—roughly that of Bertrand Russell and Martin Heidegger (Mandarins speaking for two quite different philosophical cultures)—it is an American echo, in the last part of the nineteenth century, of the British utilitarianism of the first part. What is echoed is a crass shopkeeper's sensibility that sees everything through the reductive lenses of comparative profit and loss. Jeremy Bentham and John Stuart Mill had sought a secular basis for moral, political, and social theory in the bluff bourgeois bookkeeping habits of the competitive egoist, for whom the form of a reason for action is an answer to the question "What's in it for me?" William James and John Dewey then show up as adopting this conception of practical reason and extending it to the theoretical sphere of epistemology, semantics, and the philosophy of mind. Rationality in general appears as instrumental intelligence: a generalized capacity for getting what one wants. From this point of view, the truth is what works; knowledge is a species of the useful; mind and language are tools. The instinctive materialism and anti-intellectualism of uncultivated common sense is given refined expression in the form of a philosophical theory.

The utilitarian project of founding morality on instrumental reason is notoriously subject to serious objections, both in principle and in practice. But it is rightfully seen as the progenitor of contemporary rational choice theory, which required only the development of the powerful mathematical tools of modern decision theory and game theory to emerge (for better or worse) as a dominant conceptual framework in the social sciences. Nothing comparable can be said about the subsequent influence of the pragmatists' extension of instrumentalism to the theoretical realm. In American philosophy, the heyday of Dewey quickly gave way to the heyday of Rudolf Carnap, and the analytic philosophy to which Carnap's logical empiricism gave birth supplanted and largely swept away its predecessor. Although pragmatism has some prominent contemporary heirs and advocates—most notably, perhaps, Richard Rorty and Hilary Putnam— there are not many contemporary American philosophers working on the central topics of truth, meaning, and knowledge who would cite pragmatism as a central influence in their thinking.

But classical American pragmatism can also be seen differently, as a movement of world historical significance—as the announcement, commencement, and first formulation of the fighting faith of a second enlightenment. For the pragmatists, like their Enlightenment predecessors, reason is the sovereign force in human life. And for the later *philosophes,* as for the earlier, reason in that capacity is to be understood on the model provided by the forms of understanding distinctive of the natural sciences. But the sciences of the late nineteenth century, from which the pragmatists took their cue, were very different from those that animated the first enlightenment. The philosophical picture that emerged of the rational creatures who pursue and develop that sort of understanding of their surroundings was accordingly also different.

Understanding and *explanation* are coordinate concepts. Explanation is a kind of *saying:* making claims that render something intelligible. It is a way of engendering understanding by essentially discursive means. There are, of course, different literary approaches to the problem of achieving this end, different strategies for doing so. But there are also different operative conceptions of what counts as doing it—that is, of what one needs to do to have done it. It is a change of the latter sort (bringing in its train, of course, a change of the former sort) that the pragmatists pursue. For the original Enlightenment, explaining a phenomenon (occurrence, state of affairs, process) is showing why what *actually* happened *had* to happen that way, why what is actual is (conditionally) *necessary.* By contrast, for the new pragmatist enlightenment, it is possible to explain what remains, and is acknowledged, as *contingent.* That kind of understanding whose paradigm is Newton's physics consists of universal, necessary, eternal principles, expressed in the abstract, impersonal language of pure mathematics. That kind of understanding whose paradigm is Darwin's biology is a concrete, situated narrative of local, contingent, mutable, practical, reciprocal accommodations of particular creatures and habitats. Again, the nineteenth century was "the statistical century," which saw the advent of new forms of explanation in natural and social sciences. In place of deducing what happens from exceptionless laws, these forms of explanation put a form of intelligibility that consists in showing what made the events *probable*. Accounts in terms both of natural selection and of statistical likelihood show how observed order can arise contingently, but explicably, out of chaos—as the cumulative diachronic and synchronic result, respectively, of individually random occurrences.

The mathematical laws articulating the basic order of the universe were, for enlightened thinkers of the seventeenth and eighteenth centuries, the ultimate given, the foundational unexplainable explainers, structural features of things so basic that this explanatory residue might even (as it did for the transitionally post-religious Deists) require and so justify a final minimal, carefully circumscribed nostalgic appeal to the Creator. Charles Sanders Peirce, the founding genius of American pragmatism, elaborated from the new selectional and statistical forms of scientific theory a philosophical vision that sees even the laws of physics as contingently emerging by selectional processes from primordial indeterminateness. They are *adaptational habits,* each of which is, in a statistical sense, relatively stable and robust in the environment provided by the rest. The old forms of scientific explanation then appear as special limiting cases of the new. The now-restricted validity of appeal to laws and universal principles is explicable against the wider background provided by the new scientific paradigms of how regularity can arise out of and be sustained by variability. What Hegel calls the "calm realm of laws" of the first enlightenment becomes for the second a dynamic population of habits, winnowed from a larger one, which has so far escaped extinction by maintaining a more or less fragile collective self-reproductive equilibrium. It is not just that we cannot be sure that we have got the principles right. For the correct principles and laws may themselves change. The pragmatists endorse a kind of *ontological fallibilism* or *mutabilism*. Since laws emerge only statistically, they may change. No Darwinian adaptation is final, for the environment it is adapting to may change—indeed *must* eventually change, in response to *other* Darwinian adaptations. And the relatively settled, fixed properties of things, their *habits,* as Peirce and Dewey would say, are themselves to be understood just as such adaptations. The pragmatists were naturalists, but they saw themselves confronting a new sort of nature, a nature that is fluid, stochastic, exhibiting regularities that are the statistical product of many particular contingent interactions between things and their ever-changing environments, hence emergent and potentially evanescent, floating statistically on a sea of chaos.

The science to which this later enlightenment looked for its inspiration had changed since that of the earlier in more than just the conceptual resources that it offered to its philosophical interpreters and admirers. In the seventeenth and eighteenth centuries, the impact of science was still largely a matter of its *theories*. Its devotees dreamed of, predicted, and planned for great social and political transformations that they saw the insights of the new science as prefiguring and preparing. But during this period, those new ways of thinking were largely devoid of practical consequences. They were manifestations, rather than motors, of the rising tide of modernity. By the middle of the nineteenth century, though, technology, the practical arm of science, had changed the world radically and irrevocably through the Industrial Revolution. From the vantage point of established industrial capitalism, science appeared as the most spectacularly successful social institution of the previous two hundred years because it had become not only a *practice* but a *business*. Its practical successes paraded as the warrant of its claims to theoretical insight. Technology *embodies* understanding. The more general philosophical lessons the pragmatists drew from science for an understanding of the nature of reason and its central role in human life accordingly sought to comprehend intellectual understanding as an aspect of effective agency, to situate knowing *that* (some claim is true) in the larger field of knowing *how* (to do something). The sort of explicit reason that can be codified in principles appears as just one, often dispensable, expression of the sort of implicit intelligence that can be exhibited in skillful, because experienced, practice —flexible, adaptable habit that has emerged in a particular environment by selection via a learning process.

Like their Enlightenment ancestors, the pragmatists were not only resolutely naturalist in their ontology but also broadly empiricist in their epistemology. For both groups, science is the measure of all things—of those that are, that they are, and of those that are not, that they are not. And for both, science is not just *one* sort of knowing, but its very form: what it knows not is not knowledge. But in place of the atomistic, sensationalist empiricism of the older scientism (which was later rescued and resuscitated by the application of powerful modern mathematical and logical techniques to yield twentieth-century logical empiricism), the pragmatists substituted a more holistic, less reductive practical empiricism. Both varieties give pride of place to *experience* in explaining the content and rationality of knowledge and agency. But their understandings of that concept are very different, corresponding to the different characters of the science of their times.

The older empiricism thought of the unit of experience as self-contained, self-intimating events: episodes that constitute knowings just in virtue of their brute occurrence. These primordial acts of awareness are then taken to be available to provide the raw materials that make any sort of learning possible (paradigmatically, by association and abstraction). By contrast to this notion of experience as *Erlebnis,* the pragmatists (having learned the lesson from Hegel) conceive experience as *Erfahrung.* For them, the unit of experience is a Test–Operate–Test–Exit cycle of perception, action, and further perception of the results of the action. On this model, experience is not an *input* to the process of learning. Experience *is* the process of learning: the statistical emergence by selection of behavioral variants that survive and become habits insofar as they are, in company with their fellows, adaptive in the environments in which they are successively and successfully exercised. (This is the sense of "experience," as Dewey says, in which the job ad specifies "Three years of experience necessary.") The rationality of science is best epitomized, not in the occasion of the theorist's sudden intellectual glimpse of some aspect of the true structure of reality, but in the process by which the skilled practitioner coaxes usable observations by experimental intervention, crafts theories by inferential postulation and extrapolation, and dynamically works out a more or less stable but always evolving accommodation between the provisional results of those two enterprises. The distinctive pragmatist shift in imagery for the mind is not from mirror to lamp but from telescope and microscope to flywheel governor.

These new forms of naturalism and empiricism, updated so as to be responsive to the changed character and circumstances of nineteenth-century science, meshed with each other far better than their predecessors had. Early modern philosophers notoriously had trouble fitting human knowledge and agency into its mechanist, materialist version of the natural world. A Cartesian chasm opened up between the activity of the theorist, whose understanding consists in the manipulation of algebraic symbolic representings, and what is thereby understood: the extended geometrical world represented by those symbols. Understanding, discovering, and acting on principles exhibited for them one sort of intelligibility, while matter moving according to eternal, ineluctable laws exhibited another.

On the pragmatist understanding, however, knower and known are alike explicable by appeal to the same general mechanisms that bring order out of chaos, settled habit from random variation: the statistical selective structure shared by processes of evolution and of learning. That structure ties together all the members of a great continuum of being stretching from the processes by which physical regularities emerge, through those by which the organic evolves locally and temporarily stable forms, through the learning processes by which the animate acquire locally and temporarily adaptive habits, to the intelligence of the untutored common sense of ordinary language users, and ultimately to the methodology of the scientific theorist—which is just the explicit systematic refinement of the implicit unsystematic, but nonetheless intelligent, procedures characteristic of everyday practical life. For the first time, the rational practices embodying the paradigmatic sort of reason exercised by scientists understanding natural processes become visible as continuous with, and intelligible in just the same terms as, the physical processes paradigmatic of what is understood. This unified vision stands at the center of the pragmatists' second enlightenment.

A number of these master ideas of classical American pragmatism evidently echo themes introduced and pursued by earlier romantic critics of the first enlightenment. Pragmatism and romanticism both reject spectator theories of knowledge, according to which the mind knows best when it interferes least and is most passive, merely reflecting the real. Knowledge is seen rather as an aspect of agency, a kind of doing. Making, not finding, is the genus of human involvement with the world. They share a suspicion of laws, formulas, and deduction. Abstract principle is hollow unless rooted in and expressive of concrete practice. Reality is revealed in the first instance by lived experience in the life world. Scientific practice and the theories it produces cannot be understood apart from their relation to their origin in the skillful attunements of everyday life. Pragmatists and romantics accordingly agree in rejecting universality as a hallmark of understanding. Essential features of our basic local, temporary, contextualized cognitive engagements with things are leached out in their occasional universalized products. Both see necessity as exceptional and as intelligible only against the background of the massive contingency of human life. Both emphasize biology over physics and see in the concept of the *organic* conceptual resources to heal the dualistic wound inflicted by the heedless use of an overly sharp distinction between mind and world. Whereas the European Enlightenment had seen the "natural light of reason" as *universal* in the sense of *shared,* or *common,* so that what one disinterested, selfless scientist could add as a brick to the edifice of knowledge, another could in principle do as well, the pragmatists, looking at the division of labor in what had become a modern industrial economy, saw the enterprise of reason as *social* in a more genuine, articulated, *ecological* sense, in which individuals do not make contributions that are interchangeable or fungible, but each has a potentially unique contribution to make to the common enterprise, which requires many different sorts of skills, responses, ideas, and assessments that all collectively serve as the environment in which each develops, adapts, and evolves. Here, too, they made common cause with the romantics on some general issues, while offering their own distinctive blend of rationalism, naturalism, and Darwinian-statistical scientism as a way of filling in those approaches.

Nonetheless, pragmatism is not a kind of romanticism. Though the two movements of thought share an antipathy to Enlightenment intellectualism, pragmatism does not recoil into the rejection of reason, into the privileging of feeling over thought, intuition over experience, or art over science. Pragmatism offers a conception of reason that is practical rather than intellectual, expressed in intelligent doings rather than abstract sayings. Flexibility and adaptability are its hallmarks rather than mastery of unchanging universal principles. It is the reason of Odysseus rather than of Plato. But both are thought of as part of the natural world—in the sense in which natural science is acknowledged to have final authority over claims about nature. The pragmatists are also materialists—though theirs is Darwinian rather than Newtonian materialism. Evolutionary natural history aside, the biology that inspires them is the result of the shift of attention (largely effected in Germany in the first half of the nineteenth century) from anatomy to physiology, from structure to function. The climate of German romanticism may have provided an encouraging environment for this development, but the vitalistic biology that provided their organic metaphors was by then only an embarrassing prescientific precursor of the recognizably modern sort of biology pursued in the German laboratories in which James trained.

In fact, romanticism had almost no direct influence on American pragmatism—another point of contrast with the various forms of nineteenth-century materialism in Europe. There was an indirect influence, through Hegel's idealism (which was particularly important for Peirce and Dewey), but Hegel's rationalism mattered as much for them as his romanticism. The Transcendentalism of Ralph Waldo Emerson is another conduit for idiosyncratically filtered and transfigured romantic ideas. It was pervasive, though perhaps not dominant, in the Boston milieu in which Peirce, James, and Oliver Wendell Holmes Jr. (who was a pragmatist, even though he disavowed the label because he associated it with James's "sentimental" attempt to find a place for religion in the modern worldview) were first acculturated, and it clearly affected their thought in complex ways. But the pragmatists thought of themselves as continuing the Enlightenment philosophical tradition of Descartes, Locke, Hume, and Kant—all of whom thought that being a philosopher meant being a philosopher of *science*, understanding above all what the new science had to teach us not only about the world but about us as knowers of it. The advances of nineteenth-century science were to provide the corrective needed to remedy the conceptual pathologies to which the giants of the

Enlightenment had fallen prey. Those advances, properly understood, would make it possible to reconcile its central rationalist and materialist impulses in an irenic empiricist naturalism. Although pursuing some elements of the anti-Enlightenment agenda of romanticism by quite other means, the pragmatists always thought of themselves as offering friendly amendments in support of the basic philosophical mission of rethinking inherited ideas of rationality, understanding, agency, and self in the light of the very best contemporary scientific understanding of the natural world.

2. An Ironic Story of Ideas in America

Pragmatism was a distinctively American movement of thought in ways far more important than its immunity to romantic impulses, however. We have recently been taught just how much it owes to the peculiarities of its native cultural and historical soil by a magnificent book: Louis Menand's *The Metaphysical Club: A Story of Ideas in America.*[1] It is a vast, sprawling account of the origins of pragmatism in the insular social milieu of Brahmin Boston and of the personalities, institutions, issues, and events that shaped its later course as it broke out of those confines. Many of the luminaries of late nineteenth-century American thought and culture play a role in Menand's story, introduced by deft and often fascinating thumbnail sketches. The way the same characters crisscross through the narrative, encountering each other again and again in different circumstances and with different effects is one of the joys of reading the book. It is one of the principal ways that the thick determinate texture of the culture being discussed is conveyed. In Menand's hands, the discussion of pragmatism opens up a window on this vanished world that illuminates features of our own in often unsuspected ways. It is entirely appropriate that its cover illustration literally wraps the book in an American flag—indeed, the Fort Sumter battle flag. This is a book not only about American ideas but about an idea of America. If Menand is right, the pragmatists' *semantics,* their theory of meaning and contentfulness, should be understood in large part in terms of politics—in the sense of practices of or strategies for the collective resolution of potentially incompatible practical commitments.

There are four main characters in the story: Peirce, James, Holmes, and Dewey. The last three were among the foremost public intellectuals in the America of their time. The one who was not, Charles Sanders Peirce, brilliant, spoiled, and aloof, was by far the deepest, most original, and most rigorous thinker of the group. He was one of the best philosophical logicians of his time. Perhaps his greatest achievement is his development of formal ways of expressing the inferential significance of complex sentences involving iterated quantifiers—the breakthrough that marks the first decisive advance in logic since Aristotle and the beginning of modern mathematical logic. His discovery was independent of that of the German, Gottlob Frege, from whom Russell learned about quantifiers and on which he based *Principia Mathematica*. Peirce's work in the philosophy of language, especially semiotics, was also seminal; and it is interesting to compare it with the very different approaches of logical atomists such as Russell and the early Ludwig Wittgenstein at around the same time. Peirce's work in the philosophy of science was several generations ahead of its time. His excommunication from academia—he was blackballed from professional employment and forbidden to so much as set foot on the Harvard campus—seems to have been the result, not of his financial fecklessness or even of his abusiveness (he almost certainly beat his wife and servants), but of the intersection of his extramarital affairs with his first wife's powerful family connections in Boston. He was a great philosopher, but he was also an arrogant prick. His unreliable personal habits and the catastrophic shape of his professional career kept him from ever pulling his work together into a single book. Apart from some crystalline, very influential early essays, most of what we have from him is in the form of notes and unfinished sketches of philosophical systems. Philosophers have been unearthing jewels in this treasure trove for generations, and there is no sign that the mine is playing out. In the end, though, the intellectual riches of his work must be thought of primarily in terms of the raw materials they provided, and still provide, for others.

William James popularized the pragmatism he learned from Peirce and remains its most vivid spokesman. The son of a famous Swedenborgian religious enthusiast and moral theorist, and the brother of the novelist Henry James, the young Irish American found his way to Harvard from a stratum of Boston society somewhat removed from the academic aristocracy into which Peirce was born and from the social and financial aristocracy of the Holmeses. Psychologically prone to debilitating depressions and extreme indecisiveness, he wended an extremely circuitous path to his final vocation of philosophy. Trying out a variety of courses of study, including accompanying Louis Agassiz on a collecting expedition to South America, he completed his training in medicine, then moved through physiology to the scientific psychology of which he is one of the American founders. (The building at Harvard that houses the psychology department is named for him.) Unlike his fellow Bostonian pragmatists, he was tormented by his lack of traditional religious faith—his inability firmly to endorse even the relatively relaxed metaphysical credos of the Unitarians, who formed a significant bloc at Harvard. Pragmatist ideas gave him a nonmetaphysical, naturalistic way of thinking about norms, including moral ones. He embraced pragmatism's shift of attention away from the *justification* of belief, upstream of action, to its *consequences*, downstream, as a personally liberating salvation. As he saw it, his investigations into the concepts of meaning and truth held out the promise of making intelligible the nature of practical assessments of conduct in terms of *semantics* rather than *metaphysics* and thereby finding a place for moral considerations in a scientific, post-religious world. Finishing the work of the Enlightenment was for him a personal crusade.

Oliver Wendell Holmes was the dominant legal thinker of his generation, transforming American jurisprudence by applying pragmatist ideas. A hero of the Civil War who found his ideas tested and transformed by his battlefield experiences as a young man, he was, by the end of his long career, the magisterial sage of the U.S. Supreme Court. Like Peirce and James, Holmes was man with a Father. Their personal histories are in no small part structured by their struggles to emerge from the shadows cast by their fathers' fame. While Peirce seems to have remained on uncharacteristically good terms with his father (lamenting only that his father taught him his own intellectual virtues without seeing that he needed also to be taught moral ones), and James internalized his disputes with Henry Sr., Holmes engaged in more open battles with the aptly self-named "Autocrat of the Breakfast Table," Oliver Wendell Holmes Senior, poet, novelist, and dean of the Harvard medical school, whose attitudes, values, and habits of thought were very much those of a patrician of the old prescientific, more socially homogeneous order of Boston high society—what he called "the Hub" (that is, of the cultural universe). Although they did not overlap as undergraduates at Harvard, Holmes was James's best friend for a period after the war. Like Peirce and James, Holmes was an admirer of Chauncey Wright, the brilliant, doomed "Cambridge Socrates," who resembled his namesake in being a talker rather than a writer but who also has some claim to being the original font from which pragmatism flowed. The historical episode Menand uses as a hook on which to hang his narrative is the meetings Peirce, James, and Holmes held in 1872, calling themselves the "Metaphysical Club." Almost nothing is known about what was actually said at those meetings, but Menand is surely right to see in them the birth of pragmatism as a distinguishable current of thought.

Dewey is in many ways the odd man out in this quartet. He did not go to Harvard and was not only not raised in Boston but never lived or worked there. The cultural influences he was subjected to growing up in his native Vermont were quite different from the hothouse of Transcendentalism and Unitarianism in Boston. He was not a member of the Metaphysical Club. Belonging to a younger generation, he was not personally affected by the Civil War. He never knew any of the others very well.

His greatest personal influence was his exceptionally devout mother, not his father. Perhaps for that reason, his sweet, generous, equable, and irenic temperament presents a striking contrast to the power and wildness of Peirce, the indecisive torments of James, and the autocratic complacency of Holmes. (The most violent expression of emotion Menand can catch Dewey in is his saying that Russell's repeated mischaracterization of pragmatism, even after his errors had been pointed out to him, "makes me sore.") Dewey was the only one of the four who sailed smoothly through a lifetime of employment as a university philosophy professor. Nonetheless, no history of pragmatism and its ideas can omit discussing him, and Menand's does not. It was Dewey who gave the pragmatist movement its most public voice, who applied its theoretical understanding of intelligence as in the first instance practical, experimental, situated, and problem-oriented to transforming the theory and practice of education in America. Above all, it was Dewey who made pragmatism a primary intellectual force in articulating the theory of political liberalism in the years between the world wars.

The pragmatists themselves tended to situate and motivate their views by reference to the specifically philosophical tradition. They were, after all (with the exception of Holmes), at least at some point in their careers, professional philosophers (in Peirce's case, a chronically *unemployed* professional philosopher—but the point remains). Their interpreters, also professional philosophers, have generally followed them in this practice. Menand's great achievement is to widen the cultural focus and increase the depth of field of the scene in which they show up for us. He is very good on the scientific background: both the new ideas the pragmatists adapted for their own use and the older modes of thought against which they reacted. His extended account of the thought, career, and personality of Louis Agassiz, aggressive and successful champion of the older pre-Darwinian natural history of Georges Cuvier, is particularly illuminating in this regard. And his account of the role played by the Peirces (both Charles and his famous and influential Harvard astronomer-mathematician father, Benjamin) in the sensational forgery trial of millionairess Hetty Green (known later as the "witch of Wall Street") is at once a marvelously entertaining set piece and genuinely revelatory of the importance, difficulty, and equivocal public status of the nascent statistical modes of scientific thought they displayed on this very public forensic stage.

But the context Menand provides extends far beyond the sort of philosophical and scientific considerations sketched by way of introduction above. He shows how much more there is to the history of ideas than just their intellectual history. The rise of mass democracy, the ascendancy of industrial capitalism, the institutional professionalization of university education and the high culture more generally, and the decentralization and shift of the cultural center of gravity of the country away from its original seat in Boston are all shown to so shape the development of pragmatism as to stamp it indelibly as a specifically American phenomenon. Menand deftly portrays the relations between these grand historical forces and the particularities, peculiarities, and personalities of the idea-empowered pragmatists who are his heroes. A principal limb of his argument concerns the significance of the experience of the Civil War on the birth and growth of pragmatism.

Northern politics before the war was driven by the disagreement between Abolitionists and Unionists. Abolitionists saw slavery in terms of absolute moral principles: Slavery was evil, so the country had to pay whatever price was required to eliminate it—including, if necessary, splitting the South off so as to keep the Union pure. The Unionists, by contrast, acknowledged slavery as an evil but urged that means be found to eliminate it more gradually, over a period of decades, so as to acknowledge the economic and cultural interests of white Southerners and keep the Union whole. The South's secession rendered the Unionists' arguments moot by uniting both parties as patriots of the Union. The attack on Fort Sumter made unavoidable a war that the bulk of the Abolitionists, no less than the Unionists, had neither anticipated nor desired. The horrific violence that ensued changed forever the thinking of the young generation of Harvard men who went off idealistically to fight. Holmes, who had been a staunch Abolitionist, was severely wounded more than once. James was not a combatant, but two of his younger brothers were, and one of them was seriously wounded. Peirce, like the others, had friends and classmates maimed and killed.

The men of the Metaphysical Club saw the Civil War as above all a colossal failure of American democracy. The democratic institutions on which we pride ourselves had proven themselves incapable of dealing with the high-stakes moral and economic issue of slavery. Politically unresolvable disputes degenerated into military conflict. Holmes, closest to the fighting, was also the most explicit about the lessons he drew from his experience and about their effect on the lifelong course of his thought. As Menand puts it, "The lesson Holmes took home from the war can be put in a sentence. It is that certitude leads to violence" (61). But Menand also makes a persuasive case that roughly the same dynamic moved the other founding members of the Metaphysical Club to draw the same general conclusion. What had choked democracy was inflexible, uncompromising commitment to principles. What was needed was a different attitude toward our beliefs: a less ideologically confident, more tentative and critical attitude, one that would treat them as the always-provisional results of inquiry to date, as subject to experimental test and revision in the light of new evidence and experience, and as permanently liable to obsolescence due to altered circumstances, shifting contexts, or changes of interest. Though the point is not put this way in the book, we are to see the American Civil War as playing a role in shaping the pragmatist enlightenment comparable to that played by the wars of religion for the earlier European Enlightenment.

Menand makes a cumulatively plausible case for how the climate of ideas in which pragmatism arose was shaped by the experience of passionate political convictions that overwhelmed democratic institutions and led with seeming inevitability to the sort of senseless slaughter Holmes experienced (and happened to survive) at Ball's Bluff, Antietam, and the Bloody Angle of Spotsylvania. But he is not very clear about just what sort of connection he envisages between this historical impetus and the contents of the philosophical theories the pragmatists came to hold. A number of issues need to be separated, for it could be that while pragmatism would not have arisen without the influence of the war, that merely necessary condition is of little help in understanding the thought to which it gave rise. After all, one of the crucial material conditions that made possible jazz—another distinctively American cultural phenomenon—was the flood of cheap, war-surplus trumpets and military band instruments left over from the same war. But knowing that won't tell one much about what makes the music special.

To begin with, the view that immediately emerges from consideration of the failure of antebellum (more-or-less) democratic political practices concerns *how one holds* basic, action-orienting beliefs. What rules out compromise, accommodation, and reciprocal adaptation is the sort of unshakable conviction that brooks no opposition, admits no qualification, ignores the possibility or significance of collision with other important principles, and is reckless of the practical consequences of its absolutism for the possibly worthy aims of others and the stability of the framework institutions of the community. But the pragmatists didn't just draw conclusions about the act of believ*ing*—roughly, that fallibilism is a better attitude than fanaticism. The centerpiece of their philosophical theory was an account of the *contents* that are believ*ed* or are believ*able*. To squeeze the most explanatory juice out of Menand's fascinating and instructive story, we need to know something about how an understanding of the act or attitude of believing might be thought to connect with and inform an understanding of the contents of those acts or attitudes. Again, even at the level of how beliefs should be held, the immediate lesson seems to concern *political* beliefs: the ones we use to orient our *practical* undertakings, in particular those that involve *cooperation* or decisions about what *we* all shall do. It is not obvious that considerations bearing on our assessment of admissible, desirable, or defensible features of such practical political commitments carry over to apply as well to theoretical and doxastic commitments—from claims about what *we should do* to claims about how *things are* in the natural world.

I'll say something in the next section of this essay about how one might make these connections and so fill in the philosophical lacunae in the story. Before passing to that task, however, it is worth pausing to remark on an interesting irony integral to Menand's methodology. The pragmatists' master idea about belief is that the contents of even our most abstract and theoretical beliefs are to be understood ultimately in terms of the *practical consequences* that would ensue from holding them in various circumstances. The contents of beliefs are to be understood, not in terms of the principles and premises from which they can be deduced or the evidence for them that might be adduced, but of what difference holding those beliefs would make to what one goes on to *do*. It is their role as *premises* of pieces of practical reasoning, not their role as *conclusions* of pieces of deductive or inductive theoretical reasoning, that makes them mean what they do. To understand a thought, one looks to later practical effects, not to earlier causal antecedents.

Now the account of the origins of pragmatism in reaction to the horrors of the Civil War is by no means the only string to Menand's explanatory bow. It is but one aspect of a multifaceted and multifarious story involving other intellectual movements, the transformation and growth of academic institutions, the rise and fall of social and economic classes, the interplay of complex personalities, and much more. Indeed, it is to his credit that he does not show us only those elements of the mix that directly move an argument forward. The purpose of the narrative is broad enlightenment and understanding rather than narrow establishment of a thesis. In the spirit of the pragmatists he evidently admires, Menand treats the lessons he has learned as provisional and revisable, and he is willing to have his readers draw different conclusions from the evidence he marshals. But the character of his account is resolutely *retrospective*. He follows the intellectual historian's credo epitomized by Hegel in the preface of his *Philosophy of Right*: "Philosophy always comes too late. . . . As the thought of the world, it appears only when actuality is already there finished, after its process of formation has been completed. . . . When philosophy paints its gray in gray, a form of life has already grown old, and by philosophy's gray in gray it cannot be rejuvenated, but only understood. The owl of Minerva flies only at dusk."[2] Menand tells us about the intellectual, political, social, cultural, and institutional *antecedents* of pragmatism, about the ideas, events, personalities, and forces that provided the context in which it developed. And he is wonderfully successful. His engaging, inspiring, and informative book beautifully conveys a distinctive sort of contextualizing understanding. Even philosophical specialists in pragmatism will find their horizons broadened and their understanding deepened. But what we come to understand, we do by looking *backward,* at its sources, at the reasons and causes that conditioned and elicited pragmatism, rather than *forward,* to its consequences. The intelligibility on offer is genealogical. Menand's book tells us so much about pragmatism precisely because its methodology is profoundly unpragmatist. This is the structural irony at the core of its approach.

3. Pragmatist Semantics

At the end of his preface, Menand warns us that his book is not intended to present or discuss the philosophical views of the American pragmatists in any detail. It is a work of intellectual and cultural history, meant rather to place those thinkers in a larger context. He is by and large content to offer negative characterizations of their thought by sketching the ideas, presumptions, and institutions they were reacting against. (The static, rigidly hierarchical comparative anatomy pursued by Agassiz is an index example.) Beyond that, his specifications are formal and methodological: the pragmatists were fallibilists, skeptical about inherited theories and institutions, recommending a flexible, open, experimental attitude not only inspired by but contiguous with that of the newly revolutionized natural sciences, and so on. That is all true and important, but the compelling story he tells about their origins and larger cultural surround should make us care about the ideas themselves, as well. The pragmatists were carrying forward a great sea change in the core areas of theoretical philosophy that had begun with Kant. It was a shift from epistemology to semantics, from problems concerning *knowledge* to problems concerning *meaning* or contentfulness generally. Where Descartes and the other early modern philosophers had taken for granted the intentionality or representational purport of ideas—their at least seeming to be *about* things—and had asked only after the conditions under which we could be confident of their *success* in that enterprise, after Kant the great issue became how to understand the very *possibility* of thought pointing beyond itself by normatively answering for its correctness to how it is with the things that thereby count as the *objects* of thought. It is important to appreciate the distinctive constellation of ideas the pragmatists contributed to this enterprise.

Consider the issue raised above. If, as Menand persuasively argues, the pragmatists' ideas were in fact motivated by the spectacle of abstract, absolute political principles proving indigestible by democratic institutions and leading to the most violent sort of conflict resolution imaginable, aren't they guilty of illegitimately extending a lesson appropriate to the practical sphere of deciding what we ought to do to the theoretical sphere of deciding what beliefs are true? Here is a way one might think about such a move. In the practical sphere of morality, the European Enlightenment had taught us that we need not think of our moral principles as deriving their authority from their conformity to (mirroring of) an antecedent, eternal, nonhuman ontological (theological) reality. We could and should instead think of them as products of our own rational activity —as something for which we must ourselves ultimately take responsibility. As Kant put the point in "What Is Enlightenment?" it is by acknowledging that responsibility that humanity passes from its age of self-imposed tutelage by paternal authority into the autonomous maturity of its adulthood. A second enlightenment might then repeat that lesson, only now on the theoretical side. Doing that would be seeing norms for belief, no less than for action, as our doing and our responsibility, as not needing to reflect the authority of an alien, nonhuman Reality that comes to seem as mythical, dispensable, and ultimately juvenile a conception as Old Nobodaddy came to seem to the *érudits*. Richard Rorty, inspired by Dewey and James, has been urging just such a conception of what would be required to finish the work of the first enlightenment.[3] He argues that the move from thinking of moral norms in terms of divine commandments to thinking of them in terms of social compacts should be followed by a move from thinking of the truth of belief in terms of correspondence with reality to thinking of it in terms of agreement with our fellows.

Such a conception is vulnerable to the charge that in so assimilating the theoretical to the practical, the distinction between intentions and beliefs is being elided. Intentions have a world-to-mind direction of fit: the aim is for the world to conform to our attitudes. Beliefs have a mind-to-world direction of fit: the aim is for our attitudes to conform to the world. (In her classic work *Intention*,[4] G. E. M. Anscombe illustrates the difference with a parable of a man shopping from a list, who is followed by a detective assigned to write on his own list everything the man buys. The two lists exhibit the two different directions of fit. If what is bought doesn't match what is on the lists, in the first case the error lies in what is bought, and in the second it lies in what is written.) The first enlightenment can then be seen as liberating us from inappropriate use of a theoretical, spectatorial model of the practical—as though our reasoning about what we ought to do should, like our reasoning about how we ought to believe things are, reflect an antecedent reality whose authority settles its correctness. The old picture used the wrong direction of fit for practical matters.

But surely it would be a misunderstanding of this lesson simply to turn the old picture on its head by treating the theoretical as though it had the direction of fit, and so the structure of authority and responsibility, appropriate to the practical.

But the pragmatists don't do that. They reject the dualism of a practical sphere with just one direction of fit and a theoretical sphere with just the complementary one. They start with the idea of a cyclical process of intervening and learning, of perception of an initial situation, action in it, and perception of the result, leading to new action (including the tweaking both of means and goals), with the loop repeated until it converges or is abandoned. This is what they call "experience." Talk of belief and intention makes sense for them only as the abstraction of phases or aspects from such a process. Our beliefs have practical consequences, and our intentions have theoretical conditions. In the undertaking of actual inquiries and practical projects, one does not find one direction of fit without the other. At this level, the pragmatists are not modeling the theoretical on the practical as the tradition had conceived those categories but are reconceptualizing both in terms of ecological-adaptational processes of interaction of organism and environment of the sort epitomized by evolution and learning.

What about the other charge invited by Menand's characterization of their views, that they slide from a view about *how* beliefs should be held (tentatively, provisionally, negotiably) to a view about *what* beliefs are (something like practical coping strategies)—from an insight into the attitude of believ*ing* to a claim about the contents believ*ed*? Once again, the pragmatists (in keeping with the Hegelian roots of Peirce's and Dewey's thought) seek to reconceptualize belief and meaning so as to resist a dualism of force and content, doing and thought, pragmatics and semantics. Their strategy may be thought of as coming in two pieces. First, believing or knowing *that* things are thus and so (the category of explicit, statable, theoretical attitudes characteristic of us) is to be understood in terms of skillful knowing *how* to do something (the category of implicit, enactable, practical capacities characteristic of our intelligent but not rational mammalian cousins and ancestors). Their question concerns what you have to be able to *do* in order to count as having conceptually contentful beliefs. And their answer will look to the role of those beliefs in practical reasoning, to their capacity to serve as reasons for action. For their second move is to offer a kind of *functionalism* about the propositional contents of beliefs, an account of *meaning* in terms of *use*. The contents of beliefs and the meanings of sentences are to be understood in terms of the roles they play in processes of intelligent reciprocal adaptation of organism and environment in which inquiry and goal pursuit are inextricably intertwined aspects. Functionalist (and most recently, teleosemantic) strategies in the philosophy of mind dominate the second half of the twentieth century. But the pragmatists deserve to be thought of as having pioneered them.

If that is not generally recognized, it is in part because the pragmatists did not achieve the sort of clarity of methodological self-consciousness that would have allowed them to separate the general strategy of functionalism about the relations between pragmatics and semantics (what is done with words and what they mean, or the role of beliefs in the behavioral economies of believers and the contents of those beliefs) from the specific conceptual tactics they employed to pursue that strategy. And there are some real problems with their ideas at this more specific level. For they offer an *instrumentalist* semantics, understanding content in terms of *success* conditions rather than *truth* conditions. This is not a silly idea. But after a century of intensive subsequent work in philosophical semantics, we are in a position to be much clearer about the criteria of adequacy such accounts must answer to and some of the sorts of ways they can go wrong. From this contemporary vantage point, we can see that the pragmatists' instrumentalist program involves four distinct mistakes.

First, in thinking about the functional role of belief in reciprocal interactions and attunements between believers and their environments, the pragmatists look only *down*stream, to the practical *consequences* of beliefs. That is to say that they look only at the role of beliefs as *premises* in practical inferences. They don't also look *up*stream, to the *antecedents* of belief, to their role as *conclusions* of inferences, or as the results of other processes of belief formation. In this regard, they simply invert the exclusive emphasis on the origin of belief in experience characteristic of the semantics of traditional empiricism. But each of these one-sided approaches to semantics leaves out the crucial complementary aspect of the functional role of beliefs. For whether one thinks of the role of belief as a node in a network of matter-of-factual *causal* relations, or of normative *inferential* ones—corresponding to two flavors of functionalism—one must look both to antecedents *and* to consequences. The meaning conferred on an expression by its role in a language game can be identified with the pair of its circumstances of appropriate application, specifying when it is properly uttered, and its appropriate consequences of application, specifying what properly follows from its utterance.[5] Neither one by itself will do, for sentences can have the same circumstances of application and different consequences of application, or the same consequences of application and different circumstances of application. In either case, they will have different meanings. As an example of the first kind, we could regiment the use of *foresee*, so that the sentence "I foresee that I will write a book about Hegel" is appropriately asserted (the belief it expresses appropriately acquired) in just the same circumstances as "I will write a book about Hegel." But they have different meanings, for different things follow from them, as is clear if we think about the very different status of the two conditionals: "If I will write a book about Hegel, then I will write a book about Hegel" and "If I foresee that I will write a book about Hegel, then I will write a book about Hegel." The first, stuttering, inference is as secure as could well be. The truth of the second depends on how good I am at foreseeing (and whether I am hit by a bus). To see the second point, notice that one could know what follows from the claim that someone is responsible for an action, or that the action is immoral or sinful, without for that reason counting as understanding the claims or concepts in question (grasping the meaning of the words), if one knew nothing at all about the circumstances in which it was appropriate to make those claims or apply those concepts. Empiricist, verificationist, reliabilist, and assertibilist semantic theories are defective because they ignore the consequences of application of expressions in favor of their circumstances of application. Pragmatist semantic theories are defective because they make the complementary mistake of ignoring the circumstances in favor of the consequences. In fact, both aspects are essential to meaning.

The second mistake the pragmatists make is to look only at the role of beliefs in justifying or producing *actions*. But their role in justifying or producing further *beliefs* is equally important in articulating their content, and there is no good reason to think that the latter can be reduced to, or fully explained in terms of, the former. Trying to define the contents of internal states just in terms of relations to *outputs* (even—taking on board the previous point—in terms of outputs and inputs) to the system is a broadly *behaviorist* strategy. And one of the things we have learned by chewing these things over in the last forty years or so is that taking into account also the relations of internal states to each other yields a much more powerful and plausible account. This is precisely the surplus explanatory value of functionalism over behaviorism in the philosophy of mind. Though the general considerations that motivate the pragmatists' approach are recognizably functionalist, when it came to working out their ideas, the pragmatists did so in behaviorist terms because the various distinctions and considerations in the vicinity had not yet been sorted out.

Even if these two difficulties with the pragmatists' instrumentalist semantics are put aside, they face a third. For in seeking to move from (the success or failure of) *actions* to the contents of *beliefs*, they were ignoring the necessary third component in the equation: *desires, preferences, goals,* or *norms*. Your action of closing your umbrella underwrites the attribution of a belief that it has stopped raining only against the background of the assumption that you desire to stay dry. If instead you have the Gene Kelly desire to sing and dance in the rain, the significance of that action for a characterization of the content of your belief will be quite different. And the point is fully general. What actions beliefs rationalize or produce depends on what desires, aims, or pro-attitudes they are conjoined with.[6] The conditions of the success of our actions depend on what we want just as much as they do on what we believe. Contemporary rational choice theory incorporates this insight. Coupling this fundamental observation with the insight that the semantic contents of beliefs and desires are also and equally up for grabs (contrary to the rational choice approach, which takes these for granted as inputs to its process) leads Donald Davidson to his sophisticated interpretivist successor to narrowly pragmatist approaches to semantics. It is clear in retrospect that without some such structural emendation, the pragmatist strategy cannot work.

The fourth problem is intimately connected with the third. For although the pragmatists failed to appreciate the significance of the fact that desires can vary independently of beliefs, they did not simply ignore desires. Rather, they equated the success of actions with the satisfaction of desires and wanted to attribute to the beliefs that conduced to satisfaction, and hence to success, a special desirable property: their successor notion to the classical concept of *truth.* In their sense, true beliefs were those that conduced to the satisfaction of desires. But the notion of desire and its satisfaction required by their explanatory strategy is fatally equivocal. It runs together immediate inclination and conceptually articulated commitment in just the way Wilfrid Sellars criticizes, for beliefs rather than desires, under the rubric "the Myth of the Given."[7] For on the one hand, desires are thought of as things like itches and thirst. One can tell whether desires in this sense are satisfied just by having them. If one is no longer moved to do something, the desire is satisfied. If—bracketing the previous point—one could infer from the success of an action in satisfying a desire in this sense to the truth of a belief, the pragmatist semantic strategy would be sound. The idea is to make that transition by exploiting the role of beliefs and desires in practical reasoning: in inferences leading to the formation of intentions and the performance of actions. But the desires that, along with beliefs, play a role in rationalizing actions are not like itches and thirst. They have the same sort of conceptually explicit propositional contents that beliefs do. I can't tell just by having raw feelings whether my desire that the ball go through the hoop is satisfied—never mind my desire that the engineering problem has been solved or that the chances of achieving world peace have been increased. For finding out whether desires of that sort have been satisfied is just finding out whether various claims are *true:* that the ball has gone through the hoop, that the engineering problem has been solved, or that the chances of achieving world peace have been increased. Satisfaction of the sorts of desires that are elements of *reasons* for actions gives us no immediate, nonconceptual point of entry into the conceptual realm of contents of beliefs. The *only* reason to think that explanatory ground is gained by starting with satisfaction of desires (success of actions) in attempting to explain the truth of beliefs—that is, the only reason to pursue the instrumental strategy in semantics—is that one has conflated the two sorts of desire. For what is needed to make it work is something that is like an itch, in that one can tell whether it has been scratched without needing to decide what is true, *and* like a conceptually articulated desire, in that it combines inferentially with propositionally contentful beliefs to yield reasons for action. But nothing can do both.[8] The traditional early modern conception of *experience* as *Erlebnis* wanted to have it both ways. (This difficulty is orthogonal to those caused by eliding what Sellars called "the notorious 'ing'/'ed' distinction" between acts of experienc*ing* and the contents experienc*ed*.) It is just at this point that dispositional-causal and inferential-normative functionalisms part company. The challenge behind calling *givenness* a myth is a question Kant taught us to ask: Does the experience (or whatever) merely *incline* one (dispositionally)? Or does it *justify* one in making a claim, drawing a conclusion?

From our privileged vantage point a century or more later, then, we can see that the pragmatists' instrumentalist semantic strategy for explaining *credenda* in terms of *agenda,* and so their theory of meaning and truth, is fundamentally flawed. This is, of course, not to say that they didn't have any good ideas, or that they didn't make any progress, or that we don't still have something to learn from them. I think we also know by now that the semantic strategy of the logical empiricism that succeeded pragmatism in American academic philosophy is unworkable and that its conceptions of meaning and truth are also wrong. The point is that forging, from the insights of either, a theory that fares better by the contemporary standards that were achieved with great effort in no small part by criticizing those earlier attempts will require substantial selection, supplementation, and reconstrual.

It is a useful exercise to divide the pragmatists' motivations and conceptual responses to those motivations into two categories: large, orienting, strategic commitments; and the more local, executive, tactical ones. (Example of the genre: Descartes's ontological semantics generically divides the world into representings and representeds. He then filled in that picture with a theory of representings as immediately self-intimating episodes, and of representeds as extended and moving. Even given that way of setting things up, it is a nice question whether to treat the fact that his paradigm of the representing/represented relation is the relation between discursive algebraic equations and the extended geometrical figures they specify in his algebraic coordinate geometry as a generic, framing commitment or as part of the filling-in of such a picture.) My criticisms primarily address the latter: the more detailed ways in which the pragmatists try to entitle themselves to the more sweeping framework commitments. Those framing commitments—the ones I take it they seek to entitle themselves to by doing the more detailed work—are by and large admirable.

Among the large features of the pragmatists' thought that I take to be progressive are these:

- They were Darwinian, evolutionary naturalists, aiming to reconstrue the world, us, and our knowledge of the world in the terms made available by the novel explanatory structures characteristic of the best new science of their time.
- In the service of a renovated empiricism to go methodologically with that naturalism in ontology, they developed a concept of *experience* as *Erfahrung* rather than *Erlebnis:* as situated, embodied, transactional, and structured as *learning,* a process rather than a state or episode. Its slogan might be "No experience without experiment." Representing and intervening were for them two sides of one conceptual coin—or less imagistically, reciprocally sense-dependent concepts concerning aspects of processes exhibiting the selectional, adaptational structure common to evolution and learning.
- They appreciated the explanatory priority of *semantic* over *epistemological* issues, which had been one of Kant's great lessons. So they sought to understand *content* in terms of experience (as they construed it), that is, in terms of the role in learning, rejecting an orienting goal thought of as achievement of *knowledge* as a static, permanent state, in favor of thinking of it as a dynamic process of *adaptation.*
- They understood the *normative* character of semantic concepts: that they must underwrite assessments of correctness and incorrectness, truth and falsity, success and failure. The semantic instrumentalism criticized above is the more specific strategy the pragmatists adopted in their attempt to give a naturalistic account of this normative dimension of semantic concepts.
- In semantics, they tried to develop nonmagical, indeed, scientific theories of content, in contrast to "ideas" theories, which are constructively responsive to skeptical worries about the *success* of ideas' reference to things in the world—intentionality—but not about

referential *purport.* The pragmatists tried to figure out what it is we *do*—something continuous with what preconceptual critters can do—that adds up to *thinking* or *knowing* something, even *unsuc-cessfully.* They were broadly *functionalists* in thinking about the contents of the concepts that articulate intentional states, looking to the role the contentful states play in the whole synchronic, de-veloping behavioral economy of an organism in order to under-stand the concepts they involve.

- While reason and the sort of intelligence that ultimately issues in scientific theories and technologies are given pride of place in their picture of us, they move decisively beyond the intellectualism and Platonism that had plagued the first enlightenment, by privileg-ing practical knowing-how over theoretical knowing-that in their order of explanation.

At this level of very general explanatory strategy, what one misses most in the pragmatists—at any rate, what most separates them from us— is that they do not share the distinctively twentieth-century philosophical concern with *language,* and with the *dis*continuities with nature that it establishes and enforces. The dominant philosophical lineages of the cen-tury are soaked in a sense of the centrality of language: both the Husserl-Heidegger-Gadamer line and the structuralist-poststructuralist lines that come together in Derrida, on the one hand, and the Frege-Russell line that goes through Carnap to Sellars, Quine, and Davidson, and to Wittgenstein and Dummett on the other. This is partly because of the pragmatists' assimilationism about the conceptual: their emphasizing *continuities* be-tween concept users and organic nature. That emphasis, too, has good credentials; and I think it is fair to say that even now we have not yet sorted out the tensions between naturalistic assimilationism and normative ex-ceptionalism about the discursive practices most distinctive of us. But I also take it that the philosophical way forward from the ideas of the American pragmatists must be a *linguistic* pragmatism, allied with the later Wittgenstein and the Heidegger of Division One of *Being and Time.*

4. A Political Problem for Pragmatism

At the end of section 2, I pointed out an ironic structural feature of Menand's (and any similar) explanatory enterprise directed at pragma-tism. The view he is explaining understands the meaning of a state or event by looking forward to its effects and consequences. But he makes sense of it by looking backward, to its causes and premises. Since then, by looking at semantics a little more closely in section 3, we have seen that the consequential and genealogical approaches to meaning can be seen as complementary rather than competing. Each is one-sided on its own, but together they specify the circumstances and consequences that a more adequate semantics sees as both essential aspects of meaning or significance. Indeed, by including both the noninferential circumstances of application of concepts in perception and the noninferential consequences of application of concepts in action, one gets the transactional sense of "experience" as *Erfahrung*, as a process of attunement of organism and environment through practical learning, which represents the pragmatists' best philosophical wisdom. This is the positive philosophical lesson of that structural irony.

Nonetheless, on either account, practical consequences matter to meaning. Menand closes his book with a *political* assessment of the prospects of pragmatism. He thinks that though pragmatism suffered during the Cold War, because "The Cold War was a war over principles . . . [,] [t]he notion that the values of the free society for which the Cold War was waged were contingent, relative, fallible constructions, good for some purposes and not so good for others, was not a notion compatible with the moral imperatives of the age. . . . And once the Cold War ended, the ideas of Holmes, James, Peirce, and Dewey reemerged as suddenly as they had been eclipsed" (442). Menand in effect endorses the pragmatists' view that reason (like democracy itself) should be seen as consisting in *procedure* rather than *substance*—that what matters is how a (local, temporary, provisional) result is arrived at, and what its consequences are, rather than its form (in particular, the form of universal and immutable principles). Besides the *philosophical* question raised by a genealogical account of the *experience*, in the pragmatists' favored sense, of their consequentialist, instrumentalist semantic theories, however, there is also a *political* question Menand's story raises. For he assembles all the raw materials needed to formulate another serious question about the practical political consequences and effects of the pragmatists' theories.

An important strand running through Menand's story—one that underscores once again the distinctively American character of the context and experience that gave rise to and shaped pragmatism—concerns *race*. Racial issues come up at a number of points in Menand's recounting of the social, cultural, and institutional antecedents and vicissitudes of the pragmatists and their ideas. And, as he points out, race is theoretically intricated with the advent of Darwinian natural history, which was appealed to in justifying various practical political attitudes, and with the pragmatists' own adaptation and generalization of Darwin. And once the issue has been raised by political practice, thinking in terms of the structures common to evolution and learning highlights the question of whether to treat

race as a biological category and how to see it as related to various acculturated capacities. The concept of race was a primary locus around which
emerging theoretical struggles about the interactions of nature and culture coalesced, as the pragmatists reconceived both of those notions. But it
was also a locus where this theoretical philosophical issue is reciprocally
influencing and influenced by more narrowly *political* issues—particularly
those into which the pre–Civil War disputes about slavery had been transmuted by the war and its outcome.

The pragmatists were uniquely well situated, by their suspicion of
fixed conceptual categories and of appeals to *ontology* as supposedly sup-
porting normative relations of *authority,* to see various ways in which the
concept of race as embodied in ground-level practical politics (personal
and institutional, as well as national) owed more to culture and social
prejudice than to biology and adaptive fitness—to see it as a complex,
inherently questionable product of contingent cultural significance and
given biological fact. But with the exception of Dewey, they did not rise to
the occasion. They did not apply their theories of the contents of concepts
to offer a public critical assessment of this one.

Indeed, at just this juncture, politics may have trumped philosophy.
For as Menand characterizes the conclusions the pragmatists drew from
the war, even those (such as Holmes) who went into it as Abolitionists, like
those (such as Peirce) who went into it as Unionists, came out of it
endorsing essentially the Unionist position. There was a collision between
principles of democracy—discussion among citizens of differing opinions
(or their representatives) is the only way to settle disputes among citizens
—on the one hand, and principles of human rights—slavery is not a toler-
able practice—on the other. And pragmatism, if I read Menand aright, was
one form taken by a commitment to the former value over the latter.
Unionism stemmed from conciliatory, flexible, irenic impulses. It saw a
need to accommodate concrete established practice and deeply felt commitment by softening the appropriate application of abstract principles of
justice—a view consonant with that of Edmund Burke on the French
Revolution.

Questions about the political consequences of such a conclusion are
given particular point in view of the way national comity was in fact
reestablished in response to the triumph of those Unionist impulses. For
after the war, this attitude led to the post-Reconstruction accommodation
of white Southern sensibilities by segregation sanctioned by the state in
the form of the shameful Jim Crow laws. (One telling statistic cited by
Menand: In 1896, there had been 130,334 African Americans registered to
vote in Louisiana; by 1904, there were only 1,342 [374].) Holmes, in particular, expressed his pragmatic view that talk of principles always masked

the collision of social forces ("'Justice' and 'fairness' are slogans propping up particular struggles, not eternal principles" [64]), and his conclusion was that therefore one should "shift the totem of legitimacy from premises to procedures" by endorsing this way of trying to heal the wounds the war had inflicted on the social fabric of the nation. The result was to take the issue of racial justice and civil rights for people of color (not only former slaves and their descendants) off the political table and out of the public discussion for three-quarters of a century—as thoroughly and effectively as the issue of slavery had been in the prewar years when the Senate (in the interest of being able to get on with other business in the face of intractable disagreement) adopted a rule of procedure according to which any proposed legislation that dealt with or even mentioned slavery was to be tabled indefinitely without debate. It is arguable that this period in American history—this latter-day Great Compromise—did as much damage to race relations in the United States as slavery itself had done.

Perhaps this postwar Unionism was, after all, the best policy. Perhaps a later version of Abolitionism, now addressed to civil rights, would have yet again torn the country apart in the 1890s and following decades, substituting acute, naked, uncontrolled political violence for the chronic, background political violence of Jim Crow society. Perhaps. But it is certainly not *obvious* that this is so—that such a level of injustice *had* to be tolerated, that principles of justice and rights were not worth fighting for once again. For Menand, pragmatism is above all about the idea that changing circumstances require changed ideas, that flexibility and experimentation are the essence of rationality, not the discovery of truths or principles one can hold on to. But we should ask whether that view really obliges us to draw the political conclusions he thinks and some of the pragmatists thought it does, and whether those are conclusions we *ought* to endorse.

It seems to me that when we assess the *political* consequences of pragmatist philosophical thought, as Menand has given us eyes to see them, this question is the one pressed on us most urgently. This is the arena in which we must consider whether the ideas Menand shows the pragmatists as taking away as lessons of the Civil War are ones we should want to see as guiding subsequent political practice. For it seems that we have not yet sorted out what was right about each side in the prewar dispute between the Unionists and the Abolitionists. Not only did the Civil War fail to achieve that sort of political or philosophical understanding, but subsequent history has not been a great deal of help either.

As a result, one of the great lessons I think we should take away from Menand's thought-provoking study is that we still have a lot of thinking to

do about what is living and what is dead in pragmatism—both in philosophical theory and in political practice.

Notes

I would like to thank Danielle Macbeth for useful discussions on the topics of
this essay.

1. Louis Menand, *The Metaphysical Club: A Story of Ideas in America* (New
York: Farrar, Straus, and Giroux, 2001). Subsequent references to this work are
cited parenthetically by page number.

2. G. W. F. Hegel, *Elements of the Philosophy of Right,* ed. Allen W. Wood and
trans. H. B. Nisbet (Cambridge: Cambridge University Press, 1991), 23.

3. See Richard Rorty's essay, "Universality and Truth," chapter 1 of *Rorty and
His Critics,* ed. Robert B. Brandom (Malden, Mass.: Blackwell Publishers, 2000).

4. G. E. M. Anscombe, *Intention* (1957; reprint, Cambridge, Mass.: Harvard
University Press, 2000).

5. I discuss this way of thinking about semantics further in chapter 1 of my
Articulating Reasons: An Introduction to Inferentialism (Cambridge, Mass.: Harvard University Press, 2000).

6. In chapter 2 of *Articulating Reasons,* I argue for an inferential construal of
the expressive role of statements of preference or pro-attitude, and of normative
vocabulary generally. But this reconstrual does not affect the point that there is a
further element in play besides beliefs and actions or intentions, whose variability
undercuts the possibility of any straightforward inference from things done to
things believed.

7. See Wilfrid Sellars's masterwork, *Empiricism and the Philosophy of Mind*
(Cambridge, Mass.: Harvard University Press, 1997).

8. Dewey at least appreciated and articulated this crucial distinction—but
even he did not manage to think through its consequences for fundamental structural features of his guiding methodology.

TWO

The Unexamined Frontier:
Dewey, Pragmatism, and America Enlarged

David H. Kim

In the wake of 9/11 and the contested war in Iraq, a public conversation has emerged as to whether and to what extent America is an imperial power. In the course of this discussion, it is striking how often people have adverted to America's wars in the "Orient" in trying to get a hold on the events of 9/11 and thereafter. Pearl Harbor, Japanese American internment, and especially Vietnam have become recurring tropes. Thus, American conflict in Asia and racism against Asians have offered hermeneutical structures in our assessment of current events.[1]

Of course, these structures can themselves be objects of inquiry. In fact, press hard enough, and one finds that they are linked to still earlier American incursions into the Asia-Pacific. For example, U.S. businessmen led a coup d'état against Queen Liliuokalani of the Kingdom of Hawaii in 1893. In addition, one comes upon the geographical discovery that Latin America shares this legacy of subjection. America's Monroe Doctrine of 1823, for instance, became a well-worn diplomatic path to the domination of Latin American countries. As it turns out, the United States has exercised, since roughly the mid-nineteenth century, various kinds of dominion in the American hemisphere, the Pacific, and Eastern Asia. Since some form of this hegemony persists to this day, the current Eurasian adventures of the U.S. nation-state overlap with a later stage of its ongoing "Amerasian" dominion.

This essay examines geopolitics and social thought at a time before, but not disconnected from, Iraq and Afghanistan, and Japan and Vietnam. It maps the rise and maturation of pragmatism as a distinctively American body of thought onto the large historical and geographical features of the U.S. nation-turned-empire. After the Civil War, America's most conspicuous act of national self-assertion was its short war with Spain in the Caribbean and in the Asia-Pacific. This was followed by the annexation of most of the Spanish colonies (e.g., Puerto Rico, the Philippines, and Guam) and by a longer, bloodier, and more contested war with the Philippines. Born of the Civil War and coming of age in the Amerasian wars, where did pragmatism as a self-consciously American philosophy stand morally on these two markers of its development? As an American voice of progressive sentiment, how did pragmatism understand its principles and its nation in relation to blacks' demands for equality and liberty and to various Amerasian demands for equality and national self-determination?

I offer a consideration of the latter question, focusing mostly on America's Asia-Pacific. Since little is known of America enlarged, the first section of the essay begins with reflection on the work of Louis Menand and the more familiar Civil War context of American politics and philosophy. Robert Brandom's response to Menand in the previous chapter is then used to sharpen the conceptual and historical issues at stake. Brandom's critical framework, which on my reading puts pragmatism on trial, as it were, is extended in the second section of this essay, where I discuss America's imperial self-assertion during post–Civil War reconstruction. In the third section, I consider the work of the pragmatist most identified with democratic theory, John Dewey, who largely escapes critical attention in Brandom's critique. I shall argue that Dewey's work reveals a structured absence of reflection on the expansion of American racial hegemony in spite of the fact that he was engaged seriously with the Orient and so-called Orientals and, to a lesser extent, with U.S. imperialism in Mexico. The configuration of this absence can be traced to his antidemocratic philosophical rendering of the classic frontier chronology of the U.S. nation-state. Insofar as Dewey's philosophy was formative of pragmatism, a critique of pragmatism more generally is not far removed from the concerns of this essay. But, returning to the pressing issues of race and democracy, I noted earlier that the Asia-hermeneutic in current use is significant both as a reminder of certain events and peoples of the American past and as a lasting symptom of America's geopolitical location. Because the nation uses a severely truncated version of its imperial history to understand its current hegemonic projects, it remains to be seen whether pragmatism maintains a flawed Deweyan vision or whether it really opens a path to "creative democracy."

The Price of America Reunified

Social detachment as a description or as an ideal of philosophy has had few more eloquent or persistent critics than John Dewey. He opposed, as he famously put it, the "dogma of immaculate conception of philosophical systems."[2] And his challenge came with a corollary, namely, that societies, in turn, are not purified of philosophy, that changes in philosophy, an active and self-conscious part of culture itself, will generate changes in civilization. Both aspects of Dewey's metaphilosophy converge in the following passage:

> Philosophy . . . is a conversion of such culture as exists into consciousness. . . . But this conversion is itself a further movement of civilization; it is not something performed upon the body of habits and tendencies from without, that is, miraculously.[3]

In his marvelous book, *The Metaphysical Club,* Louis Menand follows Dewey's insights and reveals how pragmatism was a conversion of postbellum culture into a distinctively aspirational consciousness and how this transpired from within the inmost chambers of the body politic. As he tells the story, the prehistory of pragmatism must be anchored to a catastrophic moral struggle, the Civil War. But the crucible within which this philosophical innovation matured was a later transitional period: the historical moment when trauma from the war opened upon an ominous new industrial age, the point when a stultifying Unionist compromise met the developing threat of a new social conflagration. As it turned out, the working out of Civil War trauma became increasingly shaped by what looked to be a growing class war. Correspondingly, pragmatism became tasked, in effect, with the prevention of another catastrophe. Menand even asserts: "In a time when the chance of another civil war did not seem remote, a philosophy that warned against the idolatry of ideas was possibly the only philosophy on which a progressive politics could have been successfully mounted."[4] But the preemptive social forces that helped select pragmatism over its contenders also gave rise to and effectively consolidated racial apartheid, for "the price of reform in the United States between 1898 and 1917 was the removal of the issue of race from the table."[5]

Now, if the "price of reform," the great Unionist compromise, had the dual effect of aiding pragmatism and consolidating apartheid, what were some links between the two effects themselves? Woven throughout Menand's narrative, sometimes in subdued fashion, is the theme of race. And, of course, how could it be otherwise? Central events in the story, like the Civil War and its civic and social aftermath, become unintelligible without reference to slavery, race ideology, lynchings, legal apartheid, the "whitening" of new European immigrants, and black nationalism. Yet pragmatists mostly evaded public conversation on these remarkable political events and forces. They certainly focused on important social matters, but from the standpoint of democracy and community, these matters taken collectively still remained incomplete without sustained treatment of the race question. Thus, to return to Dewey on consciousness and philosophy, Menand explains how a postbellum, mass-industrialized Jim Crow culture was converted into a fallibilist, prospective, race-blind consciousness, and how this consciousness influenced that culture.[6]

Robert Brandom offers a compelling perspective by which to sharpen our consideration of Menand's narrative. After summarizing and critically revising the main tenets of pragmatism, he asks us to consider two lacunae in conjunction. First, Menand's account of pragmatism is almost entirely retrospective when the philosophy under examination is marked by its consequential rather than genealogical semantics. And second, pragmatism was sorely lacking in antiracism in spite of its democratic sympathies. Putting these ideas together, Brandom enjoins us to consider the practical, in particular the political, consequences of a philosophy that regarded its commitment to flexibility, contingency, and futurity as requiring the endorsement of the Unionist compromise, which is to say a philosophy that sanctioned, in effect if not intent, reticence on the abolition of white supremacy. And he places the discussion here into a devastating framework: the consequences of this compromise, which held sway well into the twentieth century, arguably generated "as much damage to race relations in the United States as slavery itself had done."[7] As Brandom sees it, the aftermath of the Civil War witnessed the struggle between principles of democracy (the necessity of conflict amelioration) and of human rights (intolerance of grave human suppression), and the victory of the former over the latter with little pragmatist protest. Moreover, the resulting severity and longevity of racial apartheid requires pragmatism to question: (1) whether it rightly drew a Unionist conclusion from its philosophical principles; or, more fundamentally, (2) whether, by entailing that conclusion, one or another of its central principles helped to generate or at least to permit this tragedy and hence needed to be abandoned.[8]

Brandom's account is sufficient to place pragmatism on trial, as it were. But as demanding as his case may be, I contend that it does not go far enough, and perhaps this shortfall is inherited from Menand's narrative. In the next section of this essay, I offer a brief account of the geographical expansion of America's racial nationalism into the Asia-Pacific. With this expanded portrait, we can see that the Unionist compromise helped generate not only racial apartheid in the domestic scene but racial imperialism on the international front. As it turned out, pragmatism was mostly silent on this emerging condition. In its (Deweyan) role as social critic, pragmatism failed far more extensively than Menand or Brandom clarify. Thus the question that Brandom puts before us is all the more pressing.

The Price of America Enlarged

After the short and relatively bloodless Spanish-American War (1898), Rudyard Kipling delivered an infamous literary gift to a victorious America: a poem titled "The White Man's Burden." Shortly afterward, the poem's moral exhortation to heroic colonialism would be heeded on the battlefield because the Philippines would declare independence and wage a war of national liberation against its American occupiers. As it turned out, the Philippine-American War (1899–1902) produced the opening salvoes of a series of U.S. wars in the Orient. And many conservative voices conveyed premonitions of this movement of violence and devastation across the Pacific Ocean, the new, expanding racial frontier.[9]

In 1900, military strategy was added to poetry in the emerging canon of U.S. imperialism. Alfred Thayer Mahan, author of the classic military text, *The Influence of Sea Power upon the World*, contended in a sequel text, entitled *The Problem of Asia*, that

> sea power is . . . but the handmaid of expansion, its begetter and pre-server; it is not itself expansion, nor did the advocates of the latter foresee room for advance beyond the Pacific. Their vision reached not past Hawaii, which also, as touching the United States, they regarded from the point of view of defense rather than as a stepping-stone to any farther influence in the world.[10]

This passage is intriguing because it calls for a wholesale perspectival change. It starkly opposes the common idea that California is the end of the American frontier and, hence, that Hawaii is an outer satellite by which to defend the nation's perimeter from, say, the British empire in Asia or an increasingly industrialized and belligerent Japan. In place of this centrifugal outlook, Mahan calls upon America to imagine its West as having expanded considerably and remaining open for the taking.[11] The Pacific Ocean—the final ocean—is no longer a barrier but a wide conduit along which America can move into new lands and possibilities. Clearly, by the time Mahan wrote *The Problem of Asia*, Hawaii had become a "stepping stone" to farther influence—a military depot en route to the conflagration spread across the Philippine Islands.

A more general conceptual and historical rubric may be helpful to consider here. Manifest Destiny was, of course, one of the most important conceptions undergirding America's forceful incorporation of the Asia-

Pacific. It served as the massive ideological tracks along which the impetus of white nation-building pushed the United States to leave its exclusively Atlantic position to become, eventually, the greatest Pacific power to date. We know that before reaching the other shore, some of the most egregious crimes were perpetrated, including the Atlantic slave trade, slavery itself, and the displacement and genocide of American Indians and Mexicans. Once the nation-state arrived at the far shore, we might say that the so-called Orient or Far East had become, through Manifest Destiny, the Far West. But as the racial frontier moved across the Pacific, invasion, colonization, and the formal expansion of the nation-state followed. As we know, large-scale violence continued to sweep across the region in the decades to follow: the Pacific theater of World War II, the Korean War, the Vietnam War, and recently the "Eurasian wars."

It is important to recognize, however, that America *still* remains *spatially* in the Asia-Pacific. Guam, American Samoa, and various islands of what was formerly called "Oceania" remain formal colonies. Moreover, America has retained military bases, sometimes on a massive scale, in Japan, South Korea, Okinawa, various of the Pacific islands, and for many decades in the Philippines, to form a military perimeter surrounding China. Mahan spoke of Hawaii as "touching" the United States. Now we see that something similar could be said of the great arc of Asia-Pacific nations used as an American defense perimeter. As Mahan strategized and Kipling eulogized, the Orient as Far West has become the Orient as Near West and is even in part a literal territorial constituent of America enlarged. Put another way, America is the only Pacific Rim country on both sides of the Pacific and within it as well. So it is with little exaggeration that some have called the Pacific Ocean an American lake. Typically, Asian America is viewed diasporically: Asian peoples migrated to the United States to form various kinds of communities. What I have suggested is that we also view Asian America geopolitically, imperialistically, or centripetally to see that America itself migrated across the Pacific and has for more than a hundred years and counting resided *in* Asia and the Pacific.[12]

The dynamics of imperialism are more evident in periods of peace, because in times of relative stability, the conditions of economic exploitation ripen.[13] By now, many left-liberals and virtually all radicals agree that imperialism can obtain without formal dominative civic connections between two countries. In an age of global capitalism, an economic power that avails itself of the right sorts of international economic matrices can acquire informal political domination of another country. This is arguably true of the United States currently and historically. But as discussed earlier, "old school" imperialism, expressed in formal even if indirect political control, has also been one of America's lasting structures of international politics. As an aspect of foreign policy, this type of imperialism is actually codified in memos, treaties, and the like, not to mention in some highly troubling Supreme Court rulings called the *Insular Cases*.[14]

This last area of codification has some personal connection to pragmatism. Much to his credit, Dewey recognized and condemned economic imperialism.[15] Curiously, he did not speak out in any serious way against America's formal political imperialism and its justification by the Supreme Court, in spite of the profound problem posed by constitutionally justified colonialism. And it was not as if there was an absence of discussion of the matter. For example, James Bradley Thayer, one of the best legal minds of the late nineteenth century, argued famously for the allowance of colonies and for an amendment to the Constitution that would eliminate for these colonies any legal route to statehood on grounds of preserving a white Union. As it turned out, of course, colonies remain and no amendment was passed. This legal proponent of U.S. imperialism was a traveling companion of Emerson, an employer of Oliver Wendell Holmes, a friend of philosopher Chauncey Wright, and thus one of the many prominent satellites that fell into and out of the orbit of the Metaphysical Club, that network out of which pragmatist thought developed.[16] He apparently saw no argument of the abolitionist Holmes as applying to his vision of the segregation of races on the international front. Nor did he find convincing any of William James's attacks on U.S. conquest and control of the Philippines. Yet somehow he moved comfortably in pragmatist spaces, and apparently, to an extent, so did the idea of constitutionally justified colonialism.

In 1905, shortly after the spate of annexations and some of the early imperialist Supreme Court rulings, the world witnessed an international conflict that was widely regarded to be a race war in which Japan defeated Russia. Several months before the Russo-Japanese peace treaty was signed, America and Japan had concluded secret negotiations issuing in the Taft-Katsura Memorandum to ensure that their respective imperial interests would be preserved in the postwar negotiations to come. The agreement specified that Japan would have sovereignty over Korea and that American sovereignty over the Philippines would be left unmolested by Japan. Basically, Japan and the United States aimed to divvy up some of the "available" territory in the Asia-Pacific.

This negotiation heralded a more sweeping agreement at the onset of a more strained period in U.S.-Japan relations. In 1908, the Root-Takahira Agreement was signed. Its basic normative structure involved an expansion of the Monroe Doctrine (which obtained in U.S. dominion over Latin America) to the Asia-Pacific. Through this diplomatic measure, the terms of the Taft-Katsura Memorandum and inter-imperial stability were maintained. In hindsight, we can see that this piece of diplomacy ultimately failed to prevent a war—a racial and inter-imperial war.[17]

There is more here, and it has to do, not with war itself or even imperialist diplomacy or economic exploitation before or afterward. The deterioration of U.S.-Japanese relations was accompanied by America's progressive desensitization to the ongoing realities of U.S. imperialism (a phenomenon that as we shall see characterized Dewey's political outlook as well).[18] This is evident in an interesting way in the case of U.S. patriotism regarding Pearl Harbor. Even now, as then, our civic culture regards America as the victim of an unprovoked, brazen, and perhaps cowardly attack on its main naval base in Hawaii. Roughly two thousand soldiers died, and the Pacific fleet was nearly submerged or incapacitated. December 7, the day of the attack, has become bedrock for patriotic solemnity, perhaps with a kind of meaningfulness absent in the more crassly commercialized Fourth of July. Almost nowhere, however, do we hear the deeper truth that faults *both* America and Japan.

As noted earlier, Hawaii was a colony of the United States. So when Japan roughly simultaneously attacked the Pearl Harbor naval base in Hawaii and Clark Air Base in the Philippines, two of the most important colonial military outposts of the Pacific region of America's Amerasian empire became the front lines of the more savage half of World War II. But neither the United States nor Japan had any rightful claim to Hawaii (or the Philippines), even if it is true that Japan ought not to have attacked America. So Pearl Harbor was the site of inter-imperial combat. Yet somehow the idea of Pearl Harbor serves up an illusion of American democracy: "We have been unjustly attacked by a nation that ruthlessly seeks to dominate its region, and in the name of freedom we will defeat it as we will Germany." So at the same moment in which democracy is glorified upon the blood of Pearl Harbor martyrs, genuine democracy is denied. Hawaii did not become a state until 1959, eighteen years after the attack on Pearl Harbor, and this occurred along a colonial trajectory beginning with a U.S. business–led coup d'état. And now we have a civic culture in which Pearl Harbor cannot be seen as anything other than Freedom's Sacrifice, or the Cost of Liberty.

Returning to Brandom's concern, we can ask again, now with a fuller context before us, whether pragmatism rightly drew from its principles the Unionist conclusion, or whether it drew that wrongful conclusion aright and therefore must reject one or another of its deep principles. In 1959, as noted, Hawaii attained statehood; in 1946, the Philippines achieved independence; and Puerto Rico currently remains a territory. These are three different trajectories out of the pragmatist period of U.S. empire.[19] But they are morally unified by the shared experience of suppression, displacement, vulnerability, and poverty that have no accidental relation to U.S. imperialism.

What is additionally distinctive here is that America does not yet have the civic culture even to recognize this condition. Geographic expansion has been coupled with a constriction of the U.S. moral imagination across the twentieth century. I think most Americans would find claims for indigenous Hawaiian reparations and sovereignty, Philippine reparations and freedom from neocolonialism, and Puerto Rican reparations and autonomy not so much as right or wrong, but as confusing, unfamiliar, and perhaps unintelligible.[20] An early tolerance of America enlarged has now borne fruit in the unknowing of its underside.[21]

I have described, too briefly, some significant ideas and events during America's most important self-assertion after the Civil War. They coincide with the failure of Reconstruction and the consolidation of an anti-black polity, and as noted, they take shape at the same time as the rise of American pragmatism. Their relations, however, are not accidental or remote. Through Jim Crow, a hierarchy of citizens (within a polity) and, through Amerasian imperialism, a hierarchy of polities (within an empire) combined in the late nineteenth century and created an expansive form of American white supremacy. Compromise and tolerance helped to generate and certainly to consolidate this condition. Throughout, pragmatism, itself partly a product of such compromise, largely permitted or ignored this enlarged America and its disastrous consequences. I must conclude that pragmatism wrongly favored compromise and tolerance. The horrible conditions of Jim Crow and indigenous displacement already confirm this in my view—easily, in fact. And when we consider the terrible consequences of white supremacy internationalized, the confirmation is all the more overwhelming. But, significantly, the dimensions of this pragmatist error require us to consider again whether the problem lies in a faulty inference or in a suspect theory. I offer no direct response to this with respect to pragmatism as a whole. But a more limited response is given below. With the foregoing context in mind, I focus on the work of pragmatism's main social and political philosopher, John Dewey, and consider how deep the problem goes in his paradigmatic version of pragmatism.

Dewey and the Frontiers of Democracy and Philosophy

In discussing pragmatism and democracy, Dewey is obviously an appropriate focal point. I contend that his account is in need of serious reconstruction. As I shall argue, his view on race and democracy involves contradiction and expresses willful neglect. So my thesis is more extreme than that typically found in the secondary literature, which criticizes him mostly for a lack in his political practice or incompleteness in his theory. But I want to be clear that my position does not entail that we have nothing to learn from him, for that would be manifestly false.[22] Dewey's account of democracy is not only rich and textured, but its centrality to his way of thinking considerably deepens his philosophy more generally. However, it is also true that his antidemocratic philosophical rendering of the frontier myth is central, consequential, and disfiguring. In what follows, I consider Dewey on the relations between democracy, philosophy, and the frontier before turning to some criticisms.

A full account of Dewey's social philosophy would explain how democracy is connected to experience and education, the distinction between community and individuality, meliorism and the matching of means to aims, metaphysical contingency and epistemic fallibility, utopian and regulative ideals, and still other ideas.[23] But I will only discuss some aspects of how Deweyan democracy is linked to the historical context and internal structure of human living. One of the most important features of Dewey's theory of democracy is his political rendering of the psyche and his existential rendering of politics. He was at pains to clarify that ultimately democracy is not an institution or mechanism of governance. At bottom, democracy is about experience, which is understood as a liberating attunement to the world, one that provides personal meaning, increases knowledge, realizes potential, and opens the path to further experience so conceived.[24] Democracy ensures that experience grows in "ordered richness." It is, then, a condition internal to a certain structure of human living, not something applied from without. So a genuinely participatory democratic government exists only because for the majority of the citizens democracy is already a way of life.

One of the many important elaborations of this view can be found in his later essay "Creative Democracy—The Task Before Us" (1939). Recognizing the utopian and regulative nature of an ideal like democracy, he characterizes the democratic way of life in terms of faith in three areas: in the self-directive powers and possibilities of human nature, regardless of natural endowment or social position; in intelligence and action, fortified by a world-opening education; and in everyday cooperation and shared endeavor, which by its nature precludes violence and cultivates fraternity. Importantly, however, faith in human possibility, genuine agency, and real community is taken to have a special urgency, reflecting a distinctive historical and economic consciousness in Dewey. Specifically, he contends that democracy so conceived has become more difficult to achieve in twentieth-century America because an earlier democracy-facilitating environment has been replaced by a socially deadening political economy.[25] As a result, the creativity of democratic people must be equal to the difficulty of the times. Democracy in America, then, has a deeply dia-chronic and ecological nature. And any theory of democracy, not just with respect to America, must have a narrative that contextualizes this mode of human living. For Dewey, such a story is about structures of causation as well as meaning.

In America, Dewey contends, people faced a vast, open, untrammeled frontier; they were fundamentally pioneers, whatever their specific voca-tions.[26] The inviting conditions of this form of life by their very structure encouraged democratic living. The omnipresent task of converting nature into human forms powerfully united people in a common cause and community. So the experience of the frontier produced not only a valuing of exertion, vigor, and propagation, as commonly supposed, but also the attributes of generosity, fellow-feeling, and respect. On Dewey's view, this latter set of traits is the deeper effect of America as frontier.

Since the mid- to late nineteenth century, however, the land has been filled and the resources claimed. The new age is ominously industrial. Its developing economic lines of configuration divide people against each other in a way unknown in the days of the open expanse but frighteningly familiar in Europe. And even the state's coercive power is "pale in contrast with that exercised by concentrated and organized property interests."[27] But even so, the former way of life did not disappear with the end of expansion. The frontier was simply too deep a feature of American life. And this staying power of the pioneering orientation provides hope in the face of an emerging social crisis. Specifically, the lingering dispositions toward solidarity and mutual respect, if supported by education that re-claims the values of this past, will ensure that American democracy pre-vails against economic subjection. As Dewey puts it in his essay, "Na-tionalizing Education" (1916): "The virtues of mutual esteem, of human forbearance and well-wishing which in our earlier days were the uncon-scious products of circumstances must now be the conscious fruit of an education which forms the deepest springs of character."[28]

In the essay on the three democratic faiths, Dewey elaborates upon how the pioneer orientation was modified by the new economic period. He contends that pioneering as a mode of living was so deeply embedded in the American psyche that it continued to shape American beliefs. But in the face of a changed landscape, the frontier persisted in a specifically metaphorical form in the collective outlook of mid- to late-nineteenth-century America: land was replaced by resources, and opportunities now concerned monetary acquisition.[29] Interestingly, Dewey goes on to suggest a still newer phase of the modification of the frontier. There is some unclarity as to whether his account is really meant to be descriptive.

> At the present time, the frontier is moral, not physical. The period of free
> lands that seemed boundless in extent has vanished. Unused resources
> are now human rather than material. They are found in the waste of
> grown men and women who are without the chance to work, and in the
> young men and young women who find doors closed where there was
> once opportunity.[30]

Here he seems to contend that the political economy has generated a new
analogue to open spaces and unclaimed goods, namely, a huge unemployed or suppressed work force and hence an enormous reserve of un-
tapped human resources. The manner of his articulation suggests he is
describing an emerging consensus about a new phase of the American
frontier. But he gives no reason for thinking a consensus exists. So given
his castigation of the political economy that generated this beleaguered
army of workers, he could be read—and more plausibly should be read
here—as *prescribing* an extension of the earlier democratic outlook to the
conditions of this new crisis, with the hope that it will reproduce in some
form that positive pioneering orientation toward the new masses of America. Such an extension, and finding a way of rallying people around it,
demands, as he notes, a new social and political imagination.

According to Dewey, the pioneering orientation also generated a distinctive form of philosophy—pragmatism, of course. Like democracy—
indeed, as a potential instrument of democracy—philosophy too has a
history and geography that the frontier permeates and transforms. Nearly
all of the philosophical systems inherited from Europe deferred to an
exterior authority of some kind and correlatively to a predesigned and
hence normatively precompleted universe. Even though modern European philosophy shed explicit divinity, it was still heir to a "metaphysics of
feudalism."[31] And even philosophy in America sometimes reverts to this
metaphysics in one or another subtle guise. Pragmatism, however, constitutes a profound break from this tradition:

> A philosophy animated, be it unconsciously or consciously, by the striv-
> ings of men to achieve democracy will construe liberty as meaning a
> universe in which there is real uncertainty and contingency, a world
> which is not all in, and never will be, a world which in some respect is
> incomplete and in the making, and which in these respects may be made
> this way or that according as men judge, prize, love and labor.[32]

Dewey claims that a philosophy infused with democratic aspirations finds
not only its moral theory but its entire worldview transformed. Pragmatism, therefore, involves a metaphysics of the frontier, a democratic on-

tology and normative theory. Being constituted by the conditions of the frontier, pragmatism is the philosophical rendering of the pioneering ethos.[33] And this ethos, as noted earlier, involves not simply an action- and prospectively oriented disposition but a sanctification of community. So rather than looking to an agency higher than or at least external to humanity, pragmatism in some sense makes divinity immanent within human connection and endeavor. One of our most important contemporary interpreters of pragmatism describes this philosophy as "romantic polytheism."[34]

I think it goes without saying that one of the hallmarks of pragmatism is its insights on philosophy as both a barometer of culture and an instrument of its provocation. In the first section of this essay, I mentioned Dewey's claim that philosophy converts culture into consciousness and in doing so changes culture immanently. So how does this conversion and subsequent change in culture take place? According to Dewey, philosophy is criticism that examines the foundational beliefs of a culture and "terminates, whether so intended or not, in a projection of them into a new perspective which leads to new surveys of possibilities."[35]

On this account, philosophy guides the movement from culture to consciousness by means of criticism, where this is understood in a distinctly extended and propulsive sense. Of course, it involves a multidirectional and multidimensional investigation of a culture's basic beliefs: the process of distilling, tracing, contextualizing, making coherent, and critically evaluating the doxastic organization of a society. But as cited in the passage, such an analysis invariably leads not simply to new facts, ideas, inferences, and the like, but to a new *perspective*. The new outlook or framework, in turn, lights up new *paths to the future*. So insofar as fresh perspectives and novel senses of possibility produce new and perhaps also new *kinds* of action, philosophy changes culture within the terms, now extended, of its own self-understanding. Philosophy, then, is a transformative vision.

A significant feature of philosophical analysis and vision is its inductive approach, borne of a real appreciation for the diverse particulars out of which philosophy produces judgments of some generality. At one point, Dewey likens philosophy to cosmopolitan philanthropy. The latter is discredited when it is "not rooted in neighborly friendliness." Analogously, philosophy is suspect when its general claims are built up without a "profound respect for the significant features and outcomes of human experience" in its many and various media.[36] Possibly, the distinctively a posteriori character of biology, which deeply shaped Dewey's outlook, looms in the backdrop as much as the more moral considerations of respect for individual particularity.

This analytical method poses a possible problem for the Deweyan philosopher: How can one truly maintain this sort of "profound respect," this genuinely inductive approach, if one acknowledges the obvious truth that many kinds of lives, in their rich particularities, are significantly different from those of the investigating philosopher and hence constitute opaque or easily mischaracterized entities in the analysis? Dewey replies that empirical immersion, combined with "sympathetic intercommunication" with different kinds of people, can increase knowledge and correct biases.[37] He also contends that one implication of the situated character of experience, and hence of criticism, is that a community of experience, for example women, may, upon having the right opportunities, generate a novel form of philosophy bearing the marks of their collective particularity.[38]

In light of the foregoing, we can see the kind of role played by the frontier concept. The frontier concept is neither abstractly philosophical nor simply factually descriptive. It is an empirically based *perspective*. As such, it both organizes relevant factual claims into a cohering whole and bridges the descriptive whole to abstract and to normative philosophical claims. Here, this connective concept mobilizes a certain understanding of the general causal trajectory of American habits, beliefs, social criticism, and collective organization. "High theory" may consign such a concept to the merely auxiliary with others of its empirical ilk. But then pragmatism might see such a separation as further evidence of the holdover of a "metaphysics of feudalism," since presumably only a preformed metaphysics would be averse to the openness and sense of contingency involved in an empirical stance.

Having briefly discussed Dewey on democracy, philosophy, and the frontier, we can evaluate his political philosophy. The small secondary literature on Dewey's views on race has developed a consensus. Specifically, he had little to say about race and did little to directly help antiracist movements. In virtue of this paucity of antiracist work, scholarly attention has been confined mostly to three essays by Dewey: a 1909 NAACP speech that rejects biological racialism, a 1922 China lecture that explains racial prejudice, and a 1932 NAACP speech that condemns racism as a kind of class exploitation.[39] In a nation profoundly configured by racial hierarchy, with obviously violent enforcement (i.e., lynchings and legal laxity about it), the relatively little writing and acting in the service of antiracism are quite serious omissions for a leading democratic theorist and social critic. But pragmatist contributors to the secondary literature go on to assert a further claim that takes some of the sting out of Dewey's surprising reticence on race matters. They contend that whatever flaws or omissions there may be in Dewey's work, his general social and political philosophy can both aid and accommodate the best insights of recent work on race theory.[40] Consequently, there is no *deep* problem for Deweyan political theory as such.

If we consider Dewey's frontier idea, however, serious tensions within his theory rise to the surface. This part of Dewey's work has not been given due attention in the assessment of his views on race and democracy. I have already considered at some length his account of the frontier. So it is worth emphasizing some aspects of its importance for Dewey's outlook. First, as discussed, one of its features is the crucial context-giving role it plays in his theories of democracy, philosophy, and political economy, where each of these for analytical purposes can be taken individually. Second, a point that follows upon the former is how the frontier concept is significantly ramified or articulated through his normative theory generally, since his views on democracy, philosophy, and political economy, collectively, comprise a sizeable portion of his normative theory as such. Third, the normative inroads made by the frontier account can be found in appeals to it in establishing a new imperative for education and for creative politics and hence for his meliorist outlook. The frontier partly constitutes the American future, or so Dewey hopes. Fourth, the frontier concept contributes in an importantly empirical perspectival capacity for a philosophy defined by its centering of social criticism and the "problems of men." Finally, the frontier concept is configured by a distorted normative logic. As will be discussed shortly, it wrongly brings a context of innocence to assessments of wrongdoing. An important implication of all this is that quite unlike the content of the three race essays noted earlier (i.e., the two NAACP speeches and the China lecture), the frontier concept is not a philosophical area to which a preexisting normative theory is applied, since it is a conceptual structure already, from the beginning, suffused throughout much of the normative theory. Consequently, a further implication is that problems with the frontier concept are more internal to the Deweyan outlook than problems in the theoretically subsequent applied areas.

The foregoing may help clarify how the frontier vision is living tissue internally moored throughout the body of Dewey's philosophy. In light of it, how does Dewey's philosophy fare with respect to the issue of race and democracy? It is difficult to respond delicately. As history or chronology, Dewey's frontier idea is simply wrong. In its normative role, it is *deeply* antidemocratic. And in its effects, it has been potentially collusive with an expansive white supremacy. I discuss these in turn.

Regarding the historical aspect of its empirical role, there are various ways in which the frontier idea is flawed. First, it completely erases the fact that the continent was already occupied by self-governing peoples; the U.S. was not once upon a time a "large unoccupied continent" with "unused and unappropriated resources," as he described it. In our day, the literature in critical American studies makes such an error seriously inappropriate. But there was little room for excuse even in Dewey's day, when genocide, displacement, social quarantining, and all manner of exclusions were used against the indigenous population in highly public ways.[41] So the sheer basic falsity of Dewey's frontier presupposition cannot be overstated.

Second, the magnitude of the error requires consideration. Dewey's conception of the Westward vision was purely intracontinental, from Atlantic to Pacific. As I have described in section two of this essay, however, this is a factually false description of the actual longitude and latitude of U.S. expansion. In accord with Manifest Destiny, the expansion moved southward throughout Latin America and across the Pacific to the eastern side of Asia. Moreover, the Amerasian expansion was highly public, and many of the culture makers involved were well known to the American intelligentsia or personally acquainted with Dewey himself. As noted in section two, Rudyard Kipling, Alfred Mahan, and James Thayer—poet, strategist, and judge—all converged in proclaiming the significance of America enlarged and working through their various means to shape the internationalized white nationalism of their day. As we know, and far *less* vividly than Dewey's generation, this extracontinental expansion extended the longstanding violence and cruelty of intracontinental expansion. Whatever else may be true of Dewey's frontier, that stretch from Plymouth to Manila was inhabited with peoples and, later, also with apparitions.[42] And the frontier experience of the *underside* of American expansion could not have been more different from what we find in the nationalistic lore of John Dewey. Dewey's frontier was largely a colonial landscape, and the pioneer very often an invader or occupier.

Now at this point, one might think that my claims go too far, even if it seems clear that Dewey goes wrong somehow. Perhaps it might be claimed that the political netherworld I have depicted must be *complemented* by Dewey's positive vision of America.[43] There is a sense, it might be argued, in which pluses and minuses, pros and cons, should be evenly tallied up and perhaps "cancel each other out" in some way. I think this type of normative collation might be acceptable for many kinds of social wrongs and rights, but not the sort under investigation here. War, genocide, and lasting structures of subordination are by their very nature antithetical to the peaceable acquisitive activity postulated of the Deweyan pioneer. Individually, they involve a notable severity of harm and heinousness. And collectively, they form a variegated and punishing structure of racial oppression. So Dewey's problem here is not a mere gap or hole that leaves his account incomplete. It is a hole in a shape-maintaining or lode-bearing structure, so its existence leads to the deformation of much else in the account. Correspondingly, its rectification is not a mere filling in the gap, but a more wholesale renovation in perspective.

And there is more. If, as Menand and others discuss, the Civil War, its social aftermath, and the onset of a new industrial age formed the crucible of pragmatism's gestation, why is there no discussion of slavery in the frontier narrative? Even if we assume for the sake of argument that America was a "large unoccupied continent" with "unused and unappropriated resources," it would still be true that enslaved Africans were forced to occupy the continent to help white pioneers use and appropriate the available resources for themselves. At least this much *must* be conceded by Dewey. Abolition, Union, war, Reconstruction—how could he or anyone of his generation forget slavery and racial caste? Of course, nobody did. So if the frontier experience is postulated as a general causal structure explaining some part of the nation's democratic inspirations, we can turn the tables on Dewey and ask whether the experience of slavery and Northern racial caste did not also play a causal role, one that counteracted or mitigated the democratizing impulse of pioneering. If we consider the great narrative of the African American experience during this time, we come upon the story of the Exodus.[44] Dewey's paradigm is the pioneer chopping down trees, digging wells, riding across the landscape. The African American paradigm is the slave chopping down trees for a master, digging wells for a master, but in time shattering the master's manacles. None of this, however, is discussed, let alone mentioned, by Dewey. So as a purely descriptive matter, Dewey's account of the frontier is false, and because it has a perspectival structure, the error is seriously problematic. There are further relevant considerations here. I have yet to talk about the normative structure and some of the consequences of his account. So I turn to them now.

As discussed, race and empire are everywhere in the frontier, yet nowhere in Dewey's vision of it. It could well be said that for Dewey early America was the unexamined frontier. Yet the ignored facts were so obvious to Dewey's generation that one must ask why so much is pushed out of the horizon of his vision and how this ignoring is built into the conceptual structure. Ignoring, as an activity, requires us to question the aims involved, and correspondingly, an affected conceptual structure requires us to ask whether its normative orientation has been skewed in relation to democracy. Regarding the first of these, I have no real answer. Given all that has been said, I do not know for certain what compelled Dewey to see the antidemocratic frontier as a wellspring of American democracy and of the democratic aspirations of American philosophy. Of course, someone might point out that he was a child of his times, and everyone who was anyone normalized the frontier idea in some positive form or other. Perhaps this is so, but note that such a response does little to save Dewey and much to indict the general community, Dewey included.

Regarding conceptual structure, the frontier concept plays an anti-democratic normative role. A pragmatist theory of democracy is fundamentally a tool for ameliorating conditions contrary to human growth. The totalistic erasure in Dewey's frontier vision, however, not only fails to solve problems in democracy but actually exacerbates them. And to be clear, the issue here is not simply the factual inaccuracy of the Deweyan story, which any decent history book can correct, but normative interpretation. When racial oppression is systemic and historically protracted, a historically grounded normative context will not simply offer an informational penumbra around the condemnation of racism but will permeate and qualitatively change the condemnation itself.[45] However, Dewey's frontier vision, evacuated of historical reality, provides a kind of prelapsarian normativity whereby America is perpetually innocent, always flush with its democratic youth. He can denounce racism repeatedly, but each denouncement is unmoored from the actual historical context and thereby involves misapprehension. Specifically, racism will be seen as a serious problem because it is *serially extensive,* rather than because it is also qualitatively deep. There is a sense in which each act of racism is *normatively new,* even if it is recognized, descriptively, to be a further instance of an established pattern.

Relatedly, the legacies or enduring impact of earlier forms of racism may not be recognized for what they are. So, for example, if one were to look upon poverty in, say, the Philippines or Puerto Rico, one might only see tragic deprivation and governmental corruption or inefficiency, rather than the causal connections these have with U.S. imperialism. As a result, philanthropy, rather than reparations and the preemption of further imperialism, take center stage on the agenda of reform. Now if Dewey's theory of democracy is meant to be a problem-solving device, it must make forays into this deeper aspect of social transformation, into reparations and prevention more than piecemeal patchwork. But the prelapsarian frontier vision so suffused throughout his normative theory prevents these democratic advances in thinking. In fact, it could be seen as a potential tool of imperialism in virtue of its trivializing qualities. On a final note, consider that democracy is aspirational for Dewey and not yet a fully accurate description of any society. What Dewey's frontier vision offers us, then, is hope without history rather than hope forged in the face of apparent hopelessness.[46] Consequently, it conduces to democratic faith made shallow. Worse, it raises the specter that perhaps moral recovery from the awful past really is hopeless and that there is no future without its erasure. Could this be the motive of Dewey's dedicated ignoring?

Finally, I would like to consider, perhaps in good pragmatist fashion, a possible consequence of Dewey's frontier vision, namely collusion with U.S. imperialism. Bertrand Russell famously accused pragmatism of being a philosophy of ironclads and maxim guns. I do not think this is true. But there is certainly the worry that pragmatism might in some version, or possibly more generally, aid imperialism through a structure of allowances, permissions, or trivializations. In the case of Dewey, our evaluation must be ambivalent because, seen as a nexus of potential causal forces, his account is contradictory: his normative theory both hinders and aids imperialism. It rejects imperialism because it wonderfully supports a deep form of democracy, which I have described at some length. On the other hand, it is shot through with a frontier vision that trivializes imperialism and its legacies and thereby helps it move with less fetters than it would otherwise have. One way to draw this out is to consider Dewey's view of U.S.-Japan-China relations. A full discussion of Dewey's Asia is beyond the scope of this essay, but some aspects of his China and other travel writings show some concrete manifestations of how the frontier vision can serve as a kind of perpetual innocence-making machine, a wonderful device in the hands of imperialism.

In an essay entitled "Public Opinion in Japan" (1921), Dewey praises Japanese liberals, as he calls them, who had attempted to steer Japanese opinion away from further militarization, a psychology of bellicose nationalism, and imperialist tendencies.[47] He concludes soberly, however, that these liberals may ultimately be ineffectual, since Japanese public opinion seems to be overly conditioned by the warlike social climate that formed the very precondition of Japan as a modern political unit. He worries as well about a possible "explosion in the Pacific" precipitated by the Japanese out of resentment against American exclusion of Asians. Even if Dewey gets wrong some of the details here, he arguably anticipates the "Day of Infamy" discussed in brief in section two of this essay. His prescience might be applauded because of his sensitivity to Japanese political and social conditions. But he does not direct these sensitivities to an understanding of his home country, even with the benefit of *hindsight.* Strikingly, at no point and practically nowhere else in his China lectures, does Dewey seriously consider *American* militarization, *American* psychology of bellicose nationalism, and *America's actual,* not merely potential, imperialist and explosive incursions across the Pacific.[48] At the end of that lecture, Dewey does implore America to do the "square thing" and rid itself of international (and presumably also domestic) racism. But he does little to address the mechanisms of American empire I have noted above even as he addresses the mechanisms of Japanese empire.

In a later trip to Mexico, Dewey claims to have been convinced that imperialism can be developed mostly economically, as seen in the dominative relation between the United States and Mexico. He does not, however, make any concessions to the idea that the United States has maintained explicitly political imperialism as well, nor to the idea that U.S. economic imperialism is pervasive in the areas where it in fact maintains political imperialism. Still later, he does begin to see some of the extensiveness of U.S. economic imperialism, especially in Latin America:

> Our economic policy in Nicaragua goes marching on with the support of marines; but there was a time when similar interventions (with apologies to our authorities for not calling them "interpositions") went almost without notice. . . . Perception of great social changes usually lags far behind the changes themselves, so far behind that it is incapable of modifying their operation. But perception of the growth of economic imperialism is not perhaps so far behind the fact, and consequently so important, as had been the case in other matters.[49]

This signifies an important development in Dewey's anti-imperialism and correspondingly the working out of his democratic theory. The only problem is the vestiges of the frontier vision. Imperialism, as described here, is seen as relatively new and shallow, and its cessation relatively near.

An interesting confirmation of the continuing influence of the frontier vision can be found in a still-later piece, an address by Dewey to the Chinese public during World War II:

> Your country and my country, China and the United States, are alike in being countries that love peace and have no designs on other nations. . . . We are alike, your country and mine, in having a common end in this war we have been forced to enter in order to preserve our independence and freedom. . . .
> The United Nations will win the whole war, and the United States and China will win against Japan. . . . In this new world you are assured the position of spiritual leadership of Eastern Asia.[50]

The shifting position of the United States here is fascinating. American innocence in the Asia-Pacific, both in regard to conquest and to dominative diplomacy, is clearly ludicrous, as shown in section two of this essay. But in virtually perfect conformity to his frontier vision, Dewey begins by aligning the United States with a more obviously innocent China. As he tells the future he desires, the United States with China will defeat the imperialist aggressor, Japan. And in the ensuing peace, China will become the rightful leader of eastern Asia. But one cannot help but wonder, "What about the United States?" If the U.S. and China have been aligned thus far in this trajectory of the fight for democracy, then in the ensuing peace, will America become the leader of the Western world? Whatever leadership the United States holds in the new half of the century, according to Dewey, it will not be an empire, for its imperialism has not been deep or serious. And perhaps it will learn its lessons from the examples provided by Japan and Germany. Here again, then, the frontier reappears in the American future. By now, however, we are entitled to doubt whether that condition is democracy.

Possibly the Korean War and, had he lived long enough, certainly the Vietnam War would have dealt a serious blow to Dewey's view of American democracy. Unfortunately, still more has transpired. I began this essay with a note about current U.S. incursions into the Middle East, the addition of a Eurasian agenda to an earlier Amerasian empire. With the twentieth century behind us and still more racism and imperialism ahead of us, I think we must expand the pressing issue that Brandom has raised and see that pragmatism's compromises have been far more disastrous than he or Menand have noted. If pragmatism wrongly drew its tolerating conclusions from a basically sound theory, then we can move forward with the hope that pragmatism will, with the benefit of such hindsight, choose more wisely in the future. However, if pragmatism rightly drew its tolerating conclusions with such terrible effects, then pragmatism itself is in jeopardy.

My focus here has been on one paradigmatic pragmatist. But because Dewey was the leading theorist of democracy among the early pragmatists, pragmatism itself has not been far from the discussion. I have concluded that Dewey's account of democracy is seriously problematic, though not impossible to reconstruct. If my criticisms have been mostly valid, then we need to ask how Dewey's position would look, once shorn of the frontier vision ramified throughout his normative theory. For example, what would happen if we replaced it with an Exodus narrative of the kind found in the black nationalist traditions? Or perhaps it should be replaced with nothing at all, with all the resulting holes sutured somehow. Either way, the position, if it remains Deweyan, will have been substantially renovated. And perhaps it will be some such renovated account that will provide a way out of pragmatism's empire. Ultimately, however, all this seems to me to be an instance of the "problems of men." And until pragmatism makes U.S. imperialism and complicity with it one of its own urgent problems, I imagine that it will make itself largely obsolete in the underside of the world, where once it was Marxism that called people forward to faith and hope in transformation on a global level.[51]

Notes

1. Interestingly, two related events, dated after 9/11, have not received due attention in the mainstream media and in public forums: Haitian president Jean-Bertrand Aristide's public claim that he was ousted by a CIA-backed coup d'état, and Venezuelan president Hugo Chavez's public claim that a CIA-backed coup d'état was prevented in his country. It seems that the Middle East has preoccupied the U.S. critique of imperialism, with Latin America mostly dropping out of the picture. And U.S.–Asia relations forms a hermeneutic for current U.S.–Middle East imperialism, with Latin America playing less of a role in that hermeneutic. These asymmetries are beyond the scope of this essay. Another peculiarity that is beyond the bounds of this essay is the inclusion of North Korea in the "axis of evil" and the relative dearth of discussion about U.S. relations with the two Koreas.

2. Dewey, "Context and Thought," *The Later Works of John Dewy, 1925–1953,* Vol. 6, ed. Jo Ann Boydston (Carbondale and Edwardsville: Southern Illinois University Press, 1985), 17; hereafter *LW,* followed by the volume and page number.

3. Ibid. 10.

4. Louis Menand, *The Metaphysical Club: A Story of Ideas in America* (New York: Farrar, Straus, and Giroux, 2001), 374

5. Ibid.

6. The rise of pragmatism and apartheid were dual effects of the Unionist compromise. The discussion here is about how pragmatism related itself to apartheid, or failed to do so. For reasons of space, no discussion can be given here about links going in the other direction, in particular of how opponents of apartheid conceptualized or used pragmatism for their ends. Such an account would need to discuss W.E.B. Du Bois' partial pragmatist outlook, Alain Locke's overt pragmatism, and the rise of mid-century black (and Asian) social theorists, like E. Franklin Frazier, who were influenced by pragmatism through the Chicago School of Sociology and other such academic venues.

7. Robert Brandom, "When Philosophy Paints Its Blue on Grey: Irony and the Pragmatist Enlightenment," *boundary 2* 29:2 (2002), 28; reprinted as chapter 1 of this volume.

8. Ibid. 27–28. On page 375 of his book, Menand addresses, perhaps at a few steps removed, some of the ideas that generate Brandom's concerns. There he questions how pragmatism can adjudicate between the very interests that generate the focus of pragmatist analysis, that is, consequences.

9. The idea of the Pacific as a racial frontier has received a good deal of excellent discussion. See Richard Drinnon, *Facing West: The Metaphysics of Indian-Hating and Empire Building* (New York: Schocken Books, 1990); Arif Dirlik, ed., *What Is in a Rim? Critical Perspectives on the Pacific Region Idea* (Boulder, Colo.: Westview Press, 1993); Gary Okihiro, *Margins and Mainstreams: Asians in American History* (Seattle: University of Washington Press, 1994); Arif Dirlik, *The Postcolonial Aura: Third World Criticism in the Age of Global Capitalism* (Boulder, Colo.: Westview Press, 1997); Lisa Lowe, *Immigrant Acts: On Asian American Cultural Politics* (Durham, N.C.: Duke University Press, 1996); David Palumbo-Lui,

Asian/American: Historical Crossings of a Racial Frontier (Stanford, Calif.: Stanford University Press, 1999); and Colleen Lye, *America's Asia: Racial Form and American Literature, 1893–1945* (Princeton, N.J.: Princeton University Press, 2005).

10. Alfred T. Mahan, *The Problem of Asia and its Effects upon International Politics* (Port Washington, N.Y.: Kennikat Press, 1900), 7.

11. Mahan, therefore, stands in a tradition of frontier thinking that includes Emerson, Thoreau, Whitman, Frederick Jackson Turner, and, as we shall see, Dewey himself. For a sobering account of much of this tradition, see Richard Slotkin, *Regeneration through Violence: The Mythology of the American Frontier, 1600–1860* (Middletown, Conn.: Wesleyan University Press, 1973).

12. I offer a more detailed examination of this idea, including discussion of U.S. imperialism in Latin America, in "Empire's Entrails and the Imperial Geography of 'Amerasia,'" *City: Analysis of Urban Trends, Culture, Theory, Policy, Action* 8:1 (April 2004): 57–88.

13. Moreover, wars are sometimes not so much expressions of an already existing imperialism as they are a part of the exigencies by which imperialism is established in the first place.

14. Although space does not permit anything like an adequate discussion of the codifications of U.S. empire, consider that in a series of legal decrees called the *Insular Cases,* the Supreme Court developed across the first half of the twentieth century the conceptual space for a state/colony asymmetry and the acceptability of both kinds of constituents of the nation-state. This constitutional embrace of formal political imperialism in Puerto Rico and later in the Asia-Pacific remains intact to this day. Further elaboration is given in the excellent anthology edited by Christine D. Barnett and Burke Marshall, *Foreign in a Domestic Sense: Puerto Rico, American Expansion, and the Constitution* (Durham, N.C.: Duke University Press, 2001), and my "Empire's Entrails and the Imperial Geography of 'Amerasia.'"

15. See his "Imperialism Is Easy," retitled from "Our Monroe Doctrine," in John Dewey, *Impressions of Soviet Russia and the Revolutionary World* (New York: New Republic, Inc., 1929), 181–94.

16. For more on Thayer and the *Insular Cases,* see Christina D. Burnett and Burke Marshall, "Between the Foreign and the Domestic: The Doctrine of Territorial Incorporation, Invented and Reinvented," and Brook Thomas, "A Constitution Led by the Flag: The *Insular Cases* and the Metaphor of Incorporation," both in Christina D. Burnett and Burke Marshall, *Foreign in a Domestic Sense.* Chapter 9 of Menand's *Metaphysical Club* offers some context for the personal relations noted above.

17. For our purposes, we can regard this failure as an episode in a series of imperialist state actions, sometimes codified, which continued long after the annexations discussed above. The history of a nation's imperialism exceeds the focus on direct empire-colony relations. Rivalry between empires seems just as significant, even if that rivalry is depicted by historians as merely inter-state, as opposed to inter-imperial, conflicts. For more on the racial and imperialist aspects of the Pacific front of World War II, see John Dower, *War without Mercy: Race and Power in the Pacific War* (New York: Pantheon Books, 1986), and Walter LaFeber,

The Clash: U.S.-Japanese Relations Throughout History (New York: W.W. Norton, 1997).

18. The American conscience would, of course, be resensitized by the 1960s. See Mary Dudziak, *Cold War Civil Rights: Race and the Image of Democracy* (Princeton, N.J.: Princeton University Press, 2000); Gary Gerstle, *The American Crucible: Race and Nation in the Twentieth Century* (Princeton, N.J.: Princeton University Press, 2001); and Nikhil Singh, *Black Is a Country: Race and the Unfinished Struggle for Democracy* (Cambridge, Mass.: Harvard University Press, 2004).

19. The problem is more expansive, but for reasons of space I focus on these three cases.

20. Currently, a native Hawaiian sovereignty movement has gathered strength and has insisted on independence and thereby voiced a rejection of statehood. The Philippines, in spite of its wealth of resources, lies at the economic underside of the world, with a GNP that is substantially supplied by Filipinos living and working *outside* of their own country. Puerto Rico has stood at a crossroads for some time, with Hawaii and the Philippines as alternative scenarios. As Gregory Trianosky y Velazquez has described it for me, if Puerto Rico were to become the fifty-first state, it could very well be the poorest state of the union. If it became independent, would it follow the path of the Philippines and fall into a neocolonial subjection?

21. This would be another and important example of the colonial epistemology discussed by Enrique Dussel in *The Underside of Modernity: Apel, Ricoeur, Rorty, and Taylor and the Philosophy of Liberation,* trans. Eduardo Mendieta (Atlantic Highlands, N.J.: Humanities Press, 1996), and the "epistemology of ignorance" described by Charles Mills in *Blackness Visible: Essays on Philosophy and Race* (Ithaca, N.Y.: Cornell University Press, 1997).

22. See, for example, the use of Dewey in antiracist philosophy in Eddie Glaude Jr., *Exodus! Religion, Race, and Nation in Early Nineteenth Century Black America* (Chicago: University of Chicago Press, 2000), and Shannon Sullivan, *Revealing Whiteness: The Unconscious Habits of White Privilege* (Bloomington: Indiana University Press, 2006).

23. For more on Deweyan democracy, see Richard Rorty, *The Consequences of Pragmatism* (Minneapolis: University of Minnesota Press, 1982) and *Contingency, Irony, and Solidarity* (New York: Cambridge University Press, 1989); Cornel West, *The American Evasion of Philosophy: A Genealogy of Pragmatism* (Madison: University of Wisconsin Press, 1989), chap. 3; Robert B. Westbrook, *John Dewey and American Democracy* (Ithaca, N.Y.: Cornell University Press, 1991); John J. Stuhr, ed., *Philosophy and the Reconstruction of Culture: Pragmatic Essays after Dewey* (Albany: SUNY Press, 1993); Charlene Seigfried, *Pragmatism and Feminism: Reweaving the Social Fabric* (Chicago: University of Chicago Press, 1996); Larry Hickman, ed., *Reading Dewey: Interpretations for a Postmodern Generation* (Bloomington: Indiana University Press, 1998); Michael Eldridge, *Transforming Experience: John Dewey's Cultural Instrumentalism* (Nashville, Tenn.: Vanderbilt University Press, 1998); and Louis Menand, *Metaphysical Club.*

24. Dewey, "Creative Democracy—The Task Before Us," *LW* 14: 224–230.

25. We see here some of the inspiration for Menand's narrative.

26. Perhaps Dewey's earlier work on transposed psychological templates filled the backdrop of this pioneer narrative. He argued in "Interpretation of Savage Mind" that a hunting mentality is common to the so-called savage mind and that it persists, in variously changed forms, as the society in question becomes more civilized, as it were. In his own day, Dewey claimed, transmuted aspects of the hunter perspective were evident. See "Interpretation of Savage Mind," in *MW* 2:39–52.

27. Dewey, "Renascent Liberalism," *LW* 11:41–65.

28. Dewey, "Nationalizing Education," *MW* 10:202–10.

29. Dewey, "Creative Democracy—The Task Before Us," *LW* 14:224–25.

30. Ibid.

31. Dewey, "Philosophy and Democracy," *MW* 11:51.

32. Ibid., 50.

33. In a response to Lewis Mumford's criticism of pragmatism, especially of William James, Dewey's rejoinder offers more by which to consider pragmatism as a "metaphysics of the frontier." Specifically, he contends that the many distinctive features of James's philosophy—e.g., radical empiricism, pluralism, etc.—reveal the permeation of the pioneering orientation. On this basis, Dewey denies Mumford's claim that James and pragmatism merely reflect and acquiesce to what is prevalent in society. A frontier-constituted philosophy departs from Europe's feudalistic metaphysic, and it values an ethos that challenges the emerging status quo, particularly narrow individualism and class divisions. See Dewey, "The Pragmatic Acquiescence," *LW* 3:145–51.

34. Richard Rorty, "Pragmatism as Romantic Polytheism," in Morris Dickstein, ed., *The Revival of Pragmatism: New Essays on Social Thought, Law, and Culture* (Durham, N.C.: Duke University Press, 1998), 21–36.

35. Dewey, "Context and Thought," 19.

36. Ibid. 21.

37. Ibid.

38. Ibid. Of course, Dewey and others repeatedly commented upon and tried to explain regional or nationalistic differences in philosophy, like German versus American philosophy. So what makes his comment on women's philosophy striking is the background concern about democracy. As a proponent of various kinds of women's rights, he was of course aware of gender hierarchy. One expression of his challenge to this hierarchy, at least in some of its aspects, can be found in precisely this acknowledgement of the potential of women's philosophy. For more on Dewey's treatment of gender (and race), its limits and prospects, see Charlene H. Seigfried, "John Dewey's Pragmatist Feminism," in *Reading John Dewey,* ed. Larry Hickman, chap. 10, and her *Pragmatism and Feminism.* A very different contribution to this discussion is Richard Rorty, "Feminism and Pragmatism," in *Truth and Progress: Philosophical Papers,* vol. 3 (New York: Cambridge University Press, 1998), chap. 11.

39. I think the general judgment that Dewey wrote little on race needs to be

emended. If we consider his various writings on China and the Orient, we find that he had more to say about race than is contained in the three essays that most scholars tend to reference.

40. See, for example, West, *American Evasion of Philosophy,* chap. 3; Seigfried, "John Dewey's Pragmatist Feminism"; George Pappas, "Dewey's Philosophical Approach to Racial Prejudice," in *Philosophers on Race,* ed. Tommy Lott and Julie Ward (Malden, Mass.: Blackwell Press, 2002), chap. 15; Michael Eldridge, "Dewey on Race and Social Change," in *Pragmatism and the Problem of Race,* ed. Bill E. Lawson and Donald F. Koch (Bloomington: Indiana University Press, 2004), chap. 1; and Shannon Sullivan, *Revealing Whiteness,* and "From the Foreign to the Familiar: Confronting Dewey Confronting Racial Prejudice," *Journal of Speculative Philosophy* 18:3 (2004): 193–202. Among these, Sullivan's work seems to most clearly address the depth of the race problem in Dewey's philosophy.

41. In a related vein, indigenous thought actually influenced pragmatism, even if this has gone unrecognized. See Scott Pratt, *Native Pragmatism: Rethinking the Roots of American Philosophy* (Bloomington: Indiana University Press, 2002).

42. The Philippines' demands for independence was met by a massive consensus of American white supremacy, denying Filipinos the ability and right of self-governance. The ensuing war was genocidal. Moorfield Storey smuggled a photo of the slaughter at Mt. Dajo from the killing fields to the American media. As a result, Dewey's generation could not ignore the massacres splashed across their newspapers, and ours perhaps might look upon them with the eerie horror that often attends the observation of the black and white photos of large Holocaust graves filled with cadavers. For more on U.S.-Philippine relations and the war that initiated the relationship, see Angel Velasco Shaw and Luis Francia, eds., *Vestiges of War: The Philippine-American War and the Aftermath of an Imperial Dream, 1899–1999* (New York: New York University Press, 2002).

43. Dewey himself might object to my framing of the matter, as seen in his style of tallying the pros and cons of American society in his essay "A Critique of American Civilization," *LW* 3: 133–44. My comments here, then, are as much a response to that essay as to the imagined interlocutor.

44. For a superb examination of this idea, see Glaude, *Exodus!*

45. For example, is a particular episode of racial injustice an aberration of the social order? Or is it perhaps a part of the normal infrastructure of a society's day-to-day life? The same act, say, the racist denial of a job to a candidate, can be read very differently depending on the wider normative context brought to bear in the examination. What is *not* at issue is the description of the job denial itself as some form of racism.

46. See the essays in this volume by James Bohman, Max Pensky, and Mitchell Aboulafia, who use Mead to recapture history as a necessary component of democracy.

47. Dewey, "Public Opinion in Japan," *MW* 13:255–261.

48. The omissions are absolutely glaring. The most Dewey can say about the roiling conditions and consequences of America enlarged is that America is not prepared to absorb a flood of Orientals, that as a result anti-Asian immigration

law is regrettably justifiable, and that Japan may attack America out of resentment of its exclusion from America. For Dewey's peculiar condonation of anti-Asian immigration law, see his classic essay on racial prejudice, "Racial Prejudice and Friction," *MW* 13:254.

49. Dewey, "A Critique of American Civilization," *LW* 3:133–34.

50. Dewey, "Message to the Chinese People," *LW* 15:369–70.

51. For thoughtful comments and questions, I am grateful to the audience of the Pragmatism and Nationalism conference at SUNY, Stony Brook, at which a much earlier version of this paper was presented. I am especially indebted to the critical comments and editorial suggestions offered by Eduardo Mendieta and Chad Kautzer, which led to some substantial improvements.

THREE

Pragmatism and Solidarity with the Past

Max Pensky

Pragmatism—so the conventional wisdom runs—is a philosophy oriented implacably toward the future. It breaks consciously from that core commitment of Hegelianism in which philosophy is the retrospective gathering, and completion, of culture in the medium of thought. It is a democratic practice of understanding democracy, understanding itself both as a theory of democratic life and an activity dedicated to furthering a general project of democracy. It is "progressive" in both a methodological and ideological sense. It proposes to understand itself as a tool meant for advancing its political and cultural projects, and if the past is unchangeable—untouchable by anything in our philosophical toolkit—then it is useless and hence not a proper object of philosophical interest. This, at any rate, is the conventional wisdom (a phrase that John Dewey coined).

The conventional wisdom is incorrect. The social theory of the pragmatist George Herbert Mead, Dewey's student and colleague, understands the past, and the way in which temporal and historical relations are constructed, endowed with significance, and re-constructed, as eminently pragmatic operations, open to the revision of beliefs based on new experiences, and dynamic.

There is certainly an important sense in which the pragmatists did object to a particular conception of the objective or "fixed" past as an ideal order to which historical interpretation was to have some sort of privileged access, with the implication that interpretive historical knowledge was fundamentally different in kind than practical or scientific knowing.

In this sense, the pragmatists can be counted among numerous post-Hegelian philosophical schools, from Marxism through Nietzsche to *Lebensphilosophie,* in developing a suspicion, if not an outright disdain, for the damaging effects of too great an attachment to memory and history understood as an autonomous intellectual domain. Marx saw in capitalism's liquidation of traditional supports of social practices as offering an opening for a form of socialism brave enough to throw off the past, and Nietzsche reconceived the past as an organic weight of undigested matter crippling the vitality and energy of the human organism. Pragmatists insisted on history and memory as material whose value can only be assessed from the standpoint of present practice and future outcomes: What follows, from the point of view of our democratic projects, from a given construction of a collective past? Which pasts are able to justify their usefulness for our projects, and which appear, from that standpoint, as useless weight?

The critical interpretations of pragmatist philosophy developed in the first two essays in the present volume—inspired by Louis Menand's intellectual history, *The Metaphysical Club*—both develop the pragmatists' quintessentially American preoccupation with futurity and progress, one that proves so deeply troublesome in the omissions and elisions the pragmatists committed regarding the racial history of the United States. Menand's uneasy conclusion at the end of *The Metaphysical Club* was that the virtue of democratic tolerance that the pragmatists developed was a complex response to the catastrophe of civil war: pluralism, anti-idealism, and the dynamic of tolerant inclusion into American society were philosophical tools for the defusing of the violent potential of inevitable democratic faction: "Pragmatism," he writes, "was designed to make it harder for people to be driven to violence by their beliefs."[1]

But the "Unionist compromise" that pragmatism eventually endorsed virtually ensured a hundred years of savage and often spectacularly violent racial injustice following the Civil War. In David Kim's more far-reaching indictment, Dewey's embrace of a frontier thesis, and his efforts to reconcile this thesis with the core normative insights of transnational democracy, rendered him virtually silent on both ongoing racial injustice and America's growing imperial status. Menand argues that the moral force of the early pragmatists' philosophical project was the horror of civil war and the recognition that no social conflict could ever again be permitted such a violent resolution. This, in essence, is a conservative and not a progressive position, insofar as it is defined by what must *not* be allowed to happen and what must be protected from the specter of political violence. Like all progressives perhaps, the pragmatists found themselves defining what could count as democratic progress in contrast to that which could not be repeated. In a sense that Hegel would have understood perfectly, their very conceptions of newness and futurity were defined precisely by what they wanted to break from most absolutely. This indicates already that the pragmatists did not—and never could have—faced an unambiguous choice between a past-oriented and a future-oriented practical philosophy. To practice one is always to practice the other at the same time. At its core, the progressivism of the pragmatists, like all progressivist attitudes, demands the prevention of future suffering (as opposed to Hegel, whose philosophy is dedicated to the justification of past suffering).

No theory is necessary to assist in the recognition of what suffering is or why its amelioration is demanded. But the demand for a future without suffering cannot be imagined in the absence of some ongoing relationship with the suffering of a past that is not past and that still exerts claims on the present. In the works of Walter Benjamin, and especially of Theodor Adorno, the memory of historical suffering comes to occupy a central position in a powerfully moral conception of the duty to remember. While poles apart from the injunction to remember as a duty justified on theological grounds, as it was for the Frankfurt School thinkers, pragmatism contains its own powerful *hypothetical* imperative of historical memory. This demand doesn't take the form it did for their Harvard colleague Santayana (those who forget the past are condemned to repeat it), but, as I'll try to show in what follows, it is a reconceptualization of the relation of the past and present based on the pragmatic category of relevance for action. The past is constituted as the field of situations that relevantly determine and constrain action as a response to a problem; as George Herbert Mead describes it, the past is defined not as what is past but as what is still "going on." As a practical attitude toward the past, pragmatism will have to have something to say about the memory of suffering and injustice encoded in the national narrative. Quite contrary to the platitudinous version of pragmatism as a quintessentially American dismissal of the past, I think that pragmatism actually provides us with practical resources for a better account of the problems—theoretical, political, moral—that we confront as we try to understand the nature of past-present relations. And it will come as no surprise that the truest pragmatist response to this nature is to see it as a problem of how we decide what to do with one another rather than of whether we can generate a truer account of the nature of the past.

Philosophy's attempts to understand the salience of the past have blossomed, in the past decades, along with a growing cultural consensus that the injustices on which our national histories rest continue to exert claims upon us. Much of this work has centered on the Holocaust as the paradigm event for the formation of theories about collective remembrance of the victims of past injustice. In the United States, the shared past of racial injustice and its ongoing consequences for the status of African American citizens and racial relations has emerged (finally) as a matter of serious academic studies over the past decades.

Any number of theoretical approaches—Marxism, Freudian or Lacanian psychoanalysis, literary deconstruction—have been enlisted as guides for a theory of the political and normative dimensions of the shared past. Some approaches assume without much argument that "memory" is the best term to characterize both individual and social processes of encountering the past; others make elaborate distinctions between various forms of collective commemoration, representation, recollection, and so on. Some take seriously a distinction between history and memory; others do not. Collective memory has been explored in its relation to the production of subjectivities, of national identity and national consciousness, or of resistance to oppression. It has been registered through the media of literature and film, personal narrative, and historiography. Theorists of collective memory have explored the structure of collective trauma, contested strategies of representation, and fought over literary and cultural canons.

This turn to the past—to the dynamic and plastic nature of collective memory, the relation between memory and professional historiography, the role of a shared past in processes in identity-formation, both individual and collective—expresses a fundamental and welcome curiosity about the enabling conditions of our own cultural and political realities. In this sense, one important contribution is an attempt to clarify the following question: What are the *normative* stakes in discourses of collective memory, or a present society's relationship with its shared past? Asking this question is one way of pointing to an unresolved tension that is distinctive for many if not most contemporary intellectual discussions of the dynamics of collective memory. In normative terms, two distinct conceptions of the meaning of collective memory are often intertwined without any analysis. The normative weight of these two conceptions appears distinct, indeed, perhaps contradictory.

On one side, study of the dynamics of collective pasts has been highly successful in pursuing various versions of a social constructivist model. According to this model, the objectivity of an older positivist notion of a historical past is to be definitively rejected in favor of the strong view that the past is the *ongoing* product of current social, political, and cultural practices. Historical accuracy or truth-claims are hence to be taken as one of many contested and competing claims that shape the process of the production of a historical past. Present political exigencies and interests, demands for shared identities in the face of oppressions, efforts to shore up the legitimacy of existing political institutions, naked strategic interests

—all compete for influence in the process by which a shared past is continuously forged and re-forged. Here the key terms for this process are "redescription" and "negotiation": the past is negotiated, and renegotiated, across a spectrum of differing players, all of whom may have differing (even internally inconsistent) motives for the construction of a preferred version of a shared past. The past, on the social constructivist model, is therefore present. Largely for this reason, theories of the social construction of collective pasts have been largely descriptive in nature, documenting the fact of the contingency of any given version of the past on the basis of current conjunctures of power and interest.

This is not to say that "mere description" is normatively neutral. Descriptive accounts are meant to have a critical dynamic. They propose to describe better, or anew, the real processes by which the past is negotiated. By re-describing a conventional past in new terms, they disclose the processes by which persons and groups are dominated—and/or constituted—by discourses over which they have inadequate or no control. The core intuition guiding such critique is one familiar from Marx's notion of ideology-critique: the negotiated or contested character of the historical past implies the contingency of any version of the past, and this contingency, critically disclosed, is intended to undermine the claims to immutability and objectivity extended by those social actors whose interests are best served by a "fixed" or nonnegotiable version of the past. Historiography becomes critical, in other words, once we insist that *any* claim to the noncontingency of a predominant shared past ultimately functions as an ideological screen for the contingent and re-negotiable character of such a predominant past, or, alternatively, as checks to the agency of persons for whom such a past operates as a mechanism for oppression, exclusion, or invisibility.

We should notice straight away that the social constructivist approach maintains open tensions between re-description as a political practice for the present, and objectivist claims about the need to correct errors or omissions in the construction of an existing past. In this sense, David Kim argued in the previous chapter that both factual errors and politically motivated omissions were the enabling conditions for a prevailing view of America's imperial ambitions. That view was able to generate an ideology of American innocence only because it elided crucial events in the expansion and maintenance of an American imperial zone stretching across the Pacific Rim. Omission had the practical consequence of making concrete political decisions and policy positions coherent and plausible. Retelling the story of America's Pacific expansion undoes a prevailing past in both a descriptive and normative sense: by correcting errors in the historical record, retelling or "renegotiating" the past makes powerful normative claims, and these claims are not just about current American society and politics but about the rightness of broader inclusion of persons and events otherwise excluded. This melding of normative and descriptive considerations in a view to the practical consequences of various historical retellings is, certainly, a truly pragmatic way of thinking. "The frontier concept," Kim writes in chapter 2,

> plays an antidemocratic normative role. A pragmatist theory of democracy is fundamentally a tool for ameliorating conditions contrary to human growth. The totalistic erasure in Dewey's frontier vision, however, not only fails to solve problems in democracy but actually exacerbates them. And to be clear, the issue here is not simply the factual inaccuracy of the Deweyan story, which any decent history book can correct, but normative interpretation. When racial oppression is systemic and historically protracted, a historically grounded normative context will not simply offer an informational penumbra around the condemnation of racism but will permeate and qualitatively change the condemnation itself. (63)

The normativity of the social construction model rests on the notion of undoing "erasure," or, in my own preferred terms, of *broader inclusion*. This notion, in turn, depends on a normative claim, familiar from the "discourse principle" of Jürgen Habermas, expressing a fundamental democratic norm about the process of negotiating the past: persons and groups ought to be included as participants in the processes constitutive for negotiating versions of a past that can reasonably be expected to affect them in their self-conceptions as equal social members. Of course, the notion of full inclusion of affected persons and groups in memorial politics is a normative principle often unrealizable in political practice for a host of reasons. And in a pluralistic society, one cannot expect to have a free hand to write one's past just the way one likes. A critical theory of the social construction of the past would take on precisely the task of analyzing these processes in order to make visible the moments of exclusion and silencing, and come up with more compelling accounts of how, or where, such processes *ought* to be more inclusive, more transparent and accessible, where contingency *ought* to trump the fixedness of a version of the past, and so on. It seems that this is what Brandom and Kim must mean in their accounts of the political stakes in the renegotiations of the racialized effects of the Unionist compromise, or the silenced imperial history of America's expansion into the Pacific Rim.

I mentioned above the tension between two quite distinct conceptions of the normative significance of processes of collective memory-formation and history writing. The first, the social construction model, is a predominantly descriptive practice with a normative, critical intent. By contrast, study of the shared past can shift the emphasis from the *processes* by which the past is constructed and negotiated, to the *object* of such processes; that is, what, or more precisely, *who* is remembered, and *what kind of relation* is established between past and present through practices of memory. Here the operative term is not the re-description or renegotiation of the past but the acknowledgement and efforts to fulfill an *obligation* to past persons, which may be discharged by any number of practices: the disavowal of older social norms, the requirement of collective processes of reflection, new modes of historiography, the inauguration of commemorative practices, or claims for restitution of various kinds. The normative orientation to a shared past, in other words, consists in establishing and maintaining normatively relevant *relationships with past fellow members of a democratic society.*

The mode in which this obligation must be exercised is an interpretative one: from a moral point of view, the past discloses itself as a range of interpretive obligations toward those who fell victim to historical injustices. Interpretation may consist in "keeping their memory alive" or forbidding the obliteration of their existence in the past; or, alternatively, in transforming their unjust suffering to a source of moral insight and resolve in the present. Remembrance understood as assuming obligation has a range of practical consequences, from the official recognition of an injustice in the form of days of national memory, all the way to policies of reparation and restitution of injured persons or groups or their identifiable descendants. In this model, the relative weight of the normative and descriptive dimension of theory is reversed, and the theory model demands an open and powerful normativity: the political challenge of creative re-description is trumped, as it were, by the moral challenge of obligation, which in contrast appears precisely as nonnegotiable and hence fixed. Whereas social construction implicitly assumes a sort of foundational contingency in the constitution and maintenance of a shared past, the solidarity model seems dedicated to acknowledging victims of past suffering as normative *constraints* to the work of renegotiation, introducing a form of moral objectivity (of a highly problematic kind) to the play of contingency.

Social construction and solidarity with the past can be taken as two dominant models that emerge from new conceptions of the dynamic and malleable nature of the relation between present and past. Initially, it seems that these two models mutually reinforce one another and indeed offer complementary perspectives on the same phenomenon: we discharge our moral obligations to past victims of historical injustice insofar as we renegotiate or re-describe prevailing conceptions of a collective past in such a way that those persons are remembered, and their demands for justice, which went silent or were refused in their own lifetimes, are retroactively included in contemporary moral deliberation, attended and honored, if not satisfied. In confronting its own historical guilt, a self-reflecting social present refuses a comforting and familiar version of its own shared past in the same act of self-interpretation whereby it receives and offers a sort of justice to the frustrated claims of its historical victims.

This complementary relationship between social construction and solidarity with the past is not the only possibility, though. What happens when obligation to the past imposes constraints or limits on just those re-descriptions that the practically interested historian regards as normatively desirable for her own present? We can easily enough imagine a situation in which the normative core of social construction, the critical re-description of prevailing social institutions and practices in the interests of greater inclusion and enhanced agency of those affected by them, may well differ sharply from the kind of commemorative practices implied by solidarity with the past. In the Historians' Debate from the 1980s, the conservative historians who opposed Habermas's appeal to solidarity with the past justified their position with the argument that Germany's present need to rewin a healthy or at least nonpathological self-conception as a "normal" nation was a requirement for the psychic stability of its citizens and the collective capacity of the German nation to discharge its international responsibilities. Implicitly, they argued that the needs of the living trumped those of the dead.

Jim Bohman's chapter in this volume identifies why this conservative position in a controversy over social construction of the past fails to convince insofar as it fails utterly to justify its revision on the basis of historical novelty. But other forms of this argument, in an entirely different political register, are possible. The immigration of Turks to Germany in the 1950s and 60s is certainly intimately bound up with the collective history of Fascism and catastrophic war, as large numbers of Turkish guest workers were "imported" into Germany as an essential component of the economic reconstruction of a country sorely lacking in labor force. The transition from Jews to Turks as Germany's most visible ethnic minority is, in other words, seamlessly integrated into the ongoing shared social history, the material from which alternative constructions of the past arise. Insofar as Turks in Germany continue to suffer from a spectrum of exclusions, marginalizations, and silencings, and because such exclusions constitute socially embedded institutional injustices that *ought* to be redressed, the re-description or renegotiation of a shared German past that is more inclusive of its Turkish minority, that renders that minority more visible and contributes to its shared agency, is a normative demand. And it is entirely possible that a normatively oriented historian choosing to renegotiate Germany's recent history will find that the moral obligation to victims, according to which that history is centered on the implications of Holocaust memory, precludes a renegotiation of Germany's shared past that foregrounds the Turkish experience and its implications.

On another register, a retelling of American history that includes the true extent of the racial injustice of the reconstruction era might, as Menand's does, present a new insight into the effects of the Unionist compromise on race relations. A prevailing account of historical causality shifts. But how do we respond to an objection that this retelling, for all its practical uses, unjustly downplays the agency of African Americans themselves during the Reconstruction, portraying them as passive victims and thus reinforcing a consensus that denies them political agency?

It's well beyond the scope of this essay to analyze how pragmatism, in the form of George Herbert Mead's writings, can begin to address these problems, so my remarks here will necessarily be suggestive rather than systematic. Moreover, as I present in quite fragmentary form what I take to be the resources that Mead suggests, I'd like to contrast him to his historical contemporary, Walter Benjamin. The reasons for this interpretive strategy are simply that Mead and Benjamin, over the course of the 1930s, and operating from entirely different theoretical premises, developed strikingly complementary conceptions of the politics and morality of the revisable past. Neither Benjamin nor Mead developed his conception of historical time consistently, and the fragmentary nature of their writings can certainly be assembled and interpreted in strikingly different ways. But Mead's and Benjamin's thoughts on the nature of historical experience and the relation between present and past converge in a vision of a *shared* past that is *incessantly novel* insofar as the past is the ongoing production or performance of interpretive practices. These interpretive practices consist in the social construction of present, past, and their relationship; they are social insofar as they are interactive and imply the establishment and maintenance of ongoing intersubjective communicative relationships mediated by the exchange of positions. The practice of historiography, insofar as it seeks to interpret the past, necessarily entails a strongly normative dimension in both Mead's and Benjamin's work, since the relation between *our* present and *our* past consists in sustained interpretive practices in which the past is socially constructed as a conversation partner. For this reason, reading Mead and Benjamin against one another might help illuminate both.

Both Benjamin and Mead oppose a prevalent conception of historicism that presupposes an objective past-in-itself, which the historical sciences posit as a heuristic against which scientific progress would be measured. The connection between historicism and positivism is taken by Benjamin as evidence of the essentially ideological core of historicism: its complicity in a larger ideological program of covering the rifts and discontinuities of the transmission of historical memory and experience under the cloak of a homogenous and fixed past, inflexibly related to an unproblematic present and flowing in an orderly manner toward a predictable future. For Benjamin, the conception of time as an objective and stable structure was in essence a re-mythologization of past-present relations insofar as the even and orderly time of historicism mimics the mythic repetition of mythical worldviews in an attempt to stabilize the extreme disruptions of temporality inaugurated by the "creative destruction" of capitalism.

Mead regarded historicism as based on a conception of historical time that had in essence been invalidated by advances in natural science—specifically, by Einstein's special theory of relativity. In *The Philosophy of the Present,* Mead argued that the dynamic and mutable nature of the position of the subject in temporal experience implies that there is no objectively independent past against which a present can be consistently measured. Past and present are simultaneously generated as intertwined functions. The constitution of temporality itself is possible only as an emergent event interrupts the otherwise continuous flow of action, and the emergent event is in essence a frustration or check to routine, unreflective actions. This rejection of the conventional view of the past as a fixed and stable series of linear, narratable events implies the reformulation of our conception of what the present is. Mead argues for the rejection of the "knife-edge" view of the present as a moment of infinitesimal duration separating past and future, and its replacement by a "specious" present as a space in which things happen. Both Benjamin and Mead were influenced by contemporary efforts to describe this durable present in terms of the phenomenological description of the stream of subjective consciousness exemplified by Bergson. But neither was convinced that such a present could be adequately captured in terms that excluded the inherently social or intersubjective character of the present. Benjamin was of course deeply interested in the creative relationship between private and social memory. Mead, by contrast, comes close to rejecting the very possibility of a private memory in a manner reminiscent of their contemporary Maurice Halbwachs.

For Benjamin, the conventional relation of past and present had to be re-described as the emergence of moments of "legibility" of historical experience, "now-times" [*Jetztzeiten*] in which features of a social situation disrupt a received historical narration and re-juxtapose their elements, disclosing a new historical constellation in which the distance between past and present is shockingly bridged, and the *relevance* of a constellation of shared experiences comes into view. The aspect of sudden abridgement of temporal distance undermines the stability of the past-present relationship; a past "blasted out" of a mythical continuum of historical time is in this sense a past that has never before existed; a *novel* past that fuses to a now-superceded present to form a now-time.

Benjamin's conception of the now as the disclosure of a new context of relevance between us and a particular past corresponds to Mead's attempts to articulate a conception of the emergent, that is, the eruption of novelty within the unproblematic continuity of experience that serves as a point at which the novel present and the novel past reinterpret one another. As a social construction, "the" past is constitutive for a specious present, which can be seen as its entailment or outcome; at the same time, the present constructs "its" past as part of an ongoing interpretive practice. Both past and present are mutually interpretive structures that are exquisitely sensitive to novel interpretation in and through the emergent event. The objectivity of the temporal sequence of events is, in one sense, not an illusion, but it is the conditioned outcome of ongoing practice in such a way that the objectivity itself is dynamic in relation to the event; the past is constructed as what is *still relevant for the solution to the problem that the emergence of novelty constitutes,* what is still going on, and therefore not "passed" but passing. The past is hypothetical in its relation to a present in which social praxis is happening. Likewise, the present is that structure of intersubjective construction in which what is relevant happens; it determines the relevance of what is still going on, just as the past determines what can possibly be an emergent event:

> The relation of any event to the conditions under which it occurs is what we term causation. The relations of the event to its preceding conditions at once sets up a history, and the uniqueness of the event makes that history relative to the event. The conditioning passage and the appearance of the unique event then give rise to past and future as they appear in the present. All of the past is in the present as the conditioning nature of passage, and all the future arises out of the present as the unique events that transpire. To unravel this existent past in the present and on the basis of it to previse the future is the task of science.[2]

Mead thus understands a past that remains, as a matter of fact and as a principle of experience, constantly open for revision: *that* things have happened, and *that* what has happened will ramify as we confront checks to our actions, is irrevocable; but *what* has happened, and *how* the past will ramify for our impending actions, is as revocable and revisable as we care to make it. Once again, the production of historiography is less the exercise of a mnemo-technology than a specialized and highly presupposi- tioned variant of the same social practice that we, as participants in demo- cratic life, are already engaged in. The space of the present is, in other words, the democratic and agonistic space of the political itself, a pos- sibility that Jim Bohman's conception of de-centered democracy explores in detail in chapter 5.

Past, present, and future remain tense and open, ongoing social con- structions referred to one another and held together by the ethical bonds that hold speakers and hearers together. The ethical obligation to the past, for Mead, is the same one that social agents in the present understand as directing their interpretive attitudes toward the present and future. The work of writing history, then, encounters *both* a past principally open to revision *and* a past composed of members whose expectations of moral recognition is encoded in reciprocal role-taking, perspective-taking, and acts of recognition.

> The long and short of it is that the past (or the meaningful structure of the past) is as hypothetical as the future. . . . And the metaphysical assumption that there has been a definite past of events neither adds to nor subtracts from the security of any hypothesis which illuminates our present.[3]

Benjamin, by contrast, was a theoretician of crisis, not of democracy. He asserted that the task of the historian was a highly moral and political undertaking, not just insofar as the social and political present is con- structed from the past, but also, at the same time, because this very act of ongoing construction affects the past as well. Unlike Mead, Benjamin understood this fragility and openness of the past in terms of crisis. The social construction of the past confronts a structure of memory in which the status of past persons is caught between two equally horrible poles: on the one side, oblivion, on the other, assimilation into a homogenous and strategically constructed historical narrative that *preserves* past victims in an approved mode of collective memory precisely by *effacing* or forgetting their status as victims of an injustice that is itself ongoing. In this sense, Benjamin's understanding of the openness of the past, unlike Mead's, takes on a distinctly messianic political inflection toward the end of the 1930s and the end of Benjamin's life.

"Interpretation," for Benjamin, consists in the confrontation with a new constellation of meaning disclosed by the abridgement or collapse of mythic time; what is interpreted is not just the situation created by the newly disclosed historical elements but also the claims entailed by the act of disclosure itself. In the form of thwarted expectations for happiness or demands for justice, the past (in the form of past persons) *explodes* into our present as the insistence of relevance. Frustrated or unfulfilled expectations of *this* past cannot be "discharged" by memory but only by the political *praxis* that transforms the social context in which past and present are caught. To interpret that which has been as it intrudes on us through a now-time is to accept the demand for justice not as retroactive but as proactive, since the redemption of the suffering of those who died in injustice is possible only via the negation of the context of injustice itself. In this sense, historiography, which seeks to provoke now-times through the construction and dissemination of the material detritus of capitalism's unstable past, is less a technology of memory than a sociopolitical practice best understood as a sort of explosive or revolutionary interpretation. The only way to redeem the claims of the past is to explode the temporal continuum that renders those claims hypothetical. But this is just the messianic impulse, to arrest or destroy time, to interrupt and suspend it, rather than master it or reflexively appropriate it. The consistency of Benjamin's entire normative historiography depends, ultimately, on interpreting the relation of present and past from the indefinitely delayed point of view of the messianic arrest of time and history as such.

Messianic interpretation is second-order interpretation. It understands past justice-claims as intelligible only under the premise of the suspendability of a temporality interpreted now as normative, that is, as an unjust continuum of repetition. For this reason, the *obligation* to the past is also a second-order or indirect obligation. Calls for retroactive justice are reinterpreted, messianically, as calls for suspension of past-present relationships altogether. The social construction of time, in its confrontation with the normative weight of obligation to past victims, necessarily flips into the social *destruction* of time, even if this destruction is only virtually enacted through critical interventions intended to shock or awaken the present from the "dream time" of capitalism. In this sense, we might plausibly call Benjamin an anti-pragmatist, even as his work generates positions strikingly similar to those of the pragmatist Mead.

For Mead, the constitution of social time is also a normative practice. The corollary of the experience of the moral trumping of the conventional present in favor of the unjustly forgotten past is the eminently democratic practice in which a subject must appeal to a moral community *unbounded in time* when confronted with conventional norms of which she cannot approve. Such a generalized community is the "larger community of the past and future," as Mead calls it.[4] The I emerges in the projection of a discourse unbounded in historical time, encompassing all moral beings. For Mead, then, the practice of making history resides within a larger democratic practice. And insofar as this practice entails the progressive expansion of the social consciousness of temporality, we might say that for Mead the moral relationships in which the I encounters a temporally unbounded community of moral agents, in both past and future, means that solidarity with the past can no longer be conceived as a process of recuperation or reconstruction, but as the continuing task of constantly recalibrating and revising the meaning and implications of obligations through interpretive practices based on novelty, and thus demanding an indefinite expansion of the boundaries of a community of those involved in both historical time and social space.

If we analyze the normative intuitions behind the solidarity model, we see once again an articulation of the normative idea of inclusion. To acknowledge a demand for solidarity with past persons is to claim that the set of all those to whom we may be obligated—to whom we owe some form of moral recognition, justifications for our norms—ought to extend to *our* past. As a fact and norm of inclusion, solidarity, on this reading, must always be extended as far as possible; and the limit-case of this extensibility of relations of solidarity is not only spatial but temporal as well. The intuitive core of solidarity with the past thus consists of the potential *harm* to a solidary society in which solidarity does not, or cannot, extend to former members. Specifically, referring to the limiting conditions I just mentioned, the claim is that historical injustices done to former persons themselves contribute to a continuity of social structures and processes. Our relation with the past, therefore, cannot be unilaterally "negotiated" by present persons. The dynamic of solidarity as inclusion is part of a post-metaphysical conception of morality in which moral relations, as relations of symmetry and reciprocity of those in communication, are to be maximally inclusive.

Only by trying—that is, only through a morally motivated experimental attitude—can we find out whether or not solidary relations *can* be extended beyond what we currently take to be their "natural" limits. The normative principle underlying the maximal inclusiveness of solidarity is the same as that which animates the social construction principle, namely, that all those who may reasonably be expected to be affected by a norm ought to be capable of inclusion. But the pragmatic meaning of procedural terms such as "affected" or "capable of inclusion" is revisable in the context of actual practices. When we speak of a debt to the past, for instance, it is up to the unpredictable outcome of specific discourses whether or not we will end up taking this expression as a metaphor regarding the vicissitudes of contemporary memorial practices, or whether we intend to claim a kind of normative relation that our current moral vocabulary has difficulty accommodating. Likewise, when we refer to past persons as "potentially affected" by current norms, we must to some relevant degree leave it up to actual discourses to determine whether this potential refers entirely to our own "current time-slice" conception of how *our* interests are interpreted and articulated through reference to shared memories, or whether, conversely, interests of various kinds survive the physical presence of persons (as is assumed in legal instruments such as the will) and therefore remain affected in the present by the application of norms.

Where Benjamin's thought drives implacably toward a crisis model demanding the destruction of *an actually existing* version of social time, Mead's thought calls for past-present relationships to be fully included into a maximally expansive conception of a community of all those involved; in essence, Mead demands that *our* past is a fully appropriate matter for democracy.

If the relation to a specific set of past persons is expressed in terms of relevance, then one can also say that ongoing past-present relations constitute a system in which we members of a given community operate. Such a system is, like any system, continuously open to emergent events that introduce novelties into that system, forcing us to recalibrate its various relationships and reflexively adjust to a new reality. Insofar as the present is defined precisely as the introduction of novelty, we can make two observations. First, in our example of an apparent choice between present-day demands for a political reconfiguration of the past or the maintenance of a relation to a given past on the basis of obligations, on Mead's terms this choice is *not* between obligations to the past *versus* obligations to the present. The introduction of a new claim for the relevance of a given past, as an emergent, transforms just that past regardless of how the claim is resolved. By effecting a transition from one system of coordinated responses to another, or of one mode of system to a new mode, novelty inevitably *changes the past* to which we try to relate. It is just this transition from one system mode to another, in the face of novelty, that Mead understands as *sociality*. The voices from the past to whom we recognize an obligation do not, in other words, remain unchanged as we change our attitudes and reflexive relationships to them—but in this sense, the dead are no different from any other Others to whom we can relate. The relevance of *their* claim is also hypothetical and revised in light of novelties. For this reason the objectively grounded distinction between relations of obligation to the past and relations of political solidarity to the present cannot be maintained. The choice is not between the past and the present but between greater or lesser amplitudes or magnitudes of extension of a community of all those involved. And procedures for determining those amplitudes or degrees of inclusion—of solidarity—are, as Mitchell Aboulafia will explore in chapter 4, contingent, experimental, contested, emotional, and the very stuff of democratic life.

This suggests, I suppose, that there is no fact of the matter regarding potential conflicts between those, like our hypothetical Turks, who insist on a reinterpretation of the relative relevances of a community's shared past in the interest of its present, and those others who understand moral obligations to a society's past victims to constitute a kind of "no-go" barrier toward even the most beneficial re-descriptions. A society, any society, must encounter its own image, must find the means for its own self-reflexivity, in a generalized other; and this generalized other *expands* in historical time and social space insofar as a society masters its own problems through democratic means and progressively brings its own parochial problems and prejudices under universalistic normative premises. Such a pull of democratic expansion always asks for the broader context in which a parochial problem is settled and privileges the broader over the narrower context. If the voices of the past are not any longer to be interpreted as fixed and monotone in themselves, but if those very voices are inevitably transformed and seen anew in light of the incessant novelty that is intrinsic to modern societies, then in the final analysis it up to the actual outcome of democratic discourses, and not philosophical theory, to decide how those voices are to be interpreted. In just this sense, Mead's conception of social temporality consciously embeds itself in the ongoing discursive practices of a communication community with an enlarged mentality of the limits of inclusion that are normatively definitive for it.

Notes

1. Louis Menand, *The Metaphysical Club* (New York: Farrar, Straus, and Giroux, 2001), 440.

2. George Herbert Mead, *Philosophy of the Present* (Hackett: Indianapolis, 1949), 33.

3. Ibid, 35.

4. George Herbert Mead, *Mind, Self and Society* (Chicago: University of Chicago Press, 1934), 168.

FOUR

Mead on Cosmopolitanism, Sympathy, and War

Mitchell Aboulafia

Let us assume that it is possible for us to feel sympathy for the undeserved sufferings of those with whom we are personally unacquainted, and that moved by this sympathy we acknowledge and even seek to rectify the conditions that have led to this suffering.[1] Let us assume that to do so is morally praiseworthy. Let us also assume that we are more readily moved by suffering if we believe that it speaks in some fashion to our trials, concerns, and interests, that is, when we not only a have basis for sympathizing with others but for empathizing with them in a self-conscious fashion.[2] Now let us consider an instance of those with whom we are unacquainted, namely, those who have lived in other times. When considering these individuals, how are we to understand the relationship between our cares and interests and their undeserved sufferings? Would not their distance from our own parochial and historically defined interests lead us to dismiss their suffering and tempt us to use them as merely a means to our own ends, for example, through incorporating them into narratives that assist us in making sense of our times? Arendt expressed this concern regarding the narrative of progress in her commentary on Kant:

> In Kant himself there is this contradiction: Infinite Progress is the law of the human species; at the same time, man's dignity demands that he be seen (every single one of us) in his particularity and, as such, be seen— but without any comparison and independent of time—as reflecting mankind in general. In other words, the very idea of progress—if it

is more than a change in circumstances and an improvement of the world—contradicts Kant's notion of man's dignity. It is against human dignity to believe in Progress.[3]

Narratives of progress, like other historical narratives, can violate the dignity of those who have come before us, but Kant's concern, as compelling as it is, cannot be the final word. Certainly, if we are in some measure social constructionists, an appeal to a particularity independent of time cannot be a compelling posture. Yet the concern is a real one. If we see the past as simply a product of ongoing revisions in the service of the present, how are we to assure that past voices can be heard and that harms will not go unacknowledged? As Max Pensky noted in chapter 3, "The social construction of the past confronts a structure of memory in which the status of past persons is caught between two equally horrible poles: on the one side, oblivion, on the other, assimilation into a homogenous and strategically constructed historical narrative that *preserves* past victims in an approved mode of collective memory precisely by *effacing* or forgetting their status as victims of an injustice that is itself ongoing."[4]

George Herbert Mead can be a viewed as a social constructionist or, perhaps better, as a social re-constructionist. As a political progressive in the heyday of the progressive movement in the United States, Mead was clearly committed to relieving the suffering of those in his own society and ending the suffering that war inflicts on persons domestic and foreign. However, while Mead has much to offer a discussion of how we are to relate to the past, it may be the case that he and other social constructionists do not have the resources necessary to fully address our responsibility to the victims of past wrongs, which in turn has implications for how we respond to present-day wrongs and to the problems of war and nationalism. How can one, after all, be a genuine cosmopolitan if one cannot address humanity, past, present, and future? This is not to say that Mead would have been insensitive to our responsibility to the past or that there aren't insights in his work that can be of assistance. It is to ask whether Mead's version of cosmopolitanism can address the past in a manner that would satisfy the moral intuitions reflected in Pensky's statement.

Mead endorses a version of cosmopolitanism that can speak to our obligations to those who suffer, past and present, and specifically to the suffering and destruction brought about by unrestrained nationalism and war. While these issues obviously do not exhaust the field of ethics, they do say a good deal about Mead as an ethicist. My goal in this chapter is to provide an account of how his understanding of our obligations to those who suffer undeservedly is bound up with Mead's cosmopolitanism, which in turn illuminates his positions on war and nationalism. To this end I will provide a brief sketch of how Mead addresses the origin of normativity and the conditions that motivate *some types* of ethical conduct toward persons, both past and present. What is intriguing about Mead in this regard is that he appears to blend approaches to moral obligation that we often assume are in tension or are irreconcilable, for example, the universalism of discourse ethics, which views reciprocity and symmetry as grounded in the pragmatics of language, the communitarian tendencies of certain neo-Hegelians, and theories of moral sentiment.[5] That said, a caveat is in order. Mead's most sustained contributions were to social theory and social psychology. Although he was keenly interested in politics and ethics, and while he wrote and acted on these interests, those looking to Mead for a refined political philosophy and its relationship to ethics will be disappointed. Rather, one should look to his work as for insights that can inform these fields.

If we assume that cosmopolitanism entails a capacity to distance ourselves from the immediacy of the present and local, from the familiar as the true, it would be fair to ask: What resources can Mead bring to bear to help prevent the effacement of others by familiar (grand) narratives and well-worn ideologies, that is, those that conflate the local with the general or submerge the past in a present?[6] If we are to follow Mead and those who are in Habermas's camp, we will need to appeal to a notion of reciprocity and perspective sharing to assist us in answering this question. For Mead, perspective taking is basic to the development of the self as a cognitive object. As an object of cognition, the self depends on the internalization of roles, which can be viewed as perspectives. It also depends on reflexivity, a capacity for self-consciousness, which is grounded in the pragmatics of language development and the exchange of roles.[7] If we find ourselves in circumstances that generate the taking of alternate perspectives in a sustained fashion, we can develop an enlarged mentality, to borrow Kant's phrase, namely, an orientation toward others that is open to difference and communication. For Mead, we do not simply share perspectives that are always already given.[8] We continually encounter perspectives that are different and in varying degrees novel. When certain social conditions are present—for example, the absence of threats by others—these past and present perspectives aren't dismissed but are engaged, and the engagement helps to foster inclusiveness and an ability to step outside of the local. On the one hand, Mead is convinced that the greater number of perspectives that we share, the greater will become our sensitivity to others. Solidarity and inclusiveness will result. On the other hand, if we find ourselves mired in an unwillingness to grapple with new and different perspectives, we will grow less tolerant and insensitive. We will become ever more exclusionary and parochial.

There is certainly something to be said for remaining open to the novel lives of others in order to avoid effacing them with our forms of life. As Buber reminds us, one of the characteristics of the person, the Thou, is her ability to surprise us, to present us with the new. So remaining open to novel perspectives can be viewed as a way of seeking to avoid reducing others to our categories or to circumscribed narratives; that is, it can be seen as a form of respect. But why should we assume that taking alternative perspectives and remaining open to novelty leads to respect and moral growth? Perhaps engaging in perspective taking is best understood as a form of entertainment, so that we do not arrive at morally informed self, but at something more akin to a theatrical self or perhaps the aesthete in Kierkegaard's *Either/Or.* What is at stake here is whether a position that focuses on taking perspectives, on novelty, and on the reconstruction of the past in light of these experiences, what we might call Mead's social reconstructionism, can provide a satisfactory basis for grappling with our responsibilities to others, past or present. By responsibility here, I include not only an awareness of the normative but also the motivations that lead us to rectify harms and suffering. Mead certainly values inclusion, but can his model, or variants thereof, justify the ethical value of inclusiveness and provide an account of what motivates us to seek it? Specifically, can this inclusiveness be extended to respect for those who have lived in other times? I want to take up the latter question not only for its intrinsic merit but because it can shed light on the range, promise, and limitations of Mead's version of cosmopolitanism.

In the *Philosophy of the Present,* Mead seeks to develop a metaphysics that describes how the past arises and its relationship to the present. In brief, past, present, and future arise due to novel events. Without such events, Mead envisions a Parmenidian universe of stasis or being in which becoming is impossible.[9] Novel events yield differences of a sort that make temporality possible. We also learn in the *Philosophy of the Present* that neither the past nor the future is fixed for Mead, for with the upsurge of the novel event, the past has itself changed; that is, it has become a past that has given rise to an in principle unpredictable event, and so has in turn been altered. Or to put this in an alternative form: new pasts emerge with the occurrence of novel events because new presents are born with them. This follows, for Mead, because the past only exists in the present, and the present (and its relationship to the past) is transformed by the novel event. These new pasts are not simply a result of altering our "subjective" interpretations of the past. One might say that while the facticity of the past is located in the present, it nevertheless has an undeniable facticity. The past has an integrity of its own. It is what has preceded and given rise to the present, although its integrity is only vital in relationship to the present. Mead's position raises a host of intriguing metaphysical and hermeneutical questions, which are (mercifully, given the task at hand) beyond the scope of this essay.[10]

In order to address Mead's cosmopolitanism, it will be helpful to place his claims about the past in the *Philosophy of the Present*, which I've just touched on, in the context of his understanding of how the modern self arose through the development of a new relationship to the past, understood as history. In his *Movements of Thought in the Nineteenth Century*, Mead argues that romanticism gave rise to a fundamental shift in our relationship to the past. People turned to the past in order to appreciate their own present circumstances, and in so doing they organized the past in relationship to their current emerging selves:

> It is only because this new self had gone back into the past that such an organized past arose at all. . . . [W]e have to recognize that history does not exist except in so far as the individuals of the present in some sense put themselves back into the past. It is only in a process of memory—memory of the people, if you like, that history can be created. And such a reconstruction of the past is possible only when we have, so to speak, reached some such point that we can become aware of ourselves.[11]

Mead goes on to say that "such a past as that of which I have been speaking is always the creation of a new self, one that has attained content that it did not have before. . . . It is that of a self that has become aware of itself and turns back upon its own past in order to hold onto that self and, so to speak, create a past of its own."[12] For Mead, the process turning back on oneself, the reflexive moment, arises through symbolic interaction and the activity of taking the roles or the perspectives of others. Romanticism was uniquely suited to this process.

> What the Romantic period revealed, then, was not simply a past, but a past as the point of view from which to come back at the self. One has to grow into the attitude of the other, come back at the self, to realize the self; and we are discussing the means by which this was done. Here, then, we have the makings of a new philosophy, the Romantic philosophy.[13]
>
> It was because people in Europe, at this time, put themselves back in the earlier attitude that they could come back upon themselves. . . . As a characteristic of the romantic attitude we find this assumption of rôles.[14]

What romanticism provided was a new way of thinking about the self in relationship to the past that allowed for a new organization of the past. New narratives arose that entailed taking the perspective of others in ways that differed from earlier times. This, of course, is not to say that selves did not exist before romanticism. Rather, it is to suggest that the character of selves was altered by the ways in which people came to experience a multitude of others, both living and dead. For Mead, romanticism gave rise to inventive ways of engaging others through role-taking, which in turn led to the creation of new selves and new relationships to the past.

Earlier, I drew a connection between perspective taking and the notion of the enlarged mentality of the cosmopolitan. I want to develop this connection further by citing a passage from Mead's article, "The Social Self," in which he argues that when the self encounters problematic situations, some of a moral kind, the way in which the self responds results in either its transformation and growth or its stagnation. There is an old self that maintains accepted values or a new one that integrates different values, but to integrate these values it must move beyond both selfishness and self-sacrifice:

> To leave the field to the values represented by the old self is exactly what we term selfishness. The justification for the term is found in the habitual character of conduct with reference to these values. Attention is not claimed by the object and shifts to the subjective field where the affective responses are identified with the old self. The result is that we state the other conflicting ends in subjective terms of other selves and the moral problem seems to take on the form of the sacrifice of the self or the others. Where, however, the problem is objectively considered, although the conflict is a social one, it should not resolve itself into a struggle between selves, but into such reconstruction of the situation that different and *enlarged and more adequate personalities may emerge.* (emphasis added)[15]

Mead thinks that one of the advantages of modernity is that it makes available a larger repertoire of potential selves. He is a cosmopolitan who sees the expansion of communication and contact with others as sources of growth, including moral growth, which in turn has the potential to help give birth to a more democratized world order, one that is less given to strife. Old selves must be willing to give way to new selves to avoid what he terms selfishness. This will lead to an enlargement of the self, that is, a more cosmopolitan self, which is attuned to inclusion.[16]

But if we set aside for moment Mead's commitments to cosmopolitanism and inclusion, we may wish to ask, once again, what it is about taking alternative perspectives, as well as a willingness to accept novelty, that lead to moral and political growth as opposed to, say, some sort of aesthetic self-indulgence or an increased sense of mastery? There appear to be different possibilities for expanding the self, and if you start with the assumption that we are driven to "expand" the self for strategic reasons, as opposed to communicative ones, it's not clear how expanding the self will have the consequences that Mead wishes. But there is a reason why Mead believes that the moral development is a likely outcome of the expansion of perspectives, and it doesn't lie in quasi-transcendental claims regarding the pragmatics of symbolic interaction. He is, in fact, rather old-fashioned.

Mead is indebted to the Scottish and English sympathy theorists, even though he would find their accounts of how sympathy arises limited; for example, there is no self and other dialectic in this tradition, at least not one that would satisfy the neo-Hegelian in Mead. If you were to ask Mead why we should not simply dismiss those who have lived in earlier times, since we engage a past that has been transformed by novel events, you would receive at least two responses, one of which would entail an appeal to a notion of sympathy.

His first response would involve the way in which science approaches the transformation of the past. When one introduces a new biological form into an ecosystem, the novel organism may transform the ecosystem. To understand what has happened, we must make a good-faith effort to reconstruct how the transformation took place, which means understanding what existed before the transformation. This involves a commitment to intellectual integrity, and Mead would insist on this commitment, whether one is evaluating how past biological systems have functioned or examining how others have lived in the past. Mead would appeal here to C. S. Peirce's notion of a community of inquirers, for it is a willingness to participate in such a "community" that helps assure the accuracy and sustainability of our research, whether it be scientific or historical.

Before turning to Mead's second response to the past, which entails a notion of sympathy, I want to call attention to the fact that I have not been speaking of justice or injustice when discussing Mead's position. This is not because he does not address justice, but because for him it involves a form of identification with others in terms of rights, as opposed to kindly and charitable impulses, and it leads to a form of self-affirmation. Another way of stating this is to say that when I speak of sympathy in this essay, I am focusing on the more restricted meaning of the term; that is, I am stressing those feelings that are associated with kindly and charitable impulses—those, for example, which might help to lessen the effect or the likelihood of war—although there is in Mead's thought an understanding of the social that corresponds to the broader definition of the term, what at times I refer to as empathy.[17] Furthermore, it is important to note that Mead is not saying that sympathetic attachments, insofar as we are defining sympathy as a synonym for compassion, are the original source of perspective taking. Perspective taking in developmental terms is related to language development and therefore is weighted to the cognitive, although it can have emotional resonances.

As noted, in important respects Mead resembles the classic sympathy theorists, and it is in this resemblance that we can find his second answer to why we should be careful regarding how we address the past. He believes that there is a natural sympathy that people have for those who suffer and who are burdened. Through perspective taking, or what we might call self-conscious empathy, we can place ourselves in shoes of the other in a multitude of ways. Typically, we empathize without feeling sympathy, that is, when we are simply taking the perspectives, or roles, of others. When we feel sympathy, we are not only empathizing with others—that is, taking their perspectives—there is an emotional response to their pain or hardship. It's even possible to feel sympathy without empathizing—for example, when one viscerally responds to a cry of pain. However, Mead does not think that sympathetic feelings in themselves constitute an ethical response, for sympathy in and of itself does not generate obligation.

> In taking the attitude of the other who appeals to our sympathy, the conduct called out tends to maintain the other rather than the self. . . . The sympathetic identification with the individual in distress, however, calls out in us the incipient reactions of warding off, of defense, which the distress arouses in the sufferer, and these reactions become dominant in response of the one who assists. He places himself in the service of the other. We speak of this attitude as that of unselfishness or self-effacement of the charitable individual. But even this attitude of devotion to the interest of the other is not that of obligation, though it is likely to be so considered in an ethical doctrine which makes morality synonymous with self-sacrifice. *The earliest appearance of the feel of obligation is found in the appraisal of the relief to the distressed person in terms of the donor's effort and expenditure.* (emphasis added)[18]

Mead is too sophisticated a social theorist not to be sensitive to the social and historical dimensions of the experience of sympathy, but he argues that we can speak of a biological impulse to sympathy.[19] However, obligation is not located in the sympathetic feeling itself, or even in the visceral urge and reaction to assist, but in reflection on the circumstances of the distress and in a commitment to alleviate it, that is, in the "effort and expenditure" we are prepared to make in response to our sympathetic feelings. The ways in which we are prepared to alleviate distress are shaped by the sorts of generalized others that we have encountered and internalized. Mead even suggests that the social component of the self stands to impulses as form does to matter for Aristotle.[20] Generalized others involve various commitments, including those that we label normative; and the communitarian element in Mead is reflected in the importance that he places on the generalized other.

Selfishness, as we have seen, appears to inhere in an unwillingness to deal with new values that might transform the self, and moral myopia presents itself as a kind of narcissism, one that fixes on the given. Sympathetic and empathetic attachments, on the other hand, can contribute to enlarging the self. Through placing ourselves in the perspective of those in distress, which involves attending to the circumstances that have produced their suffering, we learn about the nature of their distress, which in a sense becomes our distress. Moral obligation arises when we recognize that a concerted effort on our part is required to alleviate the suffering. It's possible that one could take the perspective of the other who is in distress for the purposes of aesthetic experience; but in practice, Mead is betting that the distress of the other will at times call out an ethical response in us, and this bet is a good one, given the significance of generalized others in human development. A good pragmatic answer, then, to the question of whether we take the perspectives of others for aesthetic or moral ends is that we in fact do both. (Of course, sometimes we do neither.) If you share Mead's ethical and political views, then you will seek to nurture political and cultural climates that foster empathy and sympathy, and you will work to establish communities that support an obligation to assist others. You will do so because it is good not only for others, but potentially for your own well-being and growth. Enlightened self-interest is a respectable motivation for moral actions.

Mead's focus on politics and ethics is motivated by his desire to transform the present political and social order. In statement after statement, he argues for nurturing those behaviors that will transform the present. How then does his commitment to the resolution of contemporary problems, his emphasis on transforming the world—and, as we shall see, on addressing problems that can lead to destructive nationalism and war— relate to a moral sensibility and cosmopolitanism that can speak to past suffering? To answer this question, we turn again to Mead's account of history. For there to be history, we must be able to place ourselves self-consciously back into the past. "It is only in a process of memory— memory of the people, if you like, that history can be created. And such a reconstruction of the past is possible only when we have, so to speak, reached some such point that we can become aware of ourselves."[21] So for Mead, a reconstruction of the past yields history, and this process entails memory and self-awareness. By taking the perspectives of others and of generalized others, we become aware of ourselves; but in doing so, we also open up the possibility of becoming (self) aware of novel events, which in turn leads to the possibility of (new) reconstructions of the past. These reconstructions can be viewed as narratives that entail memories and structure memories. In terms of our attitudes toward those who have suffered in the past, Mead argues that a modern historical sensibility, nurtured by romanticism, has prepared us to expect the novel, the different. We are prepared to restructure our history, to see our personal and collective memories in a new light. When this openness is combined with our sympathetic impulses, which in turn have been shaped by taking the perspectives of others and of generalized others, we have the conditions in place that allow us to acknowledge suffering that is not directly a part of our present world.

However, this can not be the end of the matter. Why, after the initial acknowledgment of distress, whether past or present, are some individuals motivated to move beyond their feelings of sympathy and compassion to a sense of obligation, that is, to a sense that they should act in a concerted manner to alleviate distress? We might take an easy path here and say that the normative content of particular generalized others directs individuals to act in specific circumstances. But surely this in itself can not explain why some people are more motivated than others to move beyond feelings of sympathy to a sense of obligation, for those who are members of the same community can respond quite differently to suffering.

To answer this question for Mead, we begin with a truism that is based on experience, namely, that there are differences between individuals regarding the intensity of their visceral responses to the suffering of others. There are also differences in how prepared individuals are to take the perspectives of those who are in distress. The sources for these differences may be psychological, physiological, or sociological. But whatever may be the original sources for differential responses, the taking of perspectives tends to build on itself, both for individuals and for collectives. It is a form of praxis. Furthermore, we know that taking the perspective of others involves a sensitivity to the attitudinal. For us to respond to the attitudes of others, these attitudes must in some sense be part of us, and the more available they are to us, the more likely certain responses will be. How might we understand this availability? To put this in somewhat traditional empiricist terms: some individuals experience attitudes that are entailed in distress and suffering with greater force and vivacity than others. In practical terms this means that they are more prepared to take the perspectives of those in distress, which entails an urge to act to alleviate the distress because the experience of the other is in a sense their own experience. There are no guarantees here, for of course we can imagine sadistic or masochistic types who refrain from acting for opposing reasons. Moreover, obligation can not be a direct function of the intensity of our sympathy, if only because it entails a mediated relationship to the sufferer; that is, one must think about how to assist the sufferer. Nevertheless, it is a reasonable hypothesis that those who are attuned to the distress of others may be more motivated and inclined to remove their distress, and there is some suggestive empirical evidence to support this claim.[22]

Yet if intensity of sympathy inclines us to act, wouldn't it also incline us to be moved by those who are closest to us, kin and countrymen, to the exclusion of strangers? Doesn't any appeal to self-interest as a moral motivator contribute to the danger of parochialism? And wouldn't such parochialism be reflected in an inability or unwillingness to be moved by past harms and suffering? Where are we to locate the impartial spectator who prompts us away from the parochial, who calls on us to consider the stranger, who moves us to become more cosmopolitan, and who makes us think in terms of obligation and not just desires?

I can only begin to sketch here how Mead might respond, for the question of impartiality involves an extended discussion on the status of universals in Mead, which leads to a modification of the communitarian element in his thought that I mentioned earlier. Impartiality is related to the fact that generalized others function at different levels of abstraction. This, it should be noted, is an empirical claim for Mead. If we look about, we can see that not only do families have generalized others, but

> so do concrete social classes or subgroups, such as political parties, clubs, corporations, which are all actually functional social units, in terms of which their individual members are directly related to one another. The others are abstract social classes or subgroups, such as the class of debtors and the class of creditors, in terms of which their individual members are related to one another only more or less indirectly.[23]

Selves arise that correspond to these more abstract communities. But the process does not stop here. Through the practice of taking different perspectives and utilizing symbols that are more abstract, there develops a capacity to extend our horizons to communities that are tied together by increasingly abstract commitments, for example, a commitment to certain kinds of rights.[24]

> In the community there are certain ways of acting under situations which are essentially identical, and these ways of acting on the part of anyone are those which we excite in others when we take certain steps. If we assert our rights, we are calling for a definite response just because they are rights that are universal—a response which everyone should, and perhaps will, give.[25]

While Mead does not invoke the notion of an ideal communication community of the Habermasian sort, namely, one that depends on a quasi-transcendental foundation, he does suggest that we can develop a critical distance from localized claims by invoking more abstract and universal communities. For Mead, universals are first and foremost shared symbols, and a symbol can even be called a universal if it is shared by just two individuals. In this respect some symbols are more universal than others in being more widely shared, and there is a correlation between the potential for a symbol to be shared and its degree of abstractness. In an analogous manner, some communities or groups are more universal than others. "Group solidarity, especially in its uniform restrictions, gives [one] the unity of universality. This I take to be the sole source of the universal. It quickly passes the bounds of the specific group. . . . Education and varied experience refine out of it what is provincial, and leave 'what is true for all men at all times.' "[26] Mead places scare quotes around the phrase "what is true for all men at all times," for he isn't naively ahistorical. Yet we are no doubt dealing with an Enlightenment sensibility, though one that has been transformed by romantic and expressivist elements. (As an aside, I would add that this feature of Mead's thought is one that he shares with some other pragmatists, in particular Dewey.) Mead, then, is advocating what might be called a contingent universalism, that is, the claim that individuals can move beyond the immediacy of local interactions by engaging others at different levels of abstraction. It is our capacity to distance ourselves from the local that provides a counterweight to the danger of moral myopia due to a preoccupation with localized sympathetic attachments.[27] We might even speculate that our sense of obligation, insofar as it requires a mediated response to suffering as opposed to the immediately visceral, is nurtured by the detachment afforded by the abstractions of generalized others.

Here we return to one of our original questions: Does Mead the social reconstructionist have the resources to deal with intuitions such as Pensky's regarding our responsibility to the past? For Mead, there are people who have developed habits that allow them to take the perspective of historical actors more readily than others. These habits include shedding the parochial by engaging universals and sympathetically attaching ourselves to others. However, if we depend on our ability to abstract from our specific circumstances, then we may lose our connection to those who have suffered. We may approach these others at too high a level of abstraction and, for example, treat their unique suffering as generalized human suffering. They would then fade into various historical narratives, or perhaps into a general story of humanity, and their particularity would be forgotten. Yet if we emphasize sympathetic attachments to others rather than more abstract universalistic ties, we may fail to be moved and motivated by those who appear to be too different from ourselves. We may find ourselves mired in the local and particular and unable to empathize or sympathize with those who have come before us. Here then is Mead's dilemma, and perhaps our own: there appears to be a fundamental tension between the universal and the particular with regard to those who have lived at different times and, mutatis mutandis, for those who are our contemporaries.

What would be Mead's response to this dilemma? As a pragmatist, he would ask us to consider the possibility that the difficulty may not be a function of a failed analysis. It could in fact be due to competing claims that cannot be theoretically resolved. We will have to work to balance these claims in practice, and we will do so not in isolation from one another but as members of communities. We will seek to balance the abstract inclusiveness of the universal, that which provides the moment of impartiality, with the care and concern we have for those with whom we most closely identify. However, there is another sort of habit that may be of service here, namely, the habit of openness to the novel and different. If this habit could be nurtured in addition to our capacities for universalizing and sympathizing, we would have another tool for navigating these difficult shoals. We would find ourselves responsive to the claims of others, and not only in spite of their novelty but perhaps because of their novelty.

We have seen that novelty is also crucial to the very existence of the past and history for Mead. He might admonish us to avoid the bad faith involved in believing that our attitudes toward the past can be fixed. We should instead recognize that our relationship to the past will change over time because the past will no doubt be reconstructed in light of unpredictable novel events. Yes, at minimum a concern for our own moral growth should press us to make a good-faith effort to acknowledge the sufferings of others by taking their perspectives. And here one can argue that this effort would have to include those who have lived before us insofar as they have been harmed and suffered.

What then are the ethical implications of Mead's position with regard to the past? On the positive side, we cannot shirk our responsibility to the past by claiming that the past is inert and dead, and therefore without relationship to us, a claim that those in power often make in order to avoid their responsibility for acknowledging wrongs. (The pronouncement that we cannot change the past is nowadays often followed by the remark that "we need to move forward.") On the negative side, present experience, needs, and concerns may override the claims of those who have lived in earlier times, for the past only exists in the present. Mead would stress the value of universalism, a universalism that would include our connection to those who have come before us. But ultimately, for Mead, we must face the fact that the past only lives in the present. Our first moral obligation is to direct our energies to ensuring that suffering similar to that which has existed in the past does not find its way into the present, and this brings us to the problems of war and nationalism, which offer another avenue for addressing Mead's cosmopolitanism.

Mead thought that war was becoming an impossible course of action in the modern world. Following in Kant's footsteps, he argues that war has simply become too dangerous. Writing between the two world wars, he states, "Every war if allowed to go the accustomed way of wars will become a world war, and every war pursued uncompromisingly and intelligently must take as its objective the destruction not of hostile forces but of enemy nations in their entirety."[28] What has this to do with themes discussed earlier regarding the past and sympathy? Mead is not only willing to posit a modifiable biological urge toward sympathizing with the plight of others, but he is also willing to claim that there are other such impulses. Human selves arise through the molding of these impulses by language, social interaction, and societal organization.

> We are born with our fundamental impulses. . . . This primal stuff of which we are made up is not under our direct control. The primitive sexual, parental, hostile, and cooperative impulses out of which our social selves are built up are few—but they get an almost infinite field of varied application in society, and with every development of means of intercourse, with every invention they find new opportunities of expression.[29]

While we certainly would not want to confuse Mead with the Freud of *Civilization and its Discontents*—Mead never posits overarching meta-psychological and cosmological principles such as Eros and Thanatos, for example—for those used to a sanitized version of the American pragmatist tradition, one that avoids the "darker sides" of human nature, it is perhaps somewhat surprising to hear that Mead is quite prepared to say that there is an impulse to hostility as well as to unity lurking in individuals and human history, which often expresses itself in terms of war. However, for Mead war is not simply a result of hostile impulses or power politics, but it depends on the impulse and need that individuals have for unity. "Society is unity in diversity," he wrote. "However, there is always present the danger of its miscarriage. There are the two sources of its unity—the unity arising from the interconnection of all of the different selves in their self-conscious diversity and that arising from the identity of common impulses."[30]

Paradoxically, the source of hope in the modern world—the ability of human beings to abstract from the local and see themselves from ever widening vantage points, that is, to become participants in communities of increasing scope—can backfire if the promise of unity, community, remains unfulfilled. In this circumstance the impulse to unity is not modified in the direction of intelligently guided social interaction and organization; rather, it is strengthened by social forces that prey upon primal needs for inclusion, which can lead to war. We then have identification and bonding with others at the price of opposing those who are viewed as outsiders, as *not* members of the community. There is no older story, but in the modern world we face an especially pernicious version.

> There is something profoundly pathetic in the situation of great peoples, that have been struggling up through long centuries of fighting and its attendant miseries, coming closer and closer to each other in their daily lives, fashioning unwittingly larger racial, lingual, liturgical, confessional, political, and economic communities, and realizing only intermittently the spiritual life which this larger community confers upon them, and realizing it only when they could fight for it. The pathos comes out most vividly in the nationalisms of the nineteenth and twentieth centuries. These nationalisms have meant the sudden realization that men belonged to communities that transcended their groups, families, and clans. . . . The pathos lies in the inability to feel the new unity with the nation except in the union of arms. It is not that men love fighting for its own sake, but they undergo its rigors for the sake of conjunction with all those who are fighting in the same cause.[31]

On the one hand, Mead sings the praises of enlarging the circles in which we engage the perspectives of others, but on the other, he alerts us to forces that can turn this perspective taking against others by limiting its activity to a given unit, say a tribe or a nation, so that others are deemed as outside of "our" community. Mead's position, however, is that there is no turning back from where the modern world has brought us. We must find a way to feel united with others in a nondestructive fashion in a world that threatens our sense of stability and community.

> There is only one solution for the problem [of war,] and that is in finding the intelligible common objects, the objects of industry and commerce, the common values in literature, art, and science, the common human interests which political mechanisms define and protect and foster. . . . Within our communities the process of civilization is the discovery of these common ends which are the bases of social organizations. In social organization they come to mean not opposition but diverse occupations and activities. Difference of function takes the place of hostility of interest.[32]

These common interests are to be pursued within states and between states. Mead's thesis, in part, is that until there is a sense of unity in particular societies, developed through common ends and organizations that permit functional differentiation, there will be a temptation to war. Now there is much to criticize in this vision, but it is certainly consistent with his view that unalienated integration into groups, the existence of different sorts of groups, and movement between them, have the potential to nurture a kind of cosmopolitanism that will lessen hostility to "outsiders." Of course, one can immediately argue that Mead was simply naïve about political forces in the modern world and that functional differentiation can breed alienation as well as integration. I would, however, like to pass over a critique at this point in order to bring the discussion back to Mead's views on the psychology of sympathy. Certainly, the mere reorientation of the psychology of individual actors will not prevent war, but I want to make a more modest claim, namely, that Mead's social-psychological approach has something interesting to say regarding what disposes individual actors to become responsive to the plight of others, which in turn can have consequences regarding how readily they take up arms. But first a caveat: Mead was well aware of the importance of institutional and legal safeguards, especially on the international plane. He was, after all, a booster of the League of Nations. This is not to say that he had a sufficiently robust theory of the procedural for dealing with domestic or international affairs. It is to say that he was not naïve enough to believe that efforts based on social-psychological insight alone are sufficient to address the problem of war.

I began this essay by claiming that it is possible to feel sympathy for the undeserved suffering of others, and that moved by this sympathy we may acknowledge and seek to rectify the conditions that led to it. I take this to be an uncontroversial claim. Of course there would be considerable dispute among ethicists and the religiously minded regarding how we are to interpret the term "undeserved." And it's possible that some might challenge this claim based on the grounds that suffering builds character. However, those who may be tempted to make the latter assertion often confuse the hardship that stems from specific activities or experiences, which may build character, with the suffering involved in the hardship. In any case, for the purposes at hand, I am comfortable asserting that undeserved suffering should be prevented, eliminated, or ameliorated.

A clear instance of undeserved suffering of this type is the loss of life, homelessness, and serious injury that resulted from the recent earthquakes and tsunamis in the Indian Ocean. Estimates suggested that more than 150,000 people died, 500,000 were seriously injured, and five million left homeless.[33] Nations responded to this catastrophe by offering various forms of assistance, including large sums of money, even appearing to compete with one another regarding how great their assistance would be. Now there were geopolitical reasons for this assistance: concern about fragile and war-torn regimes in the region, and a desire to appear altruistic toward those of the Islamic faith for propaganda purposes, for example. But there also appeared to be a genuine aspiration to alleviate suffering, and this was reflected not only in the actions of governments, which seemed to be supported by their peoples, but in the contributions that were made by individuals throughout the world. Of course individuals felt different degrees of sympathy for the victims for various reasons, and there were those whose racism may have prevented them from seeing the humanity of those who suffered. But sympathy for the victims of the tsunamis appeared to be widespread, although how extensive is an empirical question that cannot be answered here.[34]

If we look at the world's response to this disaster, components of Mead's approach to suffering are in full view. First, many of those exposed to the images of the death and destruction had an immediate, visceral, sympathetic response to the distress of others, in spite of their physical and cultural distance. Second, for some, perhaps for many, this immediate response set the stage for taking the perspective of others—in this case, of those who suffered serious injury and/or the loss of loved ones. Third, the normative standards of generalized others came into play, bringing to bear "local" norms about dealing with those in distress as well as more abstract perspectives that allowed the victims to be viewed as members of more "universal" communities, for example, those that encompassed both victims and the empathic individuals. Fourth, the sympathetic impulse, the taking of the perspective of others, and the normative dimension of generalized others, helped generate a sense of obligation, which entailed an appraisal of the effort that was needed to alleviate the suffering. And lastly, this sense of obligation was acted on in various ways, for example, through monetary contributions or directly by those expending time and effort to help alleviate the suffering.

As noted, Mead's position entails biological proclivities to sympathy and unity whose origins are perhaps best understand in terms of natural selection, for example, that human beings are relatively fragile biological organisms uniquely dependent on others of their kind for survival. We might also speculate that this fragility can in part account for the fear that many feel when they experience instability, social unrest, and alienation. Impulses or proclivities are molded, shaped, and informed by the way in which the self develops through linguistic interaction, role taking, and the internalization of generalized others. However, while the reciprocity of social interaction is basic for Mead, it is not enough to guarantee unity.

There must also be goals in common, which can be found in organizations whose functional distinctions permit the social integration of the actors. Without common goals and/or intelligent integration of social functions, Mead fears that war will result. Why? As we have seen, Mead argues that there is an impulsive drive for unity that can be primed and activated by specific social conditions and sated by uniting with others in acts of war. Yet war, modern war in particular, is unacceptable to Mead.

I will offer a hypothesis, which Mead does not directly develop, but which should shed some light on how his cosmopolitanism and opposition to war are related: War should be viewed as a form of natural disaster for many, if not most, of those caught in its path. They neither understand nor were involved in the decisions of those who decided to go to war, yet they undeservedly suffer from its consequences. War comes to them as a tidal force—dark, uncontrollable, and lethal. Yes, a populace can be stirred into a war frenzy, but this sort of mass hysteria only supports the claim that people often do not appreciate the consequences of war for those who will be caught in its path. If we take Mead's account of perspective taking and sympathy seriously, one of the conditions that contributes to initiating and sustaining war is an inability to view others as those who can suffer undeservedly.

That war is made possible and sustained through the dehumanization of the enemy is surely a time-honored observation. Mead, however, is offering an account of the kinds of human capacities that have to be short-circuited if this is to occur. For example, if the so-called enemy were viewed as victims of a natural disaster, the sympathetic impulse, as well as our capacity to take their perspective, would diminish the urge to war. This is all the more true when pictures and videos of the human suffering involved in war are readily available. To keep individuals motivated to pursue war under these circumstances, one must convince them that there is a genuine threat from an adversary or that the adversary deserves to suffer. Why did so many Americans believe that the Saddam Hussein and Iraq were responsible for 9/11? One might say that this misperception was due to effective propaganda. And one might also say that without this belief it would have been hard to justify the suffering that ensued. Undeserved suffering must become deserved suffering, which is viewed as deserved or acceptable because of what "they" did to us. Because of what they did to us, they cannot be like us, for if they were like us they would not have acted as they did. They would have had sympathy for our suffering.

However, sympathy and a capacity for taking the perspective of others is an insufficient hedge against war for Mead, especially in the modern world. We need to become ever more cosmopolitan. We need to see that others are capable of suffering as we do, and we need to develop a sense of obligation toward them. But this will not be possible if nations are themselves divided, if alienation and instability rule supreme.

> What I am seeking to bring out is that the chief difficulty in attaining international-mindedness does not lie in the clash of international interests but in the deep-seated need which nations feel of being ready to fight, not for ostensible ends but for the sake of the sense of national unity, of self-determination, of national self-respect that they can achieve in no other way so easily as in the readiness to fight. National-mindedness and international-mindedness are inextricably involved in each other. Stable nations do not feel the need in any such degree as those that are seeking stability.[35]

If Mead's analysis is even partially on target, then he can be said to have understood factors working against the immediate realization of his own cosmopolitan "vision," namely, the expressivist sensibilities lodged in movements of national self-determination during the past two centuries. Mead was never simply an adherent of the Radical Enlightenment's notion of universality. There was too much understanding of the romantic temper in his thought. Hence, national identity and self-determination need to be achieved before cosmopolitanism can come into its own. So once again we see a tension between the universal and the particular for Mead. Perhaps the best that he could hope for in his lifetime was that tendencies to universality in the modern world would be nurtured and institutionalized —for example, through international organizations and agencies—while expectations for national and collective self-identity would be met in nonmilitaristic and nondestructive ways.

Mead's views on nationalism and war may seem old hat, a set of concerns from a time and place rapidly drifting into the past, especially as globalization in its myriad forms presses in around us. Or perhaps not.

Notes

1. There is much riding on the term "undeserved," namely, what is the source and nature of the judgment that this suffering is in fact undeserved? For the purposes at hand, all I ask is that the reader accept the claim that people suffer through no fault of their own, whether due to the calculations of human beings or to natural disasters.

2. The way in which I am using the term "empathy" here emphasizes the reconstructive dimension of Martha Nussbaum's definition: "'Empathy' is often used, as I shall later use it, to designate an imaginative reconstruction of another person's experience, without any particular evaluation of that experience; so used, obviously, it is quite different and insufficient for compassion; it may not even be

necessary for it" (*Upheavals of Thought: The Intelligence of the Emotions* [Cambridge: Cambridge University Press, 2001], 301–302). As we will see, if empathy simply refers to "taking the perspective of others" for Mead, it can be viewed in non-evaluative terms. However, for Mead there are circumstances in which the evaluative dimension of taking the perspective of others comes directly into play, for example, with certain generalized others.

3. Hannah Arendt, *Lectures on Kant's Political Philosophy*, ed. Ronald Beiner (Chicago: University of Chicago Press, 1982), 77.

4. See above, chapter 3, p. 90.

5. Or to state this in other terms, Habermas reads Mead as something of a dialogical neo-Kantian, although Mead is in fact not a post-metaphysical discourse ethicist, even though his ethics is post-metaphysical, dialogic, socially based, and universally minded.

6. Yes, no doubt cosmopolitanism can itself be utilized as a cover for a certain kinds of parochialism and ethnocentrism, but following Mead, I am assuming here that it need not be.

7. See Mitchell Aboulafia, *The Cosmopolitan Self: Mead and Continental Philosophy*, (Urbana and Chicago: University of Illinois Press, 2001), chap. 1.

8. Arendt writes, "In the *Critique of Judgment*, however, Kant insisted upon a different way of thinking, for which it would not be enough to be in agreement with one's own self, but which consisted of being able to 'think in the place of everybody else' and which he therefore called an 'enlarged mentality' (*eine erweiterte Denkungsart*). The power of judgment rests on a potential agreement with others, and the thinking process which is active in judging something is not, like the thought process of pure reasoning, a dialogue between me and myself, but finds itself always and primarily, even if I am quite alone in making up my mind, in an anticipated communication with others with whom I know I must finally come to some agreement. From this potential agreement judgment derives its specific validity" ("Crisis in Culture," in *Between Past and Future* (New York: Viking Press, 1968), 220.

9. George Herbert Mead, *The Philosophy of the Present*, ed. Arthur E. Murphy (Chicago: University of Chicago Press, 1980), 1–2, 47–49.

10. See Bohman, chapter 5, and Pensky, chapter 3, in this volume.

11. George Herbert Mead, *Movements of Thought in the Nineteenth Century*, ed. Merritt H. Moore (Chicago: University of Chicago Press, 1936), 70.

12. Ibid., 71.

13. Ibid., 60.

14. Ibid., 63.

15. Mead, "The Social Self," *Selected Writings: George Herbert Mead*, ed. Andrew J. Reck (Chicago: University of Chicago Press, 1964), 148.

16. Mead would find Arendt's position on the relationship of communication to cosmopolitanism compelling, although he would take some exception to the phrase "sheer fact of being human," in the following passage: "One can communicate only if one is able to think from the other person's standpoint; otherwise one will never meet him, never speak in such a way that he understands. . . .

Finally, the larger the scope of those to whom one can communicate, the greater is the worth of the object. . . . One judges always as a member of a community, guided by one's community sense, one's *sensus communis*. But in the last analysis, one is a member of a world community by the sheer fact of being human; this is one's 'cosmopolitan existence'" (*Lectures on Kant's Political Philosophy*, 74–75).

17. Mead, "Philanthropy from the Point of View of Ethics," in *Selected Writings*, 399.

18. Ibid., 400.

19. Mead, "National-Mindedness and International-Mindedness," in *Selected Writings*, 355–70.

20. Ibid., 358.

21. Mead, *Movements of Thought*, 70.

22. Nussbaum, *Upheavals of Thought*, 338–340. She cites a study by C. Daniel Batson.

23. Mead, *Mind, Self and Society*, 157.

24. Ibid., 89–90. "The very universality and impersonality of thought and reason is from the behavioristic standpoint the result of the given individual taking the attitudes of others toward himself, and of his finally crystallizing all these particular attitudes into a single attitude or standpoint which may be called that of the 'generalized other.'"

25. Ibid., 260–61.

26. Mead, "A Behavioristic Account," in *Selected Writings*, 245.

27. One of Mead's rather down-to-earth ways of expressing this: "The only way in which we can react against the disapproval of the entire community is by setting up a higher sort of community which in a certain sense out-votes the one we find" (*Mind, Self and Society*, 167–68).

28. Mead, "National-mindedness and International-Mindedness," 362–63.

29. Ibid., 358–59.

30. Ibid., 359.

31. Ibid., 364–65.

32. Ibid., 365.

33. Jane Perlez, "From Heart of Indonesia's Disaster, a Cry for Help," *New York Times*, 2 January 2005, 1, 9.

34. Note the appeal for assistance made by Susilo Bambang Yudhoyono, Indonesia's president: "I appeal to the world community to contribute to the reconstruction of Indonesia that has been hit by disaster and we welcome those contributions as a manifestation of global unity" (quoted in Perlez, "From Heart of Indonesia's Disaster"). After this tragedy, newscasts in the United States talked about the potential dangers of earthquakes and tsunamis in the U.S. While these newscasts can be viewed as cynical attempts to increase ratings through appeals to fear and self-interest, they also had the practical effect of motivating viewers to take the perspective of those who were suffering, that is, those with whom they may have had more in common than they realized.

35. Mead, "National-Mindedness and International-Mindedness," 367.

FIVE

Deliberating about the Past:
Decentering Deliberative Democracy

James Bohman

> In order to move forward, you must face backwards, towards the past.
> —Maori proverb

When most people think about deliberation, they have in mind something like a town meeting or a face-to-face forum of some sort or another. It is also apparent that this sort of deliberation turns out to be the exception rather than the rule in large and complex democracies. There are many benefits to such face-to-face deliberation, not the least of which comes in play when deliberators have difficulty taking the perspectives of others in situations of conflict, when each needs the presence of the other to correct for biases and misinterpretations. Unfortunately, such forums are often impossible to realize just when they are needed, as is the case in deliberation about the past. Even so, such deliberation has now become much more common, especially in societies with a history of great injustice, including both transitional and established democracies that have to face the burdens of both the recent and the distant past, as in cases of genocide, slavery, or conquest. The difficulty remains: how can deliberation about such claims to justice be public if the past cannot be fully present in the deliberation? While many easily recognize the claims of the future upon us, we do indeed recognize some continuing moral and legal obligations to the past, particularly with regard to property rights. The existence of some such obligations raises further questions about how such obligations are manifest in deliberation itself. Do we owe obligations to persons in the past directly, or to their descendents who are present to us as participants in dialogue, or both?

Some theorists of deliberative democracy have addressed similar issues related to discussions about how to go beyond the town meeting model and introduce temporally and spatially extended deliberation. Deliberation, they argue, must be "decentered," not only in the sense that it should not be identified with deliberation in a single face-to-face forum, but also in the sense that it should be spatially dispersed in many different sites as well as temporally extended to include deliberators who are not currently present. This means that decentering deliberation requires both that it should take place in many forums that are connected across potentially broad expanses of space and time and that membership in the relevant publics should always remain open to deliberative redefinition. Deliberation is decentered whenever the inclusion of new participants aims at introducing perspectives not present in previous stages of deliberation. But in what sense is such inclusion able to change the past of such a democracy? Does expanding deliberation mean that the past is just as open to change as the future? Walter Benjamin and George Herbert Mead are two philosophers who think that responsibility goes in various temporal directions, and both hold that in light of this fact, the past and the future are symmetrical with respect to their ability to obligate and thus also in respect to their openness to change.

My purpose here is to decenter the temporally bounded and presentist assumptions common in public deliberation in three steps. First, I explicate what it means for participants to take up a deliberative or communicative stance toward the past as part of an ongoing democratic community. I leave aside some of the difficult problems of the past that are specific to transitional justice, such as punishment and amnesty. Second, I argue that the past of any established, partially just democratic community ought never be regarded as final or closed. A first pass at what this might mean can be found by paraphrasing Elizabeth Anscombe: it is no more absurd to say that what happens now may change what has happened in the past than it is to say that what happens now may change what will happen in the future.[1] Deliberating about the past is not only a question of truth or evidential adequacy but also of claims to historical justice that can be made sense of only if we abandon the idea of the closed past. Finally, I turn to some examples of how public deliberation does justice to the past by transforming the moral boundaries of the polity and its conditions of membership. Deliberating about the past commonly results in decentering the historical political community itself as a necessary condition for such a community to achieve justice and to remain democratic. Honoring these direct obligations is also a means by which democratic communities remain democratic precisely when faced with the ongoing challenges of an ineluctable and unjust past.

Moral and Epistemic Obligations:
Interpretation as a Normative Attitude

The hold that face-to-face deliberation has on us is perhaps due to some deep, underlying philosophical commitments about deliberation and interpretation. The argument here is a familiar Davidsonian one: there is no independent way to predict beliefs on the basis of behavior, or behavior on the basis of beliefs. Communication and deliberation require a performative stance to the extent that deliberators take up particular *normative* attitudes toward each other as both speakers and hearers.[2] While I do not reject this dialogical conception of deliberation, very often it is too oriented to the speaker's obligations and thus pays insufficient attention to the obligations of the hearer who evaluates and gives uptake to the speaker's reasons. Speakers understand the reasons of others by evaluating them. Thus, to take up the performative attitude is not only to acknowledge the other as the self-originator of claims but also to treat claims in such a way that the hearer incurs obligations and commitments in the very act of acknowledging and responding to the other. In this way, our deliberative stance requires that we take up a relationship to the speaker, given that the act of speaking "binds the speaker to the person spoken to," and vice versa.[3]

It is crucial for my purposes to notice the extent to which such binding does not require that speaker and hearer are either temporally or spatially present to one another or even that the hearer is the intended addressee of the speaker's claim. Present or not, when hearers take up such a claim, they take up a relationship with the speaker that potentially binds them to distant or past others. When deliberating about claims of justice, this relationship is first of all a matter of respect, a matter of acknowledging the other person's having a participant's perspective.[4] The kind of second-personal status that is achieved in this way can be illustrated in Kantian terms. When Kant in his moral philosophy asks us to "respect the humanity of another," he is referring to the former rather than the latter, to moral demands of respect owed to persons with their own intrinsic ends or (to use Rawls's phrase) as self-originating sources of claims. As Kant puts it: "A human being regarded as a *person,* that is, as the subject of a morally practical reason . . . possesses a *dignity* . . . by which he demands *respect* for himself from all other rational beings in the world."⁵ Indeed, dignity is a certain moral status or authority that permits one to demand it for oneself precisely by reciprocally and freely recognizing it in others.⁶ Such a status is then tied to the rational capacities that make persons sources of value,⁷ or, as I am putting it, originators of claims to justice.

As Kant's discussion of the capacity to demand respect from others makes clear, he thought of the normative property of dignity as a status term, specifically the normative status of being a member of the moral community, a status that can be rightly demanded even when it is not recognized. We might call this status (for Kant, our humanity) as my capacity tied to freedom or claim making, "first-personal," and as a status that is recognized or acknowledged by you, "second-personal." It is second-personal in that it is a normative status realized in relations with others who also have this same status. This status is the status of membership in a community. In taking up the claims of others in the past as binding us, we recognize them as having this capacity to demand respect from us and to obligate us to honor their second-personal status as members of our community, whether it is our historical community or the community of humanity, of all those who are able to demand respect and in doing so to obligate us. If we are not so obligated second-personally, then we have forfeited this same status for ourselves first-personally. In deliberating with others so as to get uptake from my deliberative claims, it must always be possible that I acquire obligations from their deliberative claims upon me.

In the case of a face-to-face forum, such obligations are fully reciprocal so long as the conditions for successful communication are met. When taking a deliberative stance toward the past, such full reciprocity cannot be met. The past can bind us as present deliberators do when we take up the hearer role and form obligations to others by acknowledging the force of their justifications. In the same way, the past can fail to bind us when its claims, often implicit, are not acknowledged, and thus those speakers from the past have the same status as those who are excluded from deliberation as noncitizens. But such claims can be included if we come to regard ourselves as a community of deliberators from a new perspective, the perspective of the Generalized Other. Taking up this perspective in deliberation is not only critical but also, to the extent that it validates previously unrecognized claims to justice, obligation-producing. More specifically, critical reflexivity is achieved "only by individuals taking the attitude of the Generalized Other *toward themselves*" and thus by taking up new relations to others to whom we owe a justification insofar as their exclusion does not cohere with our democratic ideals.

Interpreting the Past, Obligating the Future

Consider the difficulties that a partially unjust democracy faces when deliberating about the past. If it is democratic, then some of its practices are universally inclusive in scope, allowing its citizens to participate in a procedurally adequate way in current deliberative practices. But this sort of democracy could still have deeply entrenched historical injustice that would seem to underscore the claim that they are now still unjust with regard to its treatment of past wrongs, say, through the institutional constraints on deliberation or as a consequence of various laws concerning land and property. In these cases, the past plays a role as a perspective of justification that unjust democracies cannot expect to address successfully without examining some of their current claims to legitimacy. Consider a case within a particular democratic polity that involves the recognition of new perspectives, reasons, and obligations. The Canadian Supreme Court recently expanded some standards of justification concerning aboriginal claims by establishing legal recognition of the stories of the Gitxsan people as legitimate evidence in land disputes. Is this a case of historical justice that reopens the past, turning what were previously dismissed as stories or oral history into the legal basis for property rights? Prior to being able to make such claims from their own perspective, the Gitxsan were essentially rightlesss with regard to making claims about property rights that may have been violated in the past. The achievement of such standing came from reopening the past to deliberation.

In discussing the significance of this case, Seyla Benhabib offers an interpretation based on the idea that the Court adopted the standpoint of the Generalized Other, according to a first-person-plural understanding of what that means. In this light, she argues that "what lent legitimacy to the Canadian court's decision was precisely its recognition that a specific group's claims are in the best interests of all Canadian citizens."[8] This means that the perspective of the Gitxsan becomes a potential source of obligations precisely by being included in the sovereign collective will, the now more impartially constituted "We" of all Canadian citizens rather than the perspective constituted by their individual self-interests.

But it is implausible to say that the interests of Canadians can be held constant before and after the decision, as Benhabib's analysis suggests. After the decision, the best interests of Canadians are now different, since everyone becomes members of a more multiperspectival and less dominating polity, just as after *Brown v Board of Education* the United States became a more multiracial polity than it had been before the decision. In both the American and Canadian cases, democracy has been self-correcting only to the extent that it is able to incorporate new perspectives and thus call into question its legitimacy as a democratic will. As such, the polity is reconstituted as a multiperspectival community through significant constitutional change that affects the deeper presuppositions concerning the nature of the democratic community.[9] When such change goes deep enough, it often requires several further decisions to make manifest the full membership of excluded persons as citizens through rectifying past injustices and establishing future normative powers and statuses for those who had not had them in the past.

The perspective of the past most often emerges within already constituted democracies in just such struggles over status and membership in claims to justice made by those who might be called quasi-members or denizens, that is, persons who de facto have the dependent status that Kant called "mere auxiliaries to the republic." Inclusion is not done only from this moment forward but requires changing the temporal perspective of the community to include the past. Even though the Gitxsan already formally possessed full citizenship status, it was only through the transformative effects of taking up their claims to justice that Canadian democratic institutions became the potential means to achieve justice that is appropriate to human rights, a conception of justice that previously was outside of the polity. This is true not simply because the Gitxsan people have now become part of a more fully impartial collective will or because the Canadian court ruled that accepting their claim is in the best interest of all Canadians as free and equal persons. Rather, the issue of justice at stake is more directly constitutional and thus reflexive. A constitutional democracy thus more robustly satisfies the demands of democracy when it acts as a political community open to the reinterpretation and revision of its fundamental principles in order to do justice to the claims of the past.

In discussing this or any other case of wide-ranging constitutional reform, a systematic ambiguity arises: is such a reform the restoration of genuine popular sovereignty, or is it something much more novel, such as the constitution of a plural subject that *surrenders* rather than exercises sovereignty? Democratic theorists have been interested in a particular subject of collective willing that occupies the first-person-plural perspective of "We Canadians," "We Americans," and so on. But there is another sort of plural perspective: the second-person-plural "You," the addressee of claims that asks for a response from the whole community of deliberators. As these cases of the constitutional reform of democracy show, the second-person-plural perspective of democracies cannot be limited *ex ante* to its current citizenry who are its de facto members but must rather be constituted by a more indefinite public with which democratic institutions interact. The reflexive disputability of the scope of any democratic "We" makes any particular limitation always open to the potential objection that its boundaries and jurisdictions are democratically arbitrary and potentially dominating. How does the past occupy one such specific perspective?

In the case of the Gitxsan people, the Canadian Supreme Court's recognition of the Gitxsan claim to justice opens up a new space for deliberation about the legitimacy of a democratic political community that does not fully manifest the equal status of all its members. In so doing, the Court also initiates public deliberation that may potentially develop into a fusion of horizons, a fundamentally new first-person-plural perspective that changes just "who" is "the Canadian people." The encounter with Gitxsan narratives shows the prejudices that are built into the idea of "evidence" in the courts of law, something that induced the Court to see much more than the simple facts of the case and the standard remedies (such as the usual cash payments for loss of land). Once on the terrain of human rights and fundamental justice, the Court saw itself instead as challenged and addressed by historical claims to justice that transcended the previous normative framework that Canadian institutions had used to justify their past actions. In doing so, Canada became a community of peoples, a transnational polity with pooled sovereignties. In this sense, the past now has become plural, no longer a first-person-plural narrative of an emerging inclusive and impartial identity. Rather, it is about intersecting and interacting pasts in which past others have second-personal claims to membership and justice.

As adjudicative institutions, courts can be addressed by a claim of past injustice only when who "we" are, as well as "our" rules of adjudication, are no longer regarded as constitutive of justice but are open to being challenged by claims regarding longstanding but as yet unrecognized historical injustices. Dominated groups such as aboriginal peoples may also appeal to the right to self-determination of colonized people recognized in the United Nations and argue for such shared jurisdiction over land and resources as the remedy for colonization.[10] Because these claims to shared jurisdiction are based in basic human rights (and thus membership in a larger historical community of humanity) more is at stake normatively than simply giving equal rights or equal membership status in an existing federation. Rather, the Canadian court's decision calls into question the consistency of unitary sovereignty with human rights and asks whether the existing Canadian constitution at the time in fact denied to "indigenous people the right to appeal to universal principles of freedom and equality in struggling against injustice."[11] The claims of the past thus function as a standpoint of justification by which constitutional orders can be judged just or unjust to the extent that they permit or deny such claims.

If allowing reflexive questions about the nature and scope of the polity is a fundamental feature of any democracy that is based on human rights, then a democracy cannot limit the scope of those by whom it may be potentially addressed. Indigenous peoples, in this case, have not been merely treated as members of a more inclusive nation; rather, the perspective of the past has tested and changed the idea of the right to membership. This fact requires that for a community to remain democratic, it must adopt a standpoint of justification that is open to the possibility that what "we" decide is unjust, *however much it expresses our collective will*. The novel past is a perspective that might be seen as one aspect of the perspective of the Generalized Other employed in testing the scope and depth of political rights in democratic institutions. Contrary to impartialist readings of what this means, the perspective of the Generalized Other does not always require the reconstitution of the polity into a unity, but it also permits a polity to become more differentiated and multiperspectival.

Mead's conception of the Generalized Other is not just instructive for its reflexivity but also for its construction of the community of deliberators. Mead assigns both collective and distributive meanings to the concept, taking it to be both the perspective of the whole community as a shared "We," and as the many different perspectives of each of its members taken distributively. This difference can be seen in Mead's analogy to games, in which there is both "We the Team," and the specific roles and powers of each individual member of the team that cannot be reduced to being simply a part of the whole. Each adopts not merely the perspective of the good of the team or of all of the other players on the team, but also a second-person-plural perspective in which they all assess the state of play and the expectations and possibilities of members of both teams engaged in play. In the course of interactive and creative play, there is no single authoritative perspective from which to make assessments for the good of the team. Instead, each moves back and forth between perspectives in order to see what it is that one ought to do at any particular time. Thus, to be the addressee of such creative and potentially novel play means not only that no single player controls the state of play in the game but also that, taken together, all the players are not even collectively in control of the outcome, since even players on the same team may intend quite different results from each play. The game's course, however, is a matter of all the decisions and assessments that can be made from all of the relevant perspectives. Understood in this distributive, rather than the usual impartial sense, the Generalized Other is the perspective of "an enlarged mentality." Similarly, Kant sees such a mentality in a distributive fashion, as thinking and judging from "the standpoint of everyone else."[12] Such reflexivity is part of the ongoing process of realizing a universal ideal compatible with multiple perspectives without dissolving them into a higher unity. Historically, the demand for such unity is tied to more to the state form than to democratic ideals as such.

Given that it is distributed in this way, the perspective of the Generalized Other is potentially fully inclusive of all those who have a perspective. It cannot, then, itself be *a* single perspective, but rather it is the multiplicity that results from the joining of normatively relevant perspectives as a reflective accomplishment. The Generalized Other emerges when participants are able to coordinate various perspectives in the activity of joint deliberation. When the more distributive form of the Generalized Other is involved, the outcome from deliberation has to meet the demands of "constitutional toleration" of other peoples and their intersecting pasts. Such toleration is, however, not just a matter of noninterference. By extending normative powers to other communities, the democratic community recognizes that it is composed of political communities, each with overlapping pasts and responsibilities to each other.[13] Weiler describes the European Union as "a people of others," in which "constitutional toleration" is possible for each of them to "be bound by precepts articulated not by 'my people' but by a community composed of distinct political communities."[14] This kind of constitutional toleration ought to be a feature of *any just democracy.*

The Openness of the Past

It is clear that we think of different temporal instances in the history of a political community as having claims to justice. Rawls's Original Position asks us to see ourselves agreeing to principles of justice under the constraints of the veil of ignorance. He considers the fairness of a "just savings rate" as a matter of not knowing which generation we will belong to in the intergenerational distribution of resources. It properly asks us to see the future as having a claim upon the present generation. Put in communicative terms, we might think of the past and the future as potential audiences to whom we must be answerable and to whom we are obligated, if only in virtual rather than in actual dialogue. Like many forms of the social contract, Rawls's veil of ignorance denies that the past has any standing not only because it is prior to establishing the conditions for fair social cooperation but also for seemingly commonsensical reasons. The past does not really make a claim on us, since it is not possible for us, who are now deliberating, to establish fair terms of social cooperation, to occupy the position of the past, even if we ought to deliberate in such a way that it would be possible for us behind the veil of ignorance to live in some future generation.[15]

Here we might think of Nozick's admission that even a system of fair and equal exchange may have an unjust starting point. We may think it possible to correct all such claims juridically. But Nozick argues that at some point the temporal regress of past harms must simply come to an end, and thus for the sake of stability, the past has a limited warranty that has already expired. It may not be just, but at some point a community must arbitrarily call an end to democratic justice.[16] In New Zealand, for example, some make similar claims in seeking to mark an end to the process of settling obligations to the past violations of the 1840 Waitangi Treaty between the Maori and the British Crown.[17] In fact, a Waitangi Tribunal was created to initiate this process of settlement of claims based on treaty violations. On the one hand, the ongoing Tribunal was a great achievement of historical justice, recognizing as open-ended the scope of such claims. On the other hand, the very idea of settlement suggests that at some point the past could be declared officially closed as far as the scope of democratic obligations go. Behind this thought is not a moral intuition, but rather the denial of the backward extension of a community's responsibility to the past.

The lack of responsibility to the past may, among other things, be moved by what Mead called "the metaphysical demand for a set of events which is unalterably there in an irrevocable past."[18] But this is not true of the obligations to the past that we might consider when deliberating about the consequences of obligations inherited from a past treaty. Here the past is not taken to be some independent and fixed reality, but rather precisely as open, as alterable and continuously reconstructed in an ongoing social process. The process of settling old claims creates new obligations to the past, especially as a large infusion of capital from cash settlements begins to alter political relationships, and not always for the better. Thus, the very attempt to close the past inevitably reopens it democratically, and potentially creates a novel past from which new claims of justice may emerge. Democratic communities cannot evade this responsibility even when they try to, except by making those whose rights were to be respected in the settlement process once again rightless.

Here one might object that the obligations to the past are simply a matter of finding out the facts of the matter. Surely, the Waitangi Tribunal could settle all such cases. Here past claims are regarded merely forensically. The real and more important issue for deliberating about historical injustices is not simply to say as some observer "that something has happened," but rather to say as a public "what has happened." What has happened is a matter of significance or import, not simply because of how things actually were, but rather as a matter of the constructive relationship between the past, present, and the future, of disclosing the set of possibilities for understanding the past and the present together. Thus, the descriptive finality of the past could not do justice to the very process of documenting past injustices, which may have a different significance in New Zealand now that the treaty settlement process is underway. The settlement process does not close the past so much as open up a new one. Indeed, the Tribunal permanently institutionalized this very fact not only juridically but also by creating a public forum and public record for detailed testimony and claims about the past.

Here we might consider Danto's analyses of the past in narrative sentences such as "The player scored the winning goal in the fourteenth minute" or "This battle was the turning point of the war" as showing why deliberative assessment of the past cannot be final. In this case, it is true *after* the game that it was the winning goal, but not necessarily true in the fourteenth minute of the game. But this semantic point does not yet fully capture the deliberative openness of the past. Consider instead an assessment of the Treaty of Versailles immediately after the end of World War I, and another after the emergence of the Nazi party. In this case, we see, as Danto notes in a way reminiscent of Mead, that if "the future is partially open, then the past cannot be utterly closed."[19] We see that the terms of the Treaty meant to punish German aggression did not have very desirable effects; a treaty that sought instead to promote the social transformation of Germany may have been able to do more justice to the situation. As Mead might have put Danto's point in a stronger form, "The novelty of every future demands a novel past."[20] The past is then the subject of the ongoing construction and reconstruction of its social relevance (what it is), not its reality (that it happened and has consequences that we may not be aware of). When Mead goes on to assert that "the past is like a train schedule, subject to change without notice," he has underestimated one element of the past that might be confused with finality. While the past is not closed, it is nonetheless ineluctable and thus beyond the arbitrary features of the voluntary will. The demand of the past remains as a demand on the present and future political community whether it is taken up or not. Mead's argument is that the very idea of a novel future requires recognizing what has been unrecognized in the perspectives and claims of the past on us, and thus we cannot have the novelty of the one without the other.

There is also a related confusion about the possibility of a novel past. Because of this ineluctability, the openness of the past should not be confused with the capacity of present or future generation to reinvent it or even to declare its warranty to be expired. Indeed, to regard the past as closed in this sense comes at a high democratic price. Consider the German *Historikerstreit,* the debate between Habermas and various German historians such as Nolte and Hilgruber. The controversy was not really an instance of revisionist history, since the forensic facts of the destruction of European Jewry were not at issue. But what is at stake for the revisionists was whether the German nation can now interpret this part of Germany's past in a way that denies its ineluctability and takes it as a matter of voluntary willing such that it can suddenly become no longer relevant to its current nationhood in ways that it was during the first decades of the Federal Republic of Germany. The historians argue that this past can now be closed, insofar as they can offer alternative explanations that deny the sense of ongoing the collective responsibility of a *democratic* Germany that critics such as Habermas want to affirm.[21]

It might seem that this is a case of the sort that I have described above: the reconstruction of a novel past for the sake of a novel future. But in this instance, it is for the purpose of closing the ineluctable past and undermining its perspective as a source of novelty for the future. The attempt to become a "normal" nation is the attempt to deny the "burden of the past." At the very least, it is to deny who Germans are and have become by closing themselves to their horrendous past. Above all, to deny the past discloses nothing new; it excludes the recent past as relevant and thus opens up no new possibilities for the German future. In this way it fails as an ahistorical reconstruction of the past and could not withstand the public and discursive validation of its novelty or its justice, that it has genuinely included more rather than less past perspectives. Instead, the historians sought to deny the obligation to the past but not the facts as such. For a democratic community, responsibility for the past is ineluctable but also creative—the basis of new norms, statuses, and members. Canada and New Zealand continue to deal with their ineluctable and intersecting colonial pasts in novel constitutional and juridical institutions.

This example shows why we should adopt Mead's conception of a novel past in deliberating about the past of a democratic community. Deliberation is not some world-historical process going on outside us; it is a process that is open to public testing and evaluation and that requires many different relevant perspectives among deliberators. The novel reconstruction of the past produces a wider and richer past in terms of perspectives; indeed, the loss of perspectives means the loss of creative and expressive possibilities. Finally, such a reconstruction can be judged normatively in terms of whether or not it fulfills the moral and political obligations to the past in terms of its claims to justice. Such obligations to the past provide a central evaluative perspective for any reconstruction of the past and the possibilities it opens up. In this way, the past is one perspective in the Generalized Other, the point of view of that deliberators take in the ongoing construction and interaction between past, present, and future. Very often, this is not possible without the recognition both of some substantive and continuing injustice and of the fact that the polity as it is currently constituted is unable to make good on its obligations to the past. The perspective of the Generalized Other that includes the past in the second-personal sense ought to be a constitutive feature of any just democracy.

Conclusion: Deliberating with the Past

Deliberative democracy has long been based on the idea of genuinely including all social perspectives whenever we are attempting to deliberate about issues relevant for all of society, to contribute possible solutions to problems, to interpret values, to produce good reasons and to invalidate others. Often the aim of deliberation is not merely to solve particular problems but to transform the normative boundaries, or parameters, of public opinion and will formation. This description, as attractive as it is, could simply refer to a process that takes place in a bounded group in a delimited time, perhaps issuing in the will of the people. In many cases, however, a temporal decentering of the process of deliberative testing and practically verifying outcomes necessary leaves things more open-ended than prior to deliberation. This open-endedness includes the occluded perspectives of the past and the future consequences of some decision for the future.

Despite the many cases in which deliberating about the past has had pluralizing effects, considerations related to the variety of temporal perspectives remain neglected as a way to decenter democracy. The guiding metaphor for decentering has been primarily *spatial,* usually referring to multiple forums and sites as a necessary feature of public deliberation in large and complex societies. These same facts about social processes require that democracies be able to think about the consequences of their decisions elsewhere, beyond their own political community. Once fully cosmopolitan, this kind of decentering of obligation already makes it difficult to sustain a single political subject that is consistent with the distributive understanding of the constitution of a deliberative democracy. Any democracy that denies such obligations outside of its community does so at its own peril, since to close its borders is very often accomplished at the price of its democracy within and peace without.

Temporal decentering is potentially even more radical, since it challenges the notion that the scope of typical claims to justice must be based solely in current practices and that the scope of obligations is limited to the current community. These assumptions about the temporal scope of claims to justice are particularly pernicious in understanding deliberative democracy and the value of expressive freedom within it. So, too, is the understanding of the past as a fixed and closed reality. Such a self-understanding cuts us off from significant and critical perspectives on our current practices, including limits of deliberation, when it is only oriented to present deliberators, however dispersed and diverse.

If as citizens in a democracy we are concerned with adopting the perspectives of each and every citizen in deliberation, we may do so only if we include among the sources of obligation that are to inform our deliberation the claims of the past taken second-personally, as being addressed to us by those who have lacked the standing to do so. Thus, in a real sense we do not just deliberate about the past, but rather *with* the past. We can do so only as we create the novel future democracy that will answer the claims of justice that are opened up by reconstructing the novel past. If the past of a democracy is closed, then so is its future. For this reason, democracies have obligations to past generations, some of which may not yet be part of the self-understanding of the temporal scope of the current community.

Notes

1. See Elizabeth Anscombe, "Aristotle and the Sea Battle," *Mind,* 65 (1956): 1–17.

2. Robert B. Brandom, *Making It Explicit* (Cambridge, Mass.: Harvard University Press, 1994), 21.

3. Hans-Georg Gadamer, *Truth and Method* (New York: Seabury Press, 1992), 397.

4. See James Bohman, "Critics, Observers, and Participants," in *Pluralism and the Pragmatic Turn,* ed. J. Bohman and W. Rehg (Cambridge, Mass.: MIT Press, 2001), 87–114.

5. Immanuel Kant, *Practical Philosophy,* ed. and trans. M. Gregor (Cambridge: Cambridge University Press, 1996), 553.

6. See Stephen Darwall, "Fichte and the Second-Personal Standpoint," *International Yearbook for German Idealism,* 3 (2005): 91–113.

7. See Christine Korsgaard, *Creating the Kingdom of Ends* (Cambridge: Cambridge University Press, 1995), 106.

8. Seyla Benhabib, *The Claims of Culture* (Princeton, N.J.: Princeton University Press, 2002), 140–41.

9. See Frederick Schauer, "Amending the Presuppositions of a Constitution," in *Responding to Imperfection,* ed. S. Levinson (Princeton, N.J.: Princeton University Press, 1995), 145–62.

10. James Tully, "The Struggles of Indigenous Peoples for and of Freedom," in *Political Theory and the Rights of Indigenous Peoples,* ed. D. Ivison, P. Patton, and W. Sanders (Cambridge: Cambridge University Press, 2000), 53–54.

11. Ibid., 47.

12. Immanuel Kant, *Critique of Judgment* (Indianapolis: Hackett, 1987), 40; Hannah Arendt, *Lectures on Kant's Political Philosophy* (Chicago: University of Chicago Press, 1982), 51.

13. George Herbert Mead, *Mind, Self and Society* (Chicago: University of Chicago Press, 1934), 280.

14. J. H. Weiler, "A Constitution for Europe? Some Hard Choices," *Journal of Common Market Studies* 40 (2002): 563–80.

15. John Rawls, *A Theory of Justice* (Cambridge, Mass.: Harvard University Press, 1971), particularly chapter 3.

16. See Robert Nozick, *Anarchy, State, and Utopia* (New York: Basic Books, 1974).

17. See Harry C. Evison, *The Long Dispute: Maori Land Rights and European Colonization* (Christchurch: Canterbury University Press, 1997).

18. George Herbert Mead, *Philosophy of the Present* (Indianapolis: Hackett, 1949), 28.

19. Arthur Danto, *The Analytical Philosophy of History* (New York: Columbia University Press, 1988), 196.

20. Mead, *Philosophy of the Present*, 33.

21. See Jürgen Habermas, *The New Conservatism: Cultural Criticism and the Historians' Debate* (Cambridge, Mass.: MIT Press, 1989).

PART TWO

THE RACIAL NATION

SIX

Race, Nation, and Nation-State: Tocqueville on (U.S.) American Democracy

Lucius T. Outlaw Jr.

Tocqueville and U.S. American Racial Diversity

Why Tocqueville? Following a number of leads and suggestions as a result of reading and considering other thinkers, I turned, more than half a decade ago, to Tocqueville's *Democracy in America,* a work I knew about but had not read, in search of more understanding about U.S. American *democracy* and the vexing matters of racial and ethnicity diversity. In particular, I was concerned with why animosity on the part of folks identified as racially "white" was so widespread and persistent for so long, so seemingly intractable or, at the very least, so difficult to get at and curtail. A principal impetus for turning to Tocqueville was my reading and rereading a discussion by Rogers M. Smith in his "Beyond Tocqueville, Myrdal, and Hartz: The Multiple Traditions in America."[1]

Thus led to Tocqueville, after some reading of his *Democracy in America* I was struck by the poignancy of his analysis, all the more because of the character of the man as I understood him then: a twenty-something young French aristocrat who had schemed his way to the United States. Accompanied by a close friend and co-conspirator, Gustave de Beaumont, Tocqueville came ostensibly to examine prisons, but in truth to see first-hand the unfolding of what he took to be the providential historical project of democratization—which, he was convinced, would sweep the world—in the one place where it had been developed most fully: namely, in the United States of America. Tocqueville and Beaumont spent nine months in the United States of America (May 11, 1831, to February 20,

1832). After returning to France, the first volume of *De la Démocratie en Amérique* was published in 1835; the second volume was completed in 1839 and published in 1840.[2] In order to spend more time with the master work of this fascinating observer and analyst, I contrived a seminar, "Race and American Democracy," in which I devoted half of the semester to *Democracy in America* and half to *An American Dilemma,* the report of a massive, multi-team research project devoted to an analysis of racial matters in the United States that was directed by Gunnar Myrdal of Sweden, the principal editor of the report.

I am still in pursuit of enhanced understanding of Tocqueville's work as well as of the intricacies and challenges of racial and ethnic diversity to the fuller achievement and continuation of democratic life in the United States, the challenges of resolving, among other problems, U.S. America's racial "dilemma," and thereby fulfilling James Baldwin's and Richard Rorty's desire that we "achieve our country."[3] Others, though, have had and continue to have very different ideas from Baldwin and Rorty, and from many of us, I suspect, of the country to be achieved and maintained. I seek to understand, with Tocqueville's assistance, the ideas and practices that gave shape to the country early in its development. My quest to better understand Tocqueville's account has become something of an abiding passion that is the beginning of what will become a focal research and writing project. I continue to assemble major primary and secondary texts to be read and assessed, with much work still before me. I offer for consideration, then, considerations I have formed from the attention I have given so far to Tocqueville and the subject of this essay.

For starters, I am especially fascinated by what seems to me to be a compelling, even necessary way of reading and understanding Tocqueville's *Democracy in America,* namely, as an analysis of the formation of a way of life conditioned by commitment to a dominant principle—*equality*—that, when put into play as a principle by which to organize associated life (that is to say, *politics*), would affect all persons and bring all aspects of life and culture in the society under its shaping influence, but as a way of life *by and for white folks only.* In other words, it is my working hypothesis that one should not read *Democracy in America* as an account of a novel historic instantiation of a political principle that gives rise to an exceptional nation-state "by and for *the people,*" understood as being all the persons who are or could become its citizens without regard for raciality or ethnicity (or gender). This text is not to be read—indeed, cannot properly be read—as a prescient understanding on Tocqueville's part of democracy in the United States in terms of understanding of the meaning and connotation of "democracy" shared by many of us today.

To the contrary—and this is my main contention—Tocqueville viewed the democratization of life in the United States at that time as inextricably related to the raciality of those who initiated and were, if you will, the agents of the providential process. Democratic America was being developed both by and for folks of the white race *only*, and would not, could not, include either Indians or Negroes for related, but different, reasons. And understanding Tocqueville's account of the reasons—really, of the social causality—aids greatly in understanding why racism on the part of white folks, against black folks in particular, was so deeply engrained, so widespread, and thus so persistent and difficult to curtail, let alone to eradicate. Tocqueville was convinced that white folks' antipathy to black folks would be intractable.

Of course, it is of great importance to understand just how Tocqueville understood and used the term that is translated in his book as "race." Achieving this understanding is one of the tasks I've set for myself as I continue to devote attention to the study of *Democracy in America* and other writings by Tocqueville, in particular letters he exchanged with a protégé, Count Arthur de Gobineau.[4] For now, though, it is clear to me that Tocqueville regarded raciality as a set of physical and cultural, behavioral and psychological characteristics that made up the defining and distinguishing *character* of an intimately related group, or groups, of persons such that they were not just a random, externally related collection or heap, but culturally related descent groupings that, accordingly, were a *people* shaped by, and giving shape to, the world through their distinctive *national character*. Tocqueville was convinced that this racial national character was a constitutive aspect of the causality, the *social* causality, operative in the making of democracy in North America that had to be grasped if a proper understanding of the historic process was to be achieved. Democracy in America was being made by white Anglo-Americans and would be for white folks only. Racial diversity, in his judgment, was a threat to the stability, indeed, to the very existence of the United States of America. Why so?

First, a brief rehearsal of several points from Tocqueville's discussion of the threat posed to the new nation by the presence of three races on the territory that was the land-basis of the United States as set forth in the momentous chapter of volume one of *Democracy in America*, "The Present and Probable Future Condition of the Three Races that Inhabit the Territory of the United States."[5] Then, a review of key elements in his characterization and analysis of those who founded and were fashioning democracy in North America, which elements will indicate why, for Tocqueville, the presence of three races was so untenable for the developing nation-state.

The Problem of Three Races

The problem, in a nutshell, was that the three races were *radically* different in what he termed their "immaterial interests," that is to say, their shared opinions and sentiments, their passions and "habits of the heart," their *mores,* in Tocqueville's words—we might say in their "ultimate concerns" in terms of which they gave shape and direction to, and went about, their lives. One of the decisive features of Tocqueville's orientation and methodology, if you will, was his treating social collectivities as the primary unit of human social ontology and of sociopolitical analysis and philosophy. It is a serious error, in my judgment, to regard Tocqueville's effort in *Democracy in America* as being focused on democratization as simply, or even primarily, the unfolding of *individualism,* as some scholars have claimed, as though neither raciality nor ethnicity was of any consequence for either the success or possible failure of the U.S. American experiment. To the contrary, Tocqueville understood that individuality as an achievement and expression of a democratic social order was made possible and sustained by a particular set of *social* conditions:

> Society can exist only when a great number of men consider a great number of things under the same aspect, when they hold the same opinions upon many subjects, and when the same occurrences suggest the same thoughts and impressions to their minds.
>
> The observer who examines what is passing in the United States upon this principle will readily discover that their inhabitants, though divided into twenty-four sovereignties [i.e., states], still constitute a single people. (*DA,* 392)

Even as he took great care to set forth what he believed to be the features that distinguished white folks in the North from those in the South, regional groupings of people he sometimes referred to as different "civilizations," Tocqueville nonetheless did so after first making the case that they were "a single people," at least in terms of their origins. It was the difference in *social conditions*—the organization of the South's agricultural economy and way of life on the basis of the labor of enslaved Negroes, and the prevalence and influence of the organization of associated life on the intimacies of New England townships in the North—that produced the subsequent civilizational differentiations.

Generally, for Tocqueville, each race was a distinctive *people* who had to be understood as such. Each was identified by its particular "physiognomy"—that is, the outward features of persons comprising a people that, in their similarities and commonalities, were thought to be indicative of each people's character and temperament, that is, their *national charac-*

ter. And what, for Tocqueville, were the defining characteristics of a people's "national character"? Common language, similar religious traditions and convictions, similar customs and habits, sentiments and opinions as well as their particular physiognomy. Said Tocqueville: "All these national features are more or less discoverable in the physiognomy of those Englishmen who came to seek a new home on the opposite shores of the Atlantic" (28).

Neither Indians nor Negroes had physiognomies readily similar to that of "Anglo-Americans" (Tocqueville's often-used term), nor, therefore, national characters similar to that of Anglo-Americans. But, we must take note: Tocqueville did *not* believe that "physiognomy" determined national character by way of strict, linear, physical causality (that is to say, in terms of biological descent or heritability). On this important point he disagreed with Gobineau, who believed in the natural and fixed inequality of the races and the superiority of the white race. Tocqueville too believed the white race superior to Indian and Negro races, but thought this a consequence, to a significant degree, of social conditions (cultural orientation and pride in their civilization in the case of Indians, enslavement in the case of Negroes), not of physical inherency. One of the really interesting features of Tocqueville's reasoning is his attention to the nuance and complexity of causal factors as reciprocally effective. No single-variable, one-way causality is at work in the world for Tocqueville; rather, a number of *social* causes are at work, with multiple effects. Though one should look for the *principal* cause, in doing so one should look to social conditions. And in the case of the United States, the principal cause was the *equality of condition* developing among Anglo-Americans as a consequence of the play of "equality" as the defining principle of the democratic project. As he said in the "Author's Introduction":

> [N]othing struck me more forcibly than the general equality of condition among the people. I readily discovered the prodigious influence that this primary fact exercises on the whole course of society. . . . I soon perceived that the influence of this fact extends far beyond the political character and the laws of the country, and that it has no less effect on civil society than on the government; it creates opinions, gives birth to new sentiments, founds novel customs, and modifies whatever it does not produce. The more I advanced in the study of American society, the more I perceived that this equality of condition is the fundamental fact from which all others seem to be derived and the central point at which all my observations constantly terminated. (*DA*, 3)

But this equality of condition prevailed, to the extent that it did, among persons who were white, not among persons of all three races. Why?

First, it is because the all-important "equality of condition" as the basis and key to the success of democratization included much that was covered by the notion of *race* as used by Tocqueville. Significant differences between or among races, differences of social conditions and national character, would, unless eliminated, impede the development of equality between or among them. White folks, Indians, and Negroes were so different that such equality seemed all but unlikely, if not impossible:

> The human beings who are scattered over this space do not form, as in Europe, so many branches of the same stock. Three races, naturally distinct, and, I might almost say, hostile to each other, are discoverable among them at the first glance. Almost insurmountable barriers had been raised between them by education and law, as well as by their origin and outward characteristics; but fortune has brought them together on the same soil, where, although they are mixed, they do not amalgamate, and each race fulfills its destiny apart. (*DA*, 332)

In the paragraphs that follow, Tocqueville summarizes the distinguishing characteristics and social conditions of Indian and Negro races compared to those of the white race, "the superior in intelligence, in power, and in enjoyment . . . the white, or European, the MAN pre-eminently so called; below him appear the Negro and the Indian" (*DA*, 332). The summaries are preludes to extended discussions of each race as Tocqueville attended to matters that he had spoken of previously but, in identifying and explaining the origins and impact of the laws and customs of American democracy and of the profound transforming effects of democracy (i.e., equality) on the laws and customs of the Anglo-Americans, he had, he noted, "never had time to stop in order so show what place these two races [Indian and Negro] occupy in the midst of the democratic people whom I was engaged in describing" (*DA*, 331). This and several other matters of the place of Negroes and Indians he had left for the final chapter of the volume. And we should note that Tocqueville regarded these matters as "collaterally connected with my subject without forming a part of it; they [these matters addressed in this final chapter] are American without being democratic, and to portray democracy has been my principal aim." (*DA*, 331). Indians and Negroes were part of the overall context of the developing democratic project; they were not, however, constitutive aspects of the project. The racial differences of Indians and Negroes were such that these peoples could not become part of the equality of conditions definitive of the democratic project.

The Indians could not, in short, because, on the one hand, after long years of living by the chase according to their own agendas, they were much too independent and proud to ever submit to, or willfully engage in, assimilating to the supposed "superior" way of life of Anglo-Americans (for example, by settling permanently in place and cultivating the soil—which was a necessity, in Tocqueville's view, for becoming a "civilized" people—and by giving up their prideful "indolence" and disrespect for "labor"). Hence, they (Indians) were destined to lose the contest of civilizational competition with Anglo-Americans. And on the other hand, the rapacious, insatiable greed of the Anglo-Americans for the land occupied by Indians was such that satisfying it, "backed by the tyranny of the government," would result in the annihilation of the Indian race—that is, genocide (*DA*, 350)—in part by killing off Indians' food supplies, in part by inflicting physical and social death through forced relocations:

> It is impossible to conceive the frightful sufferings that attend these forced migrations. . . . Hunger is in the rear, war awaits them, and misery besets them on all sides. To escape from so many enemies, they separate, and each individual endeavors to procure secretly the means of supporting his existence by isolating himself, living in the immensity of the desert like an outcast in civilized society. The social tie, which distress had long since weakened, is then dissolved; they have no longer a country, and soon they will not be a people; their very families are obliterated; their common name is forgotten; their language perishes; and all traces of their origin disappear. Their nation has ceased to exist except in the recollection of the antiquaries of America and a few of the learned of Europe. (*DA*, 339)

And all of this destruction of peoples was taking place, Tocqueville declared with poignant, even indignant irony, "in a regular and, as it were, a legal manner" perpetrated by both federal and state governments (*DA*, 340). He was even more direct and poignant in his condemnation: "The Spaniards were unable to exterminate the Indian race by . . . unparalleled atrocities which brand them with indelible shame, nor did they succeed even in wholly depriving it of its rights; but the Americans of the United States have accomplished this twofold purpose with singular felicity, tranquilly, legally, philanthropically, without shedding blood, and without violating a single great principle of morality in the eyes of the world. It is impossible to destroy men with more respect for the laws of humanity" (*DA*, 355). Indians, Tocqueville, expected, would be killed off and thus not continue to be a problem for the unfolding democratic project.

The Negro race, however, presented another and very different case: "The most formidable of all the ills that threaten the future of the Union arises from the presence of a black population upon its territory," to a significant degree because the two races—Anglo-American and Negro—were "fastened to each other without intermingling; and they are alike unable to separate entirely or to combine" (*DA*, 356). Why so threatening? Because the Negro race was so *very* different from the race of white folks, and so *very* inferior to them, fundamentally due to conditions and effects of enslavement. Africans had been brought to the New World as slaves and sustained in that social condition across the generations for centuries, which resulted in the production of a people so depraved and so restricted that there was virtually no possibility that white folks would allow, let alone desire, black folks' coming to enjoy conditions of equality and, as a consequence, intermingling with white folks as equals leading, ultimately, to racial "amalgamation."

Nonetheless, by virtue of the institution of racialized slavery, white folks, in the South especially, had forged a way of life intimately involved with and dependent on the presence and labors of a people whom they otherwise despised, yet a people not only prone to the attractions of *equality* but inevitably increasingly desirous of and actively pursuing them: "As long as the Negro remains a slave, he may be kept in a condition not far removed from that of the brutes; but with his liberty he cannot but acquire a degree of instruction that will enable him to appreciate his misfortunes and to discern a remedy for them. Moreover, there exists a singular principle of relative justice which is firmly implanted in the human heart" (*DA*, 373).

But white folks cultivated and perpetuated such invidious passions, sentiments, opinions, and "habits of the heart" of aversion regarding Negroes, linked to the latter's "immutable" color, so that, without substantial positive changes in Negroes' condition, they (white folks) were unlikely ever to change. And most white folks, given their prejudices against Negroes, were unwilling to foster, let alone allow, those changes of condition. The relatively "free" Negroes thus posed a particular problem regarding which Tocqueville saw but two options: "The Negroes and the whites must either wholly part or wholly mingle." The latter option he thought not at all likely: "I do not believe that the white and black races will ever live in any country upon an equal footing. But I believe the difficulty to be still greater in the United States than elsewhere" (*DA*, 373).

Why such distance between these two "families of men," as Tocqueville referred to the races? Why so much antipathy on the part of white folks? The young political philosopher and analyst gave copious reasons for the desperate, even despairing picture he painted of Negroes. It was a troublesome picture, indeed, for several reasons. First and foremost, because, contrary to his studied practice of giving firsthand attention—either through direct observation, interviews, and conversations, or through studies of relevant documents—to nearly all of the other subjects to which he gave his attention during his travels and when back in France, Tocqueville, it seems, had no direct contact, certainly no conversations or intimate, respectful time, with Negroes during his visit to the United States. In fact, in a footnote in the chapter on "The Three Races," he takes pains to indicate that it was his companion, Gustave de Beaumont, in his *Marie, Ou l'Esclavage aux Etats-Unis, Tableau de moeurs Americaines,* who "plumbed the depths of a question [i.e., "of the position of the Negroes among the white population"] which my subject has allowed me merely to touch upon." (356, n. 30). It is clear to me, however, that Tocqueville—and Beaumont too, I suspect—gained no adequate understanding of the conditions Negro life as meaningfully experienced, interpreted, and expressed by Negroes themselves. In *Democracy in America* there is no discussion, for example, of either Negro music or religion; and his discussion of Negro family life was fundamentally flawed by both the social distance from and the distorted lens through which he viewed it, a distance that could not be overcome by all of Tocqueville's formidable brilliance otherwise. His account, in many respects, is strikingly in accord with those of apologists for and supporters of slavery, though it must be said that Tocqueville embraced neither agenda.

Quite the contrary. Through his analysis he sought to make the case for the degradation of enslavement, for both Negroes and enslavers, the latter having given rise to a civilization in the South that "held idleness in honor" and thus had its sense and appreciation of productive labor corrupted, to its detriment, while slowly but inevitably going to ruin in an economic system that was anything but efficient. And what he sought to show in recounting the condition of the Negro race was why, having been created as such by prejudiced white folks, there was no likelihood, given the vast differences between the two races and the animosities of white folks, that the two races would, or could, "live on equal footing." Democracy in America, for Tocqueville, would not be a multiracial affair. Nor could it be, for it was an affair of and for *Anglo*-Americans.

Anglo-American *Democracy in America*

To return, now, to the central concern of *Democracy in America:* how the focal conviction regarding *equality of condition,* when combined with the particular geographical conditions of the North American continent and with the particular national character of the emigrants who established the colonies that united in federation to form the United States, exerted the transforming and defining influence on the new nation-state's political character, laws, and civil society, in the latter case thus on the formation of the sentiments, customs, passions, and habits—the *mores*—that constituted the culture of the Anglo-Americans. Tocqueville reasoned: "The emigrants who colonized the shores of America in the beginning of the seventeenth century somehow separated the democratic principle from all the principles that it had to contend with in the old communities of Europe, and transplanted it alone to the New World. It has there been able to spread in perfect freedom and peaceably to determine the character of the laws by influencing the manners of the country" (*DA*, 13). Essential to this historic development was the fact that it was a function of "a quiet and rational persuasion" of persons who understood themselves as equals and for whom "the authority of the government would be respected as necessary, and not divine" (*DA*, 9). This sharing of a sense of equality was facilitated to no small degree by facticities of racial sameness: the makers of American democracy were, initially, Anglo-Saxons. All other European immigrants were thought to be, generally came to think of themselves as, *white* people and thus of *the same race.*

This was a matter of no small significance to Tocqueville, who, accordingly, devoted the second and third chapters of the first volume of *Democracy in America* to "Origin of the Anglo-Americans, and Importance of This Origin in Relation to Their Future Condition" and "Social Condition of the Anglo-Americans," respectively. The significance of origins for a future condition was enunciated by Tocqueville very early in the second chapter by way of an analogy that expressed a basic conviction regarding the nature of objects of understanding that are subject to development:

> The entire man is, so to speak, to be seen in the cradle of the child.
>
> The growth of nations presents something analogous to this; they all bear some marks of their origin. The circumstances that accompanied their birth and contributed to their development affected the whole term of their being. (*DA*, 26–27)

A principal aim of *Democracy in America*, then, is to determine and assess "the prejudices, the habits, the ruling passions, and, in short all that constitutes what is called the national character" that is in play at the origination of Anglo-America. Doing so is possible because "America is the only country in which it has been possible to witness the natural and tranquil growth of society, and where the influence exercised on the future condition of states by their origin is clearly distinguishable" (*DA*, 27). It will be in terms of this "national character" that an explanation can be developed of a people's customs, laws, seemingly incoherent opinions, and even of the destinies of nations. Thus: "If we carefully examine the social and political state of America, after having studied its history, we shall remain perfectly convinced that not an opinion, not a custom, not a law, I may even say not an event is upon record which the origin of that people will not explain" (*DA*, 28).

The origin of the Europeans-becoming-Americans served to determine, thus to explain, a great deal for Tocqueville. The commonality conferred by a shared racial national character was a major factor conditioning the success of the developing democratic project. Differences among the immigrants (they "came at different periods . . . differed from each other in many respects; their aim was not the same, and they governed themselves on different principles") were trumped by their oneness as a single people: "These men had, however, certain features in common, and they were all placed in an analogous situation. The tie of language is, perhaps, the strongest and the most durable that can unite mankind. All the emigrants spoke the same language; they were all children of the same people" (*DA*, 28). There were, in Tocqueville's view, "striking similarities" among the British colonies "at the time of their origin" that made for "general uniformity," though "marked differences" would later develop between folks in the North and those in the South. Nonetheless, on this "foundation of uniformity"

> there developed in the North very different characteristics . . . the two or three main ideas that now constitute the basis of the social theory of the United States were first combined. The principles of New England spread at first to the neighboring states; they then passed successively to the more distant ones; and at last . . . they *interpenetrated* the whole confederation. They now extend their influence beyond its limits, over the whole American world. The civilization of New England has been like a beacon lit upon a hill, which, after it has diffused its warmth immediately around it, also tinges the distant horizon with its glow. (30–31; emphasis in original)

Furthermore, it was in the intimacies of associated living in the townships of New England, Tocqueville reasoned, that democracy as the practice of self-government was best incubated and nourished:

> In America [contrary to the development of political existence in European nations] it may be said that the township was organized before the county, the county before the state, the state before the union . . . The independence of the township was the nucleus round which the local interests, passions, rights, and duties collected and clung. It gave scope to the activity of a real political life, thoroughly democratic and republican. (*DA*, 40).

Yet the township was thereby also the locus of the nurturance of the habits of the heart that, in the presence of Indians and of Africans—the latter as slaves, "free," and "freed" black folks—came to define racial whiteness as a determinative aspect of citizenship, thus of rights and duties. And though slavery was ended in the North and New England long before the Civil War and the ending of slavery generally, it was still noticeable to Tocqueville (and to Beaumont) that even in this cradle of democratic life neither Indians nor free and freed Negroes enjoyed equality of conditions and democratic life with white folks. Democracy in America was, indeed, democracy of, by, and for the "Anglo-Saxon" people.

The Tocqueville Legacy

Now, what has become especially intriguing to me is a particular legacy that has been formed and mediated around *Democracy in America*. Many persons regard this work as one of the great efforts of political philosophy —perhaps the very best on "democracy" in the United States of America. In the "Editors' Introduction" to their new translation of *De la Démocratie en Amérique*, Harvey C. Mansfield and Delba Winthrop write: "*Democracy in America* is at once the best book ever written on democracy and the best book ever written on America" (*DA*, xvii). What is being affirmed with such praise? Why, still, does Tocqueville's *Democracy in America* continue to garner such praise if my reading of him is accurate: that is, that he described, analyzed, and seemingly endorsed what he took to be a providentially historic project, the agents of which were white folks? Is this the principal reason *why* it has received, and continues to receive, such praise: because *Democracy in America*, due in part to its framing metaphysic of history and racialism, came to be regarded as justifying and legitimating a nation-state building project in service to white racial supremacy, a way of receiving and mediating the texts—the first volume especially—that was aided substantially by how he positioned the discussion of "the three races" in his book: a subject "collaterally connected with my subject without forming a part of it . . . American without being democratic" (*DA*, 331)?

I believe, on my reading, we must answer, "Yes, in part." I say "in part" because there are a number of ways to read *Democracy in America*. One of these is to regard the text, given Tocqueville's emphasis on *equality*, as an investigation and endorsement of an historic instantiation of democratic individualism, a reading that is much in keeping with mid- to late twentieth century (that is to say, post–World War II, post–Jewish Holocaust, and post–U.S. Civil Rights Movement) convictions regarding the supposed "color blindness" (hence racial blindness), of the U.S. Constitution. Of course, we have the interpretive means (documentary evidence) and the compelling social and political reasons to know better: that the Constitution was neither designed nor ratified as a color-blind, race neutral foundational document. Rather, it was, though deliberately and, it has turned out, successfully foundational, a document decidedly devoted to white racial supremacy that was ratified and the Union formed as a result of agreements made during the constitutional conventions to keep as silent as possible about the enslavement of Africans and their descendants.[6] Tocqueville's sometimes poignant and ironizing criticisms of the treatment of Indian "savages" and enslaved Negroes never were advanced as challenges to the project of racialized democratic nation-state formation itself.

Quite the contrary. *Democracy in America* was published and received in the United States while the dominant mindset guiding the nation-state project was, on one account, being organized around convictions of white racial supremacy and a mission, a destiny, to achieve racial, political, and economic hegemony in the world:

> By 1850 American expansion was viewed in the United States less as a victory for the principles of free democratic republicanism than as evidence of the innate superiority of the American Anglo-Saxon branch of the Caucasian race. In the middle of the nineteenth century a sense of racial destiny permeated discussions of American progress and of future American world destiny. . . . The contrast in expansionist rhetoric between 1800 and 1850 is striking. The debates and speeches of the early nineteenth century reveal a pervasive sense of the future destiny of the United States, but they do not have the jarring note or rampant racialism that permeates the debates of mid-century. By 1850 the emphasis was on the American Anglo-Saxons as a separate, innately superior people who were destined to bring good government, commercial prosperity, and Christianity to the American continents and to the world. This was a superior race, and inferior races were doomed to subordinate status or extinction.[7]

It was into this developing cauldron of passions and ideas regarding the racialized U.S. American nation-state project that Tocqueville's *Democracy in America* landed when it was published in 1835 (volume one) and 1840 (volume two) and made for the welcome with which it was received by many as, that is, a very articulate and insightful characterization and endorsement of the political project and civilizational destiny of a racially superior *white* folk. It would be more than a hundred years, even after a civil war in which more than half a million people lost their lives to a great extent over the issue of slavery, before the notion of U.S. America as a white folks' nation-state would be dislodged from dominance by other notions (color blindness, racial-ethnic pluralism).

Conclusion

It is time, as well, to retire what I take to be a very serious misreading and mischaracterization of Tocqueville's *Democracy in America*. As is true in so many other instances, each "generation," in coming to maturity, must or should develop its own interpretations of those who preceded them as a way of assuming the responsibilities of and for making their ways through worlds largely inherited but still amenable, more or less, to modifications by their efforts. Thus, those of us who came of age during the Civil Rights, Black Power, Anti-Vietnam War, Second-Generation Women's, Anti-Racism, Multicultural, and various Left and other movements, as well as those of us not involved in such endeavors but who are, nonetheless, independent, critically minded persons who, along with movement people, are convinced and committed *democrats* of various persuasions who care for our nation-state's history as well as its future—we all must continue the challenging work of "realizing" our country. That is, we must continue the task of making more real, for more persons and peoples in the United States of America, the prospects and promises of *democracy* and justice, and doing so in ways and for persons and peoples that the founding folks could not, and *would* not, imagine as beneficiaries of what they regarded as the providential project.

For those of us who are teacher-scholars engaged in the critical mediation of works and people to successive generations of people who will inherit our nation-state, ours is the responsibility to reconsider the likes of Alexis de Tocqueville and his monumental *Democracy in America*, and, to the best of our ability, to correct the mischaracterization of the man and his work. We are compelled to do so by the continuing challenges of racial and ethnic pluralism in our nation-state, and, if we would both honor and respect Tocqueville's scholarly and decidedly political efforts, we should be compelled by him, as well, to take on these challenges, determined to resolve them without commitments to racial superiority or hegemony, and as committed democrats still.

Notes

1. In *American Political Science Review* 87, no. 3 (September 1993): 549–66.

2. Daniel J. Boorstin, "Introduction to the Vintage Classics Edition," Alexis de Tocqueville, *Democracy in America* (New York: Random House, 1990), vii, viii.

3. Richard Rorty, *Achieving Our Country: Leftist Thought in Twentieth-Century America* (Cambridge, Mass.: Harvard University Press, 1998); James Baldwin, *The Fire Next Time* (New York, Dell, 1963).

4. See James T. Schleifer, *The Making of Tocqueville's* Democracy in America, 2nd ed. (Indianapolis: Liberty Fund, 2000), 92.

5. Alexis de Tocqueville, *Democracy in America,* translated, edited, and with an introduction by Harvey C. Mansfield and Delba Winthrop (Chicago and London: University of Chicago Press, 2000), 331–434. Hereafter, references to this edition will be cited parenthetically in the text as *DA* with page numbers.

6. On this matter, see the especially poignant chapter 3, "The Silence," of Joseph J. Ellis's *Founding Brothers: The Revolutionary Generation* (New York: Alfred A. Knopf, 2001), 81–119.

7. Reginald Horsman, *Race and Manifest Destiny: The Origins of American Racial Anglo-Saxionism* (Cambridge, Mass.: Harvard University Press, 1981), 1–2.

SEVEN

William James on Nation and Race

Harvey Cormier

According to what seems to be a developing philosophical consensus, while the founders of pragmatism were good liberals of their time, they failed to appreciate and discuss the philosophical importance of race, class, and gender. Pragmatism is a kind of historicism, using all kinds of facts about the actual, contingent, historical origin of our ideas to explain what those ideas are, what they mean to us, and how some of them come to be true. The different pragmatists considered biological, psychological, social, and even economic and political facts in their story of thinking and how it works. But while things like racial divisions and categorizations have played an underappreciated role in the history of our human self-conception, the pragmatists missed their chance to show this, and thereby they missed their chance to point out great social injustices and strike blows against them. This was one of the biggest shortcomings of the original pragmatic movement, and neo-pragmatists of the present day are not doing much better.[1]

Pragmatism started life as an effort to clear away misunderstandings that blocked agreement and cooperative action. This was an admirable goal, but cooperation isn't everything. A conflict like the Civil War was a necessary part of the struggle for racial justice in America, so the pragmatic effort to mediate and find compromise in all intellectual matters was, to say the least, not entirely commendable.[2] Figures like William James and John Dewey bravely put their philosophy to use exhorting their fellow citizens to develop American democracy, but they had little to contribute concerning the most important concrete issues that troubled that democracy. Therefore, in the end they accomplished little besides intellectually comforting the materially comfortable.[3]

There is only one problem with this ever more widely held opinion about pragmatism: it's not true. At least one of the original pragmatists did, in fact, have something important and philosophical to say about race. In this essay I'll discuss the way William James made race the centerpiece of one of his best-known discussions, thereby putting it near the center of his philosophical thought. James was fundamentally concerned with freedom; even his theory of truth was designed to fit his story of a world in which we human individuals are free to be "turning-places" in the course of history. Some of James's contemporaries used "race" to explain deterministically the fates of societies and individuals in terms of inevitable natural adaptations, including mental and even moral adaptations, to different conditions of physical geography. James criticized this kind of geographical or environmental determinism, arguing that while race might be powerful, it did not hold our fate.

James did not say what we today might want him to have said about race, especially since he did not treat it as a political problem. He even thought of it in Darwinian biological terms rather than in the way many of us like to think of it today, as a matter of "socially constructed" differences. Nevertheless, I think that what James said is true and can be of value to us in our present-day discussions of racial distinctions and their political consequences in American society.

Freedom, James, and Race

One of James's most famous remarks (reproduced, for example, in brass letters in the marble lobby of the Harvard University behavioral sciences building, William James Hall) is "The community stagnates without the impulse of the individual. The impulse dies away without the support of the community."[4] James thought that human communities could and should grow or develop, and he argued that their growth was in fundamental ways dependent on the ideas and actions of individual persons. Those individuals and their ideas and acts were in an obvious way dependent on the human societies that surrounded them, but it was crucial to see that this dependence was reciprocal. While conditions in the natural world obviously had something to do with the growth and accomplishments of our communities, if human societies were to be ranked in terms of their achievements, nature was not to get sole credit for who ranked where. Individual persons provided an "impulse" necessary for community development.

This idea, which is very near the heart of James's thinking about almost everything, is in fact an idea about race. A "community," here, is what James also calls a "race" in the same essay—for example, when he refers to the "Celtic race"[5] and to the Germans as a people who might have wound up appearing to themselves to be "a race of spectacled *Gelehrten* and political *herbivora.*"[6] James had the nineteenth-century American conception of race, which did involve blood and biology but was also mixed up in many ways with the ideas of community and nationhood.[7]

Nineteenth-century immigrants to the United States were made to fill out a standardized immigration form. In the box for "race," they could select such choices as "Irish," "Hebrew," "Italian (north)" and "Italian (south)"—though an addendum of 1906 cautioned that

> "African (black)" refers to the African Negro, whether coming from Cuba or other islands of the West Indies, North or South America, Europe, or Africa. Any alien whose appearance indicates an admixture of negro blood should be classified under this heading.[8]

"Race" meant "blood" or biological connection, but it has also been tied to ideas of community and nation from the beginning, and our twenty-first-century American idea of race is not sharply distinct from those ideas either, for that matter.

In James's 1880 lecture, "Great Men and their Environment," whence comes the above remark about individuals and communities, James set out to describe the role and the power of the human individual in the growth of the biological and social entities known as human races.[9] He proposed in that lecture to lay out for the first time "a remarkable parallel . . . between the facts of social evolution on the one hand, and of zoölogical evolution as expounded by Mr. Darwin on the other."[10] This sounds like a prelude to "sociobiology," and indeed James is today regarded as a nineteenth-century patron saint by "evolutionary" biologists, psychologists, and linguists for his commitment to the Darwinian idea that many of the actions we take to originate in private perceptions and passions actually originate in instincts that have evolved over millennia in our species or our "races." For example, Leda Cosmides and John Tooby, in their essay "Evolutionary Psychology: A Primer," and Steven Pinker, in his *The Language Instinct*, refer to the same passage from James's *Principles of Psychology*:

> It takes . . . a mind debauched by learning to carry the process of making the natural seem strange, so far as to ask for the why of any instinctive human act. . . . Why do we smile, when pleased, and not scowl? Why are we unable to talk to a crowd as we talk to a single friend? Why does a

particular maiden turn our wits so upside-down? The common man can only say, Of course we smile, of course our heart palpitates at the sight of the crowd, of course we love the maiden, that beautiful soul clad in that perfect form, so palpably and flagrantly made for all eternity to be loved!

And so, probably, does each animal feel about the particular things it tends to do in the presence of particular objects. . . . Thus we may be sure that, however mysterious some animals' instincts may appear to us, our instincts will appear no less mysterious to them.[11]

Cosmides, Tooby, and Pinker cite this passage to show James anticipating their idea that very many of the ordinary human behaviors we regard as matters of individual experience, desire, and choice are in fact driven by instincts and tendencies that are naturalistically, even mechanistically, understandable. According to this view, we human animals are not primarily "fitness maximizers" but "adaptation executors." We are not, as the "Standard Social Science Model" would have it, beings who by and large act as a result of what we individually happen to value in our local circumstances; instead, we as a species have become adapted to a niche in the ecosystem, and what we individuals value and do can be understood primarily in terms of those evolutionary adaptations.

If we see James in this light, we might accordingly expect him to offer a view that diminishes the importance and power of both individuals and distinct human communities, invoking instead the fundamental power of the scientifically discoverable natural environment to shape human phenomena. But James, taking himself to follow Darwin's own path, does not do this. He sets out to explain in "Great Men" how a Darwinian account of natural selection allows for both individual human genius and real, consequential differences among human races or communities, and he tries to show how those differences among "races" depend crucially on the contributions of unique individual persons.

However, if James identifies human races as "communities" or "nations," how can he possibly be talking about a subject of biological study? Aren't communities our own human groupings of ourselves, while our various races, if there really are any such things to be studied scientifically, are nature's own categories, existing or not existing however we may decide to look at things? Perhaps our present-day conception of race is more genuinely scientific and natural than James's was, and maybe it is therefore a fundamentally different concept. Maybe that explains why we wouldn't think of a German or a southern Italian "race." Or it may be that we have the same concept and now just happen to take a different lot of groups to fall under the heading "races." Maybe believers in "race" used to think, rightly or wrongly, that the natural environment created not only the whites but also the French. Or maybe this whole issue is hopeless, since if there is any lesson to be learned from the philosophy of the late twentieth century, it is the futility of trying to assess sameness and differences among concepts.[12] In any case, let us pause here and think for a moment about the contemporary idea of a "race" in biology, focusing especially on the extent to which races are "found" rather than "made."

The reader may be as surprised as the present writer was to learn that the idea of race has been applied quite commonly in life science not only to human beings but to other animals and even to plants. Darwin hardly talks at all about humanity in his *Origin of Species,* but the full title of the book is *On the Origin of Species by Means of Natural Selection, or the Preservation of Favored Races in the Struggle For Life.* Darwin did not originally distinguish between race and species; in this, he followed common usage, which still calls the human species "the human race." Today, in biology if not in common speech, race and species are distinct ideas, but both races and species of nonhuman beings are still commonly discussed by life scientists. "Race" is basically another name for "subspecies" or "variety," which is the category below "species" in taxonomy.

Many modern biologists, especially taxonomists and systematists, have treated race as real and formally definable. Ernst Mayr, one of the main figures responsible for synthesizing the views of Darwin and Mendel in the explanation of evolution, understood races as *"kinds of animals that show no (or only slight) structural differences, though clearly separated by biological characters."*[13] Verne Grant, the theorist of plant species who is well-known for integrating the study of pollinating animal behavior into his theories of plant species development, said of animals and plants alike:

> Interbreeding is more frequent among a series of local populations in the same general area than it is between inhabitants of widely distant areas. The regional cohort of populations is a race or, more particularly, a geographical race. Because interbreeding occurs much more commonly within a geographical region than between regions . . . each race tends to possess a distinctive and unique ensemble of genetic variations and phenotypic characteristics.
>
> Races interbreed where they come into contact. This interbreeding leads to a more or less continuous intergradation between the races in their genetic constitutions and phenotypic characters. The sum total of the races that interbreed frequently or occasionally with one another, and that intergrade more or less continuously in their phenotypic characters, is the species.[14]

Thus, not only have biologists looked for races or varieties in nonhuman nature, they have been known to understand *species* in terms of *races.* The concept of race or variety has played a prominent role in several parts of life science, though it is currently controversial. Many scientists now challenge the very idea that there are different human races, and some disparage any and all biological categorizations below the species level as arbitrary and subjective matters of convenience.[15]

Still, it is clear that there are in fact genetic differences among human populations by which those populations can be sorted. Some of them match phenotypical differences in skin color, body shape, hair type and color, and physiology; and many of these differences correspond to geographic patterns. Sickle cell anemia, a disease with a genetic origin, is much more frequent in blacks of African origin than in whites, Asians, Native Americans, or "blacks" of Australian origin, probably because the carrier state of the disease gives resistance to malaria. The human blood group allele *Ib* has a frequency of about 0.10 in European and Asian populations but is almost entirely absent in Native American populations. And cystic fibrosis and suicidal depression, which both seem to have genetic causal factors, are much more frequent among whites than blacks. Things like this prompt some present-day scientists to speak of the scientific reality of human races.

These scientists include some experts in molecular biology. Armand Marie Leroi, an evolutionary developmental biologist at Imperial College in London, recently argued in a *New York Times* editorial that today, thanks to the latest researches, "if you want to know what fraction of your genes are African, European or East Asian, all it takes is a mouth swab, a postage stamp and $400—though prices will certainly fall."[16] Leroi pointed out that if several hundred variable genes in the human genome are sorted by their variations, a pattern emerges among human populations that roughly corresponds to origins in America, Africa, Australasia, Europe, and East Asia. This set of origins, in turn, corresponds roughly to one of the traditional human racial divisions.

However, as Leroi also noted, "Study enough genes in enough people and one could sort the world's population into 10, 100, perhaps 1,000 groups, each located somewhere on the map." While he evidently did not have this point in mind, it is clear that if one could find either ten groups or a thousand, then one *could* also sort all human beings into one big group, the human race, or divide the human population into those hundreds of millions of genetically distinctive groups known as "nuclear families," or regard each person as a singleton set that is just as real as her or his race. We can differentiate populations by overall patterns of genetic and phenotypic characteristics, but many different differentiations are possible, and none of them cuts human nature at its joints. No matter how scientific and realistic we may try to be in our account of the different human populations, an element of human interest will have to play a role in our accounting.

"Race" is like "place." Long Island is real, but it is no more or less so than Massapequa or New York state. A map of the region may leave off any or all of these labels, and the penalty will be diminished usefulness to some users, not diminished accuracy or honesty. Analogously, even if we are thinking about genotypes and phenotypes, it may be helpful for various purposes to divide humanity up into geographical races, but failing to do so is not misreporting the state of the real, scientifically discoverable world. Even if there are significant differences among groups of people, neither significance nor "groups" are simply found in nature by science. It is therefore a mistake to think that "races," biologically understood, are nature's own invention, whereas "societies" or "communities" of the kind James considered are mere human constructs, mere artifacts of contingent ways of looking at things.

Our human evolutionary history tells us many interesting things, but it tells us nothing indisputable about natural or real human categorizations, let alone hierarchies within those categorizations. Nevertheless, for better or for worse, we still do rank groups of human beings in terms of their accomplishments of various kinds, if not simply in terms of their natural worthiness. For just one example, the physiologist and historian Jared Diamond, in his recent book *Guns, Germs, and Steel,* sets out to answer "Yali's question," put to him by a native New Guinean politician: "Why is it that you white people developed so much cargo and brought it to New Guinea, but we black people had little cargo of our own?"[17] That is, why have white Europeans been so strikingly successful at the production of technology and material goods, while others among the world's populations have lagged behind so strikingly? There is no denying that even non-Europeans can and do use material goods and technology as one criterion of the success of a society, and almost any thinking person will be led sooner or later to wonder why some human societies have been so much more successful in these terms than others.

Enlightenment figures like Hume and Kant had said that nature made races what they were.[18] And in his antiracist way, even Diamond would agree: he argues that conditions of climate and geography made possible kinds of agriculture that in turn made it possible for Eurasians to get ahead of the rest of humanity in developing the leisure time that made technological innovation possible.[19] However, James insisted to the contrary that the greatness of a society or a "race" depended crucially on the individual "great" person and her or his individual free choices. No general facts of nature made the fate of societies. Instead, unique individuals of distinctive genius had concrete experiences, made particular decisions, and produced unpredictable consequences in their lives and their social worlds.

James's single most famous remark is probably the one he made in his diary regarding the beginning of his recovery from a depression manifested by the persisting thought that his acts were ineffectual in the universe. He wrote on April 30, 1870, as he realized that at least his attention was in his control:

> My first act of free will shall be to believe in free will. I will voluntarily cultivate the feeling of moral freedom.... I will go a step further with my will, not only act with it, but believe as well; believe in my individual reality and creative power.[20]

James would think of himself as an actor in the world, focusing his attention on his volitions and their results. This theory of himself would become a part of what and who he was, and this interpretation would in turn result in more and more powerful volitions. James was not just deciding to "act under the idea of freedom"; his decision to interpret himself this way would change who he was, would create and develop him as a free human agent.

James's whole philosophy exists in the service of this idea. His radical empiricism and pragmatism, though independent of each other, both amount to efforts to hold out the possibility that individuals can exist and have this kind of freedom. And he thinks that his archenemy in his struggle to make the world safe for this idea is Hegel. Correctly or incorrectly, James sees Hegel and Hegelians as offering a view that stamps out genuinely free individuals by merging them all into one big "block universe," all of whose parts are connected by relations of inevitability and necessity.[21] James's pragmatic theory pulverizes "truth," the single, abstract, logically understandable relation between thought and the world, into the many concrete ideas, beliefs, and theories called "truths"; and it understands those truths functionally, as contingently invented tools, or novel, willed solutions, to particular problems that individuals happen to face.[22] Moreover, James's radical empiricism understands all logical relations among things as relations among genuinely *individual* things, including individual persons, rather than as fibers connecting a lot of mere aspects of the whole into one big abstract and rationally knowable unit.[23]

James's "Great Men and their Environment" is a variation on this theme. James is, as usual, battling an organicist theory of the world that merges individuals and particular phenomena into a whole governed by necessities and inevitabilities, though this time the enemy is not Hegel, and the particularities at issue are not truths. James is battling the British philosopher, psychologist, and (perhaps the first) sociologist Herbert

Spencer over the issue of how much power is displayed in history by individual "great men." Spencer thinks that it is nature in the abstract that shapes nations and races. James will argue that individuals play a crucial role in shaping nations and races that Spencer does not see.

Spencer vs. James on the Great Individual

In his *Study of Sociology,* Spencer argues that if great human leaders and creators are not supernatural in origin and are therefore not "deputy gods,"

> then the origin of the great man is natural; and immediately this is recognized, he must be classed with all other phenomena in the society that gave him birth as a product of his antecedents. . . . You must admit that the genesis of the great man depends on the long series of complex influences which has produced the race in which he appears, and the social state into which that race has slowly grown. . . . Before he can remake his society, his society must remake him. . . . If there is to be anything like a real explanation of [the social changes he makes], it must be sought in that aggregate of conditions out of which both he and they have arisen.[24]

This "aggregate," as far as James is concerned, is too much like Hegel's "block." Explaining individuals who leave their mark on history as mere results of that aggregate rather than real initiators of change is unacceptable, not simply because it is wrong about the facts but because it will *create the wrong facts,* the wrong kind of future for human beings. Such a self-interpretation, such a reading and writing of ourselves, will make us human beings less free.

James wants to challenge the kind of necessitarian thinking evidently reflected in this particular passage, and he wants to do so while still offering a scientifically respectable picture. Can we think of ourselves and our leaders as speaking and acting originally at the same time we acknowledge that there is nothing human outside the scientifically knowable natural world? James thinks so, and he thinks, moreover, that the genuinely unscientific thinking is done by people like Spencer. He says that despite the relatedness of all things in the world, we can't as a practical matter overlook local causation and attribute all particular developments to the "aggregate" whole:

> If we proceeded on that method, we might say with perfect legitimacy that a friend of ours, who had slipped on the ice upon his door-step and cracked his skull, some months after dining with thirteen at the table,

died because of that ominous feast. . . . "There are no accidents," I might say, "for science. . . . The real cause of the death was not the slip, *but the conditions which engendered the slip,*—and among them his having sat at a table, six months previous, one among thirteen. *That* is truly the reason why he died within the year."[25]

James argues that this kind of holism is superstitious. A genuinely scientific understanding of an event like the slip on the porch, far from describing only general laws, involves attention to the specifics and particularities of the unique situation that led to this particular slip. If we look at things the way a truly scientific observer does, we will see that the initiatives of individuals can indeed cause changes in the future of the world.

James believes in a kind of metaphysical freedom of the will, but he puts that issue aside in his discussion of Spencer. Instead he argues, predictably enough for a pragmatist, that scientific thinking has practical constraints as well as purely theoretical ones:

The human mind . . . can be efficient at all only by *picking out* what to attend to, and ignoring everything else,—by narrowing its point of view. Otherwise, what little strength it has is dispersed, and it loses its way altogether. Man always wants his curiosity gratified for a particular purpose. . . . And if, in the case of the unfortunate man [who slips and falls], we lose ourselves in contemplation of the thirteen-at-table mystery, and fail to notice the ice on the step and cover it with ashes, some other poor fellow, who never dined out in his life, may slip on it in coming to the door, and fall and break his head too.[26]

Science does and should adopt the agent point of view, the viewpoint of someone who has something in particular to accomplish. It's not that we should "act under the idea of freedom," as Kant argues in his practical philosophy; instead, the practical point here is that the "little strength" of the human mind is dispersed and lost, rather than concentrated and increased, when we focus on the world as a whole and ignore particulars, including human particulars.

James is pointing out that, as a matter of evident fact, we can change what we are able to accomplish *in the observable world of our acts and their consequences* if we take up a genuinely scientific outlook on ourselves and what we can do. The point is not that our acts are not fundamentally determined, it is rather that it doesn't pay to think of them as if they are. But though this may still sound Kantian, the "idea of freedom" under which James wants us to act is not an idea of freedom from the causal motivations of nature. The payoff that we get from thinking of ourselves as free is not satisfaction of an imperceptible, purely moral interest; it is an increasing ability to satisfy the various ordinary desires that drive us through our lives in the natural world.[27]

The *why* of our cause-seeking, or the historically conditioned particular motive that sends us looking for the cause of an event, is a scientifically legitimate thing to consider as we carry on our search; and if we do consider it, we find that the causes we are led to are particularities rather than abstractions like the world as a whole. What's more, we *have to* consider our own motives if we're going to develop an understanding of the world that will allow us to make practical sense of it and change it. We must read ourselves as powerful if we want really to be powerful; we have to write our freedom if we really want to have it. We have to resist the idea that there are three separable things: facts about the world and our abilities in it, our beliefs or knowledge concerning those facts, and the goals or interests that make us seek that knowledge. It sounds like some kind of idealistic paradox identifying beliefs and realities, but the point is actually quite commonsensical. It's a standard moral of children's books: What we can do depends, in part, on what we think we can do. When we take our goals and goal-seeking into account, we change both our knowledge of our abilities and our abilities themselves.

If we consider our goals and take up an agent-centered outlook, we see the particularity and locality that both Kant and Spencer fail to see. Moreover, says James, we can see an actual case of this kind of attention to particularities in Darwin's account of evolution by means of natural selection. Spencer was an evolutionist too, of course. He read and admired Darwin, and it was he, not Darwin, who coined the phrase "survival of the fittest," which Darwin incorporated into later editions of *The Origin of Species*. But as James reads him, Spencer's holism has led him to miss Darwin's key insight. Like his forebear Lamarck, Spencer continues to think of "adaptive" changes in organisms as the main motor of evolution.

Lamarckians thought that it was the giraffe's stretching its neck to get at the high leaves—and thus, really, the high leaves themselves—that had resulted in longer-and-longer-necked giraffes. This evolutionary view explained the diversity of organisms naturalistically, but it left untouched the mystery of how some and only some acquired characteristics could be passed on to offspring. Spencer thought that natural selection solved this problem; the physical environment makes animals that will have some offspring well-suited and some not so well-suited to survive in that very environment, and it then disposes of the ill-suited ones. Spencer also thought that similar natural processes were at work on the human nervous system and hence on the human mind. The surrounding world and its difficulties and possibilities shape our selves and make us the beings we are. Ultimately, this kind of thinking led Spencer past evolutionary psychology to "social Darwinism," the idea that there is ultimately no point in using the resources of the state to help people live or be better, since the bad ones have been made bad by nature, the good ones have been made good the same way, and nature is slowly killing the bad ones off and inevitably making better ones.[28] Social welfare efforts just retard nature's evolutionary project. This kind of "rugged individualism" disregards the ability of individuals to change anything that really matters.

Spencer still has his Ayn Rand–type admirers because of this view; but Darwin, rather than looking at the whole surrounding environment as the cause of evolution, singled out what were then unknown changes inside individual organisms as the source of "spontaneous" or "acciden-tal" variations. These variations were not accidental in the sense of being undetermined by natural law; in that sense, maybe nothing is accidental. But they were "chance" occurrences relative to the rest of the surrounding environment.

Darwin saw the development and the passing on of heritable traits as a black box, and it seemed to James that they might always stay that way. He asked:

> Is it not obvious that the [molecular] cause [of the spontaneous varia-tions that lead to evolution] must lie in a region so recondite and min-ute, must be . . . an infinitesimal of so high an order, that surmise itself may never succeed even in attempting to frame an image of it?[29]

True, Mendel had already discovered his units and laws of heredity and was being ignored when James wrote this, and Watson and Crick (and Rosalind Franklin) provided the most basic details of the genetic mech-anism fifty years ago. The molecular machinery didn't turn out to be unimaginable after all; today we can even photograph it. Nevertheless, James's real point about Darwinism endures, since the best possible un-derstanding of the mechanisms that introduce and pass on "accidental" variations will not answer the questions Darwin set out to answer.

Darwin redefined the relation of the environment to the animal so that the question of biological origin was no longer the Lamarckian ques-tion, "What in the environment made the animal?" It was now whether the environment was more likely to preserve or destroy an animal because of *what was in that animal to begin with.* That question can't be answered by looking either at the molecules and their laws or at the natural world in the "aggregate." In "natural selection," one microscopic, discrete, isolated part of nature contingently creates the animal's features; and another part of nature, the large, plainly visible part, happens to select those features by preserving the animals that have them or discards those features by killing those animals off. Thus a new characteristic that can change the future of a species, or even create a new species, cannot be genuinely understood as the mechanical product of environing conditions. While we needn't see the production of new features as supernatural, it also makes no sense to think of the present environing natural world and its physical laws as the author of improvements in, or worsenings of, a species. Random developments in individuals that are independent of that environment and those laws—independent in that they might not have come along even if all the laws and all the environing conditions had been the same—have as big a role to play as the environment and its history.

The great man—or the great person, shall we say, since James does include Queen Victoria on his list of leaders and geniuses—is like a genetically determined improvement or worsening of an animal species. Her impact, that of her personality and her acts of will, can't be explained by the surrounding environment, since her personality and acts were produced in *what that environment surrounds,* an isolated and unique *part* of the world, by mechanisms that are even to this day too abstruse to know. But we can understand the accomplishments of the genius if we look back, not to what ostensibly produced her, but to *her interactions with her surroundings*—surroundings that will either preserve or destroy her—and that she herself might eventually work to preserve or destroy.

This story of the "great" person may call to mind Hegel's "world-historical individual," who also decisively changes society in cooperation with the circumstances of her or his moment in time. But James would no doubt reject Hegel's idea that such a person's passion-driven activity is fundamentally the tool of the World-Spirit as it cunningly unfolds behind the scenes of history. In fact, Hegel says, there is no point in blaming these disruptive figures for having had bad personal motives; had those particular persons not taken up their world-changing tasks, they would have "remained within the ordinary channels of human existence, and someone else would have accomplished the will of the spirit."[30] James will want to insist against both Hegel's rationalistic picture of the world and Spencer's more naturalistic one that the great persons of history really are themselves the initiators of change.

It is true enough, James thinks, that the genius and her contributions don't arise ex nihilo; they have causes in the history of the physical world. But looking to those historical phenomena to explain either her or the world she helps to make is like looking to the history of the Celts to explain the death of a sparrow when we saw the little Irish kid throw the rock. We can look forward to more sparrow deaths and the development of an adolescent psychopath if we waste our time that way. Likewise, we won't understand how the Irish accomplished all they did in the history of

Western civilization if we pay no attention to the particular Irish monks who preserved and spread classical learning during the early Middle Ages; to the particular inclinations and struggles of Wilde, Shaw, and Yeats; and to the particular works and efforts of those Irish American brothers William and Henry James.

The conditions around the Irish monks may have been necessary for their achievement—they were on an island far from the barbarian hordes tearing continental Europe apart—but obviously they were not sufficient. Isolation doesn't call up scholarship by itself; other isolated places produced no avid scholars. The Irish monks were not simply products of their environment; they were particular people who used their circumstances to change their part of the world by preserving a source of intellectual power. Just as a newly developed or introduced species can transform its environment and must be understood as a causal force there—think of the havoc wreaked by "invasive species" like zebra mussels, walking catfish, and flying Asian cockroaches—great persons, or collectives of them who decide to work together, can and do remake the physical and social conditions into which they are born or transplanted, and they too must be understood as causal forces. Social evolution, James says,

> is a resultant of the interaction of two wholly distinct factors,—the individual, deriving his peculiar gifts from the play of physiological and infra-social forces, but bearing all the power of initiative and origination in his hands; and, second, the social environment, with its power of adopting or rejecting both him and his gifts. Both factors are essential to change. The community stagnates without the impulse of the individual. The impulse dies away without the sympathy of the community.[31]

Or, at least, this is the way to see the monks and their social environment if we are to make scientific sense of them in the way Darwin made sense of species and their environment. We have to understand our human development as an exertion of force on our social environment, which reciprocates. We and our societies or our "races" develop together. And what is perhaps most important, we have to see ourselves as developing in this way, or we can't develop in this way. Once again, a Spencer-like story of race is the wrong kind of story to tell, not only because it fails to capture the scientific facts of evolution but because it makes individual thought and action more difficult. The Irish monks didn't wait for their environment to cause the preservation of Latin literature after the fall of Rome, and much of that literature might not have been preserved and reintroduced into Europe if they had; appealing to the Celtic race won't stop particular little Irish kids from feeling and exerting their power to kill sparrows; and expecting the natural and social world to deposit ashes on your icy front steps will result in more fractured skulls than there would otherwise be. We unique human beings and our various "races" can, do, and will change and develop together only so long as we individuals see ourselves as capable of creating, or at least co-creating, the future.

Nature or Nurture?

James thus sends a message not only to Spencer but to his followers, even those of the present day. Evolutionary psychologists, biologists, anthropologists, and linguists are misguided if they think that we human beings do and should do as our environment directs. James's Darwinian outlook entails that human beings are free to make and remake their environment, and he thinks that once we have this idea we can become freer and freer, more and more capable of reshaping the world.

Once again, this includes both the natural and the social worlds. To the currently very popular question, "Nature or nurture?" James will answer, "Neither." Not "both," as many social and life scientists would say today, but "neither." Neither prior physical conditions, prior social conditions, *nor their combination* makes us what we are or will become. Of course there is a sense in which we and our societies result from preexisting conditions—even nurture is a part of nature, after all, and we individuals have to learn languages and other skills from the cultures around us before we can accomplish anything distinctively human. But preexisting natural and social conditions do not therefore determine our futures or the futures of our various peoples. A truly scientific self-understanding shows us that we individual persons, like Darwinian species, are "products" that react to our environments idiosyncratically, in a way not determined by preexisting geographical conditions or even by physical laws. We, or at least some of us, are not inert sculptures but creative sculptors of our world—and ourselves. Some of us can and will work to remake "us" into a new nation or race—*if* we have the audacity to think that we can do it.

By contrast, James's Spencerian opponent, Grant Allen, contends:

> If the people who went to Hamburg had gone to Timbuctoo, they would now be indistinguishable from the semi-barbarian negroes who inhabit that central African metropolis; and if the people who went to Timbuctoo had gone to Hamburg, they would now have been white-skinned merchants driving a roaring trade in imitation sherry and indigestible port. . . . The differentiating agency must be sought in the great permanent geographical features of land and sea; . . . these have necessarily and inevitably moulded the characters and histories of every nation upon the earth.[32]

156

As dubious as this sounds, there are still writers in the present day who appeal to geographical factors as the fundamental cause of human racial characteristics and thus of differences in the level of cultural achievement among human populations. Their views are subtler than Allen's, and though some of them are scientific racists,[33] some of them are humane thinkers trying to make sense of facts that seem to cry out for some kind of scientific explanation. But to all the Spencerians, the malignant and the benign alike, James will reply: You are underestimating the immense power of individual human differences. To Allen specifically, he responds:

> No two couples of the most homogeneous race could possibly be found so identical as, if set in identical environments, to give rise to two identical lineages. The minute divergence at the start grows broader with each generation, and ends with entirely dissimilar breeds.[34]

Thus, if we could turn the evolutionary clock back and start over, leaving all the laws of nature the same, we would not find the same human cultures arising on the same continents. Indeed, if we turned the clock back far enough, we might not find human beings at all on any continents, since the dinosaurs might thrive this time. But if we only went back as far as "Lucy" in Africa, different accidental characteristics would develop among Lucy's human descendents—they would be different descendents this time, since the same parents have different children each time they conceive—and the resulting cultures would reflect those differences. Human beings can't make seagoing cultures in the desert, but if we started all over again, our cultures and the relations among them would be very different from the ones that actually developed over history; and it is entirely possible that this time around a different part of the world might wind up producing the most "cargo," to use Yali and Diamond's expression.

Individuals are small, and societies and physical environments are large, but, as James says:

> The social surroundings of the past and present hour exclude the possibility of accepting certain contributions from individuals; but they do not positively define what contributions shall be accepted, for in themselves they are powerless to fix what the nature of the individual offerings shall be.[35]

We human units cannot exercise godlike creation and make our physical or our social worlds just any way we like, but the world can't do just anything it wants (or "wants") with us, either. Both our physical and intellectual peculiarities make our contributions to the world distinctive, and they therefore give us a *vote*, so to speak, in the physical and intellectual futures of our "races"—not to mention the ability to campaign for other votes. We can see this happening among the animals, so why isn't it even more likely among human beings?[36] The individual traits of animal parents have as much to do with what kind of offspring get produced and thrive as does the environing natural setting; then the odd features of the offspring take the species, and sometimes the surrounding natural environment as well, in new directions once again. And James thinks that analogues of the kinds of oddities that pop up randomly among individual animals and shape their resulting "races" will pop up randomly among individual persons, allowing them to shape their human "races" both phenotypically and intellectually.

Moreover, though James does not emphasize this, the intellectual development may influence the phenotypical. Recall Verne Grant's account of races among animals and plants, according to which distinct races interbreed and disappear as geographical separation disappears; as Philip Kitcher has pointed out, the human "races" in the United States, especially blacks and whites, have not amalgamated, despite sharing a space on the map, because of their attitudes toward one another.[37] Those attitudes might have been entirely different if a few "great" persons had popped up and managed, with luck and cooperation, to spread more liberal attitudes in their different racial communities. (What if James Earl Ray and Byron de la Beckwith had missed?) The visible differences that we use in assigning individuals to the different "races" might well have diminished or vanished.

Conclusion

Thus, James offers at least one philosophically important message about "race," understood as a hierarchy among different human populations that is created and determined by natural conditions. He tells us there is no such thing. There are different groups of people in different physical and social circumstances, they look different from one another, some have societies that are more materially successful than others, and there may even be significant and discoverable differences among these groups at the molecular level that determines heredity. These groups can be seen and understood scientifically, and we can even call them "races" if we like. Nevertheless, there is no scientific truth to the Enlightenment-era belief that nature makes some of these groups as "great" or successful as they are. James argues that even in an entirely mechanical world, we individuals are free—or free enough, anyway—to wrestle with the world and co-create both our own futures and the futures of our communities, nations, or "races." Nature, including human nature, is our pawn to play with freely, not the other way around. We can't do just anything we like with nature, but then, we can't do absolutely anything we might like with any "pawn" or thing we can use as a tool. We are not gods, once again—as if this needed saying even once—but we individual persons are formidable powers in the natural and social world. We are free creators and free re-creators—or at least we *can* be free if we look at ourselves and the world in the right way. We can have power if we acknowledge our power.

Notes

1. Cornel West perhaps originates this line of argument in his *The American Evasion of Philosophy: A Genealogy of Pragmatism* (Madison: University of Wisconsin Press, 1989).

2. For this argument, see Louis Menand, *The Metaphysical Club* (New York: Farrar, Straus and Giroux, 2002). Robert Brandom accepts this point in his essay "When Philosophy Paints its Blue on Gray" in this volume.

3. The inadequacy of pragmatic treatments of race is a running theme of the essays in Bill E. Lawson and Donald F. Koch, eds., *Pragmatism and the Problem of Race* (Bloomington: Indiana University Press, 2004). See also David Kim, "The Unexamined Frontier: Dewey, Pragmatism, and America Enlarged," in this volume. Kim expands upon Menand's and Brandom's critique, pointing out Dewey's historicist metaphilosophy and the historical origins of pragmatism in a period of post–Civil War reconciliation and growing American imperialism in Asia. Compromises of that period "took race off the table" in both American politics and American philosophy.

4. William James, "Great Men and Their Environment," in *The Will to Believe and Other Essays in Popular Philosophy* (New York: Dover, 1956 [1880]), 232.

5. Ibid., 217.

6. Ibid., 238.

7. Compare with this the idea of the "Three Races that Inhabit the Territory of the United States" offered in the last chapter of Alexis de Tocqueville's *Democracy in America*. Tocqueville describes three "peoples," white, black, and native American, who differ in superficial "physiognomy" but are primarily distinguished by social conditions. Lucius Outlaw argues that this modern-seeming picture accounts inadequately for the role of race in the development of both democracy and white supremacy in America; see his "Race, Nation, and Nation-State: Tocqueville on (U.S.) American Democracy" in this volume.

8. Joel Perlman, "'Race or People': Federal Race Classifications for Europeans in America, 1898–1913," Washington University in St. Louis, Economics Working Paper Archive (2001), 11. http://econwpa.wustl.edu:8089/eps/mac/papers/0012/0012007.pdf.

9. James, "Great Men and their Environment," 216–54.

10. Ibid., 216.

11. William James, *The Principles of Psychology* (Cambridge, Mass.: Harvard

University Press, 1981 [1890]), 2, 1007–1008. Cited by Steven Pinker, *The Language Instinct* (New York: W. Morrow and Co., 1994), 20–21, and Leda Cosmides and John Tooby, "Evolutionary Psychology: A Primer" (University of California, Santa Barbara, 1997) at www.psych.ucsb.edu/research/cep/primer.html.

12. W. V. Quine, "Two Dogmas of Empiricism," in *From a Logical Point of View* (New York: Harper & Row, 1963), 20–46, contains the most famous attack on the idea that philosophers can "analyze" concepts or meanings and "reduce" theories, terms, or claims to other theories, terms, or claims. The idea that we can do this amounts to the idea that we can recognize sameness of meaning or conception, and Quine argues that we can make no sense of this.

13. Ernst Mayr, *Populations, Species, and Evolution; An Abridgment of Animal Species and Evolution* (Cambridge, Mass.: Belknap Press of Harvard University Press, 1970), 258; emphasis in original.

14. Verne Grant, *The Origin of Adaptations* (New York: Columbia University Press, 1963), 304.

15. R. C. Lewontin famously argued that about 85 percent of the total genetic variation in human beings is due to individual differences within populations and only 15 percent to differences between populations or ethnic groups. He concluded that the division of *Homo sapiens* into these groups is not justified by the genetic data. Many, though by no means all, life scientists have agreed with him. See R. C. Lewontin, "The Apportionment of Human Diversity," *Evolutionary Biology* 6 (1972): 381–98.

16. Armand Marie Leroi, "A Family Tree in Every Gene," *New York Times*, 14 March 2005, A21.

17. Jared Diamond, *Guns, Germs, and Steel: The Fates of Human Societies* (New York: W. W. Norton and Co., 1997), 9–32.

18. A very helpful selection of influential and currently hard-to-find Enlightenment-era writings on race is compiled in Emanuel Eze, ed., *Race and the Enlightenment* (Oxford: Blackwell, 1997).

19. Diamond, *Guns, Germs, and Steel*, passim and, especially, 408.

20. William James, *The Letters of William James*, ed. Henry James (Boston: Atlantic Monthly Press, 1920), 1:147.

21. James thinks that Hegel's block-picture of the world is too rational and tidy to represent the wild, unpredictable world of our unique human experiences. It is suited for stuffy, self-righteous "prigs" who want to rein other people in, rather than for people who are willing to roll in the dirt of the real world and make up even moral and logical beliefs as tools to make life better. James complained that:

> . . . all Hegelians are not prigs, but I somehow feel as if all prigs ought to end, if developed, by becoming Hegelians. There is a story of two clergymen asked by mistake to conduct the same funeral. One came first and had got no further than 'I am the Resurrection and the Life' when the other entered. '*I* am the Resurrection and the Life!' cried the latter. The 'through-and-through' philosophy, as it actually exists, reminds many of us of that clergy-

man. It seems too buttoned-up and white-chokered and clean-shaven a thing to speak in the name of the vast slow-breathing unconscious Kosmos with its dread abysses and unknown tides. (*Essays in Radical Empiricism*, ed. F. Bowers, F. Burkhardt, and I. Skrupskelis [Cambridge, Mass.: Harvard University Press, 1976], 277–78)

22. I argue for this interpretation of James's pragmatism in Harvey Cormier, *The Truth Is What Works* (Lanham, Md.: Rowman and Littlefield, 2000).

23. See James, *Essays in Radical Empiricism*, 266–80, for one defense of the anti-Hegelian idea that there are real individual things that are not made what they are by logically knowable relations.

24. Herbert Spencer, *The Study of Sociology* (Ann Arbor: University of Michigan Press, 1961 [1874]), 30–31. Cited in James, "Great Men and Their Environment," 233.

25. James, "Great Men and their Environment," 217.

26. Ibid., 219–20.

27. This is obviously not the place for a detailed discussion of Kant's complicated and obscure theory of freedom and noumenal causality, but it does seem clear that whatever Kant is trying to do in his practical philosophy, he is not trying to *produce or expand* our ability to act on our empirically knowable interests. I discuss similarities and differences between Kant's and James's theoretical and practical philosophies in chapter 5 of *The Truth Is What Works*.

28. A typical expression of this outlook, from Herbert Spencer:

[W]ith mankind as with lower kinds, the ill-nurtured offspring of the inferior fail in the struggle for existence with the well-nurtured offspring of the superior; and in a generation or two die out, to the benefit of the species. A harsh discipline this, most will say. True; but nature has much discipline which is harsh, and which must, in the long run, be submitted to. The necessities which she imposes on us are not to be evaded, even by the joint efforts of university graduates and workingmen delegates; and the endeavor to escape her harsh discipline results in a discipline still harsher. Measures which prevent the dwindling away of inferior individuals and families, must, in the course of generations, cause the nation at large to dwindle away. (*The Principles of Ethics, Volume I* [Indianapolis: Liberty Classics, 1978 (1897)], 204)

And for "nation," here, we may also read "race."

29. James, "Great Men and Their Environment," 225.

30. G. W. F. Hegel, *Lectures on the Philosophy of World History: Introduction, Reason in History*, trans. H. B. Nisbet (Cambridge: Cambridge University Press, 2002 [1822–30]), 88.

31. James, "Great Men and Their Environment," 232.

32. Grant Allen, "Nation Making," *Popular Science Monthly Supplement*, December (1878), 121, 123. Cited in James, "Great Men and Their Environment," 235–36.

33. For a depressing example, see Rushton, J. Philippe's review of Diamond, *Guns, Germs, and Steel,* in *Stalking the Wild Taboo,* a set of linked Web pages at www.lrainc.com/swtaboo/stalkers/jpr—ggs.html

34. James, "Great Men and Their Environment," 236 n. 1.

35. Ibid., 231.

36. James quotes A. R. Wallace's book *Malay Archipelago:* "Borneo and New Guinea, as alike physically as two distinct countries can be, are zoölogically wide as the poles asunder; while Australia, with its dry winds, its open plains, its stony deserts, and its temperate climate, yet produces birds and quadrupeds which are closely related to those inhabiting the hot, damp, luxuriant forests which everywhere clothe the plains and mountains of New Guinea" (*The Malay Archipelago: The Land of the Orang-utan and the Birds of Paradise: A Narrative of Travel, with Studies of Man and Nature* [London: Macmillan, 1883], 13). Cited in James, "Great Men and their Environment," 240.

37. Philip Kitcher, "Race, Ethnicity, Biology, Culture," in *In Mendel's Mirror: Philosophical Reflections on Biology* (Oxford: Oxford University Press, 2003), 239–45.

EIGHT

Race, Culture, and Black Self-Determination

Tommie Shelby

It is inconceivable that I feel alienated from the Western tradition; my people have contributed so much that is vital and good to it. I am alienated from the *people* who call themselves white, who think they own Western tradition.

—Nikki Giovanni, *Racism 101*

At least since the late nineteenth century, there have been prominent black intellectuals, artists, and activists who have advocated various forms of black cultural self-determination. And as William Van Deburg has observed, cultural nationalism, perhaps more than any other ideology of the Black Power era, continues to have an enormous impact on African American self-understanding, political consciousness, and social institutions.[1] In addition, the cultural politics of difference or democratic multiculturalism, which is sometimes embraced by progressives, has some striking similarities to Black Power cultural nationalism, and thus many have come to think of the politics of recognition as a component of black politics. I want to critically evaluate the claims of black cultural nationalism. The focus of this inquiry will be the philosophical presuppositions and political significance of the doctrine. I will argue that contemporary black politics should not be understood on the model of multiculturalism and that black Americans should not embrace black cultural nationalism as a component of their shared political outlook.

Tenets of Black Cultural Nationalism

Since black cultural nationalism has had defenders from different historical periods and of various ideological stripes, it takes a variety of forms. Canonical representatives include W.E.B. Du Bois, Alain Locke, Amiri Baraka, Harold Cruse, Maulana Karenga, Haki Madhubuti, and Molefi Asante.[2] Rather than discuss each historical variant of cultural nationalism, I offer here a general characterization—a sort of Weberian ideal type or heuristic construct—composed of eight tenets.[3] There may be few if any self-described cultural nationalists who have explicitly defended all of these views, but my aim has been to characterize this philosophy of culture in such a way that any proponent of black cultural autonomy would endorse some substantial subset of the tenets and would be generally sympathetic to them all.

Each of the following tenets has embedded within in it both factual (descriptive) and normative (evaluative) presuppositions. I will make these assumptions explicit and outline the basic rationale behind each tenet. Part of the aim will be to give a sense of how they fit together to form a coherent outlook—a black nationalist philosophy of culture.

1. There is a distinct black culture that is different from (and perhaps, though not necessarily, in opposition to) white culture. The "black" culture in question is sometimes understood narrowly to mean specifically African American culture (i.e., the culture of African slaves in North America and their descendents). But alternatively it may be thought to include cultures from the broader diaspora (e.g., from parts of Latin America or the Caribbean) or from sub-Saharan Africa. The relevant "white" culture is variously conceived of as Anglo-American, Euro-American, European, or Western. Within these categories, some would also distinguish between "high," "middle-brow," and "popular" culture or alternatively between fine art and folk expression. For simplicity, I will use the terms "black" and "white" to denote all conceptual variants, and I will not invoke a high/low distinction. Accounts of the specific characteristics of and differences between black and white cultures vary with the particular advocate of black cultural nationalism. Typically, however, such accounts characterize black culture as fundamentally: oral, communal, harmonious, emotive, spontaneous, spiritual, earthy, experiential, improvisational, dynamic, colorful, sensual, uninhibited, dialogical, inclusive, and democratic. White culture, by contrast, is often viewed as essentially: logocentric, individualistic, antagonistic, rationalistic, formal, materialistic, abstract, cerebral, rigid, static, bland, reserved, monological, elitist, and hegemonic. These are, as I say, typical ways of representing the differences between the two cultures. More nuanced ways of distinguishing them are of course possible.[4]

2. Blacks must rediscover and collectively reclaim their culture, developing a consciousness and lifestyle that is rooted in this culture. It is thought that this would enable blacks to form a cultural identity on their own terms, autonomously and endogenously. Some cultural nationalists concede that black culture, especially the African American variety, has been eroded or suppressed by the cultural imperialism of other ethno-national groups, in particular those of European descent. But rather than acquiesce to these pressures of assimilation, they insist that this loss of cultural distinctiveness is all the more reason for blacks to self-organize and perhaps to self-segregate in order to revive their heritage or to construct a new independent culture without the interference of non-blacks.

3. Black culture is an invaluable collective good; and thus blacks should identify with, take pride in, actively reproduce, and creatively develop this shared culture. Black culture is held to provide many benefits for blacks, including: a basis for psychological integration, sources of self-esteem and group pride, a repertoire of valued social roles, a stock of useful skills and techniques, conventions that make for ease of social intercourse, artifacts of aesthetic worth and historical import, images of symbolic significance, distinctive styles and modes of expression, a venerable intellectual tradition, and common narratives that contain vital sociohistorical knowledge. The loss or decay of this culture would be tragic, since it would mean the disappearance of an irreplaceable and multifaceted shared social good. Because they (could) benefit in countless ways from its existence and would be harmed by its extinction, blacks must do their part to preserve black culture. This may involve, among other things, contributing to the establishment and maintenance of cultural infrastructures, such as educational institutions, churches, archives, and mass media outlets (e.g., in news production, publishing, television, film, radio, recorded music, and Web sites). These black infrastructures can be used to store and disseminate black cultural knowledge and artifacts.

4. Unlike white culture, black culture provides a stable and rich basis for feelings of community and for the construction of positive individual identities. Some have maintained that many blacks suffer from self-alienation and dislocation as a result of living (or attempting to live) in accordance with the values and norms of white culture, which they regard as a racist culture that denigrates the ability, beauty, and moral character of black people. Authentic black culture, they contend, can provide black people with a sense of rootedness within a unified community, a cultural space that feels more like home. This culture contains vital means for the existential defense against madness and self-destruction in a racist social world that is hostile to the very presence of black peoples. An identity embedded within black cultural traditions will be more self-affirming and well-integrated, and thus blacks should accept cultural blackness as an integral component of their sense of selfhood.

5. *Black culture is an essential tool of liberation, a necessary weapon to resist white domination, and a vehicle for the expression of nationalist ideals.* The role of black artists, intellectuals, and social critics is thus to produce works that represent and affirm the authentic black experience and that inspire ordinary black folk to work for freedom and independence. Some black nationalists have no faith in the emancipatory potential of white culture, for they believe (or at least suspect) that it is inherently biased against black interests or that it is contrary to the true sensibility of blacks. Some maintain that no self-respecting fight for self-determination can be carried out with the cultural weapons of the oppressor group. Hence, the struggle for cultural self-determination must be prosecuted with cultural resources taken solely (or almost exclusively) from the black world. And such resources that are used should be deployed for the uplift and advancement of black people, not simply for self-expression or personal gain.

6. *The state should refrain from actions that prevent the endogenous reproduction of black culture; and non-blacks, perhaps with encouragement from the state, should cultivate tolerance and respect for black culture.* The vast majority of black Americans are not immigrants or the descendents of immigrants but the descendents of African slaves, subjugated peoples who were once in forced exile in the Americas. Although the United States did not appropriate their native land, the people of African descent in America have themselves been annexed to the United States. They thus have no obligation to assimilate to the dominant culture, as perhaps voluntary immigrants or refugees do. As a stigmatized minority culture threatened by white cultural imperialism, black culture, much like the cultures of indigenous peoples, has a right to governmental protection and social recognition. The government may even have an obligation to support black cultural infrastructures, say, through public finance or tax breaks.

7. *Blacks must become the primary producers, purveyors, and beneficiaries (financial and otherwise) of black culture.* While black culture is sometimes viewed as pathological, inferior, or unsophisticated, this has not prevented non-blacks from gaining tremendous financial profits from it, typically at considerable expense to blacks. Indeed, the exploitation of black culture (especially black music and vernacular style) by non-blacks for material gain has global reach. Moreover, though much that is valuable

in American culture springs from black creativity, blacks are rarely given full credit for their innovations and contributions and are almost never appropriately compensated for them. However, if blacks are to have cultural autonomy, they must be the ones to decide how, if at all, their culture is to be used for commercial ends. If it is to be so exploited, then blacks should be the ones who gain profit and recognition from this use.

8. *Blacks are (or must become) and should be regarded as the foremost interpreters of the meaning of their cultural ways.* This claim has a dual basis. First, some white teachers, scholars, and art critics have taken up the task of explaining the significance and value of black cultural practices to the rest of the world. Because of their white privilege and the general disparagement of black cognitive abilities, white interpretations of black culture are sometimes accepted (even among some blacks) as more authoritative than black interpretations. Second, white interpretations of black culture typically contain considerable distortion and misrepresentation, leading to greater stigmatization of black people and widespread misunderstanding of their distinctive ways of life. The source of this distortion is often antiblack racial prejudice (sometimes unconscious or unacknowledged) and an assumption of white cultural superiority. But even knowledgeable whites with genuine good will toward blacks will often mischaracterize black culture simply because, given their whiteness, they are incapable of being fully incorporated into the culture they wish to represent. Their ineradicable outsider status prevents them from fully understanding and thus appreciating the culture from the inside in the way that a black person born and raised in the culture comes to experience and take delight in it.

Which Black Culture?

One familiar criticism of black cultural nationalism attacks the claim that there exists (or could exist) a distinct black culture that is separate (or separable) from so-called white culture, thus challenging the very coherence of the idea of black cultural autonomy. Although we should reject the crude, ahistorical, and Manichean visions of black/white cultural difference that are sometimes put forward by cultural nationalists, I do not deny that it is coherent to speak of specifically black forms of cultural life. For purposes of this discussion, then, I assume that there is such a culture(s) along with a white counterpart(s). My focus will be on how blacks should think about and relate practically to these cultures.

The first thing to note is that not all who are socially designated as racially black self-identify as culturally black. The importance of this fact should not be underestimated. The cultural nationalist is not merely speaking to those blacks who already have a robust and committed black cultural identity, but also to those blacks who are tempted to assimilate culturally, who are culturally black but only marginally so, or who are not culturally black at all. Thus, whether tenet two is ultimately defensible will depend crucially on whether the cultural nationalist claims merely that it is permissible and laudable for blacks to reproduce and self-identify with their culture, or that blacks have an *obligation* to embrace black culture, where failure to do so opens one up to severe criticism.

We can agree, perhaps, that blacks should be free to develop and maintain their cultural identities without being inhibited by unjust measures or artificial barriers. But it does not follow that these cultural identities must be rooted ultimately in *black* culture. Keep in mind that cultural autonomy is a right that blacks may exercise or, if it is denied that there is such right, a goal that blacks may justly seek to achieve. It is perfectly consistent with such a right or goal that those blacks who do *not* desire this form of group self-determination are free to cultivate an alternative cultural identity, even to assimilate to white culture. On simple grounds of freedom of association, it seems clear that blacks are entitled to self-organize to preserve black culture, provided they respect the autonomy of individual blacks to exit the cultural community should they so choose. Carrying out the aims of black cultural self-determination could mean, for example, establishing separate educational, religious, and artistic institutions and maintaining historical societies and museums over which blacks committed to the cause would maintain control.

The Blackness of Whites

Tenet three, though, goes beyond this relatively uncontroversial conception of black cultural autonomy. It suggests that blacks have a positive duty to embrace black culture, perhaps exclusively. Yet it is not at all clear that just because blacks (could) benefit from the existence of black culture that they thereby incur a duty to actively preserve it. But if we do suppose that they have such a duty, parallel reasoning would suggest that they also have an obligation to preserve many aspects of what is sometimes regarded as white culture. Perhaps the cultural nationalist can concede this. Indeed, some have maintained that the creative and dynamic synthesis of European (or Euro-American) and African (or Afro-American) cultural elements is precisely what is unique about the form and content of modern black cultural expression.[5] This emphasis on hybridity is certainly a more nuanced view of diasporic blackness than is typically advanced by black cultural nationalists. The difficulty with this position, however, is that, on this reasoning, non-blacks would also have a duty to preserve black culture, since they have benefited in countless ways from its existence as well.[6] Ralph Ellison has famously emphasized this important point.[7]

Moreover, there are aspects of black culture that whites have arguably played a constructive role in maintaining and developing—for example, musical forms and literary traditions. Do their efforts make the culture any less black? Or are we operating, absurdly, with a reverse "one-drop rule" of culture—a criterion that holds that a cultural trait is black if and only if blacks *alone* invented it, and it is white if *any* whites had a hand in its creation? To say that a cultural trait is black or white depending on which racial group played the larger role in creating it is still somewhat arbitrary, perhaps even tantamount to a racialized conception of culture. But even if we accept this majority-contribution criterion for ethnocultural provenance, it is not clear why this would entail that blacks alone have an obligation to perpetuate black culture.

Yet even if we concede that the fate of black culture should rest largely in black hands, this would not, by itself, entail a duty on the part of blacks to embrace a black cultural identity. Granted, if black culture were to come under unjustified siege and as a result were threatened with extinction, then perhaps there would be some obligation on blacks to act to preserve it, especially if the state refused to help and, because of antiblack racism, non-blacks failed to see why the culture is worth preserving. Here the obligation to keep black culture alive springs from our obligation to resist the injustice of cultural intolerance. However, discharging this duty to actively preserve black culture need not involve identifying with the culture as specifically or exclusively one's own, as a part of who one "really" is.

Culture as Group Inheritance

But there is a deeper—and quite old—philosophical question here. Should a person value the elements of a culture because they are intrinsically or instrumentally *valuable;* or, rather, should she value them because they are components of *her* culture, that is, because *she* is black and because these elements are a part of *black* culture? If she should value them because they are valuable, then it is not at all clear why she, as a black person, has a special stake in black cultural forms, that is, a stake that is different from the members of other racial groups. All who view the culture as beautiful or useful, regardless of their racial identity, have a reason to value and preserve it. But if she should value it because she is black, in what way, if at all, does the proprietary claim (*it is mine*) justify or entail the evaluative claim (*I should value it*)?

Henry Louis Gates Jr. has argued that the proprietary claim itself should be questioned:

> I got mine: The rhetoric of liberal education remains suffused with the imagery of possession, patrimony, legacy, lineage, inheritance—call it cultural geneticism (in the broadest sense of that term). At the same moment, the rhetoric of possession and lineage subsists upon, and perpetuates, a division: between us and them, we heirs of *our* tradition, and you, the Others, whose difference defines our identity.[8]

Gates suggests that we abandon the discourse of cultural possession, the lynchpin of cultural nationalism. In his view, by accepting the proprietary premise, African Americans (native-born blacks who are descended from African slaves), having been dispossessed of their African national culture, inevitably end up affirming their status as cultural outsiders and interlopers in the place of their birth and the only home they have ever known. Thus, in seeking to ground the evaluative claim in the proprietary claim, the cultural nationalist must avoid this trap of cultural self-marginalization. Let's consider a few ways that this might be accomplished.

First, he could take the short road: blacks created the culture, so they should value it. But surely the fact that blacks created the culture does not, in itself, give them a reason to value it. We do sometimes create things that lack value; and it would be more than a bit paradoxical to insist that people should value things that lack value, to insist that they embrace junk. This is not to say that valuing something that lacks value is irrational. It's not always. People sometimes *confer* value on otherwise worthless things, for example, items that would be considered junk if not for their sentimental value. But our interest is in whether a black person should value the elements of a culture simply because these elements are a part of *her* culture (in a sense yet to be specified); and it would seem that the value of the culture is a necessary condition for justifying this normative claim. Let's proceed, then, on the assumption that black culture is valuable, objectively speaking. So our question becomes: assuming the intrinsic merit or instrumental value of a cultural form, is there a *further* reason to value it that springs from a proprietary claim?

Perhaps a black person should value black culture because of its role in making her who she is. So Sarah Vaughan might value black culture because its musical traditions contributed to her becoming a great jazz vocalist, a constitutive component of her self-identity, we may assume. But of course non-blacks could value the culture for this same reason, since many of them have been positively influenced by black cultural traditions. And of course there will be many blacks who cannot feel this way, for black culture may have had little impact on who they have become. Thus, while this account may provide those who already have a strong black cultural identity with a reason to value black culture, it does not give blacks, in virtue of their racial classification, a special reason to value black culture. Here the culture does not belong to me in virtue of my membership in the group; it belongs to me in virtue of the fact that it is a part of me.

A third possibility is that we can value a culture because we have *participated* in its maintenance or development, thus generating a form of pride or attachment rooted in a sense of achievement. Here we value it because its reproduction is a product of our efforts. So, for example, by participating in black rhetorical repartee—what Gates calls the vernacular art of "signifyin(g)"—one contributes to keeping this lively and enjoyable practice alive.[9] But again, many non-blacks participate—to good effect, one might add—in black culture, and there are blacks who have made little to no contribution to the preservation or advancement of black culture— some, arguably, have had a negative impact on it. Thus, some non-blacks could have an achievement-based reason to value black culture, notwithstanding the fact that the culture is not really "theirs," and some blacks will lack such a reason, despite the fact the culture ostensibly "belongs" to them.

A fourth possibility is to hold that individual blacks have a reason to value black culture, quite apart from whether they have made any contribution to it, because it is the product of the imagination and efforts of *their* people. On this view, it is because blacks view each other as constituting a distinct ethno-racial community that they can rightly take pride in the achievements of the other members of the group, in much the same way that a child might take just pride in his mother's achievements, even though he has had little to do with her success and indeed may have been a hindrance to it. It is this familiar sense of "we-ness" or shared belonging, rooted in mutual recognition, that underpins the special claim that all blacks have on black culture. Whites may indeed have benefited from, been shaped by, participated in, or contributed to black culture. But because they lack the descent relation and somatic characteristics that are necessary for being classified as racially black, they are not recognized members of the black nation and thus cannot possess this unique reason for valuing "its" culture.

It is no objection to this idea of black peoplehood to point out that black racial identity has its origins in the ideological fiction of "race." Other national identities are derived from similar myths—think of American narratives about being a "free country" even while it allowed slavery. The trouble with the position under consideration is not that blacks are not a people, but rather that it does not follow that blacks have a *duty* to embrace black culture simply because they are racially black. At most, black peoplehood makes it permissible for blacks to take special pride in black culture and thus to value it as uniquely their own. Such identification is indeed a kind of birthright. Yet it does not, in itself, entail that blacks cannot fully participate or find fulfillment in white culture. But for those blacks who do not strongly or primarily identify with blacks as their people or with black culture as uniquely their own, they have no special obligation in virtue of their being racially black to take up a black cultural identity. The recognition of the group must be reciprocated to produce this result. In this way, being entitled to identify with black culture as one's own entails having the freedom *not* to exercise this right. Thus, without denying who one is as a black person, one may legitimately reject one's black cultural heritage.

Instability, Hybridity, and Rootlessness

However, tenet four of black cultural nationalism suggests an additional reason why blacks should cultivate such an identity. It insists that black culture can provide blacks with a better and more stable basis for communal fellowship and identity construction than white culture can. Before considering the plausibility of this claim, we should note that cultural identities are never static but shift with changes in the sociohistorical context.[10] Such contextual factors will include prevailing economic conditions, state policy, material interdependence of cultural groups, relative group physical integration or isolation, social pressures to assimilate or remain separate, and the number and kinds of cultural groups living in close proximity or otherwise having access to each other's cultural ways. We should also keep in mind that there has been significant black immigration to the United States in recent years from Africa, Latin America, the Caribbean, and Europe, and these black peoples have quite diverse cultural and national identities.[11] Their presence in America has clearly altered the contours and content of the greater black cultural milieu, extending and reshaping our sense of the scope of black diasporic culture. Given the external and internal forces that create cultural dynamism, it is difficult to see how there could be a stable black cultural identity in contemporary America.

We must also come to terms with the fact that the increasing commercialization of culture, especially youth culture, has had a profound effect on the meaning and content of black culture, not only in the United States but around the world.[12] Symbolic blackness, particularly in the form of ghetto outlaw images, is a tremendous source of profit in the world market, exacerbating the already contentious debate among blacks over what constitutes authentic black culture and over what represents cultural exploitation and "selling-out." As Paul Gilroy puts it: "Black culture is not just commodified but lends its special exotic allure to the marketing of an extraordinary range of commodities and services that have no connection whatever to these cultural forms or to the people who have developed them."[13]

Furthermore, the metropolitan cultures of the world are becoming increasingly hybrid. In order to find favorable markets—for labor, goods, services, or investment—people are perpetually on the move, migrating when possible to where they are likely to acquire material advantages or to avoid material disadvantage.[14] This has the inevitable consequence that cultures are changing, sometimes dramatically and rapidly, because of cultural imposition, diffusion, emulation, and fusion. Although the cultural bases of black social identities are not, and cannot be, stable, the velocity and scope of global cultural exchange has made a vast array of cultural resources readily available to blacks, especially to those in the United States. Black identity construction can therefore take place using cultural materials drawn from diverse sources.

There is a tendency among some black nationalists to exaggerate the "problem" of black cultural homelessness. As the epigraph from Giovanni suggests, blacks rightly feel alienated by white racism, but not all blacks feel out of place in or ambivalent about white culture. In fact, while some are reluctant to admit this, many blacks do not feel particularly at home in even the most revered black cultural spaces. For example, the traditions and modes of expression that are characteristic of many black churches are widely thought to be paradigmatically black.[15] Yet those blacks raised in other religious traditions may not feel affirmed and content in black churches. Certainly, there is no reason to assume that those blacks who are committed to other faiths or to no religion at all will find peace and security in black churches simply because these institutions embody black cultural traditions. Moreover, white and black cultures are not the only alternatives. Some blacks may choose to identify with another ethno-racial culture altogether (e.g., black Puerto Ricans who identify culturally as Latino/a, or black Jews who are committed to Judaism). Or some may simply opt for a more self-consciously, hybrid ethno-cultural identity, notwithstanding the (unsubstantiated) charge that such identities are especially incoherent and anomic.[16]

Now, the cultural nationalist may nevertheless insist that blacks *should* feel more comfortable within black culture, notwithstanding its dynamism, fuzzy boundaries, hybridity, and diverse roots. But why should they? If the different cultures of the world are learned and reproduced through socialization or acculturation rather than genetically predetermined, as they surely are, then no culture is more "natural" to a particular individual than any other.[17] A person's comfort with a particular culture will depend, among other things, on which culture she was initially socialized into, which cultures she has subsequently come in contact with, the freedom she has to experiment with different ways of living, and her personality and temperament. But it will not depend solely if at all on what race she belongs to.

Tools Are Tools

Tenet five maintains that black culture is an important emancipatory tool, one that black artists and intellectuals should make use of, perhaps exclusively, in the collective struggle for freedom and equality. Here the interest in expressive culture is explicitly instrumental; it is a question of which cultural resources will make effective weapons of resistance or vehicles for propaganda. But if this is so, then we should use the cultural resources that would advance black interests and discard or avoid whatever would impede them, regardless of their ethno-racial pedigree. Celebrating the emancipatory potential of black culture should not be allowed to blind blacks to the instrumental value of some non-black ideas and practices.

There is, however, a more plausible version of this tenet. It holds that white cultural forms may be acceptable as tools in the struggle, particularly among the black elite and middle class, but black political mobilization requires black artists, cultural critics, and intellectuals to use familiar black cultural forms to inspire working-class and poor blacks to progressive action. There are at least two ways to defend such a view. One assumes that many blacks regard white culture with suspicion. Thus, if black artists and intellectuals are to energize and enlighten the black masses, they will have to do so with cultural tools that have greater legitimacy among blacks. If this assumption about working-class and poor blacks is sound—which is by no means obvious—then on pragmatic grounds it may make sense for those who are seeking to start or energize a mass movement to work within cultural idioms that are more to the liking of most black people. Yet insofar as the intelligentsia wants to play a leadership role, it must be willing to challenge prejudices among blacks. False assumptions about white culture —or black culture—must be questioned. As Henry Louis Gates Jr. and Cornel West put it: "Being a leader does not necessarily mean being loved; loving one's community means daring to risk estrangement and alienation from that very community, in the short run, in order to break the cycle of poverty, despair, and hopelessness that we are in, over the long run."[18]

According to a slightly different view—one to which both Gates and West seem sympathetic—white culture is not viewed as necessarily problematic from the standpoint of most black people, but it is held to be unfamiliar or opaque to many working-class and poor blacks. Thus, if the black intelligentsia is to get its message across to most black folk, it will have to "speak their language," that is, to use a cultural idiom that they can more readily understand. Again, this may at times be pragmatically necessary. Yet in accounting for this communication divide, we should not exaggerate the extent of black/white cultural differences. Blacks and whites have a lot of experience interacting with each other, if not in common residential communities and schools (due, say, to de facto racial segregation), then certainly in the workplace, marketplace, and public sphere. Misunderstanding between members of the two groups certainly happens. How could it not? It must nevertheless be relatively rare that dialogue breaks down because blacks fail to understand the cultural ways of white folks.

Most importantly, we must also be careful not to confuse differences in cultural traditions with differences in education. What is sometimes regarded as "white culture" is simply that variant of postindustrial mass culture that prevails in the United States, that familiar set of standardized meanings, assumed common knowledge, and basic competencies that all adult citizens must master if they are to live a minimally decent life in modern commercial society. This common culture, which is largely transmitted through educational institutions, allows citizens from diverse ethnic and class backgrounds to communicate with one another, to coordinate their actions, and to conduct their common affairs. Because of substandard public schools and unequal educational opportunity, far too many people in America (and a disproportionate number of blacks) have underdeveloped verbal and analytical skills, deficient knowledge of history and world cultures, little familiarity with different political traditions, and low reading levels. Rather than emphasize the need to recognize black cultural difference, then, it is more urgent for black progressives to push for reforms in our failing public school system.

Some will be made nervous—if not put off—by this prioritizing of educational problems over misunderstandings born of cultural differences. They will fear that it gives comfort to racists who denigrate black cognitive ability and who maintain that black underachievement is due to the cultural pathology of blacks. Others will take it to be an expression of elitism, as contempt for the "uncultured masses." However, I would not suggest for a moment that blacks are intellectually inferior to whites or that black expressive culture is an obstacle to learning and educational achievement. Nor do I think that well-educated blacks are inherently or culturally superior to blacks with limited education. Rather, the point is that the struggle for equal education regardless of race—or gender, class, ability, national origin, and region—is especially pressing and that the demand for equal educational opportunity must be a central component of any progressive black agenda.[19] The first impulse of the pragmatic nationalist must of course be to defend black humanity against insult. To do any less would show a lack of self-respect, group pride, and commitment to defending the dignity of the least advantaged in the black population. But if such solidarity is not to be merely symbolic—or, worse, reactionary—then it must clearly distinguish between the depredations of white cultural imperialism and differential educational opportunity.

Ethnocentrism, Cultural Intolerance, and Race Prejudice

This leads us to tenet six, which demands both state-sponsored protection of black culture against the forces of white cultural imperialism and public recognition of the equal worth of black cultural contributions. Such measures might be justified in principle, but as a practical matter they are unnecessary. To see why, we should, following Oliver C. Cox, first distinguish between ethnocentrism, cultural intolerance, and race prejudice.[20] *Ethnocentrism* is "a social attitude which expresses a community of feeling in any group—the 'we' feeling as over against the 'others.' "[21] This is simply a matter of group solidarity, which is not necessarily "racial" in character but could be rooted in cultural traditions, national origins, or common experience. Both dominant and subordinate groups in a stratified society can be ethnocentric, and typically are. *Cultural intolerance* is "social displeasure or resentment against that group which refuses to conform to the established practices and beliefs of the society."[22] Whites would be culturally intolerant toward blacks, then, if they had negative attitudes toward blacks because blacks refused to take up the beliefs, values, and practices of the white majority or if they put social pressure on blacks to abandon their cultural identity. *Race prejudice*, according to Cox, is prejudice based on somatic characteristics; it is characterized by an emphasis on obvious, visible, physical characteristics (skin color, hair type, facial features, physique, and so on). In the case of blacks, such traits carry the stigma of inferiority; they represent diminished social status.

White racism is not the same as white cultural intolerance. In addition to being subject to race prejudice, those American Indian, Latino/a, Asian, Jewish, Hindu, or Moslem persons who maintain their distinctive ethnic identities are often unfairly disadvantaged in the United States by Anglo or Christian cultural intolerance. As a condition of full citizenship, they are pressured to give up practices, especially linguistic and religious practices, that set them apart from most whites. Being English-speaking Christians, the vast majority of native-born black Americans are primarily oppressed by race prejudice, not cultural intolerance. African Americans are not currently subject to strong pressures to assimilate to the cultural ways of white people—though obviously their African ancestors were. Rather, they are primarily *prevented* from fully assimilating and becoming equally valued members of the American multicultural nation. Indeed, those black Americans who have fully assimilated to the dominant culture nevertheless remain vulnerable to race prejudice.

It is not that African Americans never experience cultural intolerance. Rather, the point is that white cultural intolerance is not currently a significant threat to the way of life or cultural identity of most African Americans. Black "difference," where this has negative implications for the life prospects of African Americans, has mainly to do with a somatic profile that is associated with African origins and that signifies inferior social status. If African American cultural difference is similarly stigmatized, which at times it surely has been and to some extent still is, it is not primarily because of the qualitative features of their cultural practices but because it is a culture associated with blacks. Indeed, the mere fact that other Americans readily adopt so many aspects of African American culture should enable us to see that it is not the intrinsic features of black life that grounds antiblack beliefs and attitudes. Nevertheless, the slightest perception of black cultural difference (e.g., a dropped 'g' in a gerund or a 'be' where one would normally expect an 'is') can serve as a convenient *excuse* for antiblack prejudice in an era when overt expressions of racism are no longer tolerated.

Now, historically some whites have explicitly sought or encouraged the degradation of blacks by denying them access to education. Some whites have also rebuffed attempts by blacks to take on what is regarded as a "white" cultural identity. These were attempts to keep blacks "in their place," that is, subordinated to the white majority, not to absorb them culturally. What is at issue here is not expressive culture but the cultivation of a repertoire of marketable and politically valuable skills. To the extent that whites possess these skills and blacks do not, black progress toward racial equality is impeded. The fact is, some whites would be quite content, some enthusiastic, if blacks were to insist on remaining "different," since this would buttress white privilege and exacerbate black disadvantage in at least three ways. First, to the extent that blacks could be successfully portrayed as unable to meet accepted meritocratic standards, blacks would be more vulnerable to being socially excluded from valued and powerful positions in society. Second, because of their relative lack of educational and social capital, some blacks would become or remain a cheap source of labor that could be easily discarded when the economy is receding or when low-skilled laborers from poor countries are willing to work for lower wages. And third, black economic disadvantage could be rationalized by pointing to the unwillingness of African Americans to conform to mainstream norms of conduct.

However, some black nationalists are not primarily concerned with cultural intolerance. Instead, their main demand is that black culture be given public and equal *recognition*. What underwrites their position is the fact that non-blacks often regard black culture with disdain or as inferior to other ethno-racial cultures. But it is hard to imagine what practical measures blacks could take to extract the desired form of recognition from the state or their fellow citizens. In a society that rightly treats freedom of expression as a basic right, the only way to engender the wanted recognition is through education and persuasion. The state could, and no doubt should, require a multicultural educational curriculum in the public schools.[23] Yet if the root cause of contempt for black culture is not a lack of knowledge of the culture but race prejudice, then such educational efforts, while perhaps welcome on other grounds, are not likely to achieve the desired goal of equal public recognition.

Production, Distribution, and Rewards

Tenet seven takes up the question of black cultural exploitation directly. Understanding the meaning of black cultural exploitation depends on making sense of the idea of a culture belonging to black people, such that an exploiter can be said to have wrongly appropriated it. We found that a cultural element could be said to belong to the culture of black people if (1) the cultural item is rooted in or derived from traditions initially developed and commonly practiced by black people; and (2) blacks identify with each other as a distinct people, forming an ethno-racial community of descent. This makes cultural possession a matter of cultural provenance and the communal relations that exist between the originators of the culture and their descendents.

Tenet seven can then be broken down into three claims about the primacy of blacks in relation to their culture. The first requires that blacks be the primary *producers* of their culture. This does not necessarily exclude non-blacks from participating in the culture; it only requires that blacks be the predominant agents behind its reproduction and development. It does not matter, in principle at least, how many non-blacks participate in black culture or how few blacks do, provided blacks retain primary control over how it is practiced and extended. The point of this aspect of cultural autonomy is to preempt the threat of cultural distortion or erosion due to non-black involvement in black practices.

The second claim requires that blacks be the primary *disseminators* of their culture, which can be understood as their having primary control over the public and private circulation of the culture. If we set aside who stands to profit from the diffusion of black culture, the point of the present requirement is to prevent cultural misrepresentation or perversion. But if blacks maintain control over their cultural practices and non-blacks distribute only what is culturally inauthentic—a watered down appropriation or pathetic imitation—then such items are not "really" elements of black culture at all, but are merely some bastardization thereof. The worry expressed in the second sub-claim of tenet seven thus becomes this: the uninformed or naïve will mistake the fake stuff for the real thing, perhaps coming away with a distorted view of the value of the original or failing to recognize its black origins altogether.

The third claim focuses more directly on the question of cultural exploitation, for it concerns who *benefits* from the production and dissemination of black culture. It demands that blacks be the primary beneficiaries of the production and dissemination of their culture. There are benefits of intrinsic enjoyment (use-value); benefits of prestige (status-value); and the financial benefits gained through the commercial use of the culture (exchange-value).

With respect to use-value, cultures are to be shared. Not even the most militant black nationalist would want to deprive others of the richness of black cultural forms. If we separate the status-value of black culture from the money that is to be made from its commodification, then the benefits of prestige are derived from public opinion about the worth of the culture. Black cultural nationalists want blacks to be esteemed because black cultural contributions are regarded as valuable, and they naturally want this admiration to be grounded in an accurate understanding of what is distinctive and praiseworthy in the culture. To the extent that *black* opinion is the desired source of this esteem, blacks could advance this goal by observing tenet two: by their growing in their knowledge, appreciation, and affirmation of black culture. To the extent that *non-black* opinion is the desired basis for such prestige, realizing the program embodied in tenet eight, that is, blacks coming to be regarded as the foremost interpreters of the meaning and value of black culture, would achieve this goal. Non-blacks would then be obliged to defer to black judgment on the worth of a putative instance of black cultural expression, thereby ensuring that those who deserve the prestige associated with black culture are the only ones to receive it. What is at stake in tenet seven, then, is not who may legitimately benefit from the use-value or status-value of black culture but who may legitimately gain pecuniary benefits from its exchange-value.

We should also distinguish between the exploitation of black (creative) labor and the exploitation of black culture. The powerful should not use their power to forcibly extract labor from those who are economically or otherwise disadvantaged. But the cultural nationalist who defends tenet seven wants to go further. He contends that when non-blacks use black culture for financial profit, not only is the labor-power of black artists and performers exploited, but so are black people taken as a whole. The basis of this latter claim is that the traditions that enable these artists and performers to invent marketable, expressive culture ultimately spring from black *collective* creativity, from a longstanding tradition that has been reproduced and developed by black people through many generations.

Now, even if we allow that black cultural traditions are a resource that belongs to blacks as a people, it is not a resource in the same sense that land, natural resources, and other material assets are. The commercial appropriation or adaptation of a cultural practice by another group is not necessarily a financial loss to the originators of the practice, even if the cultural interlopers fail to share the profits. The commercial use of black culture by non-blacks does not, in itself, preclude a similar use by blacks. In fact, the broader distribution of elements from black culture by white capitalists may actually increase the demand for them, thus allowing blacks to gain more financially from its use than they otherwise would. Consider, for example, the commercial success of hip hop music. Many rappers from the ghetto, given their minimal access to capital, would not have been able to make millions of dollars from their record sales had corporate American not created a global market for the genre. Moreover, this wide exploitation of black culture has at times increased black access to the products of black culture. For instance, the "race" records from the 1920s made the blues widely available to black America.[24]

All three components of tenet seven, then, have to do with blacks acquiring and retaining control over their culture. It is not clear, however, through what mechanisms blacks could gain and maintain the requisite kind of control. Complete exclusivity in the realm of culture is simply impossible. There is no way to fully control the flow of social meanings. Capitalists are not patriots or nationalists but are driven by profit, whatever its ethno-racial pedigree or geographical source. Given the exigencies of market competition, they must market their goods and operate their businesses in whatever part of the globe will allow their capital assets to grow. Black capitalists in the culture industry will be subject to the same economic forces.

Mysteries of Blackness and Privileges of Whiteness

Finally, we come to tenet eight, which demands that non-blacks defer to blacks on the meaning and value of black cultural forms. This clearly cannot mean that any non-black person, no matter how knowledgeable about black history and culture, must defer to any black person, no matter how ignorant and misinformed he or she is. Thus we might interpret the tenet as holding that a "true" or "deep" understanding of black culture requires the interpreter to view it from the standpoint of the black experience, where the requisite black consciousness entails being racially classified as black. The suggestion here is that a non-black person can have only a superficial comprehension of the meaning and worth of black culture. If non-blacks want to get at the profound core of black culture, they will need to acquire it second-hand from those who are black.

It is true that participating in black culture as one who identifies and is publicly regarded as black will likely feel experientially different from the way it would feel if one were, say, white. But does the black experience really provide one with privileged insight into the meaning and value of black *culture*? Or rather, more plausibly, does it simply give one insight into the subjective consciousness of black people, in particular into how they *experience* their culture? Of course, no one can have direct and complete access to the subjective consciousness of others. Imagination, empathy, concerted attention, study, and dialogue can all help in bridging the gap, but they cannot erase it altogether. And if the point is to understand how black people experience their culture, then blacks have a kind of access to this knowledge that non-blacks cannot, a kind of access that philosophers call first-person authority. But if the point is to understand and appreciate the culture of black people, a culture that could exist independently of black interpreters (though not independently of the interpretations of its participants), then it is far from clear that being black is a necessary or sufficient qualification.

The confusion here is twofold. First, there is a hasty generalization from the fact of first-person authority—which concerns how an *individual* relates to the contents of his or her own subjective consciousness—to the claim that blacks have privileged access to their *collective* consciousness. Here we find the implicit positing of a black plural subject, the function of which is to underwrite the idea of a unique experience that all blacks share. But while some rough generalizations may be possible here, there is no reason to think that blacks, given the many differences that exist between them, experience their culture (or anything else for that matter) in precisely the same way. Differences in gender, class, education, sexuality, age, region, religion, values, political ideology, and many other things will all affect how blacks experience and relate to their culture. However, even if there were something like a collective black experience, it would not follow from the presumption of first-person *plural* authority that blacks thereby have privileged access to the meaning of black culture.[25] The only way such authority could be justified is if we simply assumed that to (really) understand and (fully) appreciate black culture is to do so from the "black point of view." But this begs the question, since the possibility of non-blacks fully comprehending the richness of black culture is precisely what is at issue.

Now, being black does give one an advantage in understanding black culture—or, conversely, not being black is a handicap in appreciating it. Yet this is because, given the history of racial antagonism in America, blacks are often reluctant to accept non-blacks into black practices as equal participants. Thus, to the extent that blacks maintain some control over their cultural institutions and restrict access to participation in them, it will be easier for blacks to come to understand and evaluate black culture for the simple reason that they have greater freedom to enjoy and learn about it. Accordingly, a more tenable reading of tenet eight is that a black person's interpretation of some putative item from black culture is, all other things being equal, to be accepted as more authoritative than a non-black person's. The justification would then be the access advantage that is afforded by being a recognized member of the black community.

This principle is better from a theoretical point of view but is of negligible practical significance. For while there might be a justified prima facie presumption that a black person's interpretation is to be given greater weight than a non-black's, further information about the relevant credentials of the parties to an interpretive dispute could easily overturn this presumption. The problem is that once we acknowledge the relative advantages and disadvantages of racial group membership for interpreting black culture, things are rarely equal in all other relevant respects—for example, with respect to sociohistorical and cultural knowledge, active participation and engagement, and aesthetic judgment and intellectual acumen. This means that we can never rule out the possibility that some non-black person will have as much if not more standing as some black person to judge the meaning and value of a particular black cultural item or performance.

I would like to close this chapter by raising a final worry about tenets seven and eight. Such arguments can be easily turned around to restrict the access of blacks to so-called white culture and to question the standing of blacks to interpret and evaluate non-black modes of cultural expression. Should blacks be denied the opportunity to participate in, disseminate, consume, profit from, and assess white cultural ideas and practices? Because blacks lack the "white experience"—the experience of living with the bodily badge of whiteness and the privileges that this entails—does this disqualify them as equal participants in white cultures? Such arguments about the esoteric character of black cultural difference and the fundamentally alien character of white culture could lead us down this unfortunate path. Indeed, at a time when there is a black-white educational achievement gap—which in the absence of affirmative action will inevitably produce racially disparate access to well-paying jobs—to suggest that there is some unbridgeable cultural gap between blacks and whites is to play right into the hands of those who would prefer to see blacks remain socially subordinate. Moreover, those of us who believe that we have important and original things to say both within and about the Western *philosophical* tradition should be especially concerned about the exaggerated claims of black cultural nationalism.

The black struggle for social equality has traditionally included the fight for each black individual to be viewed as an equal participant in the multicultural mix of America. This is a legacy of the black freedom struggle that should earnestly be kept alive, for it expresses a cosmopolitan ideal well worth striving for, though no doubt utopian at the moment. But cultural nationalism is not a suitable vehicle for bringing about this post-ethno-racial utopia, since its basic tenets are plagued by a number of conceptual and normative difficulties. My alternative suggestion is that we focus our critical analyses and political activism on continuing racism, persistent forms of socioeconomic inequality, unequal educational opportunity, and racialized urban poverty, for it is these that give rise to unflattering and disrespectful views of black people and thus of the cultural forms associated with them.

Notes

1. William L. Van Deburg, *New Day in Babylon: The Black Power Movement and American Culture, 1965–1975* (Chicago: University of Chicago Press, 1992).

2. W.E.B. Du Bois, *The Souls of Black Folk*, edited with an introduction by David W. Blight and Robert Gooding-Williams (Boston: Bedford Books, 1997); Alain Locke, "The New Negro," in *The New Negro*, ed. Alain Locke (New York: Atheneum, 1969); Amiri Baraka (LeRoi Jones), *Blues People: Negro Music in White America* (New York: William Morrow, 1963); Harold Cruse, *The Crisis of the Negro Intellectual* (New York: William Morrow, 1967); Haki R. Madhubuti, *From Plan To Planet: Life-Studies: The Need For African Minds and Institutions* (Chicago: Third World Press, 1973); Maulana Karenga, "Society, Culture, and the Problem of Self-Consciousness: A Kawaida Analysis," in *Philosophy Born of Struggle: Anthology of Afro-American Philosophy from 1917*, ed. Leonard Harris (Dubuque, Iowa: Kendall/Hunt, 1983); and Molefi Kete Asante, *The Afrocentric Idea* (Philadelphia: Temple University Press, 1998).

3. For a discussion of the meaning of "ideal type," see Max Weber, *Economy and Society: An Outline of Interpretive Sociology*, ed. Guenther Roth and Claus Wittich (Berkeley: University of California Press, 1978), 18–22; and Max Weber,

The Methodology of the Social Sciences, trans. and eds. Edward A. Shils and Henry A. Finch (New York: Free Press, 1949), 89–101.

4. See, e.g., Lawrence W. Levine, *Black Culture and Black Consciousness: Afro-American Folk Thought from Slavery to Freedom* (Oxford: Oxford University Press, 1977); Sterling Stuckey, *Slave Culture: Nationalist Theory and the Foundations of Black America* (Oxford: Oxford University Press, 1987); Henry Louis Gates Jr., *The Signifying Monkey: A Theory of African-American Literary Criticism* (Oxford: Oxford University Press, 1998); Wilson Jeremiah Moses, *Black Messiahs and Uncle Toms: Social and Literary Manipulations of a Religious Myth*, rev. ed. (University Park: Pennsylvania State University Press, 1992); and Tricia Rose, *Black Noise: Rap Music and Black Culture in Contemporary America* (Hanover, N.H.: Wesleyan University Press, 1994).

5. Sidney W. Mintz and Richard Price, *The Birth of African-American Culture: An Anthropological Perspective* (Boston: Beacon, 1976); and Paul Gilroy, *The Black Atlantic: Modernity and Double Consciousness* (Cambridge, Mass.: Harvard University Press, 1993).

6. Stuart Hall, "What Is This 'Black' in Black Popular Culture," in *Black Popular Culture*, ed. Gina Dent (New York: New Press, 1998), 22.

7. Ralph Ellison, "What America Would Be Like Without Blacks," in *The Collected Essays of Ralph Ellison*, ed. John F. Callahan (New York: Modern Library, 1995).

8. Henry Louis Gates Jr., *Loose Canons: Notes on the Culture Wars* (Oxford: Oxford University Press, 1992), 109.

9. See Gates, *Signifying Monkey*, esp. chap. 2.

10. See Chandran Kukathas, "Are There Any Cultural Rights?" *Political Theory* 20 (1992): 105–39; and Seyla Benhabib, *The Claims of Culture: Equality and Diversity in the Global Era* (Princeton, N.J.: Princeton University Press, 2002).

11. Mary C. Waters, *Black Identities: West Indian Immigrant Dreams and American Realities* (Cambridge, Mass.: Harvard University Press, 2001).

12. See Clarence Lusane, *Race in the Global Era: African Americans at the Millennium* (Boston: South End Press, 1997), 85–116.

13. Paul Gilroy, *Against Race: Imagining Political Culture Beyond the Color Line* (Cambridge, Mass.: Harvard University Press, 2000), 214.

14. David Held, Anthony McGrew, David Goldblatt, and Jonathan Perraton, *Global Transformations* (Stanford, Calif.: Stanford University Press, 1999).

15. E. Franklin Frazier, *The Negro Church in America* / C. Eric Lincoln, *The Black Church Since Frazier* (New York: Schocken Books, 1974). Also see Cornel West, *Prophesy Deliverance! An Afro-American Revolutionary Christianity* (Philadelphia: Westminster Press, 1982).

16. See, e.g., Molefi Kete Asante, *The Afrocentric Idea* (Philadelphia: Temple University Press, 1998).

17. For more on this point, see Bernard R. Boxill, *Blacks and Social Justice*, rev. ed. (Lanham, Md.: Rowman and Littlefield, 1992), 182.

18. Henry Louis Gates Jr., and Cornel West, *The Future of the Race* (New York: Vintage, 1996), xvi.

19. See Jennifer L. Hochschild, *The New American Dilemma: Liberal Democracy and School Desegregation* (New Haven, Conn.: Yale University Press, 1984).

20. See Oliver C. Cox, *Caste, Class, and Race: A Study in Social Dynamics* (New York: Monthly Review, 1959), chaps. 18 and 25.

21. Ibid., 321.

22. Ibid., 321.

23. See Robert Gooding-Williams, "Race, Multiculturalism and Democracy," *Constellations* 5 (1998): 18–41.

24. Baraka, *Blues People,* 98–112. Also see Evelyn Brooks Higginbotham, "Rethinking Vernacular Culture: Black Religion and Race Records in the 1920s and 1930s," in *The House That Race Built,* ed. Wahneema Lubiano (New York: Vintage, 1998), 157–77.

25. See Clifford Geertz, *The Interpretation of Cultures* (New York: Basic Books, 1973).

NINE

Prophetic Vision and Trash Talkin': Pragmatism, Feminism, and Racial Privilege

Shannon Sullivan

In his review of Cornel West's groundbreaking *The American Evasion of Philosophy: A Genealogy of Pragmatism* (1989), Richard Rorty criticizes West's notion of prophetic pragmatism as incoherent. According to Rorty, a prophet is someone who has a specific vision of a different and better future. Because they can make a positive contribution to society, prophets are valuable and powerful instruments of social change. Philosophers, especially pragmatists, also may contribute to social change, but only through the negative role of tearing down old ideas to clear space in which prophets can perform their imaginative work. The most that pragmatist and other philosophers can do is to "clea[n] up rubbish left over from the past."[1] When they try to do more than this, mistakenly thinking that they can be creative architects of society, philosophers tend to fall into essentialism, representationalism, and foundationalism.[2] Prophets inspire and create; pragmatist philosophers merely clear away intellectual garbage. For this reason, Rorty argues, "the term 'prophetic pragmatism' [should] sound as odd as 'charismatic trash disposal' " (75). In Rorty's view, West should abandon the idea of being a prophetic philosopher working for racial and other forms of social justice. While West's work may be "as likely a source of specific, concrete, patriotic, prophetic vision" as the United States has today, philosophy has no special role to play in creating that vision (78).

At the same time that Rorty trashes West's prophetic pragmatism, however, he claims that "feminist *philosophers* like Marilyn Frye may be the closest thing we have to prophets these days" (77, my emphasis). The contrast between Rorty's dismissal of West and praise of feminist philosophy for what seem to be the same prophetic tendencies is striking—and potentially disturbing, for on a first glance, the main difference between West's and feminism's prophetic philosophies is that West concentrates on race and racism, while feminism concentrates on gender and sexism. Rorty's differential treatment of West and feminism thus might appear to be the product of his disregard for issues of race, which is one of the forms that white privilege and white domination historically have taken and increasingly take as Western liberal societies strive to become "color-blind."[3] Rorty's dismissal of West's prophetic pragmatism can seem to smack of racism, in other words, even if that racism is unintentional.

The story is more complicated than this first glance reveals, however. Race does play a role in Rorty's contrasting judgments of West's and feminism's prophetic philosophy, but indirectly, as race is filtered through the prism of religion. West's prophetic philosophy is explicitly Christian, while that of most feminist philosophy in the United States is decidedly secular; and it is this difference that makes the crucial difference in Rorty's treatment of the two. But before I turn to the role of religion in both West's pragmatism and feminist philosophy, I will examine in more detail Rorty's account of pragmatist philosophy, including its relationship with prophecy. The anemic version of pragmatism with which Rorty operates is responsible for the sharp opposition between philosophy and prophecy in his work. If, instead, pragmatist philosophy is richly conceived in a more Deweyan vein, then prophetic pragmatism need not be tossed away as charismatic trash.

At least since the publication of *Philosophy and the Mirror of Nature* (1979), Rorty has been concerned with philosophical trash disposal. In this influential book, Rorty throws out the epistemological garbage of representational theories of knowledge and correspondence theories of truth. Those theories follow a model of mind as a mirror of nature: knowledge and truth occur when the mind accurately copies objects in the world. Philosophy's task, on this model, is to help ensure that an exact match between internal mind and external world is obtained. Philosophy is centered on epistemology, and epistemology is a quest for indubitable foundations in knowledge allegedly provided by a perfectly functioning mirror.

For Rorty, as well as for his intellectual forbearers Dewey, Wittgenstein, and Heidegger, there are two significant problems with this model of philosophy. First, it is "an attempt to escape from history" by treating as eternal a culturally and historically specific way of conceiving of knowledge.[4] Representational theories of knowledge came to prominence in the seventeenth century via Locke's and Descartes' complementary accounts of mental processes. They were taken up and consolidated by Kant's account of pure reason, the nineteenth-century neo-Kantians who followed him, and then much of twentieth-century analytic philosophy.[5] Especially, given the current dominance of analytic philosophy, representational theories of knowledge can seem like the only philosophically respectable game in town. But as Rorty's mini-genealogy suggests, those theories have specific historical origins that established mirroring nature as a particular philosophical problem. That problem does not so much need to be solved as to be dissolved by throwing out the problematic philosophical assumptions that underpin it.

Central to those assumptions is that human knowers are separate from the world rather than a part of it. This is the second significant problem with the mirror of nature model: it divorces human beings from the world they inhabit and then struggles to figure out how humans can know anything about it. It implicitly treats human beings as if they were little gods hovering outside the world rather than active participants in it. But if human beings are part of the world, then there is no gap to overcome. The project of mirroring a distant world to an isolated mind thus is irrelevant; a different set of questions emerge for philosophy to confront. Once human beings' historical embeddedness in the world is taken seriously, philosophers, Rorty hopes, will realize that "the notion of knowledge as the assemblage of accurate representations is optional—that it may be replaced by a pragmatist conception of knowledge which eliminates the . . . contrast between contemplation and action, between representing the world and coping with it."[6]

Rorty doesn't say much about this new conception of knowledge. Instead, he concludes *Philosophy and the Mirror of Nature* with an argument in favor of hermeneutics over epistemology. Hermeneutics abandons the idea that there is a neutral framework that indisputably establishes the truth and falsity of different knowledge claims. Without such a framework, any resolution of differences must be achieved through dialogue and debate in which one side tries to change the language with which the other describes the world; and the goal of a liberal culture should be to keep that conversation going, especially when incommensurable viewpoints confront one another. Creative and imaginative uses of language are crucial to this process, for there is no neutral language that captures reality in a bias-free way. Thinking that there is an objective reality apart from the language, concepts, and ideas with which we describe it is part of the epistemological garbage that needs to be thrown out. And philosophy's contribution to this cultural conversation is to do precisely—and only—that. Ironically (or perhaps, fittingly), given its production of so much epistemological trash, philosophy's revamped role in society is to keep it clean of appeals to foundationalism, essentialism, and representationalism so that ongoing creative conversations that give birth to new ideas and forms of life can take place.

For Rorty, those new creations include feminist alternatives to sexism and male privilege. In the early 1990s, he wrote two essays that praised feminism for its attempts to create a new society in which women count as full persons and that explained how pragmatist philosophy can assist these efforts.[7] But these essays also contain a stern warning to feminists and other intellectuals who look to philosophy for substantial help with their political projects. They must accept philosophy's limited role as garbage disposal and not think it can provide an "objective" foundation for their claims. A pragmatist approach to feminism, for example, would not argue that women really are equal to men and that this reality has been distorted by those who perpetuate patriarchy and male domination. This is because there is no reality apart from the language, discourse, and social concepts that help construct it. According to Rorty, all that pragmatism, and philosophy more generally, can do for feminists is help them show that, like any other sociopolitical system, systems that support male privilege are social constructs. They are not based in any sort of nondiscursive nature, and there is no fixed human nature that necessitates male domination of women. Male privilege thus is not inevitable, and this realization is a very important step toward its possible dismantling. But neither is the respectful and equal treatment of women inevitable. Nothing about nature or human nature requires that women be thought of or treated as full persons: "The enslavement . . . of human females by human males is not an intrinsic evil."[8] So pragmatism cuts both ways: against what Rorty calls masculinism, but also against feminism insofar as it looks for an absolute foundation on which to ground its claims. For Rorty, "pragmatism— considered as a set of philosophical views about truth, knowledge, objectivity, and language—is neutral between feminism and masculinism. So if one wants specifically feminist doctrines about these topics, pragmatism will not [and cannot] provide them."[9]

Likewise, pragmatism cannot provide specifically antiracist doctrines that would help philosophers and other intellectuals dismantle white supremacy and white privilege. In Rorty's view, thinking that pragmatism could help provide an antiracist vision for the future is precisely where Cornel West's version of philosophy gets into trouble. Rorty criticizes West for what he sees as a crucial unresolved tension in *The American Evasion of Philosophy*.[10] As the title of the book suggests, American philosophy (and pragmatism in particular) evades what John Dewey called "that species of intellectual lock-jaw called epistemology" that has dominated mainstream

Western philosophy.[11] West's evasion of epistemologically centered philosophy is, of course, something of which Rorty wholeheartedly approves. But then West combines the wish to evade philosophy with the hope that philosophy can prophetically sketch a new and better future, one that "confronts candidly individual and collective experiences of evil in individuals and institutions . . . [and] that holds many experiences of evil [such as racism and sexism] to be neither inevitable or necessary but rather the results of human agency, i.e., choices and actions."[12]

Herein lies the problematic tension for Rorty: pragmatism cannot fulfill both of West's desires because "pragmatism is merely a way of evading the usual boring skeptical conundrums about truth, knowledge, the deep nature of things, and the relation between language and the world," and so "it is neutral between alternative prophecies, and thus neutral between democrats and fascists," as well as racists and anti-racists.[13] Rorty clearly supports a future world in which human agents make less evil choices and engage in less evil actions, but he claims that pragmatism cannot provide societal "microscopes that make precise diagnosis [regarding how to create that world] possible."[14] For Rorty, "pragmatism is [not] a good place to look for prophecy, or for the sorts of rich possibilities which the prophetic imagination makes visible."[15] All that pragmatism has to offer intellectuals striving for social change, as Rorty tells feminists, are "occasional bits of ad hoc advice."[16]

Rorty operates with a false dilemma on this point, however, and it is this false dilemma that makes his version of pragmatism anemic. Pragmatist philosophy can do more than dispose of epistemological trash and offer ad hoc bits of advice, and it can do so without resorting to foundationalism, essentialism, or representationalism. In his comments on feminist philosophy and West's prophetic pragmatism, Rorty repeatedly opposes philosophical practices of trash disposal and road-clearing to misguided philosophical efforts to plan the details of a future world by "unlock[ing] the secrets of history or of society."[17] As he does so, Rorty offers a number of historical examples of oppressive leaders who followed "Marx's bad example" by using philosophy to further their political goals: "Remember Lenin on Berkeley? Stalin on language? Mao on contradiction? If Sendero Luminoso bombs its way to the top, we can count on Abimael Guzmán—Ph.D., Philosophy, San Marcos U, c. 1970—to add another short, peppy, masterwork to the Little Library of Socialism—one that everyone up and down the Andes, from the starving schoolchildren to the village elders, have to memorize."[18] Presenting this grim picture as the only alternative to philosophy as garbage disposal, Rorty makes garbage disposal seem like a reasonable and sufficient role for philosophy to play.

Even with the best of intentions, when philosophy strays from this role, it more often than not only makes things worse.

Rorty's grim example plays on the fears of feminists and other leftist intellectuals and can, in so doing, prevent them from noticing the very non-pragmatist, quasi-foundationalist role that Rorty would have pragmatist philosophy play. Similar to the way that Descartes's *Meditations on First Philosophy* sought to raze the epistemological ground so that only beliefs of which he could be certain were retained, Rorty's pragmatism seeks to clear a blank slate on which creative prophets can build a different future. Rorty does not follow Descartes in Descartes' project of rebuilding, of course, and in that sense Rorty's philosophy indeed is anti- or non-foundational. But the spirit of its methodology is remarkably close to that of Descartes. A whiff of foundationalism lingers about Rorty's pragmatism in that the need for road-clearing or ground razing is central to it, just as it is for Descartes' philosophy.

What would it look like if pragmatist philosophy fully lived up to Rorty's goal of avoiding foundationalism? To begin, it would resemble John Dewey's version of pragmatism considered apart from Rorty's reading of it. Rorty dismisses Dewey's claims that philosophical problems are—or at least should be—inseparable from "real life" social issues, stubbornly insisting that these claims be read "in the road-clearing sense."[19] While Dewey does say in "From Absolutism to Experimentalism"—in what must be Rorty's favorite Dewey quote—that "a chief task of those who call themselves philosophers is to help get rid of the useless lumber that blocks our highways of thought,"[20] Dewey also insists, in *Reconstruction in Philosophy*, that

> when it is acknowledged that under the disguise of dealing with ultimate reality, philosophy has been occupied with the precious values embedded in social traditions, that it has sprung from a clash of social ends and from conflict of inherited institutions with incompatible contemporary tendencies, it will be seen that the task of future philosophy is to clarify men's ideas as to the social and moral strifes [*sic*] of their own day. Its aim is to become so far as humanly possible an organ for dealing with these conflicts.[21]

While clearing away useless "lumber" might be an important component of philosophy's struggle with contemporary social and moral conflict, the latter cannot be reduced to the former. Rorty likes to overlook the reconstructive aspect of pragmatism, but to do so is to severely truncate what Dewey's philosophy, and the classical origins of pragmatist philosophy more generally, are all about.

As Dewey, as well as Charles S. Peirce, William James, and W.E.B. Du Bois, explicitly argued, there is no possibility for philosophy to begin with a blank slate. Nor is there any need for it to do so. Reconstruction—imaginative creation and visionary rebuilding—always takes place in the midst of the old structures that are being replaced. Even stronger, often the old is the very material out of which the new is formed, so from a Deweyan point of view, reconstruction and creation tend to be transformations rather than abruptly new formations disconnected from what came before them. This does not mean that nothing original or different ever occurs, but that a sharp conceptual division between clearing away the old and creating the new artificially separates what, in human experience, tends to be organically intertwined.

Cornel West's prophetic pragmatism appreciates Dewey's classically pragmatic understanding of reconstruction and avoids the error of thinking that visionary creation is divorced from critical analysis ("road-clearing") of the old. As he explains,

> Prophetic thought and action is preservative in that it tries to keep alive certain elements of a tradition bequeathed to us from the past and revolutionary in that it attempts to project a vision and inspire a praxis that fundamentally transforms the prevailing status quo in light of the best of the tradition and the flawed yet significant achievements of the present order.[22]

And the point could be made even more strongly: not only are critical analysis and visionary creation not radically divorced so that the former prepares the way for the latter, but envisioning a different future often is what enables effective criticism of the past. Sometimes it is only when an alternative to the present can be seen, or at least sketched out, that one can see how and why the present is problematic. Pragmatism (understood as "road-clearing") might not so much pave the way for prophecy as it follows in prophecy's wake.

Rorty himself seems to admit this point when he says in the context of feminism, "Only if somebody has a dream, and a voice to describe that dream, does what looked like nature begin to look like culture, what looked like fate begin to look like a moral abomination."[23] It is when feminists began to create new language and concepts to understand women's experiences that criticism of particular features of the world as oppressive to women became possible. For example, drawing on one of Rorty's favorite feminists, Marilyn Frye, we can say that it is when a woman begins to envision the possibility of life apart from any men that she can critically see when and how her independent interests and will have been "metaphysically cannibalized" by that of the men around her.[24] Apart from prophetic feminist vision, women's subordination of their persons and lives to men—metaphysical cannibalism—can seem, to women as well as men, like something very different, namely love. In fact, conflating romantic love with metaphysical cannibalism has been one of the most effective ways for male-dominant societies to perpetuate women's subordination.[25] But this criticism of love as oppressive only became possible as feminists began to envision different forms of loving, including love between women as well as between women and men.

If Rorty's pragmatism fully lived up to its Deweyan inheritance and its own goal of avoiding foundationalism, it also would include a richer understanding of philosophical method. According to Rorty, Dewey's fallibilism, which involves being open to the likelihood that one's goals will change in the process of pursuing them, entails that "there is no method or procedure to be followed [in the pursuit of one's goals] except courageous and imaginative experimentation."[26] Courage and imagination should be relied upon when envisioning a new future, not allegedly neutral criteria.[27] And Rorty is right that successful experimental inquiry involves these traits. What is lacking, however, is an indication that experimentation means for Rorty anything other than imaginative guesswork or courageous ad hoc suggestions. In his positive comments on prophecy, imaginative "experimentation" often seems like a lightening bolt that strikes as if from nowhere. A visionary prophet can only hope to get lucky by being struck; there is no other method that could guide his or her creative work. Rorty's appeal to courage and imagination thus tends to work hand in hand with his reduction of pragmatism to road-clearing. With the road completely cleared and the slate wiped totally blank, there is little concrete to work with as one begins to envision something new.

For Dewey, experimentation meant something very different. Championing scientific inquiry as *the* methodological model for non-foundational philosophies, Dewey argued that science begins with a problematic situation, develops a hypothesis that suggests a possible solution, and then tests the hypothesis in lived experience to see if the desired results occur. The development of a hypothesis worthy of testing is rarely, if ever, a random trial-and-error affair. Scientists use the results of previous experiments to guide them as they formulate possible solutions to the new problems they face. The key word here is "guide." Previous experiments do not determine which hypothesis a scientist will produce, nor do they provide an exact recipe for a scientist to follow as she tries to develop a plausible hypothesis that fits the current situation. Imagination and creative insight often are crucial to the shift from past to present that is involved in the scientific development of new hypotheses. But previous experience also can provide resources to assist with that shift. Critically and imaginatively reflected upon, it can suggest which future paths might be dead ends and which are likely to be fruitful, based on similar problematic situations that occurred in the past. Not only is there is no need to clear the road of previous experiences and possible solutions to problematic situations, such road-clearing would interfere with the production of creative alternatives for the future.[28]

Dewey admired the experimental inquiry of actual scientists, but his point about experimental method concerns much more than the work that goes on in labs. For Dewey, scientific inquiry is a method for the production of knowledge that everyone can and should engage in. When faced with a problematic moral situation, for example, an individual is going to have much more success in dealing with that situation if she develops a hypothesis about it based on previous experience rather than isolating it from other similar experiences and then taking a stab in the dark (albeit, a courageous one) about its cause, meaning, and solution. This does not mean that one is confined to the moral language already in existence. New moral concepts can be created, but their creation does not occur in a vacuum.

Marilyn Frye reveals the importance of previous experience to prophetic vision in her account of an all-white group of feminist women that assembled to explore racism in their own lives with an eye for dismantling it. A black woman strongly objected to the formation of such a group, challenging its members' notion that they could achieve their goals by working in an all-white space even though Frye's group explained that it never intended their group to be the only way that its members worked on problems of racism. Nothing Frye's group could say satisfied the black woman, and Frye found herself thinking that the woman seemed crazy. It was at that moment that Frye was stopped short: she "paused and touched and weighed that seeming. It was familiar. [She knew] it as deceptive, defensive."[29] Reflecting on how lesbians, feminists, and women often have been posited as crazy in order to dismiss their claims against a male-privileged society, Frye heard what the black woman was saying in a different way. The black woman who objected to the all-white group could see, as the group could not, that the group members were exercising their privilege as white people to decide when to relate to people of color. They were, in other words, uncritically engaging in the very racial privilege that they thought they were challenging.

Frye faced a problematic situation when confronted by her black critic: what to do in response to the black woman's "crazy" accusations—and, more broadly, is there any way for white people to decide to work against racism when liberty of decision is itself an instance of white privilege? Frye then developed a hypothesis in response to this situation. Distinguishing between phenotypic and political whiteness (being white versus being White), Frye gave herself "the injunction to stop being White." This injunction is something for her (and her readers) to test in lived experience, to see if it improves white people's ability to struggle effectively against white domination. By reflecting on previous experiences in which she herself was posited as "crazy," Frye was able to develop a much more meaningful and helpful hypothesis about what to do in the situation of the all-white group than her initial reaction allowed. And at the same time that her hypothesis drew on the past, it also "invite[d] the honorable work of radical imagination" to figure out what being white but not being White might mean.[30]

A more robust version of pragmatism than Rorty offers shows how philosophy and prophecy complement each other. Clearing away existing philosophical concepts that are problematic can and often does work hand in hand with the creation of new language and concepts for the future. The visionary creation of the prophet does not take place in a vacuum. It is nourished by, and feeds back into, criticism of existing experiences and worldviews.

That said, one would expect Rorty's anemic account of pragmatism to be equally dismissive of prophetic philosophy whenever and wherever it is pursued. But this is not the case. In his criticism of West's prophetic pragmatism, Rorty admits that William James and John Dewey "were lucky enough to combine, to some extent, the roles of [philosophy] professor and prophet."[31] But he claims this was only because the intellectual right of the early twentieth century still used foundational arguments— sometimes religious, sometimes rationalist—to justify their positions against racial equality, labor unions, and so on. In that context, pragmatist arguments against religious and rationalist claims made by political conservatives were useful. They helped build a different future as they cleared away foundationalist trash. In contrast, according to Rorty, "Nowadays nobody even bothers to back up opposition to liberal reforms with argument."[32] They merely complain about high taxes and reverse discrimination, and these emotion-based complaints serve as a firewall that blocks any engagement with argument.

I'll set aside the question of whether the times indeed have changed in the way that Rorty claims. The effect of the story he tells about James and Dewey is to sever West's prophetic pragmatism from any prophetic tradition in classical American philosophy. Maybe the so-called founding fathers of pragmatism engaged in prophecy, but West cannot ground his claims to prophetic pragmatism in that heritage. According to Rorty, even if professional pragmatist philosophers once played the role of cultural and social prophet, this role is no longer available to current philosophers.

This makes it all the more remarkable Rorty's granting that feminist philosophers can be prophets. After claiming that philosophers could only cheer from the sidelines during the civil rights movements of the 1960s and 70s, Rorty allows that philosophy has been socially useful in the case of feminism. "Feminist members of the academy are inventing new ways of speaking about the relations between men and women," Rorty asserts, "founding something like a new cultural tradition." In fact, "feminist philosophers like Marilyn Frye may be the closest thing we have to prophets these days."[33] Likewise, in his essay on "Feminism and Pragmatism," published the same year as his review of West, Rorty praises Catherine MacKinnon for the prophetic tone of her feminism. Commenting on MacKinnon's remarks that "we have no idea what women as women would have to say" and that they "might say something that has never been heard," Rorty urges that passages such as these "be read as prophecy rather than empty hyperbole."[34] Feminist philosophers such as MacKinnon, and especially Frye, are not talking about how to view reality in an undistorted way, but rather how to weave a new web of meaning in which women are thought of as full persons.[35]

Rorty's dismissive remarks about prophetic philosophy are reserved for West and do not target feminist philosophers. How can this inconsistency be explained? While West's work concerns much more than racial oppression (for example, heterosexism, and especially class and economic oppression), race, and specifically African American traditions, play a central role in West's prophetic pragmatism. Does Rorty's inconsistency mean that he thinks gender, but not racial inequality, is a legitimate topic for prophetic philosophy? Or, more cynically, that white intellectuals (women) can manage to combine philosophy and prophecy, while black intellectuals (men) cannot? I think the answer to both of these questions is no, but I also think that race nonetheless plays an important role in Rorty's views about the possibilities for prophetic philosophy. What is significant about West's prophetic philosophy is that it is explicitly religious, more specifically, Christian, whereas the prophetic philosophy of Frye and Mac-Kinnon is secular and even hostile to religion on occasion. Rorty is allergic to religion, and because of this allergy, he is unable to take seriously a prophetic philosophy that would intertwine itself with Christianity.

First, a few words about the secular nature of most contemporary feminist philosophy in the United States before turning to the crucial role that religion plays in West's work. And in the case of Frye's and MacKinnon's philosophies, I literally mean a few, because neither of these women tends to mention religion in her work. In the introduction to *The Politics of Reality*, as she explains her occasionally idiosyncratic grammar, Frye briefly remarks that "though my use of upper case letters is normal for the most part, I do not dignify names of religions and religious institutions with upper case letters. Hence the word 'christian,' used either as noun or adjective, is not capitalized, nor is the word 'church' or 'catholic', etc."[36] The topic of religion does not appear elsewhere in the book, except in Frye's biographical statement, where she mentions, among other things, that she was reared in a "devoutly christian family."[37] It is striking that Frye makes a point of explaining her treatment of religious names when they virtually never appear in her book and certainly play no significant role in its creative vision. While the alleged goal of her grammatical explanation is just that—explanation—the effect of her remark, if not also its ultimate goal, is to let readers know that religion has no place in the women-friendly world that Frye courageously imagines. The implication is that religion has been complicit with, perhaps even a major source of, male domination, and that feminists who wish to effectively challenge that domination thus must condemn any and all forms of religion as sexist.

MacKinnon's work, which focuses on sexual harassment and pornography as forms of sexual discrimination and more recently on rape as an act of genocide in international conflicts, also rarely mentions religion.[38] When religion is discussed, it tends to be treated solely as a conservative and thus problematic support for laws that give women fewer rights than men.[39] In general, however, MacKinnon's feminist legal theory, like that of most of contemporary feminist philosophy, isn't so much openly hostile to religion as it is generative of a chilly atmosphere for religious concerns through its silence about them. Feminist philosophy of religion exists as a small sub-field, and important philosophical work has been done on the intersections of religion, women's lives, and male domination.[40] But religion is only occasionally at the center of contemporary feminist philosophy, and often when it is focused on, the focus is critical rather than visionary. The effect is similar to that which Charles Mills has called the silence of exclusion.[41] Mills explains how the silence about race and racism in most of mainstream Western philosophy implicitly excludes people of color from participating in the field. The message sent by this exclusion is that people of color do not matter enough even to be acknowledged in philosophical discourse. Likewise, feminist silence about religion is not neutral. It sends a message that religion has no positive role to play in feminist philosophy.

West's prophetic pragmatism, in contrast, carves out a significant place for black Christianity in its visionary work for the future. West begins with "the biblical injunction to look at the world through the eyes of its victims," and this reveals to him not only suffering and oppression but also important sources of sustenance for the world's victims.[42] The entire world over, religion is "a crucial element of the culture of the oppressed," a fact that leftist Marxists arrogantly refuse to take seriously.[43] In the midst of African Americans' physical and ontological mistreatment as slaves, for example, the black church helped African Americans survive and see themselves as more than commodities or animals to be bought and sold. It sustained hope and made black solidarity possible in a virulently antiblack society. This was never about escapism, according to West. "The major focus of the *prophetic* black Christian worldview . . . was on marshaling and garnering resources from fellowship, community, and personal strength (mediation, prayer) to cope with overwhelmingly limited options dictated by institutional and personal evil."[44] Even today, West claims, "black people do not attend churches, for the most part, to find God, but rather to share and expand together the rich heritage they have inherited."[45] Black Christianity is about the here and now, helping the exploited and oppressed find joy and patience as they struggle to meliorate the tragic situation in which they live.

But by embracing Christianity, does West's prophetic pragmatism give up on the American project of evading philosophy (epistemology) and resort to foundational claims about, for example, the existence of God and the truth of the Christian gospel? The answer is no, but that answer is helpful only if the project of evading philosophy is understood in West's terms. From this perspective, West's title for his genealogy of pragmatism, *The American Evasion of Philosophy,* is unfortunate because it suggests that West is interested only in the trash-dumping work that Rorty allows philosophy. But West makes clear in the body of the book that his "evasion of epistemology-centered philosophy . . . results in a conception of philosophy as a form of cultural criticism in which the meaning of America is put forward by intellectuals in response to distinct social and cultural crises."[46] Even more explicitly, West claims that "prophetic pragmatism understands the Emersonian swerve from epistemology—and the American evasion of philosophy—not as a wholesale rejection of philosophy but rather as a reconception of philosophy as a form of cultural criticism that attempts to transform linguistic, social, cultural, and political traditions for the purposes of increasing the scope of individual development and democratic operations."[47] While Rorty equates philosophy with epistemology and wishes to abandon both, West refuses to reduce philosophy to epistemology and believes that philosophy can be a social force for positive change. West does not give up on the project of evading philosophy, *and* his prophetic pragmatism avoids foundationalism in that evasion.

An example of this can be found in West's pragmatic response to the question of whether Christianity is true. After presenting a rich account of how and why he locates his prophetic pragmatism in the Christian tradition, West finally acknowledges that "the fundamental philosophical question remains whether the Christian gospel is ultimately true." West has put off this question until the last few pages of *The American Evasion of Philosophy,* I think, because it is asked in a non-, even anti-pragmatist spirit. The question asks, for example, does West think that the New Testament account of Jesus' resurrection accurately matches what happened in Galilee over two thousand years ago? The question assumes, in other words, the representational account of truth that West's pragmatism evades, and for that reason it is not very relevant to his philosophical project. West's response to the question is a brief, fallibilist yes: "I reply in the affirmative, bank my all on it, yet am willing to entertain the possibility in low moments that I may be deluded."[48] He then directs readers to his essay on "The Historicist Turn in Philosophy of Religion," which explains more fully his refusal of dogmatism or claims to religious certainty about God.[49] The point of West's prophetic pragmatism is not to proclaim whether or not God really exists. It is to live in the uncertainty of God's (non)existence while drawing upon religious and other resources to foster hope and eliminate oppression and despair.

Even in this non-foundational form, however, religion makes Rorty uneasy. In his review of West's book, Rorty tries to distance himself from leftist intellectuals who find religion to be a tiresome holdover from childhood. Rorty claims that the fact that Martin Luther King was and Jesse Jackson is a preacher and that Malcolm X was a Muslim is embarrassing to "most white leftists," who "wish that African Americans would grow up, would find some firmly secularist leaders." After also explaining white leftists' ridicule of patriotism and romanticism, Rorty says, "so much the worse, in my view, for that Left."[50]

But Rorty's claim that he is not part of the Left that dismisses religion is unconvincing. A decade later, in an essay that backpedals on his earlier criticisms of religion, Rorty distinguishes between ecclesiastical organizations, which he strongly objects to, and religion at "the parish level," which he does not. The distinction made here is between the institution and the faith. Rorty claims that once religion is pruned down to the latter, religion should serve only as a source of personal meaning for some individuals, not as an institution that guides believers, wielding economic and political clout, and not as a social movement that attempts to fight injustice. This is because a mature society no longer needs public expressions of religion. As Rorty explains, "We secularists have come to think that the best society would be one in which political action conducted in the name of religious beliefs is treated as a ladder up which our ancestors climbed, but one that now should be thrown away."[51] For Rorty, a society that continues to mix religion with politics is a society that has yet to grow up.

Even in Rorty's chastened restatement of his views, religion has no legitimate role to play in social struggles for political change. In line with the sharp public/private distinction that he makes in *Contingency, Irony, and Solidarity,* Rorty restricts religion to the realm of the private. This restriction occurs not because Rorty thinks religion is a fruitful source of ironic self-creation but because he claims it interferes with liberal attempts to reduce suffering. Examples of religion's making a positive difference in the public world are only exceptions in Rorty's view: "We [secularists] grant that ecclesiastical organizations have sometimes been on the right side, but we think that the occasional Gustavo Guttierez or Martin Luther King does not compensate for the ubiquitous Joseph Ratzingers and Jerry Falwells. History suggests to us that such organizations will always, on balance, do more harm than good."[52] Rorty also restricts religion to the private sphere because he claims that strongly held religious convictions tend to produce an impasse in political debates, shutting down public conversation. Those debates should be limited to premises that all participants can or do share in common so that the conversation can continue. As Nicholas Wolterstorff's explains, the message from Rorty is loud and clear: "Religion must shape up if it's to be tolerated in our liberal democracy. Its shaping up must take the form of privatizing itself."[53]

This message, in turn, sends another clear message to feminist and pragmatist philosophy: the concerns of people of color are not their concerns.[54] Excluding religion from public life and political struggle has racialized effects for both feminist and pragmatist philosophy. As Cornel West has explained, "The culture of the wretched of the earth is deeply religious," and many of those wretched worldwide are people of color. "To be in solidarity with them requires not only an acknowledgement of what they are up against but also an appreciation of how they cope with their situation," which includes appreciation of the place of religion in their life-world.[55] To say, then, that religion has no place in feminist or pragmatist philosophy is effectively to say that people of color also have no place in it—at least, not *as* people of color. In general, only if people of color have been willing check their race at the door when they enter the whitewashed halls of philosophy could they enter at all. The result was and is the demographic and conceptual whiteness of philosophy.[56] Philosophy in the northern and western hemispheres tends to be populated by white people who then take up their concerns as if they were universal, without acknowledging or even seeing their false universalization. No wonder then that philosophy, including feminist and pragmatist philosophy, often does not appeal to students of color.

Feminist philosophy in the United States has struggled for decades with this problem. It is a problem that Rorty recognizes, if only briefly and without much insight into why it occurs. After praising Marilyn Frye as a feminist philosopher and prophet, he says, "But although feminists are painfully aware that they speak for middle-class women, and would love to link up feminism with the struggle of the weak against the strong (which, in the United States, in inseparable from the struggle of blacks against whites), they have not come up with anything very convincing." Rorty singles out feminists' attempts to create a "unified theory of oppression" dealing with gender, race, and class, claiming that they have "have produced little of interest."[57] However, more of the blame should be laid on the way that the initial projects and concerns of contemporary feminist philosophy were designed by white, western, middle-class, secular, straight women. It should be no surprise that asking women who do not fit this description to join up and work toward goals that do not include their needs and interests produced little interest. The exclusion of religion from feminist philosophy is not the only reason that women of color sometimes avoid it, but it is an important one.[58]

Just as feminist philosophy can and should be inclusive of religious concerns, so too should pragmatist philosophy.[59] Religious beliefs can be a source of inspiration for political struggle against white domination and other forms of oppression. And as Cornel West in particular has shown, drawing on religion for this inspiration need not conflict with a pragmatist commitment to non-foundationalism. With West, I want to emphasize that my claim "is not that [all] American philosophers [should] become religious, but rather that they [should] once again take religion seriously, which also means taking culture and society seriously."[60] Rorty's anemic version of pragmatism does not take culture or society seriously enough, which is a significant factor in his dismissal of religion as a potentially positive force for social and political change.[61] His attack on and distrust of institutional religion misses the point that many religious movements are also social movements. Rorty describes his work as "distinguish[ing] public from private questions, questions about pain from questions about the point of human life," as if questions about pain and the point of life could not be deeply connected.[62] But deeply connected they often are for many people, but in particular for many black people in the United States, who struggle with slavery and its aftermath. The black church, for example, historically focused on "com[ing] to terms with the absurd *in* America and the absurd *as* America" and, in so doing, "transformed a prevailing absurd situation into a persistent and present *tragic* one."[63] The existential situation of black slaves and their descendents was one of pain and suffering at the hands of white people and institutions—as well as joy, resilience, and humor in response to them—that was inseparable from questions about the point of life in an insane world. Religious traditions and institutions have helped nourish an existential freedom for black people that concerns both the "public" pain of being degraded as a sub-person and the "private" need for meaning and fulfillment as a full person.[64]

Catherine Wilson has objected to Rorty's self-described "horror of women," which she claims grounds his pragmatist approach to feminism.[65] In the passage in which Rorty mentions this horror, he also expresses guilty relief at not being born black, gay, or mentally disturbed.[66] While the term "horror" might be too strong for it, Rorty also has a strong aversion to the thought of a life filled with rich religious convictions and beliefs. Rorty simply does not "get" religion. He does not understand how religion can be a source of the creative redescriptions of self and world that he seeks. Nor does he understand how religion could, in West's words, "bequeath to us potent cultural forms of ultimacy, intimacy, and sociality" that sustain and nourish human life.[67] As a result, Rorty does not see how religion, and Christianity in particular, could be part of a prophetic tradition that envisions a better future through criticism of the past and present. Prophetic pragmatism is much more and much different than charismatic trash disposal. Its openness to religion is something that could open up Rorty's philosophy, as well as the philosophy of many other pragmatists and feminists, to transformative possibilities for lived experience and social justice that they otherwise might not imagine.

Notes

Thanks to Chad Kautzer and Eduardo Mendieta for their helpful comments and editorial work on this essay.

1. Richard Rorty, "The Professor and the Prophet," *Transition* 52 (1991): 75.

2. Rorty suggests that these not only are philosophically problematic positions, but they also, when combined with political programs, can contribute to totalitarianism regimes (ibid.,72). Subsequent references to this review are cited parenthetically in the text.

3. For criticisms of "colorblindness" as an antiracist strategy, see Eduardo Bonilla-Silva, *Racism without Racists: Color-blind Racism and the Persistence of Racial Inequality in the United States* (Lanham, Md.: Rowman and Littlefield, 2003), and Shannon Sullivan, *Revealing Whiteness: The Unconscious Habits of White Privilege* (Bloomington: Indiana University Press, 2006).

4. Richard Rorty, *Philosophy and the Mirror of Nature* (Princeton, N.J.: Princeton University Press, 1979), 9.

5. Ibid., 3–5.

6. Ibid., 11.

7. See Rorty, "Feminism, Ideology, and Deconstruction: A Pragmatist View," *Hypatia* 8:2 (1993): 96–103, and "Feminism and Pragmatism," in *Truth and Prog-*

ress: Philosophical Papers, Volume 3 (New York: Cambridge University Press, 1998), 202–27.

8. Rorty, "Feminism and Pragmatism," 207.

9. Rorty, "Feminism, Ideology, and Deconstruction," 101.

10. Cornel West, *The American Evasion of Philosophy: A Genealogy of Pragmatism* (Madison: University of Wisconsin Press, 1989).

11. John Dewey, "Does Reality Possess Practical Character?" in *John Dewey, The Early Works*, ed. Jo Ann Boydston (Carbondale: Southern Illinois University Press, 1977), 4:138n.

12. West, *American Evasion of Philosophy*, 228.

13. Richard Rorty, *Contingency, Irony, and Solidarity* (New York: Cambridge University Press, 1989), 75.

14. Rorty, "Feminism and Pragmatism," 214.

15. Rorty, *Contingency, Irony, and Solidarity*, 75.

16. Rorty, "Feminism, Ideology, and Deconstruction," 101.

17. Rorty, "Feminism and Pragmatism," 215.

18. Rorty, *Contingency, Irony, and Solidarity*, 72.

19. Rorty, "Feminism and Pragmatism," 215 n. 26.

20. John Dewey, "From Absolutism to Experimentalism," in *John Dewey, The Later Works*, ed. Jo Ann Boydston (Carbondale: Southern Illinois University Press, 1988), 5:160.

21. John Dewey, *Reconstruction in Philosophy*, in *John Dewey, The Middle Works*, ed. Jo Ann Boydston (Carbondale: Southern Illinois University Press, 1988), 12:94.

22. Cornel West, "The Crisis in Contemporary American Religion," in *The Cornel West Reader* (New York: Basic *Civitas* Books, 1999), 357.

23. Rorty, "Feminism and Pragmatism," 203.

24. Marilyn Frye, *The Politics of Reality* (Freedom, Calif.: Crossing Press, 1983), 65–66.

25. Ibid. 169.

26. Rorty, "Feminism and Pragmatism," 217.

27. Ibid., 218.

28. John Dewey, *Logic: The Theory of Inquiry*, in *John Dewey, The Later Works*, Vol. 12, ed. Jo Ann Boydston (Carbondale: Southern Illinois University Press, 1991).

29. Frye, *Politics of Reality*, 112.

30. Ibid., 127.

31. Rorty, "The Professor and the Prophet," 75–76.

32. Ibid., 76.

33. Ibid., 77.

34. Rorty, "Feminism and Pragmatism," 202, 206.

35. I say "especially" since Rorty notes that MacKinnon sometimes slips back into realist claims about women. See Rorty, "Feminism and Pragmatism," 208.

36. Frye, *Politics of Reality*, xvi.

37. Ibid., 175.

38. See Catharine MacKinnon, *Feminism Unmodified: Discourses on Life and Law* (Cambridge, Mass.: Harvard University Press, 1987), and *Are Women Human? And Other International Dialogues* (Cambridge, Mass.: Harvard University Press, 2006).

39. See, e.g., MacKinnon, *Are Women Human?* 128–29.

40. See, e.g., Pamela Sue Anderson and Beverley Clack, eds., *Feminist Philosophy of Religion: Critical Readings* (New York: Routledge, 2004).

41. Charles Mills, *Blackness Visible* (Ithaca, N.Y.: Cornell University Press, 1998), 3.

42. Cornel West, "The Historicist Turn in Philosophy of Religion," in *Cornel West Reader,* 360.

43. West, "Religion and the Left," in *Cornel West Reader,* 478. See also West, *American Evasion of Philosophy,* 233.

44. West, "Prophetic Christian as Organic Intellectual: Martin Luther King, Jr.," in *Cornel West Reader,* 427; emphasis in original.

45. West, "Subversive Joy and Revolutionary Patience in Black Christianity," in *Cornel West Reader,* 437.

46. West, *American Evasion of Philosophy,* 5.

47. Ibid., 230.

48. Ibid., 233.

49. West, "The Historicist Turn in Philosophy of Religion," 360–71.

50. Rorty, "The Professor and the Prophet," 70.

51. See Rorty, "Religion in the Public Square: A Reconsideration," *Journal of Religious Ethics* 31, no. 1 (2003): 142.

52. Ibid.

53. Nicholas Wolterstorff, "An Engagement with Rorty," *Journal of Religious Ethics* 31, no. 1 (2003): 129–39.

54. Thanks to Alex Stehn and especially Mary Alessandri for helping me think about the racialized and racist effects of excluding religion from philosophy.

55. West, *American Evasion of Philosophy,* 233.

56. Mills, *Blackness Visible,* 2.

57. Rorty, "The Professor and the Prophet," 77.

58. Another one is separatism. bell hooks has argued that a feminist insistence on separatism has implicitly excluded women of color, who often work closely with men of color in political struggle against racism. See hooks, *Feminist Theory: From Margin to Center* (Boston: South End Press, 1984), 67–81.

59. For a collection of pragmatist work that takes religion seriously, see Stuart E. Rosenbaum, *Pragmatism and Religion: Classical Sources and Original Essays* (Urbana: University of Illinois Press, 2003).

60. West, "The Historicist Turn in Philosophy of Religion," 368.

61. As James Flaherty notes, neither Dewey's nor James's richer versions of pragmatism would privatize religion as Rorty does. See Flaherty, "Rorty, Religious Beliefs, and Pragmatism," *International Philosophical Quarterly* 45:2 (2005): 175–85.

62. Rorty, *Contingency, Irony, and Solidarity,* 198.

63. West, "Prophetic Christian as Organic Intellectual," 427.

64. In a complementary vein, Mary Doak objects to Rorty's isolation of the individual in the private realm, questioning whether human beings "can live creative and fulfilled lives without addressing the material conditions of [their] lives and interactions with other people" ("Pragmatism, Postmodernism, and Politics," in *Pragmatism, Neo-Pragmatism, and Religion: Conversations with Richard Rorty,* ed. Charley D. Hardwick and Donald A. Crosby [New York: Peter Lang, 1997], 153).

65. Catherine Wilson, "How Did the Dinosaurs Die Out? How Did the Poets Survive?" *Radical Philosophy* 62 (1992), 24.

66. See Rorty, "Feminism and Pragmatism," 224.

67. West, "The Historicist Turn in Philosophy of Religion," 369.

PART THREE

The Tragedy and Comedy of Empire

TEN

The Unpredictable American Empire

Richard Rorty

As Michael Ignatieff has pointed out, a country that has military bases around the world, commands military force capable of overwhelming any opponent, displays increasing arrogance in its attitude toward other nations, and sees international agreements and institutions as tools to be manipulated in its own interests, can plausibly be described as an "empire."[1] Still, the contrast between empire and republic can be misleading. For when we think of the transition from the Roman Republic to the Roman Empire, we think of two quite different things—the imposition of the *pax Romana* on places far away from the imperial capital, and an increasingly authoritarian internal regime.

The United States, like the Roman Republic, is a corrupt plutocracy, but it is not an authoritarian regime. It is still a constitutional democracy in which elections make a difference. The press and the universities are free, and the judiciary remains independent. The world is lucky that the country that serves as a global policeman—the one that guarantees the counterpart of the *pax Romana*—is not yet one in which an autocrat can do whatever he likes.

Under the bad caesars, the only remedy was the assassination of the tyrant. In the United States, a bad president can still be removed by the decision of the electorate. There is still plenty of internal debate going on in the United States about how to play our policing role and whether and how to try to shift this role to the United Nations. The appalling document published by the Bush administration—"The National Security Strategy of the United States of America"—would not have been issued by a Gore administration, and Gore would have been elected had he received the three million votes that American leftists gave to Ralph Nader.

The rest of the world should not think that someone like Bush—an ignorant and arrogant president, without either internationalist ideals or an aspiration for social justice—is the inevitable consequence of America's rise to unchallenged hegemony. He is just a piece of very bad luck. But of course he also represents a very great danger. If there are further successful terrorist attacks on the scale of 9/11, the Bush administration will almost certainly use them as an excuse to put the country under what amounts to martial law. This administration has no respect for civil liberties and would cheerfully turn the FBI into a Gestapo if it thought it could get away with it.

Even if there are no new terrorist attacks, the United States may well become even more of a garrison state than it already is. If future decisions on foreign policy are made by as small a cabal as the one that decided to invade Iraq, then the United States will remain a republic only in a very tenuous sense. If we see a series of Republican administrations and of Republican-dominated Congresses stretching over the next two decades, the American public will probably become accustomed to seeing our military forces suddenly dispatched abroad for reasons that are even vaguer and more confusing than those that were used as a rationale for the Iraq War. The opinions of the Democratic minority in Congress and of the liberal media (the *New York Times*, for example) will be brushed aside without a thought, and without the courtesy of a response, by Republican chieftains who think the affairs of the world too important to be entrusted to the judgment of the electorate.

If this pessimistic scenario were to play out, then the parallel with Rome would become complete. The shift from constitutional democracy to autocracy can become irreversible before anybody quite realizes that it is taking place. If the Democratic Party gradually ceases to function as a counterweight to bellicose White House cabals, historians may some day compare the "splitter" role of Nader's Green Party in 2000 to the refusal of the Communists to make common cause with the Social Democrats in Germany in 1932.

My topic in this paper, however, is not the current situation. Rather, I want to go back over some of the ground covered in my book *Achieving Our Country*,[2] and to describe the split between two self-images of the United States that have emerged in the decades since the 1960s. One of these self-images is of a republic that is always in danger, thanks to its ever-increasing wealth and power, of becoming an empire. The other is of a country that has always been imperial and hypocritical, one whose pretensions to moral worth have always been undeserved.

One convenient way to follow recent debates about the nature of the United States is looking at the academic discipline called "American Studies"—a discipline that is barely fifty years old. Within that discipline, a massive shift has occurred, one that has made a great difference in what American university students are told about the history and the nature of their country. There has been a change from a triumphalist, exceptionalist, and hopeful view of the United States to a depressed and skeptical view.

This shift in perspective is the central topic of a much-cited essay by Gene Wise, "'Paradigm Dramas' in American Studies."[3] On Wise's account, which perfectly fits my own memories, most American intellectuals prior to the 1960s took for granted what he calls "the Parrington paradigm." Those who did so believed that there was such a thing as the American Mind, and that it was importantly different from the European Mind.

This earlier generation took for granted that American thinkers and poets had long since done what Emerson hoped they might do: ceased to listen to "the courtly muses of Europe" and become inspired instead by "the spirit of American freedom." They agreed with Whitman that "Americans of all nations at any time upon the earth have probably the fullest poetical nature." They looked with scorn on the huge colonial empires that the European powers had grabbed in the course of the nineteenth century. Conveniently forgetting the Mexican-American War, they thought that their country's virtue was demonstrated by its having been content, at the end of the Spanish-American War, with very modest spoils.

These pre-1960s intellectuals also took for granted that their forefathers had brought forth upon the American continent a new birth of freedom, just as Lincoln had said. They saw the oppression of American workers by American capitalists and of American blacks by American whites as a tragic, but corrigible, failure to live up to ideals that remained central to the nation's self-image. They thought of the aggressive expansionism of the Mexican-American War, and of the annexation of Puerto Rico and the occupation of the Philippines at the beginning of the twentieth century, as unfortunate but long past episodes—events that were not really important to the nation's story.

Many of the pre-1960s intellectuals I am describing called themselves socialists, but few of them were Marxists. Most of them thought the New Deal had shown that violent social revolution was unnecessary, and that social justice at home, like de-colonization abroad, could be brought about by gradual, step-by-step, top-down measures. All of them, white as well as black, were angry at the humiliation and misery still being inflicted on African Americans, but they assumed that this problem, like that of poverty, could be solved by federal legislation.

Up until the mid-1960s, I whole-heartedly shared all the assumptions and attitudes I have been sketching. The people among whom I was brought up, and who shaped my political consciousness, knew very well, and helped publicize, what American whites were doing to American blacks. They also knew how viciously the bosses were still fighting the labor unions and how easy the rich found it to corrupt the American government. They agreed with Mencken and Veblen about the sad vulgarization of American middle-class life. Nevertheless, they did not doubt that the United States was the greatest and freest country that had ever existed. When Stalinist intellectuals defended the gulag by asking, "What about the lynchings of blacks in the United States?" these people replied that there was no comparison between a free country stained with racial hatred and a cruel tyranny. They conducted the struggle to make America a more just society in a spirit of sentimental patriotism. They regarded Gore Vidal's claim that we were rapidly moving from republic to empire as hysterical overstatement.

Things changed in the mid-1960s as more and more troops were sent to fight more and more hopeless battles against the Viet Cong. As Wise's article reminds us, the great post–World War II expansion of American higher education meant that most of the people of my generation who would, in my parents' generation, have become freelance writers and literary bohemians, became professors instead. So by 1965 almost every intellectual in the United States found himself teaching students who were quite likely to be drafted out of the classroom and sent off to fight in the jungles of Southeast Asia.

This created problems for those of us who wanted to be both patriots and social critics. The wars we and our parents had lived through—World Wars I and II—seemed to us to have been good, just wars. So, up until Vietnam, had the Cold War. The bad wars the United States had fought— the Mexican-American and Spanish-American Wars—were for us just memories of what the United States had been like in the bad old days before FDR. So to find our country once again waging a patently bad, unjust war made us question the faith in which we had grown up.

As people like me gradually realized both that the Vietnam War could not be won and that our government seemed nevertheless prepared to wage it forever, our image of our own nation began to change. We began to wonder how it must look not only in the eyes of our draft-age students, but in the eyes of the Vietnamese villagers we were napalming. This led us to realize how the United States had looked to Latin Americans ever since the CIA, in 1952, overthrew a left-wing Guatemalan government whose policies might have endangered the profits of the United Fruit Company. We began to see the Cold War, not just as a great and necessary crusade, but as a process that had subtly and silently corrupted our country from within. What Wise says about teachers of American Studies in this period—that they felt they must "assume an adversary role against the culture"—was true of many other academics, particularly those teaching in the social sciences and the humanities.

There was, however, a split between those who thought that the adversary was simply the American government of the moment and those who thought it was something deeper and more entrenched—the culture. We professors who had taken part in Martin Luther King's civil rights march on Washington in 1963 and who by 1968 were joining anti-war marches through the streets of New York City were divided into two camps. There were some who thought that the good old Emerson-Lincoln-Whitman-Dewey story about America had been hypocritical self-delusion. They began to describe the United States as a racist, sexist, imperialist nation. They read Marx and Marcuse, and they started telling their students that reform was obviously never going to work, that revolution was the only answer. But there were others, of whom I was one, who thought that the image of America as lighting the way to freedom and justice might still be preserved.

People in my camp continued to think of the Cold War a justified crusade against an evil empire, but we were gradually forced to admit that prosecuting that war had caused the government to fall into the hands of what President Eisenhower called "the military-industrial complex." This realization did not cause us to repudiate our country or our culture. We did not think that the story of America needed to be retold. We simply wanted to take the country back from the Pentagon and the corporations. If America would return to its senses and live up to its glorious past, we thought, it could continue to prosecute the Cold War, but in ways that did not commit it to the support of despotisms run out of the American embassy.

Even Cold Warriors like myself have now come to admit that we are citizens of something more like an empire than like the republic Emerson described and Whitman hymned. We still hope that the people might some day recapture the government from the control of the military-industrial complex and that someday our country will cease to be a garrison state. But we have to acknowledge that vast areas of national life have been turned over to the so-called "iron triangle" that links corporations, the Pentagon, and the Senate and House Armed Services Committees. The Congress, heavily bribed and deeply corrupt, never seriously debates life-

and-death issues such as nuclear disarmament any more than it shows genuine concern for the needs of the American poor. It never discusses what to do about America's role in the international arms trade. That is why the collapse of the Soviet Union made so little difference to defense expenditures, why we still have enough nuclear warheads to destroy civilization, and why President Bush can repudiate treaties without much public outcry.

Our radical colleagues agree with all this, but they think that recent changes have simply made it easier to see what America has always been like. They see the Vietnam War as continuous with the Mexican-American War and the occupation of the Philippines. On their view, the contempt for non-whites that all three episodes revealed was of a piece with the racism that has always permeated American society. They see leftist reformers like myself as naïve, desperately trying to preserve the Parrington paradigm in the face of the facts.

We reformists, however, think that the radicals' picture of America as pretty much irredeemable is just a way of evading questions about how to change our country for the better. The radicals rejoin that electing liberal Democrats rather than conservative Republicans will never make any real difference to the country's behavior. As they see it, we liberals are those who, long after the Roman Republic has been succeeded by the Roman Empire, still worried about who would become consul.

The split within the ranks of American intellectuals that I have been describing is epitomized in the contrast between the views of David Hollinger, perhaps our most eminent scholar of American intellectual history, and those of Nikhil Pal Singh, who teaches American Studies at New York University.

Hollinger is, like myself, a social democrat and an admirer of Dewey. He wants American intellectuals to pay less attention to identity politics and to think more about what political initiatives to support. In 1995 he published a book called *Postethnic America: Beyond Multiculturalism* in which he tried to revive the pre-1960s idea of America as an inclusive, pluralist society.[4] His subtitle, "Beyond Multiculturalism," was in part a protest against the way in which the term "multiculturalism" had become the watchword of the radicals—the term used to describe their skepticism toward the very idea of "American culture."

Hollinger's book was of a piece with books published around the same time by Todd Gitlin, Arthur Schlesinger Jr., and myself.[5] All four of us argued that it was time to stop emphasizing diversity and conflict and to try to formulate a consensus around which leftist intellectuals and the public as a whole might rally. What the country needed, we said, was not identity politics but what Gitlin called "majoritarian" politics—that is, political activity aimed at winning elections, getting bills through Congress, and filing suits that would produce court decisions favorable to liberal causes. We wanted intellectuals to let up on criticism of the culture and switch to criticism of, and changes in, the laws and in administrative policies. In particular, we wanted the intellectuals to talk less about race and more about class, because we hoped that a political majority might be formed if poor white people and poor black people made common cause.

The opposing, radical point of view was laid out in a 1998 article by Nikhil Singh titled "Culture/Wars: Recoding Empire in an Age of Democracy."[6] This was a comprehensive and very thoughtful overview of the radical-vs.-liberal opposition in American intellectual life in the course of the last six or seven decades. In it, Singh set his face against the whole cluster of ideas and attitudes common to Schlesinger, Gitlin, Hollinger, and myself. He sees our efforts as reactionary. He urges specialists in American Studies not to be seduced into reaffirming a discredited "universalism."

Singh's central criticism of Hollinger's project is that the attempt to revive a patriotic sense of common citizenship is "mystificatory" in that it obscures both racial and class conflict. "The problem," Singh says, "is that the concept of universalism in this discussion remains too closely aligned with the idea of nationalism and especially with the achievement of a hegemonic social formation capable of transcending differences, social antagonisms, and divisions."

I agree with Singh when he says that "the epistemic, historical, moral and worldly political status of internalized/externalized exclusion and inequality, perpetuated by the civic nation, constitutes the proper, if vexed, terrain of the culture wars." But I disagree with him when he goes on to say, "In this conflictual, communal conversation, the reassertion of American universalism actually provides few solutions; it only begs more questions." It seems to me that the only thing that can provide solutions is a shared sense of citizenship, a sense of participation in a social formation capable of transcending differences, antagonisms, and divisions.

Singh and his fellow radicals think that any such sense of participation would be self-deceptive. Their point is that the rich and powerful whites who have manipulated American public opinion ever since the country's foundation created a series of fictions, including the fictions purveyed by Lincoln in the Gettysburg Address (a speech that all students in my elementary school were required to memorize). Singh and many other specialists in American Studies think that the principal task of scholars in this field is to debunk the Parringtonian and Lincolnesque story of America as a land of freedom. Hollinger and those like him reply that the work of demystification has been accomplished, that we do not need to do it again and again, and that it is time to get back to consensus-building. Our central argument is that that there is a difference between fictions and ideals, and that you cannot have change for the better without an ideal to strive for.

To judge by the content of *American Quarterly*, and in particular by the tenor of recent presidential addresses to the American Studies Associations, Singh's point of view is now dominant among American academics who belong to that Association. But Hollinger thinks, and I agree, that it would be a great misfortune for our country if our students were won over to Singh's way of thinking of the United States. On our view, one of the few things that might help ensure that we remain a republic would be the sense, in the rising generation, that our country's ideals have been betrayed.

Addressing the Brazilian Association for American Studies, Hollinger took pains to note that "the need to confront, rather than 'erase' conflicts 'of regions, race, class, gender, and sexuality' has long been accepted in a variety of academic settings in the United States and was a well-established mantra against the 'consensus' school even in the 1970s." He went on to say that "if someone is looking for ways to *innovate* in American Studies, or if one wants to develop a perspective influenced by one's position as an outsider to the United States, the place to look is *not* the differences by region, race, class, gender, and sexuality."[7] He was trying to warn his Brazilian audience against repeating a familiar mantra under the illusion that they were boldly breaking new paths.

Hollinger's speech in Brazil runs counter to a warning uttered by Janice Radway in her 1998 Presidential Address. There she said that the American Studies Association must "ensure that its very name does not enforce the achievement of premature closure through an implicit, tacit search for the distinctively American 'common ground.'" What Hollinger views as ceasing to repeat a mantra is viewed by Radway as "premature closure." Radway continues by noting that in her address she will not use the pronoun "we," in the sense of "we Americans," because she wishes to refuse "the presumptive and coercive enclosure it usually enacts when used in institutional situations of this kind." "I have resisted," she continues, "the comforting assumption that there is an unproblematic 'we' as a way of recognizing that the many who associate their work with American studies often have distinctly different interests, agendas, and concerns."[8]

Radway may here be making implicit reference to a well-known paper by Hollinger titled "Expanding the Circle of the 'We.'" There Hollinger treats the process of taking account of the needs and concerns of blacks, women, gays, lesbians, and recent immigrants to the United States as attempts to make phrases like "we, the people of the United States," or "we fellow-citizens" cover more kinds of people than they had in the past. He sees the search for greater social justice as the attempt to change "them" into "us," to include the concerns of the previously excluded in deliberation about what, politically, is to be done. He views the various movements toward including the excluded as not so much recognition of difference—cultural or otherwise—but of incorporation in a larger unity.

This strikes people like Singh and Radway as condescending—as a perpetuation of the attitude that says "You people down at the bottom should be patient until we wise and good middle-class white males have the time to raise you up to equal status with ourselves and then to assimilate you." This sort of condescension was, they point out, the customary attitude of men toward women who asked for the right to vote, of Southern whites toward African Americans who asked not to be lynched, and of Northern whites toward blacks who asked to be hired on the same terms as their white competitors. Practitioners of "cultural studies" such as Singh and Radway want the various disadvantaged and oppressed groups within U.S. society who have been subjected to such lofty condescension to resist and want each of them to retain a kind of proud autonomy rather than simply hoping to be assimilated into the larger society. This is why they distrust Hollinger's proposal to stop practicing identity politics and why they refuse to switch from criticism of American culture to criticism of the American government.

From Hollinger's and my point of view, this justified suspicion of condescension goes too far when it expresses itself as suspicion of any attempt to get a consensus among Americans—any attempt to unite Americans behind ideals which, though dishonored in the past, have some chance of being honored in the future. We are particularly dubious about Radway's argument that "the state and the political economy of the United States are themselves entirely dependent on the internal, imperial racialization of the population" and that the United States "is thus utterly dependent on its obsession with 'blackness' . . . that obsession is constitutive of the state." "Entirely" and "utterly" seem to us rhetorical overstatements, essentialistic over-simplifications, ways of avoiding asking how things might be changed.

Liberals like Hollinger and myself are dubious about identity politics because we think that it is merely mystificatory to run together a community of interest with an "identity" or with "a shared culture." We see the black poor and the white poor in the United States as having a shared interest, and we regard the question of whether they share a common culture as politically irrelevant. From the point of view of our radical opponents, however, this distaste for identity politics is a result of our failure to realize how deeply the black-white contrast permeates our culture. Our insistence on thinking in terms of competing, and possibly cooperating, interest groups rather than in terms of cultural differences signalizes our failure to realize that the difference between African Americans and Americans of other ethnic backgrounds is not much like that between, for example, Irish Americans and WASP Americans, or between Jewish Americans and Arab Americans. In particular, we fail to grasp the implications of the fact that the conviction that "one drop of black blood pollutes" is not matched by any similar conviction in regard to Irish or Jewish or Vietnamese or Hispanic blood.

We liberals respond to this line of criticism by saying that the United States has always been a multicultural society, one that in the past has often been united by a sense of shared citizenship and of shared hope for political change. We think it essential to keep both of these alive. We have to concede to the radicals that for African Americans, and for the Japanese Americans who were interned after Pearl Harbor, the promise of equal citizenship was not fulfilled. We also have to concede that the belief that "one drop of black blood pollutes" means that intermarriage will probably not break down barriers for African Americans in the way it did for immigrant groups in the past (and probably will for Hispanic and Asian Americans). But we think it important to reemphasize that the promise of equal citizenship *was* fulfilled, eventually, in respect to the immigrants who arrived from Europe between 1850 and 1920. Insofar as "multiculturalism" simply means "antiracism," then liberals can be as good multiculturalists as can radicals. But the radicals seem not to think "antiracism" is an adequate synonym. We liberals cannot see what more "multiculturalism" *could* mean.

The disagreements between liberal and radical scholars in the United States about the nature of our country are mirrored by their respective ways of looking at the Bush administration's overweening arrogance since 9/11—its assumption that U.S. hegemony should go unquestioned and that the other nations should be content to have the United States police the world.

From the point of view of the radicals—people whose view of the United States is taken from the writings of Noam Chomsky and Gore Vidal—this arrogance is a matter of our having finally stripped off a mask, thus making the true nature of the United States becoming obvious to all. From the point of view of liberals like myself, however, it is a result of our having elected a particularly bad president in 2000. The radicals say, "America has finally unmasked itself, revealed itself as an unashamed imperial power." The liberals say, "Of course the people around Bush would like us to exercise unquestioned imperial hegemony, since that will increase American corporate profits, but their current dominance does not entail that they will always get their way." The difference is analogous to that between those who say, "Germany revealed its true nature when the Nazis took over," and those who say, "Germany had catastrophically bad luck in 1933 but proved able to overcome its own misfortune."

Liberals like myself are quite willing to drop the triumphalist Parringtonian paradigm, but we do not want to substitute a debunking, pessimistic account of the true nature of our country. As good pragmatists, we think that our country has a history, but not a nature. That history can be narrated in many different ways, but these narratives cannot be graded according to how close they come to an account of what our country *really* has been. None of them give us knowledge of an underlying national nature.

Those who, like myself, compose narratives in which our country figures as a symbol of the triumph of leftist ideals hope that the United States will have the power to act so as to realize and spread those ideals. There is a perfectly good leftist case for using the military power of democratic countries to conquer countries ruled by tyrants and to replace them with democratic regimes. That this excuse for invasion has been used disingenuously by, among others, Napoleon, Mussolini, Stalin, Mao, Eisenhower, Nixon, and Bush does not mean that it has to be used that way. To be leftist is to be internationalist, and to be internationalist is to believe that when a man such as Kim Il Song, Saddam Hussein, Pinochet, Milosovic, or Mugabe is victimizing the people of his country or of a neighboring territory, the peoples of the rest of the world should try to overthrow him.

The question of which country or international organization should do this, and whether it is to be done by invasion, assassination, or support of internal dissidence is a matter of calculating consequences, not one that can be settled by appeals to principle. Until the United Nations is transformed into what Tennyson called "the Parliament of Man," it will be up to individual democratic nation-states and coalitions of such states to overthrow tyrants. Recently, this has meant that it has been up to the United States. Sooner or later the European Union may pull itself together, increase its military budget, adopt a foreign policy of its own, and stride forth onto the world stage. But until that happens, the United States is the only nation likely to use its military power to right wrongs.

In the present situation—one in which a *pax Americana* is the best we can reasonably hope for—the American left should not try to make things easier for itself by adopting isolationism as a counterweight to oppose Bush's hypocritical interventionism. It should not worry about whether the United States is *really* a republic or *really* an empire, since it is obviously both. It should stick to the question of how we are going to use our imperial power—a question that is, precisely because we still are a republic, a matter for public debate.

As many commentators have been saying recently, the period of American imperial power is bound to be short-lived. We may be in the last decade of the *pax Americana*. People in the Bush administration seem honestly to believe that we can maintain our overwhelming military superiority forever; the "National Security Policy of the United States" makes this belief explicit. But nobody outside Washington takes seriously the idea that both China and Russia will be content to sit back and let the United States run the world for more than another few years. It is quite likely that the next time the United States embarks on an adventure abroad, its European allies, including Great Britain, will simply turn their backs on America and start sounding out the leaders of Russia and China about the possibility of forming a new peacekeeping coalition.

Still, with a great deal of prudence on America's part, plus a great deal of luck, the decline of American imperial power might see a transition to something better than the *pax Americana*—to a recognition by all the nuclear powers, including China and Russia, that they must work together to prevent an otherwise inevitable series of conflagrations. Whether America will have the necessary foresight and exercise the necessary prudence to make this transition possible will be determined, not by anything intrinsic to its nature or made inevitable by its history, but rather by a few million swing voters during the next three or four national elections. That is one of the splendors, as well as one of the miseries, of a republic.

Notes

1. Michael Ignatieff, "The Burden," *New York Times Magazine*, 5 January 2003.

2. Richard Rorty, *Achieving Our Country: Leftist Thought in Twentieth-Century America* (Cambridge, Mass.: Harvard University Press, 1999).

3. Gene Wise, "'Paradigm Dramas' in American Studies," *American Quarterly* 31.3 (1979): 293–337.

4. David A. Hollinger, *Postethnic America: Beyond Multiculturalism*, rev. ed. (New York: Basic Books, 2000).

5. Todd Gitlin, *The Twilight of Common Dreams: Why America Is Wracked by Culture Wars* (New York: Owlet Press, 1996); Arthur M. Schlesinger Jr., *The Disuniting of America: Reflections of a Multicultural Society*, rev. ed. (New York: Norton, 1998); Richard Rorty, *Achieving Our Country: Leftist Thought in Twentieth-Century America* (Cambridge, Mass.: Harvard University Press, 1999).

6. Nikhil Singh, "Culture/Wars: Recoding Empire in an Age of Democracy," *American Quarterly* 50.3 (1998): 471–527.

7. David Hollinger, "Foreign Area Studies and the Promise of a More Comprehensive Scholarly Engagement with the United States," *Transit Circle; Revista da Associacao Brasilera de Estudos Americanos,* 1999. Hollinger argued that American Studies programs should not think of themselves as developing a distinct scholarly discipline of that name, replete with a method and a central task, but rather on the model of what are called "area studies programs" in the United States—loose assemblages of people from different disciplines who share a common interest in a certain part of the world.

8. Janice Radway, "What's in a Name?" *American Quarterly* 51.3 (1999): 1–32.

ELEVEN

Transcending the "Gory Cradle of Humanity": War, Loyalty, and Civic Action in Royce and James

Eduardo Mendieta

Pragmatists take questions of what something is and translate them into questions of what something is *for*. Concepts do not refer to things, but to possible actions. Entities do not have an ontological status independent of how they relate to human praxis. In this sense, pragmatists are radical critics of all forms of metaphysics. They find ontological questions useless at best and mystifying at worst. The pragmatist attitude toward "profound" philosophical quandaries is not to insist on their timelessness and deepness, but rather to invite us to cease to talk about them in old and confusing language and to develop new languages—languages that allow us to articulate the issue in different, perhaps more useful ways.

Pragmatists thus are romantics, who, like Karl Marx and Friedrich Nietzsche, subordinate all systems of thought to human purposive action, and who in similar ways announced the "death of all gods," where "gods" stands for anything that is thought to be independent of human action, purpose, and the ability to transform and refashion.[1] A pragmatist, therefore, would not ask, What is the essence of war? Nor would a pragmatist ask whether war is an ineluctable dimension of all human existence, or whether war is intrinsic to the human essence. Instead, a pragmatist would ask whether war performed any function in human history, whether war responds to specific needs, and whether those needs could be fulfilled by other means. A pragmatist would bracket the question about the inevitability of war and instead ask how it affects our ways of seeing the world and what kind of role it performs in our present way of thinking. Most importantly, a pragmatist would ask about the immediate relevance of the question about the whither and purpose of war in a given context.

In the following discussion, we will be guided by this pragmatic agnosticism about the nature of war and will seek to answer two related questions: How has war affected the emergence of pragmatism as a distinctively U.S. philosophical tradition, and to what extent has that influence framed and conditioned the philosophical attitude and method of analysis of pragmatism? In order to approximate an answer to these two questions, we will have to engage in a bit of historical reconstruction. What is noteworthy, although not altogether unexpected or strange, is that most of the classic pragmatists—with the glaring exception of C. S. Peirce[2]—as well as many neo-pragmatists, made substantive and lasting pronouncements on war. However, I will restrict myself to two key pragmatists: Josiah Royce and William James. This restriction is not entirely arbitrary. I have decided to focus my discussion on these two figures because, first, Royce and James shared some common ideas about the function of war in society and what it would take to bring about its abolition or sublimation. Moreover, both had as an explicit philosophical contender the ethnologist Rudolf Steinmetz, who is mentioned in their respective writings on war. In 1907 Steinmetz published a substantive book of 352 pages with the provocative title *Die Philosophie des Krieges* (The Philosophy of War), which seems to have been the synthesis of years of research.[3] As Steinmetz notes in the foreword, this book was not the first time in which he has expressed his views on war, and he lists in a footnote three publications— one in French, another in German, and another in Dutch—all dealing with war. As we will see, Steinmetz articulated a view of war that sought to ontologize it, rendering it into an immutable aspect of human existence. Steinmetz proffered a philosophical apologia for war that must have struck both Royce and James as precisely the philosophical attitude that both found anathema, if not precisely what they sought to overcome.[4]

If space had permitted, I would also have discussed the views of George Herbert Mead and John Dewey. Mead is an obvious point of reference for any discussion dealing with pragmatism, pacifism, and internationalism. He was one of the most socially progressive thinkers in the pragmatist tradition,[5] but he also shared with Royce and James the philosophical and sociological concern with achieving a social answer to the enduring need to utilize war as a motivating and cohesion-granting device, as Aboulafia discusses in this volume. Like Royce and James, Mead thought that war could be abolished if we made a transition from an emotivistic type of social integration, which mobilizes blind allegiance and the passions of hate that call for the elimination of the enemy, to a deliberate and rational form of both individuation and socialization that sought an enlarged mentality that synthesized concern for one's nation with internationalism. Mead, in fact, explicitly, albeit critically, commented on and based some of his own analysis of the obsolescence of war on James's famous essay, "The Moral Equivalent of War."[6]

The focus on John Dewey would also have been amply warranted because he lived through two world wars and was actively engaged in the public debates concerning U.S. participation in both wars. The shift in Dewey's views and analysis of war from World War I to World War II and the onset of the Cold War would allow us to offer a litmus test of the non-metaphysical, non-foundationalist pragmatist attitude toward war that I think is the background assumption of pragmatists and neo-pragmatists.[7] Furthermore, in discussing Dewey we would also have had an opportunity to analyze Randolph S. Bourne's trenchant and pungent criticism of Dewey, his teacher, mentor, and philosophical idol until their break in the late teens.[8] In studying the Dewey-Bourne debate, we would have arrived at perhaps the most explicit articulation of what I take to be the two central themes of a pragmatist approach to war: (1) its social uses; and (2) the possibility of sublimating its virtues and powers to mobilize humanity toward great deeds of sacrifice into the virtues of democratic temperance and cosmopolitan loyalty, which dispenses with the fear of the absence of fear and celebrates the moral and civic genius of a people, to use James's language. Fortunately, this discussion has been carefully taken up by several contributors to this volume and documented and studied by two superlative intellectual historians, Robert B. Westbrook and Steve C. Rockefeller. What I could add here would pale in comparison with what both have already written.[9]

Why Are People Willing to Die for Ideals?

In his Pulitzer Prize–winning book, *The Metaphysical Club*, intellectual historian Louis Menand frames the emergence and eventual eclipse of pragmatism between two wars: the Civil War and World War II.[10] The Civil War was an existential shock to many of the classic pragmatists. William James's brothers fought in it, and one of them died of wounds he suffered in battle. Oliver Wendell Holmes Jr., whom Menand restores to the classical pantheon of the founders of pragmatism, was wounded twice in the war. The destruction, both personal and national, brought about by the Civil War made a profound impact on the founding generations of pragmatisms. Menand goes further. He argues that it was precisely against the passions of certitude and the certitude of passions that resulted in the upheavals of the Civil War that pragmatism was developed as an antidote.

If violence resulted from a blind allegiance to beliefs, pragmatism sought to make it harder for people to "be driven to violence by their beliefs"[11] by making our allegiance to our beliefs conditional on their efficacy. A belief was worth our loyalty so long as it contributed to the defusing of the violence of abstractions. As a philosophical response to the Civil War, pragmatism, in Menand's view, became "a style of thought that elevated compromise over confrontation."[12] It was this very attitude that spelled its eclipse after World War II and the onset of the Cold War, for these two wars were fought over principles, principles that are mutually exclusionary and that prevent any compromise and negotiation. While pragmatism may have been a style of thought that served the healing nation by articulating a tolerant and ecumenical way of looking at disagreement and dissent, it became obsolete and even an obstacle when questions of principle came to the foreground. Curiously, Menand notes that the major social and political transformations in the U.S. polity, namely, the civil rights movement, did not stem at all from pragmatism, but from the religious communities, in particular the black Southern Baptists. Menand notes: "Martin Luther King, Jr. was not a pragmatist, a relativist, or a pluralist, and it is a question whether the movement he led could have accomplished what it did if its inspirations had come from Dewey and Holmes rather than Reinhold Niebuhr and Mahatma Gandhi. Americans did not reject the values of tolerance and liberty during the Cold War—on the contrary—but they replanted those values in distinctly non-pragmatic soil."[13]

Menand's analysis of the impact of the Civil War on the founding generation of pragmatists is surely right, although the conclusion he draws concerning their support for the Unionist compromise is rightly challenged by Brandom and Kim in this volume. Yet to bracket pragmatism between the Civil War and the Cold War is doubtless contestable. James and Royce, as well as Dewey, were deeply disturbed and critical of the U.S. intervention in Cuba and the Philippines. Menand neglects the role of the Spanish-American War and what many, including James, considered to be a form of imperialism. World War I had a profound impact on the development of Dewey's political philosophy, as we will see. Most importantly, however, the development of pragmatism did not halt with the Cold War, even if one can partly assent to Menand's claim that pragmatism suffered an eclipse by the professionalization of philosophy. Menand neglects the role of Vietnam and the 1960s in the education of the neo-pragmatists. It can be argued that the work of neo-pragmatists like Richard Rorty, Richard Bernstein, and Cornel West were unmistakably marked not just by the Cold War but also by the reactions to it that culminated in the Vietnam debacle. At the very least, one has to challenge Menand's rather jejune view that U.S. history, in general, and U.S. intellectual history in particular, can be neatly sandwiched between these two major wars: between the war that forged a nation and the war that forged the supposed empire of the good.[14] U.S. history, sadly, has been marked indelibly by many wars, most of which cannot be easily assimilated into the kind of Whiggish and sanitized history that Menand presupposes when he unfolds a narrative that goes from national trauma to global ascendancy over the forces of intolerance, authoritarianism, and dictatorship.

Additionally, while Menand's book has done a great service to the history of pragmatism and the history of ideas in the United States, especially as it has forcefully and eloquently argued for a greater recognition of the role of Darwin and the philosophy of law (via Holmes) in both histories, Menand's conclusions seem not to have absorbed a central lesson of all the founding pragmatists, namely, that selves are neither Cartesian homunculi nor Kantian disembodied moral subjects. In chastising pragmatists for offering a type of thinking that "explains everything about ideas except why a person would be willing to die for one,"[15] Menand takes us behind pragmatism's development of what has been called the dialogic or mediated self.[16] Ideas, as Menand right notes, are just tools, which may indeed lead us to want to die for them, or to kill for them. But for all pragmatists, from Peirce through West, more important than ideas are the types of selves that we think we should be. Menand, in order words, manages to re-epistemologize and re-mystify the social self into an epistemic machine that gives and accepts reasons while submitting them to a preexisting set of adjudicating norms.

For pragmatists, the issue is not what kind of ideas social agents can entertain, but rather how social agents are socialized in such a way that they are vulnerable or resistant to the dogmatism of certain ideas. Pragmatism is a philosophy of social agents, not of ideas that exist in some metaphysical realm. Thus, Menand's formulation about how pragmatism does not explain why a person should die for a certain idea manages to reverse pragmatism's fundamental insight into the relationship between ideas and persons. The issue is not what kind of ideas we should die for, but what kind of person is it that would die for an ideal or idea. When we reframe the issue in that way, we immediately recognize that all pragmatists, perhaps with the exception of Peirce, sought to answer these questions: What kind social arrangements produce agents that would be willing to die for specific ideas? and Can we develop new social formations that would give birth to persons who would replace dying and killing for certain ideas with other social values and forms of social interaction? It is this latter question that particularly preoccupied Royce, James, and Mead.

From the Philosophy of War to the Philosophy of Loyalty

Josiah Royce "confesses" quite early in his book *The Philosophy of Loyalty* that he had entitled his lectures thus because of a book he had read early in the summer of 1907.[17] The book was Rudolf Steinmetz's *Die Philosophie des Krieges* (The Philosophy of War). Royce notes that "war and loyalty have been, in the past, two very closely associated ideas. It will be part of the task of these lectures to break up, so far as I can, in your minds, that ancient and *disastrous* association, and to show how much the true conception of loyalty has been obscured by viewing the warrior as the most typical representative of rational loyalty."[18] Royce is here immediately taking distance from Steinmetz, even as he confesses that it was Steinmetz who not only suggested the title for his own book, but also the very theme of loyalty. According to Steinmetz, Royce proceeds, "war gives an opportunity for loyal devotion so notable and important that, if war were altogether abolished, one of the greatest goods of civilization would thereby be hopelessly lost." And then Royce adds emphatically: "I am keenly conscious of the sharp contrast between Steinmetz's theory of loyalty and my own."[19] What was Steinmetz's view?

As was noted above, Steinmetz was an important ethnologist, even a pioneer of sociology. His *Die Philosophie des Krieges* was the summation of years of research and also a kind of manifesto. The work is a methodical analysis of the role of war in history, relying on his substantive knowledge of the subject. Steinmetz explores: "war as a cultural instinctual power [*Triebkraft*]"; the disadvantages and advantages of war; the "essential and still valid function of war"; the replacement of war through international agreements; the process of collective selection through war; the resistance to that selection; the ineluctable law of the increase in military budgets; future war; the curtailment of the martial spirit; peace congresses and their ineffectiveness; and, finally, the enemy. Steinmetz's approach is unmistakably marked by a form of social Darwinism, for which war is a selection mechanism that eliminates unworthy races and nations and exalts those who have survived the fire and iron of the canons of war. Steinmetz's work is in fact very similar to that of Friedrich Ratzel, the father of modern German geopolitics. And perhaps not coincidentally, Steinmetz's book was published as part of a series that included Ratzel's works as well as those of other racialists such as Hans Driesch and Rudolf Eisler.

Steinmetz espouses the view that we should view the state as a vital organism, one that both expresses and preserves the vital force, or instinctual powers, of a race. The vitality of a state is the vitality of a race or people. War is an indispensable means for the preservation of that vitality and for the *Kollektivauslese* that eliminates those who represent a social pathology and preserves those who augur the health of the fatherland and state. It is the glory of the state and the fatherland that compels individuals to rise above their egoism and the fear of their lonely deaths. Without those ideals, individuals would not be compelled to rise above their individual preservation. Indeed, argues Steinmetz, whoever contemplates the highest achievement of human life as an ideal must be willing to accept the love of the fatherland, and naturally also its presupposition, namely, the sacrifice and compassion that is commanded by it. As he puts it bluntly: "For its full existence, the state, as well as the individual, requires: Danger, need, and struggle. Whoever loves humanity should not want to spare it these. This is, I think, generally acknowledged and has simply become trivial wisdom. The same applies to the state."[20] Or, as he puts it: "Peoples, like individuals, need distress (*Not*), suffering and danger for their development, as well as for their life" (221). To want to die for the glory of one's nation and for the strength of its state is to want to die for posterity. In dying for the state and the fatherland, we live forever in the memory of the victorious people. As Steinmetz writes: "The state, fatherland and war are simply irreplaceable, and that is why they demand their sacrifice" (200). It is for this reason that Steinmetz reformulated Hegel's famous statement about history into "war is world-judgment." "War is both a judge and reformer at the same time" (222). War, in short, is indispensable for the spiritual development of an entire people. War is the source of the moral and physical health of the people (237). Or, as he provocatively formulates it: "If there were no war, we would have to invent it" (290).

Royce's "sharp contrast" with Steinmetz could not be sharper. Steinmetz subordinates any kind of moral values or social virtues to the vitalistically construed people, race, nation, and state. It is the glory of these that exacts from us loyalty. Here loyalty is at the service of a warrior people and state. For Royce, on the contrary, loyalty is the very foundation of morality, one that is implicitly universalizable, as he elaborates later on; it is the expression of the moral commandment itself. When properly defined, for Royce, "loyalty is the fulfillment of the moral law."[21] For loyalty is the deliberate, conscious, and practical "devotion" of a person to a cause. Loyalty is the self-subjection and self-giving of a person to a cause, a cause that is also the cause of another. It is very evident in Royce's language that he is explicitly appropriating and translating Kant's moral philosophy, but in terms of Peirce's semiotics, as we will see later. For loyalty is a self-relation mediated by a community of interpretation. We don't adopt a cause, any cause, without a context. We submit in devotion to those causes that are shared by others with whom we have entered into a process of interpretation. Communities of loyalty are communities of interpretation. To be loyal is by definition neither a solipsistic nor an egotistical act.

Loyalty is a form of witnessing: of oneself as a principled individual before others, a community of moral accountability. We submit before and for others, self-consciously. We affirm our autonomy by willingly subjecting ourselves to a cause. This autonomy is just another expression of our rational self-consciousness. Thus, for Royce, loyalty is the summation of both self-legislation and rational self-consciousness. I am the author of my own subjection, but only insofar as it is rationally evident to myself. For Royce, as for Socrates, Augustine, and Kant, "moral authority for each of us is determined by our own rational will."[22]

Royce explicitly addressed the obvious question of what happens when two different loyalties confront each other. In fact, it is in addressing this question that he comes to one of the strongest theses of these lectures, namely, that all "commonplace virtues" are but expression of "loyalty to loyalty."[23] Loyalty to loyalty, in fact, becomes a moral compass for Royce that directs us to respect the loyalty to loyalty of other persons. Royce writes that "a cause is good, not only for me, but for mankind, in so far as it is essentially a *loyalty to loyalty*, that is, is an aid and a furtherance of loyalty in my fellows. It is an evil cause in so far as, despite the loyalty that it arouses in me, it is destructive of loyalty in the world of my fellows. . . . In so far as my cause is a predatory cause, which lives by overthrowing the loyalties of others, it is an evil cause, because it involves disloyalty to the very cause of loyalty itself."[24] Inasmuch as loyalty to loyalty is a form of self-subjection, or, as Royce calls it, "to have a cause" by which one lives, it is a form of self-reflexivity that exhibits both consciousness and will. Our loyalty to loyalty, however, is betrayed, becomes an evil, if that same ability to be loyal to loyalty is denied in others. Perhaps, not unlike Kant's categorical imperative with its four different formulations, the imperative to be loyal to loyalty entails also the reverence and respect of the same ability in every other human being.

For Royce, like Kant, the supreme expression of our humanity lies in our living in accordance with a moral law that is to be respected in every human being. There is a simultaneous universalizing and constraining, or self-curtailment, of this supreme moral duty: loyalty to loyalty demands that I constrain my loyalty to those loyalties that do not curtail or destroy another fellow's own loyalty to loyalty. Loyalty can't be blind, boundless, and unreasoning. On the contrary, argues Royce, it is only insofar as it is an expression of my rational will that loyalty is loyalty to loyalty, that is, to that ability to submit ourselves to causes and ideals that would, or could, command the same loyalty from other human beings. In the end, Royce's thesis is strong and unequivocal: "*All those duties which we have learned to recognize as the fundamental duties of the civilized man, the duties that every man owes to every man, are to be rightly interpreted as special instance of loyalty to loyalty.* In other words, all the recognized virtues can be defined in terms of our concept of loyalty."[25]

Royce returned to the questions of loyalty and war in a series of lectures he delivered on the occasion of the twenty-fifth anniversary of the Philosophical Union of the University of California. Soon after Royce had delivered the lectures in the summer, World War I began.[26] The manuscript of the lectures underwent revisions in light of the war, but it was published in 1914 under the title of *War and Insurance: An Address.*[27] In fact, Royce sought to make the final manuscript a manifesto against the war and, significantly, once again makes an explicit reference to Steinmetz that demands quotation:

> Sebald Rudolf Steinmetz is professor of Ethnology at the University of Amsterdam. His "Philosophie des Krieges" was published in 1907 and has much influenced the train of thought which was first set forth in the present writer's "Philosophy of Loyalty" (New York, 1908), and which has gradually led, through a series of intermediate books, to the present Address. That this influence has partly been due to my own opposition to certain of the theses of Steinmetz is obvious. But I hope that section II of this Address clearly shows that in certain respects I stand greatly indebted to Steinmetz for some of his views regarding the war-like aspects of human essence. (83)

Part II of Royce's *Address* is entitled "The Neighbor: Love and Hate." In this section, Royce addresses how the martial spirit mobilizes both hate of the enemy and love of one's compatriots. At the heart of Royce's preoccupation in this chapter, as well as throughout the whole book, is to understand how it is that war, or the war-like spirit, draws on the spiritual side of the human being. As he puts it, in war's appeal to the spiritual in the human being "lies its appeal to what is best in man" (19). We cannot properly address the endurance and perpetuation of war if we simply dismiss the war-like spirit as an atavistic and regressive leftover from earlier stages of social evolution. Nor can we deal properly with war in terms of love and hate relations. Love of one's neighbor and hate of one's adversary are expressions of a more fundamental form of love: loyalty. Thus, Royce is appealing to his earlier work on loyalty. The issue is how to transform the love and hate that the martial spirit exploits and mobilizes into a different form of love, or rather loyalty. For Royce, the issue is to redirect these forms of affect and emotional attachment to other forms of social cooperation and cohesion. With Steinmetz, then, Royce agrees that challenges, need, and danger raise human beings to higher levels of moral and spiritual achievement; but against Steinmetz, Royce think that it is not the state, the nation, or war that should be the object of our faith, devotion, and loyalty. Instead, and here Royce stays with Kant, the solution to war is the development of a higher form of loyalty, or loyalty to a more encompassing social whole: humanity as a community of interpretation. This is where Royce's "insurance" in the title of his book comes in, as well as Peirce's semiotics.

Basing himself on Peirce's semiotics, Royce developed the notion of a "community of interpretation" that involves at the very least three elements: An interpreter, an interpretant, and an interpretee, which correspond to Peirce's symbol, sign, and icon. Royce also puts it this way: a community of interpretation consists "in what is usually called a *principal,* of an *agent,* and of a *client,* or other such man, *to whom the agent represents the principal"* (45). Royce identifies three special forms of communities of interpretation: the judicial community, the banker's community, and the community of insurance. Nonetheless, what is of utmost importance for Royce is the specific quality of all communities of interpretation, which is that insofar as they abolish all dyadic relations, they dilute, decrease, and even abolish all possible conflict. Since all relations are now triadic, differences have to be mediated, negotiated, interpreted, and resolved in terms of some sort of consensus, or cultivated rational persuasion. A pair, alone, is a dangerous relation. A triad augurs peace, or at least "negotiation." Not unexpectedly, Royce develops his critique of "dyads" with reference to Kant's notion of the "unsocial sociability" of the human being.[28] Royce is quite blunt: "*Dyadic, the dual, the bilateral relations of man and man, of each man to his neighbor, are relations fraught with social danger. A pair of men is what I may call an essentially dangerous relation*" (30). Once we enter into relations with others, others that are more than a pair, that is, we have entered relations that command our loyalty. Triadic relations are correlated with loyalty and peacefulness, whereas dyadic relations entail hostility and conflict. Thus, Royce concludes that war persists because nations continue to relate to each other on the basis of dyadic relations: "War is simply one case whereby to illustrate how dangerous the dyadic relations are in the social world; and how a dangerous community is one which has the form of a pair either of individual men or individual nations" (40).

This is where the community of insurance enters into Royce's overall argument and proposal. The solution to the endurance and perpetuation of war is to develop an international system of insurance that would begin with the establishment of an international bank to aid its participants in the eventuality of national crises due to natural catastrophes. A community of insurance would develop as a community of interpretation that would command the loyalty of its members. In this way, war would be from the outset outlawed and eventually made obsolete. The aim of this community of insurance would be to help each other but also to secure the mutual respect and loyalty that triadic relations presuppose, according to Royce. Through the kind of mutual aid and accountability that developing a community of insurance would instigate in its participants, we would have an instance of Abraham Lincoln's famous triadic statement: "government of the people, by the people, and for the people." As Royce summarizes and re-states in the language of an original draft of these lectures, *"whenever insurance of the nations, by the nations, and for the nations begins, it will thenceforth never vanish from the earth, but will begin to make visible to us the holy city of the community of all mankind"* (40). This holy city would be the "great community" of humanity that would have abolished war and sublimated the spiritual side of war into an "enlarged loyalty"—to use Richard Rorty's language.[29]

From the "Gory Cradle of Humanity" to the "Blessing of Civic Genius"

It could be argued that William James's famous essay from 1910, "The Moral Equivalent of War," has unfortunately eclipsed an equally, if not more powerful statement of James's views on war, namely his 1897 oration on Robert Gould Shaw,[30] delivered on the occasion of the dedication of the monument to Shaw and his regiment designed by August Saint-Gaudens and Sanford White. Shaw was the white Union colonel who led the all-volunteer African American Massachusetts Fifty-fourth Regiment. He was killed in battle on July 18, 1963, as he was leading his regiment in a charge on the Confederate Battery Wagner. After the failed charge, resulting in the death of nearly half of his regiment, he was stripped of his uniform and buried in a common grave with his black soldiers. The Confederate troops meant this to be an insult and desecration of an officer whom they must have taken to be a race traitor. Saint-Gaudens and White's monument portrays Shaw on horseback, looking forward, austere, stoic, and resolute, sword in hand, as if ready to lead in a charge. He is flanked by his regiment of black soldiers, whose faces are carefully cast, fully individualizing each soldier's face in fine lines of pride, resoluteness, courage, and even joy. The monument is majestic in the way it brings holistic and unifying motion but also careful individuation and personalization. As Harvey Cormier put it, Saint-Gaudens and White's monument succeeded "strikingly in representing for all the men of the Fifty-fourth not only a single, unified, purposeful motion but also their full human individuality."[31] It is undoubtedly a powerful and moving monument, which is why it has been deemed one of the most important nineteenth-century American sculptures. William James's oration is equally moving, ceremonial, and philosophically enlightening.

From the outset, James makes it clear that this monument should not be understood to be celebrating military victory, or the martial virtues of those who died in the Civil War. The monument to Shaw and his soldiers is a very different type of monument than those that have long ago been, and will continue to be, erected to the "great generals" and the abstract soldiers. James spoke the following words: "Our nation had been founded in what we may call our American religion, baptized and reared in the faith that man requires no master to care of him, and that common people can work out their salvation well enough together if left free to try."[32] And this is what Shaw and the Fifty-fourth both stood for and died for. Their genius, as James argues, was in fact to show that "Americans of all complexions and conditions can go forth like brothers, and meet death cheerfully if need be, in order that this religion of our native land shall not become a failure on earth" (67). Yet it is not the glory of dying that James underscores; nor does he offer a laudation to the "spiritual" side of war, as important as it may be. James is explicit and adamant about distancing himself from any kind of militaristic celebration, even as he is dedicating a monument to soldiers who died in war. He writes: "War has been much praised and celebrated among us of late as a school of manly virtue; but it is easy to exaggerate on this point. Ages ago, war was the gory cradle of mankind, the grim-featured nurse that alone could train our savage progenitors into some semblance of social virtue, teach them to be faithful one to another, and force them to sink their selfishness in wider tribal needs" (72). Indeed, this is why war and war's heroes continue to be sung by the poets of nations. And for this reason there is no need to press the point on the military heroism of Shaw and his men, argues James. But there is a more noble and difficult achievement that is too easily forgotten, in James's view. It has not been bred into the bone of human beings by the survival of the fittest, but rather, it is a "lonely kind of courage (civic courage as we call it in peace-times)" (72). It is to this lonely, civic courage that the monuments of nations should be erected, of which the one to Shaw and the Fifty-fourth Regiment is an example. In juxtaposing military heroism and virtue that has been bred into human beings by history, with civic courage, which is an acquired social virtue, James then provides an encomium for what he calls civic genius:

> The deadliest enemies of nations are not their foreign foes; they always dwell within their borders. And from these internal enemies civilization is always in need of being saved. The nation blest above all nations is she in whom the civic genius of the people does the saving day by day, by acts without external picturesqueness; by speaking, writing, voting reasonably; by smiting corruption swiftly; by good temper between parties; by

the people knowing true men when they see them, and preferring them as leaders to rabid partisans or empty quacks. Such nations have no need of wars to save them. (72–73)

What the Civil War has taught us is that social evils have to be checked in time, before they grow into bellicose causes. War leaves in its wake misery, increased powers of government, corruption, inflated budgets, and thus the seeds of future wars, "unless the civic virtues of the people save the State in time" (73). War is neither the health of the people, nor of the state. Rather, it is the active civic genius and courage of citizens that saves the people and the state from war.

James returned to the question of war toward the end of his life in a series of public interventions, one of which carried the title "The Psychology of the War Spirit,"[33] and which eventually became his famous "The Moral Equivalent of War"—rightly deemed one of the best American essays of the century.[34] This text revolves around the question of explaining the role of the martial spirit and its enduring relevance. James claims that pacifists have to directly address the psychological and moral relevance of the war spirit. Simply calling for the abolition of war will not do. The first three-quarters of "The Moral Equivalent of War" is devoted to analyzing a variety of pro-war arguments, or more precisely, philosophies that celebrate and foreground the importance of war in the education of humanity and the exaltation of nations. James is adamant that, even as an avowed pacifist, he will not speak of the "bestial" side of war. Rather, he wants us to understand why war enthralls and inflames our imaginations with its pomp, romance, and heroes. As James overviews different arguments that capitalize on this aspect of war, he discusses Steinmetz's *Philosophie des Krieges*. He writes that Steinmetz's work is a good example of the celebration of the moral and spiritual side of war, thus articulating a far more complex and sophisticated view. James offers a very good summary of Steinmetz's arguments:

> War, according to this author [Steinmetz], is an order instituted by God, who weighs the nations in its balance. It is the essential form of the State, and the only function in which peoples can employ all their powers at once and convergently. No victory is possible save as the resultant of a totality of virtues, no defeat for which some vice or weakness is not responsible. Fidelity, cohesiveness, tenacity, heroism, conscience, education, inventiveness, economy, wealth, physical health and vigor—there isn't a moral or intellectual point of superiority that doesn't tell, when God holds his assizes and hurls the peoples upon one another. *Die Welgeschichte ist das Weltgericht*"[35]

Steinmetz, continues James, is a "conscientious thinker" but the overall argument can be summarized in a formulation by Simon Patten, "mankind was nursed in pain and fear," and the transition to a "pleasure-economy" may be fatal to humanity. James turns this phrase into an even more insightful one: "If we speak of the *fear of emancipation from the fear-regime*, we put the whole situation into a single phrase; fear regarding ourselves now taking the place of the ancient fear of the enemy."[36] Those who worship the gods of war preserved a religion that is the continuation of human immaturity, subordination, and moral tutelage. The unwillingness to face this fear of ourselves free from the disciplining and commanding fear of the enemy is in fact an unwillingness to engage our moral and aesthetic imaginations. And this is why James finds the pacifist position inadequate—not because it rejects war, whose horrors and tragedy are all too evident, but because it fails to offer both moral and aesthetic alternatives to the seductions and passions of war. "So long as anti-militarists propose no substitute for war's disciplinary function, no *moral equivalent* of war, analogous, as one might say, to the mechanical equivalent of heat, so long they fail to realize the full inwardness of the situation."[37] James's moral equivalent of war is what he called in his oration on Shaw the development of civic courage and genius:

> The martial type of character can be bred without war. Strenuous honour and disinterestedness abound elsewhere. Priests and medical men are in a fashion educated to it, and we should all feel some degree of it imperative if we were conscious of our work as an obligatory service to the state. We should be *owned*, as soldiers are by the army, and our pride would rise accordingly. We could be poor, then, without humiliation, as army officers now are. The only thing needed henceforth is to inflame the *civic temper* as past history has inflamed the military temper.[38]

As a superseding equivalent for the blinding and inflaming passions of war, James proposes the fearless and self-conscious *civic temper* of civic genius. If war continues to visit humanity with its scourge, plagues, and seeds of future wars, it is because we have failed to rise as a democratic nation. Greater than the fear of the enemy is the fear that holds back a nation from exercising its moral imagination and commanding the loyalty of citizens to its own civic genius.

Conclusion: "Fighting Terrorism with Democracy"

Fred Anderson and Andrew Cayton open their sweeping, timely, and indispensable *The Dominion of War: Empire and Liberty 1500–2000* by urging us to imagine walking around the Washington D.C. Mall during the winter, when most of the trees have lost all their leaves and we have unimpeded views of most of the buildings.[39] More specifically, they urge us to imagine what we would see as we stood right at the vortex of Maya Lin's Vietnam Memorial, where the black wall inscribed with the 58,000 names of U.S. soldiers who died in that lost war, "the names of the dead hang[ing] over us with an almost unbearable weight," turns obliquely, forming an angle. From that intersection our sight of vision is turned in two directions: toward the Washington Monument in the East, and the Lincoln Memorial in the West. Why is our gaze directed to these two particular monuments? Anderson and Cayton ask. What about the other war memorials in the Mall: the Korean War memorial, across the reflecting pool on the south side, or the World War II memorial "bestride the Mall as the head of the Reflecting Pool, claiming a place as central as Washington's obelisk and Lincoln's Doric Shrine"? They then go on to summarize, in essence, the central thesis of their book:

> Silent though their stones may be, the monuments on the Mall speak unmistakably to Americans about the relationship between, and their relative importance of, five wars—the Revolution, the Civil War, the Korean Conflict, the Vietnam War, and World War II. Even stronger implicit messages can be discerned in the *absence* of monuments commemorating other conflicts: the War of 1812, the Mexican-American War, the Spanish-American War, World War I, numerous military interventions in the Caribbean and beyond, and three dozen or more Indian wars by which the citizens of the Republic appropriated lands that native peoples had called home for a thousand generations.

If we add to their catalogue of wars that gathered by William Blum in his *Rogue State: A Guide to the World's Only Superpower*, it becomes overwhelmingly difficult not to conclude that war has punctuated the life of U.S. citizens on a yearly basis.[40] It is similarly difficult not to find the influences of such wars on the development, eclipse, and eventual resurgence of pragmatism over the last century. Menand's claim about the centrality of the Civil War in framing the emergence of pragmatism is right, but as to what happened afterward, his analysis has to be seriously revised, especially his central claim that pragmatism has been useless in confronting the war of ideas and the idea of war of the second half of the twentieth century. It has been my contention in this essay that pragmatism is a philosophy that has opposed, challenged, and critiqued the war spirit in American life. Even when pragmatists have not been self-confessed pacifists, they have argued that there are other alternatives to war. At the core of the reconstruction of philosophy, social theory, and social psychology that pragmatists undertook has been the project of offering alternatives to the meaning-granting function that societies have bestowed on war and war-making. At the very least, running as a recurring theme, and even a philosophical tenet, through some of works of the most important pragmatists has been suspicion of the claim that, as Bourne put it, "war is essentially the health of the State," and conversely that "the ideal of the State is that within its territory its power and influence should be universal."[41]

John Dewey, the target of intense criticism by Bourne, would eventually come to share Bourne's views on war and the rise of a militaristic, anti-democratic state. Late in his life, Dewey argued against U.S. intervention in the then-dawning global conflict by arguing: "It is quite conceivable that after the next war we should have in this country a semi-military, semi-financial autocracy, which would fasten class divisions on this country for untold years. In any case we should have the suppression of all the democratic values for the sake of which we professedly went to war."[42] For Bourne and Dewey as well as for Royce and James, as I have shown here, war eviscerates the democratic institutions and temper of a republic while subjecting its citizens to the reign of fear and terror of a state apparatus that grows more powerful as it grows more secretive and punitive. Republics whose civic genius and democratic intelligence are vital and vibrant have no need for wars, argued both Royce and James.

I want to close by noting that Richard Rorty shared this quintessential pragmatist suspicion of war, even if his contribution in this volume may seem to suggest otherwise. Toward the end of his life, Rorty published a couple of very pointed essays in which he expressed great concern with the possibility of the destruction of American democracy through its militarization. In October of 2002, as preparations for the invasion of Iraq were set in motion, Rorty wrote in *The Nation:*

> If we cannot forestall such attacks [terrorist attacks with nuclear weapons], we may nonetheless be able to survive them. We may have the strength to keep our democratic institutions intact even after realizing that our cities may never again be invulnerable. We may be able to keep our moral gains—the increase in political freedom and in social justice—made by the West in the past two centuries if 9/11 is repeated year after year. But we shall only do so if voters of the democracies stop their governments from putting their countries on a permanent war footing — from creating a situation in which neither the judges nor the newspapers can restrain organizations like the FBI from doing whatever they please, and in which the military absorbs most of the nation's resources.[43]

In a piece published in the April 1, 2004, issue of the *London Review of Books,* Rorty once again expressed his concern for the future of American and Western democracies were more terrorist attacks to take place. Criticizing Christopher Hitchens's jeering remarks about American leftists, namely, that they are more afraid of John Ashcroft than of Osama Bin Laden, Rorty said, "I am exactly the sort of person Hitchens has in mind. Ever since the White House rammed the USA Patriot Act through Congress, I have spent more time worrying about what my government will do than about what the terrorist will do."[44] Rorty ended his essay with a sobering and bleak warning that echoes not just Bourne but also Dewey and James, two of his most adored pragmatists and surely the ones who influenced him the most: "In a worst-case scenario, historians will someday have to explain why the golden age of Western democracies, like the age of Antonines, lasted only about two hundred years. The saddest pages in their books are likely to be those in which they describe how citizens of the democracies, by their craven acquiescence in governmental secrecy, helped bring the disaster on themselves."[45]

The greatest enemies of a democratic republic, warned James, are not foreign adversaries, or terrorists in our day, but the genuflection before and surrender of our democratic institutions to a state that sacrifices the civic genius of a nation to wars that only seed future wars, increase economic inequality, and squander the life of younger generations. Pragmatists are romantics that ask how an idea or institution can enhance the life of citizens (but here romanticism and realists converge, if only too infrequently); and war is one of those institutions that has at the very least outlived its usefulness and at worst become a major threat to our political freedoms and social justice, or what Rorty called our moral gains. War may have been the grotesque nurse of humanity, but we have entered the youth of our democracy, what Kant with Emerson, Dewey, Rorty, and West's assent, called our entry into maturity.

Notes

1. The best articulation of this view of pragmatism is to be found in Richard Rorty's essay, "Pragmatism and Romanticism," in *Philosophy as Cultural Politics, Philosophical Papers, Volume 4* (Cambridge: Cambridge University Press, 2007), 105–19.

2. See Joseph Brent, *Charles Sanders Peirce: A Life*, rev. ed. (Bloomington: Indiana University Press, 1998), 61–62. Not only did Peirce seek to evade military service, but he also had no particular sympathy for the abolitionist cause.

3. S. Rudolf Steinmetz, *Die Philosophie des Krieges* (Leipzig: Verlag von Johann Ambrosius Barth, 1907).

4. Martin Woessner has pointed out that Oliver Wendell Holmes Jr. glorified the soldier's spirit, and that my overall argument that pragmatists challenge it

needs to be attenuated. Martin may be right. Holmes, of all pragmatists, suffered most personally the effects of the Civil War. He surely was profoundly proud to have been a soldier, as is perhaps underscored by story that he kept in his closet the uniform he wore as a solider, with the holes where he had been wounded. In his famous Memorial Day speech from May 30, 1895, Holmes said, perhaps criticizing views like those espoused by Royce and James: "For although the generation born about 1840, and now governing the world, has fought two at least of the greatest wars in history, and has witnessed others, war is out of fashion, and the man who commands attention of his fellows is the man of wealth. Commerce is the great power. The aspirations of the world are those of commerce. Moralists and philosophers, following its lead, declare that war is wicked, foolish, and soon to disappear." It is against this view, that he then affirms the soldier's faith: "Behind every scheme to make the world over, lies the question, What kind of world do you want? The ideals of the past for men have been drawn from war, as those for women have been drawn from motherhood. For all our prophecies, I doubt if we are ready to give up our inheritance. Who is there who would not like to be thought a gentleman? Yet what has that name been built on but the soldier's choice of honor rather than life? To be a soldier or descended from soldiers, in time of peace to be ready to give one's life rather than suffer disgrace, that is what the word has meant; and if we try to claim it at less cost than a splendid carelessness for life, we are trying to steal the good will without the responsibilities of the place. We will not dispute about tastes. The man of the future may want something different. But who of us could endure a world, although cut up into five-acre lots, and having no man upon it who was not well fed and well housed, without the divine folly of honor, without the senseless passion for knowledge outreaching the flaming bounds of the possible, without ideals the essence of which is that they can never be achieved? I do not know what is true. I do not know the meaning of the universe. But in the midst of doubt, in the collapse of creeds, there is one thing I do not doubt, that no man who lives in the same world with most of us can doubt, and that is that the faith is true and adorable which leads a soldier to throw away his life in obedience to a blindly accepted duty, in a cause which he little understands, in a plan of campaign of which he has little notion, under tactics of which he does not see the use" (Oliver Wendell Holmes Jr., "A Soldier's Faith," online at www.globalfuture.com/memorial-holmes1895.htm). This passage allows us to speculate that Steinmetz may not have been the only point of reference for Royce and James. It is very likely that James had read or heard about Holmes's Memorial Day speech; thus, we can speculate that his "The Moral Equivalent of War" is a response to Holmes's "A Soldier's Faith."

5. See Hans Joas, *G. H. Mead: A Contemporary Re-Examination of His Thought* (Cambridge, Mass.: MIT Press, 1997 [1985]), and especially Dimitri N. Shalin, "G. H. Mead, Socialism, and the Progressive Agenda," in Mitchell Aboulafia, ed., *Philosophy, Social Theory, and the Thought of George Herbert Mead* (Albany: SUNY Press, 1991), 21–56.

6. See George Herbert Mead, *Selected Writings,* ed. Andrew J. Reck (Chicago: University of Chicago Press, 1981). See especially, "The Psychology of Punitive

Justice," and "National-Mindedness and International-Mindedness," 212–39, and 355–70, respectively.

7. See Kim's essay, chapter 2 in this volume.

8. See Westbrook's discussion of Bourne's critique, chapter 12 in this volume.

9. See Robert B. Westbrook, *John Dewey and American Democracy* (Ithaca, N.Y.: Cornell University Press, 1991), especially chapter 7, "The Politics of War"; and Steve C. Rockefeller, *John Dewey: Religious Faith and Democratic Humanism* (New York: Columbia University Press, 1991), especially chapter 6, "Pragmatism, Progressivism, and the War." See also Westbrook's outstanding piece "Bourne over Baghdad," *Raritan* 27 (Summer 2007): 104–17.

10. Louis Menand, *The Metaphysical Club: A Story of Ideas in America* (New York: Farrar, Strauss and Giroux, 2001). See in particular the epilogue, where Menand makes explicit this framing. In a public, albeit unpublished, lecture entitled "War and Pragmatism" (2001, manuscript), Menand expanded on this framing of his history of pragmatism, linking it to the then-recent events of 9/11.

11. Menand, *Metaphysical Club,* 440.

12. Ibid., 441.

13. Ibid.

14. See Dagmar Barnouw, *The War in the Empty Air: Victims, Perpetrators, and Postwar Germans* (Bloomington: Indiana University Press, 2005), and my essay "The Literature of Urbicide: Friedrich, Nossack, Sebald, and Vonnegut," *Theory & Event* 10, no. 2 (2007), online at http://muse.jhu.edu.libproxy.cc.stonybrook.edu/journals/theory—and—event/vo10/10.2mendieta.html.

15. Menand, *Metaphysical Club,* 375.

16. See Mitchell Aboulafia, *The Mediating Self: Mead, Sartre, and Self-Determination* (New Haven, Conn.: Yale University Press, 1986), and *The Cosmopolitan Self: George Herbert Mead and Continental Philosophy* (Urbana: University of Illinois Press, 2001).

17. Josiah Royce, *The Philosophy of Loyalty* (New York: Macmillan, 1915 [1908]).

18. Ibid., 12–13, emphasis added.

19. Ibid., 13.

20. Steinmetz, *Philosophie des Krieges,* 199. Translations from the German are my own. Subsequent references are given parenthetically in the text.

21. Royce, *Philosophy of Loyalty,* 15.

22. Ibid., 26.

23. Ibid., 129.

24. Ibid., 118–9, italics in original.

25. Ibid., 139–40, italics in original.

26. See John Clendenning, *The Life and Thought of Josiah Royce* (Madison: University of Wisconsin Press, 1985), 376–90.

27. Josiah Royce, *War and Insurance: An Address* (New York: Macmillan, 1914). Subsequent references to this work are given parenthetically in the text.

28. See section III of *War and Insurance* for Royce's discussion and use of Kant.

29. See Richard Rorty, "Justice as a Larger Loyalty," in *Philosophy as Cultural Politics: Philosophical Papers, Volume 4* (Cambridge: Cambridge University Press, 2007).

30. See William James, *Essays in Religion and Morality* (Cambridge, Mass.: Harvard University Press, 1982), 64–74.

31. Harvey Cormier, *The Truth Is What Works: William James, Pragmatism, and the Seed of Death* (Lanham, Md.: Rowman and Littlefield, 2000), 155. See Cormier's wonderful discussion of both the monument and James's analysis of it.

32. James, *Essays in Religion and Morality,* 66. Subsequent references to this work are given parenthetically in the text.

33. See the editorial note on "The Moral Equivalent of War" in James, *Essays in Religion and Morality,* 252–53. Note especially the transcription of what James is supposed to have said in a panel discussion held February 21, 1906.

34. See Joyce Carol Oates, editor, and Robert Atwan, co-editor, *The Best American Essays of the Century* (New York: Boston and New York: Houghton Mifflin Company, 2000).

35. William James, "The Moral Equivalent of War," in William James, *Writings 1902–1910* (New York: Library of America, 1987), 1286.

36. Ibid., 1287.

37. Ibid., 1288.

38. Ibid., 1292, italics added.

39. Fred Anderson and Andrew Cayton, *The Dominion of War: Empire and Liberty in North America* (New York: Viking, 2005). All quotations are from the introduction, page x.

40. William Blum, *Rogue State: A Guide to the World's Only Superpower,* new updated edition (London: Zed Books, 2002).

41. Randolph S. Bourne, *War and the Intellectuals: Collected Essays 1915–1919* (Indianapolis: Hackett, 1999), 69.

42. John Dewey, "No Matter What Happens—Stay Out," in John Dewey, *The Later Works: 1925–1953. Volume 14: 1939–1941* (Carbondale: Southern Illinois University Press, 1981), 364.

43. Richard Rorty, "Fighting Terrorism with Democracy" *The Nation,* 21 October 2002, online at www.thenation.com/doc/20021021/rorty.

44. Richard Rorty, "Post-Democracy: Richard Rorty on Anti-terrorism and the National Security State," *London Review of Books,* 1 April 2004, 10.

45. Ibid., 11.

TWELVE

Pragmatism and War

Robert Westbrook

Pragmatism, the "American philosophy," has developed in an intimate relationship with American participation in the wars of the twentieth century. While it would be mistaken to suggest that this is the only or perhaps even the most important context in which to place the development of pragmatist thought, it certainly has been a pivotal one.

The dominant impulse among those American intellectuals who have identified themselves as philosophical pragmatists has been to lend their support to the nation's wars.[1] Louis Menand has contended that "pragmatism explains everything about ideas except why a person would be willing to die for one."[2] But this claim would puzzle the many pragmatists who have tried to explain to their fellow citizens why they should do just that.

From John Dewey in World War I, to Sidney Hook in the Cold War, to Arthur Schlesinger Jr. in the Vietnam War, to Richard Posner in the current "war on terror," leading pragmatists have called for war (or "war"), backed the growth of the American national-security state, and sometimes waved aside concerns about the threat each may pose to liberty, equality, and human dignity. So much so, that antiwar critics from Randolph Bourne to Dwight Macdonald to Noam Chomsky to David Cole have suggested that there is something about pragmatism as a moral philosophy that inclines it toward an acquiescence to war and numbs the critical faculties of pragmatist intellectuals, who because of their pragmatism are predisposed to be compliant servants of the masters of war. If, as Richard Rorty has said, pragmatism "names the chief glory of our country's intellectual tradition,"[3] then, such critics respond, so much the worse for our country.

This view, though understandable, is, I believe, a distortion. Without denying that over the course of the century many pragmatists have rushed in unseemly fashion to be compliant servants of masters of war from Woodrow Wilson to George W. Bush, I would argue that they might well have done otherwise without abandoning their pragmatism. Pragmatist ethics has the resources to give peace and liberty their every due, if not the resources to insist that they trump war and national security in every instance.

Moreover, in a culture such as that of the contemporary United States, I would suggest that public debate in the face of war and other contentious issues of great moment will tend to take a pragmatist turn as policymakers (and their critics) struggle to mobilize support. That is, for better or worse (I think for better), when we argue among ourselves as citizens about war, we Americans are likely to argue as pragmatists.

Unprincipled

At the heart of the criticism of pragmatic moral reasoning is the charge that it is "unprincipled." Generally, critics do not mean by this that pragmatists are altogether without principles, but rather that they tend to hold their principles too loosely—so loosely that they sometimes fall from their grasp. This criticism has become embedded in ordinary speech in which a "pragmatist" is someone (more often than not a politician) who is willing to settle for a glass half empty when standing on principle threatens to achieve less. Pragmatists are concerned above all with practical results; they are willing to compromise their principles in exchange for power. The bitter opponent of the compromising pragmatist is the rigidly principled, often powerless "true believer."

Philosophical pragmatism is grounded in the claim that a judgment is warranted because it serves human needs, not that it serves human needs because it is warranted. Warranted judgments are those that solve our problems. When pragmatists say a judgment is justified, they are paying a compliment to its usefulness. By virtue of this claim that warranted judgments are serviceable judgments, philosophical pragmatism has been tinged with the opportunism that the popular usage of the term suggests. Nothing, it would seem, is more useless or less serviceable than a principle on which we are powerless to act.

This way of thinking, critics contend, has drawn intellectuals to the flame of power. For this reason, the argument goes, in time of war, at which the impulse to serve the powers that be is heightened, pragmatists are more likely than other intellectuals to lose their grip on inconvenient principles, particularly on those principles that are in tension with the central imperative that war itself imposes on the nation state: the efficient defeat of the enemy.

The locus classicus of such criticism is Bourne's essay "Twilight of Idols" (1917), in which he attacked Dewey and other pragmatist intellectuals for backing Wilson's war. "War," he said, "has a narcotic effect on the pragmatic mind." Though Bourne's slants at Dewey himself were qualified, his assault on Dewey's acolytes was unsparing. "The war has revealed a younger intelligentsia, trained up in the pragmatic dispensation, immensely ready for the executive ordering of events, pitifully unprepared for the intellectual interpretation or the idealistic focusing of ends. . . . There seems to have been a peculiar congeniality between the war and these men. It is as if the war and they had been waiting for each other." These intellectuals had been drawn by "the allure of the technical" and lost sight of democratic principles. "Our intellectuals have failed us as value-creators, even as value-emphasizers," Bourne said. He acknowledged that Dewey himself had called, however vaguely, for "a more attentive formulation of war-purposes and ideas, but he calls largely to deaf ears":

> His disciples have learned all too literally the instrumental attitude toward life, and being immensely intelligent and energetic, they are making themselves efficient instruments of the war technique, accepting with little question the ends as announced from above. That those ends are largely negative does not concern them, because they have never learned not to subordinate idea to technique. Their education has not given them a coherent system of large ideas, or a feeling for democratic goals. They have, in short, no clear philosophy of life except that of intelligent service, the admirable adaptation of means to ends. They are vague as to what kind of a society they want, or what kind of society America needs, but they are equipped with all the administrative attitudes and talents necessary to attain it.

In their quest to be serviceable, Bourne concluded, pragmatists had shown themselves prone to "a flagging of values, under the influence of war."[4]

Bourne's worries about the marriage of pragmatism and war have been echoed again and again, often knowingly, over the course of the last ninety years. A good recent example is the criticism directed at the most practically powerful philosophical pragmatist in contemporary American life, federal judge Richard Posner, who has argued, on the basis of his pragmatist theory of judicial reasoning, for a substantial narrowing of civil liberties in the face of the exigencies of the threat of international terrorism.[5]

Posner's normative theory of judicial judgment is a specialized variation of pragmatist ethics. Like Dewey, he argues for a method of ethical reasoning centered on what Dewey termed a "dramatic rehearsal." That is, faced with a morally problematic situation, one in which we are torn between values, we rehearse in our mind various courses of conduct and estimate their consequences. On the basis of these estimates, we choose that course of conduct that will most fully redeem the values at stake.[6] More often than not, we will be unable to find a course of action that will fully satisfy all the values at stake, since they are at odds, so we opt for the most inclusive choice. Usually, as William James put it, "some part of the ideal must be butchered," so we aim to do as little butchery as we can.[7] Individuals and communities of individuals are guided in this balancing act, this weighing of consequences, by ideals of individual and collective character: we chose that balance of values, that butchered ideal, that—on balance—best serves the sort of person or society we hope to be. Since these ideals vary from individual to individual and from society to society, we can well expect that the balance that will appeal to one individual or society will have less appeal for another. Even in a culture in which most people feel the tug of the same values, there is considerable room for dispute.

As Posner sees it, the U.S. Constitution is a repository of many of the values and principles to which the American people have committed themselves, but not a set of mechanically determinative rules and standards. Instead, "constitutional rights are created mainly by the Supreme Court of the United States by 'interpretation' of the constitutional text." And—whether they own up to it or not—the Court's judges interpret the text pragmatically. They "find themselves making decisions in much the same way that other Americans do—by balancing the anticipated consequences of alternative outcomes and picking the one that creates the greatest preponderance of good over bad effects."[8]

Posner applies this pragmatic method to the legal issues raised by the Bush administration's "war on terror," those in which the balance to be struck is between the values of public safety and personal liberty. His conclusions are good news for the Bush administration, and Bush might well wish he had Posner in the Supreme Court (at least on these matters). Considered pragmatically, Posner concludes that:

> the measures taken in the wake of the 9/11 attacks to combat the terrorist threat do not violate the Constitution, except the effort to deny the right of *habeas corpus* to U.S. citizens—a measure that the Supreme Court invalidated—and to foreign terrorist suspects captured in the United States. Terrorist suspects are entitled to due process of law, but they can

be tried as unlawful combatants before military tribunals (the constitutionality of which is at this writing pending in the Supreme Court) and thus denied most of the constitutional rights possessed by criminal defendants. Additional counterterrorist measures, in particular in the related areas of electronic surveillance and computerized data mining, could be taken without violating the Constitution (even if there were a clear constitutional right to informational privacy), especially if the effect on privacy is minimized by a strict rule against using information obtained through such means for any purpose other than to protect national security. More can be done to deter the leaking of national security secrets to the media, and if necessary (I do not think it yet necessary), to crack down on extremist speech. Coercive interrogation up to and including torture might survive constitutional challenge as long as the fruits of such interrogation were not used in a criminal prosecution.[9]

Posner's arguments have, not surprisingly, elicited howls of protest from civil libertarians, protest that has extended beyond these particulars to his "unprincipled" pragmatism ("always Posner's North Star," as one reviewer commented).[10] Labeling Posner's views "alarming" and "chilling," *New York Times* reviewer Michiko Kakutani characterized his pragmatism as "a depressing relativism in which there are no higher ideals and no absolute rights worth protecting." Dismissive of "enduring values," she said, Posner had turned the Constitution into "a fantastically elastic proposition that can be bent for convenience's sake," little more than "an old piece of parchment." Similarly, legal scholar David Cole complained that "the problem with Posner's [pragmatist] approach is that it does away with the animating idea of the Constitution—namely, that it represents a collective commitment to principles." Constitutional interpretation calls for something other than Posner's sort of cost-benefit analysis: "it requires an effort, guided by text, precedent, and history, to identify the higher principles that guide us as a society, principles so important that they take precedence over the decisions of democratically elected officials. . . . [T]he Constitution embodies a commitment to principle over ad hoc judgments alleged to be pragmatic, and in particular to the principles of liberty, equality, and dignity, which cannot easily be balanced away." Posner's contributions to debates over liberty and security, Alan Ryan has wryly remarked, are "an elegant illustration of what is lost by pragmatism's abandonment of principle."[11]

Principles without Foundations

As these remarks suggest, the unease that pragmatism creates in its critics —their conviction that it is "unprincipled"—is often rooted in one of pragmatism's most important features: what has come to be termed its "anti-foundationalism." Pragmatists uniformly deny that human beings can secure the God's-eye view of the world that the pursuit of absolute, universal, and incorrigible foundations for knowledge seeks. For them, the attempt to find foundations for human knowledge outside of human practices is, as Dewey said, a futile, self-defeating, necessarily fruitless "quest for certainty."

Pragmatists insist that this anti-foundationalism does not make them skeptics, either epistemologically or ethically.[12] In order to understand pragmatism, one has to wrap one's mind around the possibility of an unskeptical fallibilism, of a way of thinking that, as Hilary Putnam has said, avoids "both the illusions of metaphysics and the illusions of skepticism."[13] Pragmatists, as Cheryl Misak has nicely put it, avoid "high-profile" conceptions of truth in epistemology and ethics, but they do so in favor of "low-profile" alternatives. For the pragmatist, inquiry of all sorts, including moral inquiry, is "truth-apt" and "a true belief is one that would withstand doubt, were we to inquire as far as we fruitfully could on the matter. A true belief is such that, no matter how much further we were to investigate and debate, that belief would not be overturned by recalcitrant experience and argument." But since no inquiry can be exhaustive, we can never know for sure that any of our beliefs are true, however indubitable they may seem at present. Truth is thus a "regulative ideal"; it is "what inquirers must *hope* for if they are to make sense of the practices of inquiry." Truth is the aim of moral inquiry, but the best that can be secured at any moment in its course is well-justified belief, which is not necessarily true. Beliefs about matters that are in doubt are always forged against a background of beliefs about matters that, for the moment at least, are not—these fallible yet undoubted beliefs provide the warrants for new belief. Hence, beliefs can be deeply embedded in history and established cultural practices and nonetheless be well-justified (if not necessarily true).[14]

In face of arguments such as this, pragmatism's critics would probably admit that the charge that pragmatist ethics is "unprincipled" is excessive and unfair. Pragmatists—even Posner—clearly have their principles. Yet the unease remains. The pragmatist's principles strike many as too loosely anchored, too low-profile. Above all, they have no extra-human, extra-social, extra-historical authority (in God or nature, for example) to back them up. Pragmatism's critics want some guarantee that somewhere, somehow, there is to be found a realm of truth and justice over which the human serpent does not trail. They want assurance that we need not rest content with well-justified but perhaps false beliefs and butchered ideals born of weighing incommensurable values and the imponderable consequences of acting on them. And guarantees and assurances of this sort, pragmatists readily admit, they cannot provide.

Immanent Critique

In a fierce exchange with David Cole, Posner dismisses Cole's appeal to a "Constitution of principle" as a lovely but empty sentiment. The Constitution is, he says, filled with principles, including several in tension with one another. The pragmatist balancing that Cole deplores, he suggests, is not really pragmatist balancing as such but the particular pragmatist balance that Posner has struck. "The reason [Cole] dislikes the administration's counterterrorism measures is that he thinks they impose greater costs, in harm to civil liberties, than the benefits that they convey in reducing the risk of further terrorist attacks. The rest is rhetoric."[15]

Posner has a point. And indeed, one of the striking things about much of the criticism of pro-war pragmatist thinking by antiwar critics over the course of this past century is the extent to which it is itself, often despite itself, cast in a pragmatist frame. For example, apart from "Twilight of Idols," and even in parts of that essay, Bourne's is essentially a Deweyan, pragmatist criticism of American intervention in World War I. Bourne demanded that Dewey and other progressive intellectuals provide him with a compelling pragmatist case for American intervention in the war, that is, a good argument that would demonstrate that war was an effective means to the democratic ends that they sought—and that he shared with them. When none was forthcoming, Bourne instead made a pragmatist case against intervention, one cast within the framework for ethical deliberation he had learned from Dewey. That is, he turned Dewey's own "logic of practical judgment" on the illogic of the judgments that Dewey made about the war.[16]

Bourne's argument fell on deaf ears. But it was, nonetheless, a powerful one. In a brilliant article titled "The Collapse of American Strategy" published in August 1917, Bourne argued that, if the end for which the United States entered the war was, as Wilsonians claimed, the creation of an international order that would prevent the recurrence of world war, it was worth asking, if one was a pragmatist, how entering the war was to serve, and whether, since April, it had served as a means to this end. The country entered the war in the face of the resumption of German submarine attacks, pro-war progressives argued, not to secure an Allied victory but to prevent a German victory and secure a negotiated "peace without victory" that could serve as the basis of the international organization necessary to prevent future conflicts. At the time, Bourne said, "realistic pacifists" like himself had argued for the use of naval force to keep the shipping lanes free, a policy of "armed neutrality" aimed directly at the submarine problem. If it was successful in rendering submarine warfare ineffectual, such a policy might have convinced the Germans that they could not win, while at the same time it might preserve the possibility of a negotiated settlement mediated by the United States. By entering the war, the United States lost any leverage it may have had for securing "peace without victory" and, indeed, lifted the hopes of the Allies for "*la victoire intégrale,*" a "knockout blow" against the Germans. If American participation in the war was supposed to liberalize the war aims of the Allies, it had been a miserable failure. Instead, American war aims themselves had been transformed. The nation had been effectively enlisted on behalf of the reactionary goal of an Allied "peace with victory," and "American liberals who urged the nation to war are therefore suffering the humiliation of seeing their liberal strategy for peace transformed into a strategy for a prolonged war."[17]

The collapse of American strategy was compelling evidence, Bourne argued, that war was as nearly inexorable as a social phenomenon could be. "War-technique" set its own end, victory, and its own means, whatever was necessary to that end; and it rode roughshod over any attempt to control it for other ends or to tame the bloodshed and repression it brought to the single-minded pursuit of its goal. Tied to any but its own purposes, war was among the most unpredictable and inefficient of means. True to his pragmatism, Bourne declared that he would not yield his fear of such inefficient means. He would resist the war-technique even when it came "bearing gifts," and any philosopher "who senses so little the sinister forces of war, who is so much more concerned over the excesses of the pacifists than over the excesses of military policy, who can feel only amusement over the idea that any one should try to conscript thought, who assumes that the war-technique can be used without trailing along with it the mob-fanaticisms, the injustices and hatreds, that are organically bound up with it, is speaking to another element of the younger intelligentsia than that to which I belong."[18]

Not only was Bourne's attack on Dewey mostly pragmatic in character, but Posner is correct to say that the sharpest criticism of his defense of Bush administration policy is cast in (sometimes ill-disguised) pragmatist terms. For example, the moment at which Cole admits that the principles "enshrined" in the Constitution that act as "critically important constraints and guides to constitutional decision-making" are nonetheless both in tension and substantially (if not wholly) indeterminate, he has moved onto pragmatist ground. And at the point that he, and other Posner critics, move from rhetorical invocations of principle (to which no pragmatist would object) and begin to hammer out opposing consequentialist arguments about torture, warrantless wire-tapping, and ethnic pro-filing, they are even more decidedly on that ground—even as they weigh the imponderable costs and benefits quite differently from Posner. Pos-ner's particular pragmatist arguments are indeed troubling, but they are so for reasons that a good pragmatist might well discern.[19]

The Pragmatist Face of Modernity

The decidedly pragmatist cast of much antiwar criticism of pro-war prag-matism indicates that Bourne and others were wrong to think that prag-matism has a bent for war and the prerogatives of the national security state (or for that matter for peace and expansive claims for civil liberty). But it also leads me to a wider and more speculative hypothesis with which I would like to conclude: might not pragmatism have become the default frame for public debate in the United States?

I have myself made light of Richard Rorty's dream of a "pragmatized" American culture, offering up a satirical Rortyean version of the open-ing lines of the Declaration of Independence that such a culture would require:

> We ethnocentrically hold these warranted assertions to be the product of the justificatory practices of our community, that all men are born equal, endowed by our community, at least for the moment, with in-alienable rights, that among these are life, liberty, and the pursuit of happiness.[20]

But perhaps I was too quick to disparage Rorty's dream. Even though I suspect many, perhaps most, Americans would be loathe to admit it, has not pragmatism become increasingly the mode of argument in public life for most Americans—Christian fundamentalists and secular humanists alike? Even if we are, with Kakutani, alarmed and chilled by the thought, do we Americans not nonetheless feel compelled to argue as pragmatists when we argue in public and with our fellow citizens?

I would suggest that we often do, and that the reason we do is that as our liberal society has grown more pluralistic and marked by a diversity of what John Rawls termed comprehensive moral and religious doctrines, the ticket to participation in public debate in which those possessed of different, sometimes clashing, comprehensive doctrines argue with one another has steadily become a willingness to accept this pluralism and admit that "under the political and social conditions secured by the basic rights and liberties of free institutions, a diversity of conflicting and ir-reconcilable yet reasonable comprehensive doctrines will come about and persist." Oppression, most of us agree, is the only means to secure the hegemony of single, foundational comprehensive doctrine. Hence, "pluralism is a permanent feature of a free democratic culture."[21]

My contention is that insofar as we accept the moral pluralism Rawls described, we will argue in public (if not necessarily in private) in a pragmatist frame. We will, with Rawls, turn historicist, not foundationalist, in quest of an "overlapping consensus" of shared, constitutional values. We will, with Rawls, then resort in our political debates to a "public reason" that is recognizably pragmatist. Pragmatism or something very much like it is the default mode of argument in a pluralist, liberal democracy such as ours—and is likely to remain so as long as we remain a pluralist, liberal democracy. Like it or not (and many still do not like it), pragmatism is a public philosophy well-suited to a fractious, quarrelsome people who would nonetheless hope to remain politically one.[22] Such a people may or may not go to war, but whether they do or not, they will act under the banner of pragmatist arguments.

Notes

1. The most notable antiwar stance by a leading pragmatist was William James's bitter opposition to the American suppression of the Philippine nationalist insurgency led by Emilio Aguinaldo that followed the Spanish-American War (which James did support).

2. Louis Menand, *The Metaphysical Club* (New York: Farrar, Straus and Giroux, 2001), 375.

3. Richard Rorty, *Consequences of Pragmatism* (Minneapolis: University of Minnesota Press, 1982), 160.

4. Randolph Bourne, "Twilight of Idols," in *The Radical Will: Randolph Bourne Selected Writings, 1911–1918*, ed. Olaf Hansen (New York: Urizen Press, 1977), 337, 342, 345, 344.

5. Richard Posner, *Not a Suicide Pact: The Constitution in a Time of National Emergency* (New York: Oxford University Press, 2006).

6. John Dewey and James Tufts, *Ethics* (1908), *Middle Works, Volume 5*:292–93.

7. William James, "The Moral Philosopher and the Moral Life," in *The Will to Believe* (Cambridge, Mass.: Harvard University Press, 1979), 154.

8. Posner, *Not a Suicide Pact*, 17, 24.

9. Ibid., 151–52. It should be said that not only Posner's position on *habeas corpus* but his dissent from the administration's "extravagant interpretation of presidential authority" grounded in his or her role as commander in chief distinguishes his views from the administration's most hidebound defenders, such as former Justice Department lawyer John Yoo, author of the notorious "torture memo." This latter argument, Posner says, "confuses commanding the armed forces with exercising dictatorial control over the waging of war, the kind of

control exercised by a Napoleon or a Hitler or a Stalin" (68). On the other hand, Posner's positions on electronic surveillance, prior restraint and punishment of newspapers and other media inclined to publish leaked national security information, and the repression of Islamic hate speech, are more extravagant than those advanced publicly by the administration. Posner's position on torture is intriguing: he thinks it would be better not to justify it legally in exceptional circumstances but rather to hope that government officials will torture suspects in dire circumstances as acts of civil disobedience—acts that courts might regard leniently in the event of prosecution. Cf. John Yoo, *Powers of War and Peace: The Constitution and Foreign Affairs after 9/11* (Chicago: University of Chicago Press, 2005), and *War by Other Means: An Insider's Account of the War on Terror* (Chicago: University of Chicago Press, 2006).

10. Emily Bazelon, "Maximum Security," *New York Times Book Review,* 10 September 2006.

11. Michiko Kakutani, "Constitution Bending: A Jurist's Argument," *New York Times,* 19 September 2006; David Cole, "How to Skip the Constitution," *New York Review of Books,* 16 November 2006, 21, 22; Alan Ryan, "The Legal Theory of No Legal Theory," *New York Times Book Review,* 14 September 2003.

12. Posner is the perhaps the pragmatist (a good argument could be made for Stanley Fish) least concerned about courting the charge of skepticism. See especially Posner, *The Problematics of Moral and Legal Theory* (Cambridge, Mass.: Harvard University Press, 1999).

13. Hilary Putnam, *Renewing Philosophy* (Cambridge, Mass.: Harvard University Press, 1992), 180.

14. Cheryl Misak, *Truth, Politics, Morality: Pragmatism and Deliberation* (London: Routledge, 2000), 49, 98, 69.

15. Richard Posner, "'How to Skip the Constitution': An Exchange," *New York Review of Books,* 11 January 2007.

16. I am summarizing and compressing the argument I make at greater length in Robert Westbrook, *John Dewey and American Democracy* (Ithaca, N.Y.: Cornell University Press, 1991), 195–212, 367–69. I have argued for the pertinence of Bourne's arguments to the Iraq War in "Bourne Over Baghdad," *Raritan* 27 (2007): 104–17.

17. Randolph Bourne, "The Collapse of American Strategy," in *War and the Intellectuals: Collected Essays 1915–1919,* ed. Carl Resek (New York: Harper and Row, 1964), 22–35.

18. Bourne, "A War Diary" (1917), in *Radical Will,* 324–325; "Twilight of Idols," 336.

19. As it happened, as I was writing the initial version of this essay, Cole delivered a lecture at the University of Rochester in which he argued against Bush administration policy in largely consequentialist, pragmatist terms. See *Campus Times* (University of Rochester), 22 February 2007. For other examples of the sort of pragmatist response to Posner I have in mind, see John Mueller, *Overblown: How Politicians and the Terrorism Industry Inflate National Security Threats, and Why We Believe Them* (New York: Free Press, 2006), and David Luban, "Eight

Fallacies about Liberty and Security," in *Human Rights in the "War on Terror,"* ed. Richard Ashby Wilson (Cambridge: Cambridge University Press, 2005), 242–57.

20. Robert Westbrook, *Democratic Hope: Pragmatism and the Politics of Truth* (Ithaca, N.Y.: Cornell University Press, 2005), 160.

21. John Rawls, *Justice as Fairness: A Restatement* (Cambridge, Mass.: Harvard University Press, 2001), 33–34, 36.

22. I should perhaps emphasize that my contention here leaves us far short of Rorty's fully pragmatized public culture. Insofar as Americans have increasingly resorted to a pragmatic public reason, many, perhaps most, have done so strategically and not as a matter of principle. To use Rawls's terms, they have adopted it as a *"modus vivendi,"* not as an abiding commitment to an "overlapping consensus." But, as he argued, this may be the first step toward principled pragmatism.

THIRTEEN

Laughter against Hubris:
A Preemptive Strike

Cynthia Willet

Tragic Beginnings

For twelve years, the United States had stood alone and uncontested as the sole world superpower. Then came the terror of September 11, the crumbling World Trade Center towers, the damaged face of the Pentagon, and thousands dead. The deaths and destruction prompted much speculation on the reasons for anti-American sentiments and on how the United States might exert its power with a sense of cosmopolitan responsibility. The terror also brought about widespread sympathy for the United States. When French President Jacques Chirac proclaimed that "we are all Americans now," there was a real chance for the United States to exercise global leadership and to lay the groundwork for world peace. But then something went wrong. Instead of seeking world peace, the United States announced a thinly veiled and highly risky strategy for global domination. We were to be engaged in a war against terrorism without definition or end. With plans to invade Iraq, the United States lost the sympathy it had gained from the attack, and France joined with Germany to lead world opinion in the United Nations against American aggression. "When France is accusing the U.S. of arrogance, and Germany doesn't want to go to war, you know something is wrong," philosopher-at-large Chris Rock quipped—and for good reason.[1] To be sure, the United States has a sporadic history of imperialist invasion, taken up in good measure by David Kim in this volume, but the post-9/11 agenda shifted that imperialism into high gear.

254

The anger unleashed in the 9/11 attacks surprised Americans, who were for the most part genuinely unaware of our long history of imperialist invasion and the hostility that cultural and economic domination, let alone the presence of U.S. troops, can generate abroad. Mainstream historians have preferred to portray the United States as a passive defender of democracy, not as an active imperialist power. Those historians who portray the United States as an active empire typically insist that this imperial role is for the good.[2] Prominent historian John Lewis Gaddis, for example, claims that the politics of the Cold War required that the United States assert its power as "a new kind of empire—a democratic empire."[3] Only a few historians have seen through such claims of American innocence as one more romance with American exceptionalism. And yet extensive empirical research demonstrates fairly clearly that, in the words of historian Marilyn Young, "U.S. foreign policy aims first and foremost for a 'world safe and assessable for the American economic system.'"[4] The United States rarely advances pro-democracy programs, and only then when the costs are perceived to be slight. The typical consequence of American imperialism is to subjugate foreign people, viewed as racially or culturally inferior, and to drain their resources. Even the high moral rhetoric commonly used to defend an American empire is hardly exceptional. The French and the British empires also claimed to bestow the rule of law and democracy on inferior populations. Regardless of the rhetoric, imperialism's strategies are sadly the same: to tear down and replace preexisting socioeconomic structures with hitherto unknown systems of dependency.

Whatever we might think about the historical likelihood of a moral empire, the ironies that characterized the surge of patriotism following the 9/11 attack are telling. Stunned by terror in the homeland, citizens who had enjoyed, somewhat cynically perhaps, the stock market bubble of the 1990s asked what they might give back to a nation in need. In the mood of shock and mourning that followed the terror, these citizens seemed poised to break out of the exaggerated schedules of work and consumption that had shaped the years before. President Bush, claiming to be, if not our popularly elected leader, at least our "moral leader," did not call out to us to respond to the crisis with a republican ethic of sacrifice. We were not asked for the sake of the nation to ration, buy savings bonds, or trade in the keys for our SUVs for some hybrid model. On the contrary, we were asked to spend and spend lavishly as though our lives would depend upon it. In a time of crisis, we peered into the soul of our nation and found it difficult to see past the veneer of materialism that continues to both mesmerize and disturb us. The president's redefinition of duty brought to national consciousness the impact of an economy rooted more in consumption than in production, and even more precariously, in consumer confidence. And so, in the anxiety of post-9/11, we were called upon, not to make sacrifices, but to consume and to do so with undaunted confidence. Of course, the call to consume came to constitute an exceedingly pleasant if somewhat unusual embodiment of citizen duty. Many of us were ready to do our part.

The hedonistic embodiment of patriotic duty was, however, definitely going to mess with some basic philosophical distinctions that had emerged in the twelve years of the post–Cold War era. In the carnivalized atmosphere of globalization that followed the fall of the Berlin wall, the world-system *seemed* to divide between what German philosopher Cornelia Klinger portrays as the postmodernism of the rich and the communitarianism of the poor.[5] For those who could enjoy the elite postmodern lifestyle, globalization might be experienced as the freeing of the subject from essentializing categories of identity, patriotism among them. This was to be a time for enjoying bodies and their pleasures, the narcissism of unencumbered individualism, the negative freedom of fluid boundaries in a transsexual, transgender, and transnational world. It seemed as though this could be paradise. On the underside of the world system, disenfranchised populations were left struggling for a sense of belonging or recognition, a positive sense of identity and freedom, and new forms of communitarianism, nationalism, and fundamentalism.

Or so, as I say, it seemed. For it was never so clear that pomo-consumerism, at least the American brand, was not a way after all to write upon the world an American identity—in other words, just one more form of nationalism. The beauty of the first response to 9/11 was that we could have it all. We could be nationalistic citizens and pleasure-loving consumers—indeed, ever more the one as the other. We could wave our flags as proud Americans and yet yield to our most hedonistic urges—as long as these urges could be satisfied in the malls and not on the streets. (Buying drugs, according to the ongoing national campaign, finances the terrorists.) What could be more safely delicious?

And yet, as easy as this first response to 9/11 was to be, it was not going to satisfy our nation's conservative moral leadership. Perhaps the emphasis on consumption seemed a bit too feminine—not quite manly enough.[6] In any case, over the next few months, the administration would exploit the sense of national emergency and compensate for any perceived passivity in our nation's identity with a more kick-ass model of citizenship. This second response took the shape of the 2002 National Security Strategy,[7] a project originally laid out by Paul Wolfowitz in 1992 and proposed by Bush as part of his rationale for invading Iraq. The new policy would entitle the United States to so-called preemptive strikes against perceived enemies—indeed, against any power that challenges U.S. global supremacy.[8] This policy turn promised to be full of risk, excitement, and adventure—and manlier, too.

The beefed-up role of patriot as warrior of an active empire (and not merely as consumer in a passive empire) may or may not serve to advance the cause of freedom. Much depends on how freedom is defined. Certainly, the double role of consumer and warrior is geared to add overwhelming military force to make the world "safe and assessable for the American economic system" and its ideology of free markets. But the doctrine of preemptive strike would also begin to cast dark shades of meaning on the motto of mall culture, "Shop till you drop." If just prior to 9/11, Young could draw the conclusion that the United States aims to be "at once powerful and passive," the National Security Strategy of 2002 changed all of that, and for clear motives. The new get-tough security policy redresses a degree of vulnerability that mainstream America has not known before and compensates for whatever hint of passivity there may be in a service economy—countering any force that threatens to feminize us. After seeing the 1999 film *Fight Club*, I am inclined to view our national evolution to the Wolfowitz doctrine through Brad Pitt's "Project Mayhem."[9] "Let's evolve," Brad Pitt says to the timid Ed Norton. Of course, Paul Wolfowitz is not as cool as Brad Pitt, and George W's Project Mayhem (I take the W as standing for George's alter ego, Wolfowitz) does not target the credit companies; George W's Project Mayhem is aggressively pro-capitalist, capitalist with a vengeance, perhaps even a tragic kind of vengeance—or at least this has been the widespread concern.

It is said that as Americans we lack a sense of the tragic. Certainly, the miscalculations of the Bush administration brought this country more trouble than it was ever able to foresee. The weird mix of consumer capitalism and Project Mayhem militarism, symbolized in the minds of our frightful enemies by the World Trade Center and the Pentagon, profile the dangers of excess and arrogance that we have become. In the ancient logic that Defense Secretary Donald Rumsfield dismissed as part of "Old Europe," these twin dangers spell hubris. And the tragic consequences, in political theater as in classic drama, have been clear in advance to all but the doer of the deed. Old Europe's tales warn that it is of the nature of unrivaled power to overstep limits, setting loose the furies that bring it down. Of course, it has been a genuine hope among some that the United States would avoid the usual traps and use its immense power for moral purposes. The liberal philosopher, journalist, and human rights advocate Michael Ignatieff has made perhaps the most thoughtful case for the moral use of our imperial power, and I will examine his arguments more carefully in a moment. But as allies and enemies warn, the imperial logic of the superpower may not allow for the happy ending to which America aspires.

Unchecked and unbalanced, power cannot sustain a clear moral path if ever there was one.[10] Power breeds hubris, and hubris brings about resentment, anger, and doom. The intentions, moral or not, hardly matter.

After 9/11, worldly neoliberal capitalists joined with flag-waving republican patriots to rally behind an active role for an American empire and spread freedom abroad. Ignatieff, among others, termed this active power "liberal imperialism." Of course, future administrations may lead the United States to a more cautious style of imperialism, one that operates more carefully through economic partnerships with powerful allies. However, this return to pre-Bush style imperialism does not address the underlying hubris that brought about 9/11 to begin with. One wonders if our country is doomed to repeat a formula of capitalism and militarism, narcissism and nationalism, excess and arrogance—a very old logic of tragic recoil that we cannot even see. Is there an alternative role for a superpower?

Martha Nussbaum contrasts the sense of inevitability one finds in classical tragedy with the comic mindset of the American sensibility.[11] If ancient tragedians mourned the blunders that bring about downfall, the comic sensibility acknowledges vulnerability and dependence on others and thereby avoids tragic ruin. Nussbaum does not herself explore the ethics of comedy beyond her brief allusion to its formal character, the avoidance of conflict. But what if we were to play along with Nussbaum's broader claim and grant that she has steered us toward a truly salutary element of mainstream American identity? Might we find on the surface of American culture some profound comic insight that takes us beyond the blindness to excess and arrogance that the American disavowal of tragedy otherwise implies?

That Awesome Thing: Liberal Empire

In a January 2003 *New York Times Magazine* article, "The Burden," Ignatieff gently urges the United States to wake to its new responsibility as empire: "Ever since George Washington warned his countrymen against foreign entanglements, empire abroad has been seen as the republic's permanent temptation and its potential nemesis. Yet what word but 'empire' describes the awesome thing that America is becoming?" He continues: "The 21st century imperium is a new invention in the annals of political science, . . . a global hegemony whose grace notes are free markets, human rights and democracy, enforced by the most awesome military power the world has ever known. . . . In this vein, the president's National Security Strategy . . . commits America to lead other nations toward 'the single sustainable model for national success,' . . . free markets and liberal democracy."[12]

Ignatieff cautions that this mission is not without its danger. "As the United States faces this moment of truth, John Quincy Adams's warning of 1821 remains stark and pertinent," he writes. Citing the words of the famous founding father, we have "to ask whether in becoming an empire [America] risks losing its soul as a republic." "What every schoolchild also knows about empires is that they eventually face nemeses. . . . To call America the new Rome is at once to recall Rome's glory and its eventual fate. . . . [T]he city on a hill . . . now has to confront . . . a remote possibility that seems to haunt the history of empire: hubris followed by defeat."[13]

Ignatieff is among a booming chorus of voices that warn the United States of its arrogance. In 1999, before 9/11 alerted the American public to the hostility that imperial power provokes abroad, Thomas Friedman reported on a shift in the discourse of our extreme critics in the Middle East. In 1996, "Iran's mullahs had began calling America something other than the 'Great Satan.' They had begun calling it 'the capital of global arrogance.' "[14] The shift from the theological language of good and evil to the older language of hubris reflects in part the need to forge a political ethics that translates across cultural boundaries. The Bush administration might take note: the pagan discourse of hubris may indeed garner a transnational appeal that the self-righteous quasi-Christian discourse of good and evil lacks. "Enron embodies Nobel-class hubris," we hear after the corporation's fiasco.[15] This is a deregulated world of out-of-control corporate monopolies, a post-Columbine world of queen bees and out-of-control bullies in the public schools, a global society in which one super-power is no longer balanced by another.[16]

The resentment toward the hubris of the American lifestyle of deregulated power not only resonates at home, but it crosses boundaries. The toned-down accusations of the mullahs might not have shifted the brunt of the perception of fanaticism away from the Islamists toward the Americans. The language does, however, reflect substantial ethical concerns with the single-mindedness of monopolistic capital and unipolar power. Friedman gave us a glimpse into how American zeal is viewed across the world in the same 1999 article: "We Americans are the apostles of the Fast World, the prophets of the free market and high priests of high tech. We want 'enlargement' of both our values and our Pizza Huts. We want the world to follow our lead and become democratic and capitalistic."[17] But if the internationalist agenda of prior administrations made enemies, the Bush sabotage of internationalism and the subsequent bravado of its National Security Strategy seems destined to do more than make enemies; the Bush sabotage, to cite a line from Aristotle's study of tragedy, has made "enemies out of our friends."[18]

The tragic warnings against hubris echo back before the days of Rome. In his genealogical studies of moral terms, Nietzsche contrasts the theological language of good and evil with the pagan ethics of the Greeks.[19] He explains that the common people, or *demos,* of ancient Athens used the category of hubris as a tool for restraining not only tyrants but all kinds of elites. While the Hellenic people encouraged competition (*agon*) for honor and status, they thought to establish restraints on power so that contests would not degenerate into what Nietzsche describes as "a fight of annihilation." We might ponder, Nietzsche writes, "the original meaning of ostracism. . . . 'Among us, no one shall be the best; but if someone is, then let him be elsewhere'. . . . Why should no one be the best? Because then the contest would come to an end and the eternal source of life for the Hellenic state would be endangered." What becomes of those whom the gods behold without a rival? They are "seduce[d by these same gods] to a deed of hubris," madness, and doom.[20]

Despite the reference to the gods, Nietzsche's statement coheres with contemporary scholarship. This scholarship corrects the traditional view, which reduces hubris to the attitude of pride or a religious offence against the gods.[21] As N. R. E. Fisher writes, what liberals explain in terms of the "basic rights of the citizen not to be abused, or exploited or treated violently, Greeks often preferred to express . . . in terms of honour and shame." Charges of hubris were directed on behalf of conquered people or lower classes against imperialist states and the rich or ruling classes as "peasant-citizen democracy" grew more effective in Greek states. An attack on the honor of the individual or group was viewed as a major crime, destabilizing the community and risking social unrest or revolution and war. Because of the danger of the elites, the people (or *demos*) demanded laws and ethical codes to protect them against hubris as well as to secure some degree of redistribution of the wealth.[22] Those who were the target of hubristic acts or policies were expected to act out in rage and seek revenge. While classic scholarship traces the ethical codes against hubris at least as far as Egypt, Wole Soyinka observes that the codes extend into Sub-Sahara Africa.[23]

Today we understand the logic of nemesis less in terms of the fatal cycles of anger and revenge than of rational decisions and political fact. "Since the beginnings of the state system in the 16th century, international politics has seen one clear pattern—the formation of balances of power against the strong," observes Fareed Zakaria shortly after the invasion of Iraq in his *Newsweek* article "The Arrogant Empire."[24]

It is odd that contemporary defenders of an active American empire invoke the mythos of hubris repeatedly, as though compelled by some force that (after that theorist of madness, Freud) I am tempted to call a death wish. In any case, after invoking the specter of hubris, they do not back down. They prefer instead the bolder move and demand more, not less, power: "The question," Ignatieff writes, "is not whether America is too powerful but whether it is powerful enough."[25] Similarly, citing foreign policy expert Michael Mandelbaum, Friedman writes just before the Iraq invasion, "'The real threat to world stability is not too much American power. It is too little American power.'"[26] One has to wonder what perverse pleasure comes from tempting the fates.

The decision to invade Iraq is a case in point. Jonathan Schell observes that the global protest against the invasion of Iraq on February 15th of 2003 "will go down in history as the first time that the people of the world expressed their clear and concerted will in regard to a pressing global issue. . . . On that day, history may one day record, global democracy was born."[27] From these multitudes who spoke together against the tyranny of the United States emerged the voice of the *demos* of a global community. Perhaps this proclamation has turned out to be a bit optimistic, but still the irony of imposing democracy from above is clear. Such a politics may give rise to a democratic uprising, but it's not the democracy that the powers-that-be had in mind.

The apologists for the invasion of Iraq continue to claim to fight the forces of evil and to have moral right on their side. It may be that the Cold War is over, but the new world system is also bipolar, insists Thomas Friedman among others in order to justify their norm-imposing imperial discourse: "Instead of being divided between East and West, it is divided between the World of Order and the World of Disorder."[28] Friedman's imperial discourse may be a toned-down version of Samuel Huntington's 1993 article "The Clash of Civilizations?" As the Cold War gave way to the culture wars, Huntington wrote, "It is my hypothesis that the fundamental source of conflict in this new world will not be primarily ideological or primarily economic. The great divisions among humankind . . . will be cultural."[29] But if Friedman lacks the cheap melodrama of the clash of civilizations, it nonetheless disguises a fact: there is a single major actor on the world stage, and that actor refuses all restraint. Given that our days are limited (think China and India), it might be wise to join with other nations to lay down some international rules for restraint. And in fact, Ignatieff seems to have something like this in mind.

But for Ignatieff, it is not unrivaled power but the cheap use of power that finally concerns him. "After 1991 and the collapse of the Soviet empire, American presidents thought they could have imperial domination on the cheap, ruling the world without putting in place any new imperial architecture—new military alliances, new legal institutions, new international development organisms—for a postcolonial . . . world," he writes.[30] Ignatieff shares the concern for a multilateralism and an internationalism that neo-pragmatists have carried forward from the Cold War days. "Putting the United States at the head of a revitalized United Nations is a huge task. . . . Yet it needs to be understood that the alternative is empire: a muddled, lurching America policing an ever more resistant world alone, with former allies sabotaging it at every turn. . . . Pax Americana must be multilateral, as Franklin Roosevelt realized, or it will not survive," Ignatieff writes in the fall of 2003 as the postwar chaos in Iraq began to threaten greater danger to U.S. hegemony than the ousted tyrant.[31] To be sure, Ignatieff's neo-pragmatism takes a step in the right direction, but the perception of U.S. arrogance predates the post-9/11 mayhem; in fact, it predates the collapse of the Soviet empire. The perception of arrogance has haunted what is called the American century, and Ignatieff's gracious offer for the United States to head the United Nations is not going to make this perception go away, at least not anytime soon.

Aristotle contrasted legitimate and illegitimate regimes of power based on whether they aimed for the moderate social life that he termed "friendship."[32] A U.S.-led alliance of nations with or without the former imperial powers of Old Europe does not constitute the moderate life that he had in mind. He explains ostracism as the banishing of men or cities of outstanding influence (1284a17). Cities of such excellence and ambition may be humbled by other cities "made presumptuous by memories of having once had an empire themselves" (1284a17). One may protect oneself from the politics of leveling that hubris invokes by forming stronger alliances, but it is a misunderstanding to assume that multilateral coalitions serve in themselves to preempt charges of arrogance. As Aristotle makes clear, perverted regimes arise from an "abundance of connections" as well as excesses of wealth or power (1284b22). Only true excellence can serve to legitimate the unbalanced rule of the few. But then who can legitimately claim such unqualified excellence? The assertion of the claim itself provides grounds for the charge of tyranny. When has power ever exerted restraints on itself? It is "better policy," as Aristotle remarks, "to begin by ensuring that there shall be no people of outstanding eminence, than first to allow them to arise and then to attempt a remedy afterwards" (1302b5).

It is a mistake to understand the struggle against Westernism and its arrogance in the terms of the extremists who concocted the terror of September 11th. But the aftermath of 9/11 should sound an alarm for those lured by any new romance with American exceptionalism. The old claim that the United States escaped the class warfare of Europe and its subsequent flirtation with Marxism, reasserted recently by Richard Rorty, downplays the nation's original dependence on slave labor and the violent politics of race.[33] Today, as our corporations move their sites of production oversees, our nation continues to depend on cheap labor and natural resources from disenfranchised populations. Under the conditions of neocolonial dependency of developing countries on rich nations like the United States, it is difficult to claim for the United States the status of a uniquely moral empire or, as Ignatieff prefers, liberal leadership. A simple return to the multilateralism of the Clinton era does not suffice to foster the kind of friendship that world stability would demand.

This is because any liberal defense of an American empire with or without its expensive alliances is in fact not even liberal, at least not if by liberal we mean to include a system of checks and balances that establishes firm limits on power. Ralph Ellison restates and appropriately radicalizes the liberal suspicion of power in the ancient idiom of tragedy as he tracks the psychic and social imbalances of white supremacy in race-torn America: "If the philosopher's observation that absolute power corrupts absolutely was also true, then an absolute power based on mere whiteness made a deification of madness."[34] The tragic echo of the terror of hubris may not be audible in American culture, but it is not absent either.

The romance of America as the moral center of a new world order blinds us to the ambiguity of the moral status of any unbalanced power in a unipolar world. Beware of your enemy, echoes an ancient claim, for your enemy is who you are destined to become. Even before 9/11, dissident voices were asking rather pointedly if "globalization and the political discourse of terrorism [share] a common root in fundamentalism . . . [for they] respectively hegemonize the markets and religion with limited participation from other sources?"[35] As the United States, now armed with the doctrine of preemptive strike, prepares to face off with one evil enemy after another, voices around the world can be overheard pondering how to balance the demands of one kind of tyrant with another. Is there any way out of this uncanny hall of mirrors?

International capitalism penetrates every facet of culture and politics on a scale that is global. Some internationalists speculate that capitalism in one form or another might very well upstage even such a powerful nation-state as the United States. If so, U.S. nationalism no less than religious fundamentalism is doomed to be an ineffective if persistent reassertion of symbolic power against the neoliberal onslaught of capital. The romance of the American empire would be just another defensive shield against the demise of the nation-state, as reactionary as any other identity politics, in the face of the transnational meltdown of global capital.

Still Ignatieff gives us reasons to think that nationalism is not a thing of the past even if it is not the sole force on the world scene. He contrasts the "postmilitary and postnational" identity sought by European countries with the United States, which has remained "a nation in which flag, sacrifice and martial honor are central to national identity." If it seemed as though neoliberalism would render American-style nationalism a relic of the past, "Sept. 11 rubbed in the lesson that global power is still measured by military capability."[36] At this time, only one nation possesses this kind of capability. For Ignatieff this means that the United States alone among nation states is in the position to write the terms of the new world order.

Ignatieff's profound hope is that the United States will use its power to promote an international legal and economic system that protects a minimal list of basic human rights. Prominent on the list are the classic liberal rights to free expression in speech and religion, property, and due process, or what Ignatieff's teacher Isaiah Berlin clarified as forms of "negative liberty." Following Berlin, he insists that these liberal rights protect individuals against the tyranny of families, churches, and organic communities. As Ignatieff admits, America's critics challenge the underlying individualism of liberalism as prejudicial against non-Western cultures and proclaim a proposal to universalize a particular conception of right as "arrogant." But Ignatieff defends the minimal, liberal concept of right, and its underlying individualism, on the basis of its universal moral merit. His claim is that a list of rights that protect individuals from the tyranny of the family or community secures the greatest hope for freedom. He cannot imagine any better moral language for a global community than the liberal vision of negative freedom and the individualism that this vision protects. And he wonders what proposal of moral right could be more free from arrogance than one that grants to each individual the agency to choose the life that is best for him- or herself.[37]

Curiously, the kind of freedom of which Ignatieff speaks, the uprooting of the individual from the family, church, and state, can also be viewed as much as the effects of capitalism as of liberalism—a view systematically pursued by Hegel in his *Philosophy of Right*, for example. If capitalism together with liberalism liberates individuals from authoritarian codes of meaning, it nonetheless produces its own blind power. In the eyes of the global community, however moral the intentions, an unchecked and unbalanced superpower already entails hubris, and this hubris unravels the social bonds that any minimal system of justice requires. The National Security Strategy pushes the logic of hubris one step further, daring to nihilate (borrowing Nietzsche's language) those who challenge American supremacy. Ignatieff warns against the patent arrogance of the Wolfowitz strategy, and he is right to do so. But he does not always seem to see the hubris that any assertion of a superpower status entails. However moral its intentions, the United States cannot escape the charge of hubris as long as it aims to occupy the position of an unrivaled world power. An unrivaled power constitutes a threat to the multitudes that compose the global community. The ancient democrats referred to any form of unrivaled power as tyranny, and they let it be known that for the sake of the community this kind of power must be brought down.[38]

The Trick of Comedy

In *Upheavals of Thought*, Martha Nussbaum writes of a "characteristically American conjuring trick, turning tragedy into good news. . . . Does this determination to turn bad news into good show that . . . America . . . lack[s] a full-fledged sense of tragedy? If a full-fledged sense of tragedy entails giving up the hope that things can become better in this world, the answer to this question must be yes."[39] If Nussbaum is right, then how does this characteristically American conjuring trick work? And could it bring good news today?

Nussbaum refers us to the preface to the revised edition of *Fragility of Goodness* for further discussion.[40] While the preface does not elaborate directly on the nature of comedy, it does give hints about how tragedy might be avoided. Her claims regarding tragedy in the preface have shifted significantly from the major arguments of the book itself. I shall recount her earlier and later views briefly in order to take them a bit further. Both earlier and later arguments focus on the vulnerability of the individual to external circumstances, obscuring the political ethics of hubris and the central role of social relationships for individual well-being.

Consider her early account of the two causes of tragedy. One typical cause of tragedy, Nussbaum explains, is bad luck.[41] External circumstances can bring bad luck upon a basically good character. Her example is the somewhat rash but otherwise basically good character of Oedipus. The second cause of tragedy, according to Nussbaum, is hard choices forced on characters by external circumstances. For example, Antigone and Creon must choose between conflicting duties to family and state. In both kinds of tragedy, the audience feels fear and pity for noble characters who are not wicked and do not deserve to suffer.

Nussbaum's view of the tragic buttresses her modern liberal moral philosophy and neglects the communal context of ancient Greek tragedy. A partial clue to the communal context can be found in Aristotle's observation that tragedy enacts an ironic reversal of plot that turns friends into enemies. Aristotle himself does not develop the meaning of this ironic reversal and also indicates no interest in the role of hubris in tragic drama. However, his remarks on the tragic do point to the fact that the destruction of friendships is not incidental; the damage to friendships is part of the essence of tragedy. For a communal culture, the destruction of the web of connections leads to self-ruin. This is the meaning of tragic irony.

Following Aristotle, the early Nussbaum dismisses any claim that the noble protagonist of tragedy is hubristic on grounds that the audience would fail to identify with him or her. For Nussbaum, audience identity is important because it fosters the sympathy that she places at the center of a liberal moral education. A sympathetic response to the fallen characters prepares the audience to acknowledge a universal vulnerability to external circumstances. Friendships are consigned to external conditions for individual well-being (rather than part of one's identity). Bad luck or a difficult decision can alienate friends, and we depend upon friendships and other external conditions for a full and happy life.[42]

Choruses of classic tragedies such as Sophocles' *Oedipus* sing of bad luck, but more poignantly yet, they warn of hubris. Listen to the chant of Sophocles' chorus: "Hubris breeds the tyrant, violent hubris, gorging, crammed to bursting with all that is overripe and rich with ruin—clawing up to the height, headlong pride crashes down the abyss—sheer doom! But the healthy strife that makes the city strong—I pray that god will never end that wrestling."[43] These are the lines that motivate the defense of democratic moderation in Nietzsche's early philosophy. Nietzsche's reflections on the crime of hubris interprets this crime correctly as a provocation that disturbs the very friendships that sustain the self. Certainly, flashing forward to the provocations of an American empire, the loss of allies cannot be understood as a simple case of bad luck. The loss of friendships comes about as a direct effect of hubris. The loss of friendships is not a mere secondary effect of a hard life. The consequence of damage to others is a weakening of the self. It is characteristic of liberal theory to obscure this irony of tragic self-ruin.

In the newer Preface to *Fragility of Goodness,* Nussbaum shifts the focus of her reading of tragedy from a moral to a political context. Now she argues that an Aristotelian appreciation of our common vulnerability to external conditions (including wealth, friends and family, honor and citizenship) articulates a liberal policy that goes beyond mere moral sympathy for bad luck. Reflections on tragedy support a full-fledged economic argument for the redistribution of wealth. Moreover, Nussbaum no longer interprets the aristocratic characters in ancient drama as basically good. Our sympathies are now viewed as turning against these characters in favor of the victims of their egregious power. Human tragedy does not come from bad luck per se so much as from "defective political arrangements" and that these tragic circumstances are the result of "ignorance, greed, malice, and various other forms of badness." Her early work, she now believes, was too quick in its criticism of a Hegelian-style "synthesis" that would happily overcome bad political arrangements, including the clash of demands from the private and public spheres. As she explains, conflict between duties to family and career may make life difficult, but social policies might re-adjust the structure of employment to reflect the facts of family life. The trick of preempting tragedy, say of transforming the struggles of Antigone and Creon into a harmless battle of the sexes, is to set in place good social policies. "We must never forget that trage-dies were vehicles of political deliberation and reflection at a sacred civic festival—in a city that held its empire as 'a tyranny' and killed countless innocent people," she writes.[44] The comic sensibility, or at least, the op-timistic mindset of American life strives against such tragic vices as selfish ambition by cultivating both moral sympathy and structural change.

Nussbaum's new reflections take us far but still fall short of the dialec-tic of hubris that tragedy portends. This tragic dialectic renders what might otherwise be interpreted as a banal vice, such as vanity or greed, into the terrifying madness that hubris unleashes. Hubris, unlike any simple vice, does not just happen to leave the protagonist alone and with-out friends. Hubris names an assault on the web of friendships that con-stitute who we are. The consequences of destruction on self and other can be horrifying.

Does the logic of hubris carry any force in the contemporary world? No doubt the dialectic of tragic recoil seems to be of little relevance for a republic that not only takes itself to be immune from the old logic of Europe but also thinks of itself as disconnected from the rest of the world, disconnected even from its own past. But September 11th and its discon-certing aftermath should have changed all that. Our new world should give us some glimmer of awareness that U.S. policies abroad will sooner or later boomerang to have consequences here at home. Moral sympathy and generous American liberal institutions are good, but they are not enough. A political ethics for a world that is in fact defined by interdependence and not independence (or, what Nussbaum defends as the ontological separat-ism of liberal individualism) profits from a deeper understanding of the communal context of ancient theater than Nussbaum's liberalism allows.

Nussbaum interprets the demands of social justice entirely within the parameters of liberal individualism. Without an understanding of the social ontology of interdependence, it is difficult to grasp the impact of hubris.[45] Perhaps it is not surprising then that liberals, however well-intentioned, remain vulnerable to charges of arrogance from all over the world. The offer of the stronger to help the weaker by imposing liberal val-ues just does not suffice. Neither nations nor individuals can claim to stand alone, and yet liberalism relegates social interdependence to background conditions for self-flourishing. As a consequence, liberalism misses the symbolic gestures of domination (including forms of cultural imperialism) that can accompany even its most sincere moral claims. Nor does liberalism give serious consideration to the dependencies of strong nations on weaker ones (today we might think of the importance of oil for the over-industrialized nations or the reparations owed by Europe and the United States to the colonized) and the dialectical ironies that these dependencies portend.

The choruses of ancient tragedy represented the communal cry of the *demos* against hubris and the cycles of rage and terror that this crime would provoke. This old language of hubris translates across cultures and nation states and provides elements of an ethics for a global community, what Schell calls "the will of the world." But is the United States then doomed to be the scapegoat for this re-emerging logic? Is there in American culture any basis for joining our voice with, and not against, the multitudes? Any distinctly American wisdom that might allow us to stand with, and not against, an emerging global community?

A headline in a *New York Times Magazine* article written just after the Iraq invasion reads, "My French neighbors like 'Rugrats' and Tex-Mex. It's our soul they don't want to import."[46] Tex-Mex is delicious, but it is the French fascination for American comedy that is interesting in our context. Nussbaum has claimed that ancient tragedy offers a liberal moral education about liberal virtues, especially generosity. Nietzsche, influenced by the dialectical thought of Hegel, encourages us to extend the lesson beyond liberal virtues to a tale about hubris and the irony of power. Might we not find some corresponding wisdom in mainstream American comedy, a genre that otherwise seems to exhibit nothing more than our passive delight in easy-to-consume pleasures? Might the American preference for the apparent superficialities of the comic demeanor open a deeper perspective on freedom and democracy that could revitalize our sense of who we are, one that could steer us away from the hubris of the flag-waving, honor-seeking nation-state or even of downward-looking liberal sympathy and toward a pleasure-loving social ethic of freedom? The *New York Times* article alludes to what our alienated European allies like and do not like about American culture: "They don't want to be American, because being American implies to them a willful amnesia, a loss of familial and societal ties," the author writes. Our comedies are popular abroad, while our liberal individualism and our neoliberal values are not. But then do our comedies reveal a larger vision of America, one that unmasks our high-flying moral rhetoric and rigid individualism—preempting tragic hubris through self-humbling laughter?

Rugrats is typical of American comedy, a genre that, Northrop Frye explains, portrays a society controlled by types of bondage transformed to one of "pragmatic freedom."[47] "Comedy usually moves toward a happy ending, and the normal response of the audience to a happy ending is 'this should be,' which sounds like a moral judgment. So it is, except that it is not moral in the restricted sense, but social," Frye observes.[48] Comedy does not employ bipolar moral discourse that opposes good and evil, lest it risk its humor. But if American comedy offers a romantic vision of things, not as they are or ought to be, but as they should be, what is the pragmatic freedom that this broader vision portrays? What is this sense of things as they should be?

Two Concepts of Social Freedom, One Tragic, One Comic

The aftermath of September 11th brought conservative and liberal strategists to reconsider John Adams's famous warning that in becoming an empire the United States risks losing her soul as a republic. As the country comes to terms with its vulnerability to external forces, the model of the enclosed nation-state (with its illusion of separatism and self-sufficiency) has given way to the moral (i.e., naively self-righteous) claims of a liberal empire (needing oil). Of course, any project for American hegemony, even one that works through alliances, is going to be perceived by those who are excluded from its circle of power as hubris and may fuel what the Pentagon now calls "blowback." Hence the need for a third model of the nation-state, one that rests on interdependence in a global community. This third model would avoid imperialism's rhetoric of good and evil and would heed voices wary of arrogance and liberal empires. The comic element of U.S. culture offers us some glimpse into this alternative political ethics, one that deflates the arrogance of moralizing perspectives. The classic liberal conception of freedom as one version or another of independence does not address what a more full-bodied freedom might mean for a partner in the global community. Popular comedy, oddly enough, does.

At the beginning of the Cold War, Isaiah Berlin contrasted two concepts of freedom that continue to frame American moral and political thought and yet fail to capture what is at stake in global politics. The first concept, "negative" freedom, anchors standard American liberalism. Berlin locates this freedom as an answer to the question "'What is the area within which the subject . . . is or should be left to do or be what he is able to do without interference by other persons?'" The second concept, "positive" freedom, "is involved in the answer to the question 'What, or who, is the source of control or interference that can determine someone to do, or be, this rather than that?" Berlin traces back this second concept to Kant's notion of rational autonomy. The Kantian notion severs from the empirical self an ideal self. For continental thinkers who came after Kant, including Hegel and Marx, this ideal self could only be liberated in a rational society. Such a society, Berlin warned, may open the door to the dangers of communist, nationalist, authoritarian, or totalitarian creeds.[49]

While Berlin's Cold War–era essay is focused on defending liberalism against the authoritarian dangers of this second concept of freedom, he ends the essay with a truncated discussion of a third concept of freedom. Berlin points out that the central aims of anti-colonial and nationalist movements have never been properly addressed by the first and second concepts of freedom. In response to these movements, a third freedom emerges, one Berlin insists is not truly a quest for liberty or even equality but a struggle for status and honor. More recently, since the culture wars of the 1990s, multiculturalists have reinterpreted this third freedom (via Hegel) in terms of the politics of recognition. Berlin's neglected remarks on the third freedom shed light on these contemporary debates.

Berlin explains that positive and negative conceptions may acknowledge our interaction with others, but "I am a social being in a deeper sense. . . . For am I not what I am, to some degree, in virtue of what others think and feel me to be?" "I desire to be understood and recognized, even if this means to be unpopular and disliked. And the only persons who can so recognize me . . . are the members of the society to which, historically, morally, economically, and perhaps ethnically, I feel that I belong," a society in which I am "recognized as a man and a rival." "It is this desire for reciprocal recognition that leads the most authoritarian democracies to be, at times, consciously preferred by its members to the most enlightened oligarchies."[50] Berlin notes that this third concept, really a hybrid notion, is referred to as "social freedom." It is "akin to what Mill called 'pagan self-assertion'" but extended beyond the individual to the personality of a class, group, or nation. Berlin suggests that this concept is involved in the question of "Who is to govern us?" and he observes that the focus of this freedom is on assaults on social identity that are experienced as insults. "It is the non-recognition of this psychological and political fact . . . that has, perhaps, blinded some contemporary liberals."[51]

Liberals may aim less to be tragically blind to these social forces than for a degree of autonomy, if not anonymity, from conventional norms of honor and status. Nussbaum, for example, explicitly warns against the illiberal pursuit of honor and wealth, and she emphasizes the importance of valorizing the individual choice instead.[52] As we have said, she rests her liberalism on an ontological commitment to the existence of separate individuals, and she opposes this liberal ontology rather sharply to any romantic view that subordinates the individual to an organic whole.[53] What such a sharp opposition misses is a rich third alternative. However much Nussbaum addresses the importance of friendship for individual flourishing, her characterization of friendships as "external goods" and her portrayal of the social realm as a locus of dependency, neediness, and vulnerability (all forms of the devalued heteronomy) leaves individual autonomy as our first and foremost moral and political value. This view fails to bring to the foreground of discussion the intersubjective realm where vital, complex, and troubled dimensions of the social being take root and where a progressive theory of social freedom might be worked out. Compare Berlin's claim that the aims of nationalist and postcolonial peoples are thoroughly heteronomous and threaten true liberty.[54] Excluded from liberal theory is a third possibility for the free life beyond liberalism's autonomy/heteronomy dichotomy.

In an essay called "Home," Toni Morrison writes of concerns for "legitimacy, authenticity, community, and belonging" that motivate many of the narratives of freedom in American slave and post-slavery society.[55] At first glance, these concerns for belonging would seem to recall the struggle for recognition that Berlin finds in nationalist projects, but in fact they diverge. As Morrison reflects upon her own literary project *Paradise,* a novel that juxtaposes two kinds of communities, one that is black nationalist and male-dominated in its inclinations and the other that is not, she writes of the need to transform the "anxiety of belonging" away from the dangerous moral psychology of honor and revenge to more forgiving "discourses about home" (5). She wonders if "[black] figurations of nationhood and identity are . . . as raced themselves as the [white] racial house that defined them" and if there is not another image of the "world-as-home" (11).

Of course, since Homer's *Odyssey,* finding home has defined the center of comedy. But could the metaphor of home have any significant political value (that is, apart from the nationalist one that Morrison eschews)? Morrison offers another glimpse into the political meaning of the metaphor by drawing our attention to a popular misreading of her novel *Beloved,* one that "works at a level a bit too shallow" (7). The penultimate line of the novel ends with the word "kiss"; it is this word that she suspects may cloud the novel's driving force, as she explains: "The driving force of the narrative is not love, or the fulfillment of physical desire. The action is driven by necessity, something that precedes love, follows love, informs love, shapes it, and to which love is subservient. In this case the necessity was for connection, acknowledgment, a paying out of homage still due" (7). The repetition of the word "necessity" indicates a drive that is not a choice because it is not an option. Some vague notion of belonging characterizes a vital human need.

Morrison understands the web of connections that define us in part through a sense of debt to the past, and for an African American writer, this includes unknowable ancestors and their unspeakable pathos. The term "home" names better than love or compassion the sense of connection that is for Morrison both spiritual and selfish and that compels the individual to encounter sources of meaning outside the self that also lie within. In its final pages, *Paradise* turns from bleak tragedy to a vision of "going home" that is almost comedy (and that invites comparisons with the third part of Dante's *Divine Comedy*). "There is nothing to beat this solace . . . of reaching age in the company of the other," the narration ends.[56] That is paradise.

Liberalism's individualism makes it difficult to understand the need for connection, acknowledgment, or homage still due as core political concepts. Standard political discourse, with its socially minimalist rhetoric, too readily flattens these needs to forms of security. In contrast, romantic comedy opens beyond liberal political dichotomies of autonomy vs. heteronomy, the individual vs. authority, or independence vs. dependence, toward a more complex meaning of a free life. To be sure, like liberalism, comedies deflate the conventional values of status and honor and the political battles that ensue. But rather than cultivating a stoic indifference to the heteronomous claims, romantic comedy engages the free life through comedy's presiding genius, Eros.[57]

Interestingly, Patricia Hill Collins enlists the term "eros" to characterize the force that is at stake for women in the African American community.[58] In *Fighting Words*, Collins defines as a "visionary pragmatism" a theory of justice that fosters an "intense connectedness," and she cites Morrison's novel *Beloved* as exemplary.[59] To develop the novel's central theme, she draws upon the classic essay by Audre Lorde, "The Uses of the Erotic."[60] Oppressive racial systems, Collins writes, "function by controlling the 'permission for desire'—in other words, by harnessing the energy of fully human relationships to the exigencies of domination."[61] It is this specific concept of oppression that Collins finds in *Beloved*. For the characters of Morrison's novel, "freedom from slavery meant not only the absence of capricious masters . . . but . . . the power to 'love anything you chose.' "[62]

But then how can we conceptualize the novel's vision of freedom? Lorde's essay offers two elements. First, Lorde locates at the core of the person, not the cognitive and individual capacity for self-reflection, but a libidinal capacity for creative work and meaningful social bonds. In contrast with the Freudian view of the erotic as fully sexual, Lorde explains that "the very word *erotic* comes from the Greek word *Eros* . . . personifying creative power."[63] A liberal theory typically focuses on the damage that oppression does to the capacity to reflect and make viable choices for oneself; and oppression can and does inflict this kind of harm. But of course oppression also sharpens critical insight into fundamental choices. Lorde focuses on assaults on the erotic core of the person. Oppression may render the individual unable to feel properly, and it is this emotional incapacity that defines for Lorde the salient political threat.

A second contrast concerns the direction of the psyche. The liberal view valorizes the capacity to turn inward and reflect upon motives and beliefs. Lorde does not take this capacity lightly, but she alters its focus to the growth that begins, and culminates, in relationships. The idea of expanding the self by turning outward appears throughout American visions of individuality, including John Dewey and W.E.B. Du Bois as well as Morrison. In *Beloved,* Morrison describes love through the image of a turtle able to stretch its head outside of its shell, or defensive "shield."[64] As Lorde explains, the Greek term "eros" names, not a turn inward, but a centrifugal pull of the self outward. The individual grows with, not in reflective distance from, the community.

Lorde's poetic essay on erotic drive takes us some way toward understanding the visionary pragmatism of U.S. culture and its multidimensional quest for freedom. Still, the ethic of eros will strike the liberal defender of autonomy as overly sentimental, and in part for good reason. As we have seen, Morrison herself cautions against overemphasizing the importance of love in her novel. Lorde's essay, written in the cultural climate of the 1970s, articulates libidinal sources of selfhood but does not lay out in full the sense of connection that defines the center of Morrison's work. The driving force of the narrative is not love, Morrison notes, or at least not the "fulfillment of physical desire."[65] The driving force of the novel is not love but precedes love. Collins glosses freedom in Morrison's *Beloved* as "the power to 'love anything you chose' "; but Morrison had not written the word "power." Morrison's text reads: "a place where you could love anything you chose. . . . *that* was freedom."[66] Instead of power, and indeed, what might be reduced to nothing more than an individual capacity, she had written of freedom as though it were a place, a haunted but necessary place.

We can understand the connections that enjoyed and suffered in terms having less to do with the sublimation of libidinal desire, as Lorde's essay would suggest, than with a sense of responsible connection with the past as well as the present and the future. Place as a web of belonging names what a people in diaspora may most of all seek.

A liberal conception of autonomy acknowledges that social relations play a role in individual well-being but consigns them to the background, as props for the care of the self-reflective subject. The primary focus of the liberal subject is on a first-person narrative of self-ownership. A larger pragmatist vision (pragmatist in Frye's sense) focuses on social entanglements and unfolds in a drama of relationships. Relationships move to the foreground of the plot.

In order to capture the "intense connectedness," we might rename the force that drives Morrison's narrative "social eros." The term fits with Morrison's reference to ancient Greek and African cultures to articulate the American sensibility that she explores. She explains that "a large part of the satisfaction I have always received from reading Greek tragedy, for example, is in its similarity to Afro-American communal structures (the function of song and chorus, the heroic struggle between the claims of community and individual hubris) and African religion and philosophy."[67]

But if social eros were to replace autonomy on the central axis of normative theory, then what term best names the harm that oppression does? Morrison meditates on "the concept of racial superiority," and she describes this concept as "a moral outrage within the bounds of man to repair."[68] "Moral outrage" is a common translation for the Greek term *hubris*. In "Unspeakable Things Unspoken," she points out that the struggles of the community against hubris often define the plot of tragic drama. In Greek tragedy, it may be the function of the chorus (representing the *demos*, or common people) to warn against hubris. Not surprisingly, Morrison lists as characteristic of black art: "the real presence of a chorus. Meaning the community."[69]

Aristotle defined hubris as an "insult," or "a form of slighting, since it consists in doing and saying things that cause shame to the victim . . . simply for the pleasure involved. . . . The cause of the pleasure thus enjoyed by the insolent man is that he thinks himself greatly superior to others when ill-treating them."[70] Today, in the context of both domestic and international politics, we might think of hubris as an act of arrogance, or a crime of humiliation, and understand its perverse pleasure as what those who are morally righteous sometimes seek. The ancient Greek *demos* established codes against hubris and invoked these codes in an effort to control the elites. Morrison returns to ancient sources of democracy through her interest in classical tragedy, but she does not take as central to society the values of honor and status, and the contests in which these stakes were claimed.

If we join with liberal theorists to disparage the culture of honor, we might nonetheless re-engage a vision of the free life that classic comedy relates. Morrison's romantic vision of a home reinvents the meaning of democracy—and of what one might call, after Berlin, a new type of social freedom. The central axis of ethical discourse does not turn around the poles of autonomy and heteronomy. Morrison's focus is neither on liberal independence nor nationalist struggles for honor and recognition. Her central focus is on the acknowledgment of friendships and communities, the outrageous acts that tear these bonds apart, and the comic wisdom that allows for their repair. If the comic mindset frames a prevailing American conception of freedom, then it might be mined for something more than its form alone. From the comic vision, we might find a political ethics of eros and hubris that represents the field of force that Morrison calls home.

Notes

Thanks to Tim Craker, Robert Frodeman, Eduardo Mendieta, Harvey Cormier, Kelly Oliver, and most of all to Chad Kautzer for their helpful comments on earlier versions of this essay. Thanks also to Eduardo Mendieta and Harvey Cormier for organizing the "Racism, Pragmatism, and Nationalism" conference at SUNY-Stony Brook in May 2003, where I originally presented the essay.

1. Niall Ferguson, *Empire: The Rise and Demise of the British World Order and the Lessons for Global Power* (New York: Basic Books, 2004); Michael Ignatieff, *Empire Lite: Nation Building in Bosnia, Kosovo and Afghanistan* (London: Vintage, 2003). For a critical overview, see Eduardo Mendieta "Imperial Religions, 'Clash of Civilizations,' and the People's Church," 10th Annual Hispanic Lecture in Religion and Theology, Drew University, April 20, 2005.

2. This is the perspective of Rorty's essay, "The Unpredictable American Empire," in this volume. There he argues that "there is a perfectly good leftist case for using the military power of democratic countries to conquer countries ruled by tyrants and to replace them with democratic regimes" and that the American Left "should stick to the question of how we are going to use our imperial power" for the good.

3. Cited in Marilyn B. Young, "The Age of Global Power," in *Rethinking American History in a Global Age,* ed. Thomas Bender (Berkeley: University of California Press, 2002), 279.

4. Ibid., 279.

5. Cornelia Klinger, "The Subject of Politics—The Politics of the Subject," in *Democracy Unrealized,* ed. Okwui Enwezor et al. (Ostfildern-Ruit, Germany: Hatje Cantz, 2002), 285–302; references to anthology hereafter cited *DU*.

6. For a definitive study of what counts as manly, see Harvey C. Mansfield's *Manliness* (Cambridge, Mass.: Harvard University Press, 2006).

7. The quite radical doctrine in the 2002 version of the annual National Security Strategy (NSS) has not, to this day, been substantively altered.

8. The difference between preemptive war and preventive war should be noted here, since the former is technically a "defensive" response to an imminent attack, which is what the 2002 NSS claims it advocates, while the latter is a war of aggression initiated without such a threat: what happened in the case of the U.S. invasion of Iraq, which was a clear violation of international law. The obfuscating rhetoric of the 2002 NSS intentionally blurs this distinction, writing that "we" will "defend ourselves, even if uncertainty remains as to the time and the place of the

enemy's attack" (NSS, 19). Of course, even imminent threats are uncertain as to time and place, but the important move in the NSS document is the dropping of "imminent" while still calling it "defensive" or "preemptive." See www.white house.gov/nsc/nss.pdf

9. For an interesting discussion of the novels of *Fight Club*'s author, see Eduardo Mendieta, "Surviving American Culture: On Chuck Palahniuk," *Philosophy and Literature* 29 (2005): 394–408.

10. As *New York Times* columnist reporting on the ongoing wars in Africa explains, even in a "magical world where great powers always have good intentions," no outside intervention—whether by American, European, Asian, African or United Nations force—would be likely to solve the problems of ethnic division and conflict that rage in East Europe, the Middle East, or the Congo: "'Nation building' by outsiders is inherently arrogant and risky, and there are few success stories." See Adam Hockschild, "Chaos in Congo Suits Many Parties Just Fine," *New York Times*, "The World," 20 April 2003, 3.

11. Martha C. Nussbaum, *Upheavals of Thought: The Intelligence of the Emotions* (Cambridge: Cambridge University Press, 2001), 675.

12. Michael Ignatieff, "The Burden," *New York Times Magazine*, 5 January 2003, 22, 24.

13. Ibid., 24, 25.

14. Thomas Friedman, "From Supercharged Financial Markets to Osama bin Laden, the Emerging Global Order Demands an Enforcer: That's American's New Burden," *New York Times Magazine*, 28 March 1999, 43.

15. William Greider, "Enron's Rise and Fall," *The Nation*, 24 December 2001, 1.

16. For the best among a wave of new books on bullying among girls in the schools, see Rachel Simmons, *Odd Girl Out the Hidden Culture of Aggression in Girls* (New York: Harcourt, 2002).

17. Friedman, "From Supercharged Financial Markets," 43.

18. Aristotle, *Poetics*, trans. Richard Janko (Indianapolis: Hackett, 1985).

19. Friedrich Nietzsche, *The Birth of Tragedy and The Genealogy of Morals*, trans. Francis Golffing (New York: Random House, 1956); for hubris as "active sin," see *Birth of Tragedy*, 64; on genealogy of moral terms, see esp. "First Essay" in *Genealogy of Morals*, 162.

20. Friedrich Nietzsche, "Homer's Contest," in *The Portable Nietzsche*, ed. and trans. Walter Kaufmann (New York: Viking Press, 1974), 36, 38.

21. N. R. E. Fisher, *Hybris: A Study in the Values of Honour and Shame in Ancient Greece* (Warminster, England: Aris and Philips, 1992), 1–2.

22. Ibid., 493–94, 505.

23. Wole Soyinka's remarks at his seminar on African Philosophy and Literature, February 1999, Emory University.

24. Fareed Zakaria, "The Arrogant Empire," in *Newsweek*, 24 March 2003, 24.

25. Ignatieff, "The Burden," 27.

26. Thomas L. Friedman, "Peking Duct Tape," *New York Times OP-ED*, 16 February 2003, 11.

27. Jonathan Schell, "The Will of the World," *The Nation*, 10 March 2003, 3.

28. Friedman, "Peking Duct Tape," 11.

29. Samuel P. Huntington, "The Clash of Civilizations?" *Foreign Affairs* 72:3 (Summer 1993): 22–49.

30. Ignatieff, "The Burden," 53.

31. Michael Ignatieff, "Why Are We in Iraq? (And Liberia? And Afghanistan?" *New York Times Magazine,* 7 September 2003, 85. Hussein's execution in early 2007, after a highly politicized trial whose legitimacy was never recognized by the international community, has only further incited sectarian divisions, particularly after leaked videos of the execution recorded the sectarian tauntings of the executioners just moments before Hussein's death.

32. Aristotle, *Politics,* trans. Ernest Barker (Oxford: Oxford University Press, 1995), 1288ob29. Subsequent references are cited parenthetically in the text.

33. See Richard Rorty, *Take Care of Freedom and Truth Will Take Care of Itself: Interviews with Richard Rorty,* ed., Eduardo Mendieta (Stanford, Calif.: Stanford University Press, 2006), 152–53. Cf. Charles Mills, *The Racial Contract* (Ithaca, N.Y.: Cornell University Press, 1997). See also Lucius T. Outlaw Jr.'s and Shannon Sullivan's chapters in this volume. Outlaw analyzes the racialized foundations of Tocqueville's concept of equality in his notoriously classic *Democracy in America,* and Sullivan provides a trenchant critique of the exclusionary repercussions for a discourse and politics of race that are implicit in Rorty's rejection of prophetic pragmatism.

34. Ralph Ellison, "An Extravagance of Laughter," *Going to the Territory* (New York: Vintage, 1986), 172.

35. See "Preface" in *Democracy Unrealized,* ed. Okwui Enwezor et al. (Ostfeldern-Ruit, Germany: Hatje Cantz Publishers, 2002), 10.

36. Ignatieff, "The Burden," 50.

37. See Ignatieff's essays, "Human Rights as Politics" and "Human Rights as Idolatry" in *Human Rights as Politics and Idolatry,* ed. Amy Gutmann (Princeton, N.J.: Princeton University Press, 2001), 3–98.

38. Montesquieu had a similar understanding of tyranny. As Hannah Arendt writes: "Montesquieu realized that the outstanding characteristic of tyranny was that it rested on isolation—on the isolation of the tyrant from his subjects and the isolation of the subjects from each other through mutual fear and suspicion—and hence that tyranny was not one form of government among others but contradicted the essential human condition of plurality, the acting and speaking together, which is the condition of all forms of political organization. Tyranny prevents the development of power, not only in a particular segment of the public realm but in its entirety; it generates, in other words, impotence as naturally as other bodies politic generate power" (Arendt, *The Human Condition* [Chicago: University of Chicago, 1958], 202).

39. Nussbaum, *Upheavals of Thought,* 675–76.

40. Martha Nussbaum, *The Fragility of Goodness* (New York: Cambridge University Press, 2001), xiii–xxxix.

41. On the topic of "bad luck," see also Rorty's chapter and Mendieta's interview with Cornel West in this volume.

42. Nussbaum, *Fragility of Goodness,* xiv, 387.

43. Sophocles, *Oedipus,* in *The Oedipus Cycle: Oedipus Rex, Oedipus at Colonus, Antigone,* trans. Dudley Fitts and Robert Fitzgerald (New York: Harcourt, Brace & World/Harvest Book, 1977), lines 873–80.

44. Nussbaum, *The Fragility of Goodness,* xxii, xxx, xxxviii.

45. This social ontology is considered in several essays in Part I of this volume, particularly by Aboulafia, Bohman, and Pensky.

46. Fernanda Eberstadt, "The Anti-American Lifestyle," *New York Times Magazine,* 23 March 2003, 16.

47. Northrop Frye, *Anatomy of Criticism* (Princeton, N.J.: Princeton University Press, 1957), 169. Romantic comedy is often also associated with a critique of the work ethic.

48. Ibid., 167.

49. Isaiah Berlin, "Two Concepts of Liberty," *Four Essays on Liberty* (Oxford: Oxford University Press, 1969), 121–22.

50. Ibid., 155–57.

51. Ibid., 160, 162.

52. Martha C. Nussbaum, *Sex and Social Justice* (Oxford: Oxford University Press, 1999), 12, 11, 6.

53. Ibid., 10.

54. Berlin, "Two Concepts of Liberty," 156.

55. Toni Morrison, "Home," in *The House that Race Built,* ed. Wahneema Lubiana (New York: Random House, 1998), 5. Subsequent references to this work are cited parenthetically in the text.

56. Toni Morrison, *Paradise* (New York: Plume, 1999), 318

57. Cf. Frye, *Anatomy of Criticism,* 181.

58. See Patricia Hill Collins, *Black Feminist Thought* (New York: Routledge, 1991), 166.

59. Patricia Hill Collins, *Fighting Words: Black Women and the Search for Justice* (Minneapolis: University of Minnesota Press, 1998), 188.

60. Audre Lorde, *Sister Outsider* (Freedom, Calif.: Crossing Pres, 1984), 53–59.

61. Collins, *Black Feminist Thought,* 182.

62. Ibid., 166.

63. Lorde, *Sister Outsider,* 55.

64. Toni Morrison, *Beloved* (New York: Alfred A. Knopf, 1987), 105.

65. Ibid., 7.

66. Ibid., 105.

67. Toni Morrison, "Unspeakable Things Unspoken: The Afro-American Presence in American Literature," In *The Black Feminist Reader,* ed. Joy James and T. Denean Sharpley-Whiting (Malden, Mass.: Blackwell, 1984), 25.

68. Ibid., 39.

69. Toni Morrison, "Rootedness: The Ancestor as Foundation," *Black Women Writers,* ed. Mari Evans (New York: Anchor Press, 1984), 341.

70. See glossary entry for "wanton aggression" in Aristotle, *Nichomachean Ethics,* trans. Terence Irwin (Indianapolis: Hackett, 1985), 432.

Interview with Cornel West, Conducted by Eduardo Mendieta

[Cornel West's Office, Princeton University, April 6, 2004]

Eduardo Mendieta: Is the United States a republic or an empire?

Cornel West: It's both. We're in the moment where the American empire is devouring American democracy and we have to fight it. But it's both. The United States has 650 military facilities in 132 countries, a ship in every major ocean, a presence on every major continent other than Antarctica, and 1,450,000 soldiers around the globe. It is the uncontested military power and the cultural mover in terms of shaping people's utopian desires and ideals and so on. Starbucks and Wal-Mart and McDonalds—you go right across the board, because the dollar is the currency other nations invest their financial resources in for security. It is an uncontested empire and yet, at the same time, domestically, there are democratic procedures and processes that are not dead. They've been deeply assaulted, but they're not dead. And so we've got this simultaneity: democratic practices constituting still a kind of republic representative government, and at the same time this empire. And they're in deep tension—both creative and destructive tension. Right now the Bush administration, of course, is the deep imperialist strain that is claiming to be the defender of democracy.

EM: Do you think that the present Bush administration is an example of very bad political luck, or is it indicative of something much more endemic to America?

CW: Oh, no, it's endemic, because America has always had this deep battle between imperialist strands and democratic strands. America was born as

279

an empire on indigenous people's lands and on indigenous people's backs, with the use of African labor constituting a slave, not just class, but a slave foundation—an economic foundation of the nation. The same would be true for Mexican laborers with the moving border. There is the American manifest destiny, which is nothing but imperialist ideology to justify expansionism for resources and for land and so forth. The same would be true for Asian workers being brought in and ordered to perform certain kinds of cheap labor and then sent out. So you have this long history of American imperial expansion, and alongside that you have what I call a deep democratic tradition.

EM: But don't you think that the hard power is going to overwhelm the so-called soft power, when you have an annual 400 billion dollar investment in the world's largest military-industrial complex?

CW: Here I think Sheldon Wolin is very important. Democracy is always a matter of ordinary people taking back their powers and targeting consolidated elite power. And no matter how much money and how many cannons or missiles the elites might have, they still have to, in the end, deal with the incorporation of the *demos,* of we plebeians, as it were. And so in an ironic way, what appears to be weak can turn out to be very strong, which has to do with democratic energy from below. The question is how long it can be contained. How long it can be amused and mis-channeled and so forth. And that deep democratic tradition, really, that goes all the way from both the founding fathers who had a revolutionary energy that was quite impressive against the British as just as many were fearful of unruly *demos* once they pushed the British out. But that's part of a deep tradition. And I think when you look at Emerson, when you look at Melville, when you look at Eugene O'Neill, Tennessee Williams, when you look at the best of the populace, the best of the progressivist movement, the best of the feminist movement, and, most importantly for me, the struggles against white supremacy.

EM: Is there a relationship between pragmatism as a philosophical spirit of the United States and U.S. imperialism?

CW: Well, again, pragmatism here, I think, is a very complicated intellectual tradition because there is no one-to-one correspondence between pragmatist views on truth, knowledge, and so forth, and pragmatist politics. You can be left, center, or right and that's very important. One has to be very Gramscian about this in terms of what the context is, in terms of what the temperament is of the particular pragmatic philosopher. But pragmatism, I think, is on the one hand very much a part of the democratic spirit in terms of its deep suspicion of authority, in terms of its preoccupation with preserving individuality—very different than "posses-sive individualism," now—but which is a democratic individuality, self-interrogation, self-scrutiny, and so on. The problem with pragmatism has always been that it has no significant understanding of the role of struc-tures and institutions, not just within nations but across nations. So that even William James's exemplary anti-imperialist critiques were moralistic critiques, you see. There's nothing wrong with moralism; we want to be certain kinds of persons. *Paidea* does matter. But there's no understanding of the structural, institutional practices linked to these imperial projects. Especially of his day. Especially of our day. So that pragmatism can actu-ally end up being used by elites to contain democratic energies, even though it does embody, in its own views of the world, deeply democratic sensibilities. It's a fascinating kind of juxtaposition there, and I've always felt that about pragmatism—years ago and I see that now.

EM: A parallel question: Do you think pragmatism was, is, a nationalistic philosophy in the ways that Hegel and Kant and in the 20th century Scheler and Heidegger's philosophies were nationalistic? Was Dewey nationalistic? Was James nationalistic?

CW: Well, you know it's interesting. I think that in the great pragmatists Pierce, James, Dewey, you have a cosmopolitanism there. Now, it is a cosmopolitanism that oftentimes is Eurocentric. It's like Goethe, it's like Matthew Arnold, it's like Wieland, who were the creators of a notion of this world literature. And by world literature they still meant the best of Europe across national boundaries in Europe, for the most part—with a few excep-tions of maybe Persia, and one or two poets in the East or something, you know what I mean. But what's fascinating about James and Dewey is that James's preoccupation with the democratic individuality and Dewey's pre-occupation with democratic community led them to an allegiance to democratic ideals that could easily have taken them beyond national boundaries. That's what I love about them. That's part of my own interna-tionalism as a democrat—that you can tease that out of there. And in some ways, it goes back to Emerson, really. I think Stanley Cavell is probably right that Emerson is American in terms of his roots, but he's international in terms of his routes. They take him out, you see. And I think Dewey and James, especially in their essays on Emerson, had this sense of democracy, of individuality that cuts across. And so, again, there is an ambivalence there, I think, when it comes to the national character.

EM: Do you think that a judicial pragmatism, of the kind espoused by Richard Posner and Justice Stephen Breyer, is a liability or an asset in the Supreme Court?

CW: In the Supreme Court itself?

EM: Yeah.

CW: Well, I think Breyer is a very brave man, a very decent man. I thank God he's on the Court, but that's a relative judgment. You measure him against Scalia and you want to have a party, right? [laughter] At the same time, I think that when it comes to the larger issues regarding the philosophy of law and so on and so forth, I've always viewed pragmatism in its relation to the law, going all the way back to Holmes, as [on the one hand] liberating—in terms of getting beyond certain narrow forms of legal positivism, and trying to take history and experience seriously, and the dynamism of the law I like. But [on the other hand] I always thought there was a certain parochialism to pragmatic thinkers reflecting on the law, because, you see, [when it comes to] the relation of the law to economic structures, the relation of the law to power dynamics in the nation-state, in foreign policy as well as domestic policy—there is very little talk about that when it comes to pragmatism and law. They carve out their little domestic space, criticize their positivist interlocutors, and so forth, and you get the feeling "Thank God they're doing that kind of thing," but in the end it's just so limited. When I think of people who think seriously about the law, in that broader sense of Roberto Unger—people who have a vision of the complex relation between legal practices and economic structures, and foreign policy as it's linked to the nation-state and it's bureaucracy (State Department, Pentagon, and CIA). These are very important kinds of issues that we ought not leave to journalists, and there's a sense in which a lot of philosophers of law left it to journalists to tell those stories.

EM: Do you think there is anything worth preserving in patriotism?

CW: Oh sure!

EM: Is patriotism a form of virtue?

CW: Absolutely. I believe that piety is an appropriate virtue.

EM: So patriotism is a form of piety?

CW: Oh absolutely, absolutely. We have to pay debt to the sources of our being. That includes mom and dad. That includes the community that shaped you. That includes the nation that both protects you as well as gives you some sense of possibility. And for religious folk, of course, it includes God. Now, the problem is there has to be some Socratic energy in one's piety. Piety ought to be inseparable from critical thinking, but the critical thinking is parasitic on who one is and where one starts. And who one is and where one starts has to do with what has shaped you from womb to tomb. Part of the hollowness and shallowness of some of modern thinking is to think that somehow one gives birth to oneself and therefore one has no debt to anybody who came before—as if you can have a language all by itself, as if you could actually raise yourself from zero to five, and so forth and so on. So that I look at my beautiful daughter and I give her all the love that I can. And as she gets older, she is going to feel a certain kind of relation to me. In the end, she may characterize that as a debt that she feels to me because of the love that I gave her. I think that's appropriate. I don't do it for that reason, but I think that's appropriate. I certainly feel that with my parents, and I feel that with my neighborhood. I feel that with my black church. I feel that with the nation, and I also feel that with my intellectual ancestors. I think I have a deep debt to Chekhov and a deep debt to Coltrane. I have a deep debt to Hilary Putnam and Stanley Cavell, and these people who were so very kind to me. That doesn't mean I uncritically accept what they have to say. I wrestle with them, but I'm thinking of a kind of critical, Socratic patriotism. Let's call it that.

EM: What's the difference between patriotism and nationalism?

CW: I think patriotism works at that psychic, existential level in terms of debt. I think nationalism is a particular ideology that was forged as the European empires began disintegrating. You needed different units to be constituted to deal with the dynamics of power, so you ended up with these nation-states with their institutions of administration and their control over the instrumentalities of violence. And it has become the most powerful modern ideology in some ways. As the empires underwent metamorphosis, some of them collapsed, some of them reconstituted and so on. A very powerful ideology.

EM: Is there a link between black nationalism and U.S. nationalism?

CW: Absolutely. Absolutely. It's ironic because nationalism itself is a European construct, and we get black folk—who are victimized mainly by Europeans tied to vicious notions and practices of white supremacy—using a European ideology to counter. I can understand that; we have to use any weapon we can. But we have to be cognizant of its limitations, how tainted it is, and especially how morally tainted it is in terms of not allowing our internationalism and universalism to become more pronounced. But, of course, the problem has always been that the black nationalist movement has no land, no territory, and so it becomes symbolic. A way of trying to organize . . .

EM: Cultural?

CW: A cultural nationalism or a kind of psychic nationalism. A control over community in terms of the flow of capital, as opposed to having one's own nation-state that you can control the boundaries and borders and so forth. People like Elijah Mohammed—I have great respect for him in terms of his willingness to live and die for black people. I have a devastating critique of him in terms of the limitedness of his vision: the xenophobia, the uncritical appropriation of a nationalist ideology that has wreaked havoc on so many other peoples. And similarly with Louis Farrakhan—I have a great love for him in terms of his love for black people and his willingness to live and die for black people, and yet at the same time—and he's still alive, thank God, so we can argue about these things, about my critiques of his nationalist projects and the patriarchy and the homophobia that often go with nationalist ideology: You need some other human to be, if not demeaned, then certainly to be defined over against. You see, as a radical democrat I am very suspicious of it.

EM: Are you suggesting that black nationalism has become historically obsolete?

CW: No.

EM: Is there a role for it still?

CW: Absolutely. As long as white supremacy is around, there will be black nationalism—and progressive black nationalism will be more common. I think that's true for any kind of nationalism. I'm critical of a Zionist project because it is a form of nationalism of oppressed people just like black nationalism is a form of nationalism of oppressed people. But progressive Zionists are my comrades, because as long as racist forms of anti-Semitism are around, then you're going to have nationalist responses to it. Zionist responses vis-à-vis anti-Semitism, black nationalist responses vis-à-vis white supremacy, and so forth and so on. When I said "progressive" what I mean is those particular nationalists who accent the democratic dimensions of their projects—and there are significant democratic dimensions of the Zionist project, of the black nationalist project, of the American nationalist project. Ralph Ellison, I'm going to lecture on him today. This man is a thoroughgoing American nationalist—patriot to the core. You know, one of the great geniuses of the American literary tradition—much too nationalist for me. But the democratic dimension of his American nationalism is very rich.

EM: Do you think that the African American reaction to 9/11 was different from that of Anglo-Americans, or does it make any sense to talk about this split?

CW: It was very different. It was very different. To be a nigger in America meant to be unsafe, unprotected, subject to random violence and hated. America experienced that as a nation for the first time on 9/11, so the whole nation was niggarized. Black people began to say, "You beginning to get the sense now what it is I have to deal with"—this terrorized condition, you see. And I think that black folk, therefore, were less likely to engage in an adolescent lust for revenge, because they've got long traditions of over-coming that kind of spiritual immaturity. Well, you say, revenge is an instinct when you're terrorized. But when you come out of a people who have been terrorized, over time you recognize that your survival will not be procured by revenge. If we had the voice of a Martin King or the voice of a [?], as the dominant responses to American terrorism, you wouldn't get the Lone Ranger, cowboy-like attitude of George Bush and others.

EM: *Do you think, notwithstanding that difference, that African-American intellectuals and spokespersons have been cowered into silence and acquies-cence for fear that they might be called unpatriotic?*

CW: Early on that was the case, absolutely. Barbara Lee, my dear sister, stood up—all by herself and under death threats for weeks—before Con-gress to vote against Bush pushing that through immediately after 9/11. Part of the problem is that the market-driven media is just not interested in some of the more significant truth-tellers coming out of the black community. So if you actually look at the black press, the black radio, or even Tavis Smiley's C-SPAN show on the black response to 9/11: You probably had more truth-telling on that show about America than you had on any other show. And it's mainly because black people been dealing with American terrorism for hundreds of years. So we could trash, call into question, all forms of terrorists—be they American, be they Islamic, be they Christian, be they Jewish, be they whatever. Whereas America became so obsessed with this particular terrorist attack, which was vicious and wrong and cowardly, but didn't want to look at itself, and therefore fell into that typically adolescent pure victim/impure victimizer, us versus them—the Manichean vision that we hear Bush articulating day in and day out.

EM: *We'll come back to that Manicheanism later on. Do you think there's a continuum between the slave plantation, Jim Crow, the ghetto, the ethno-racial prison, and the present use of the death penalty as a form of "legalized lynching," as Jesse Jackson calls it?*

CW: Yeah, I think Angela Davis and others have been quite brilliant on this issue. What we're talking about is the excessive use of repression and violence to contain and control significant slices of the black community, especially, more and more these days, the poor black community. And that black encounter with the violent face, with the repressive face of the American state has played a crucial role in shaping black people's perception of America. And it goes from the whip on the plantation, to the lynching of the lynching tree, to the trigger-happy policing, on to the death penalty and the criminal justice system and the prison-industrial complex. Absolutely. Absolutely. A number of mediations: shifts in space from rural to urban, shifts in class location from pre-industrial labor to industrial labor to post-industrial labor, shifts in educational sites and so on. But the progress goes hand in hand with the underside of the progress, which is what you're actually . . .

EM: Right. Now you might know these lectures from 1976, which I think you actually anticipated in Prophecy and Deliverance, on the genealogy of racism: Foucault's lectures of 1976, which are called Society Must Be Defended. There he talked about racism for the first time very explicitly. He talks about racism as a racial war against a biological or social threat. That's why society must be defended. Now, if we keep that in mind, can we say that in fact if we look at these institutions—the plantation, the ghetto, the lynching, Jim Crow, and today the death penalty—what we're facing is a racial war against African Americans?

CW: The problem with the metaphor of war—and this goes back to Clausewitz—is that it tends to put a premium on the point at which contestation is accented, whereas black people's labor, black people's bodies, black people's styles are preconditioned for the American project. So the given impression that is first and foremost of war is that they want to annihilate black people. They can't annihilate black people. If they had annihilated 22 percent of the inhabitants of the thirteen colonies who were keeping the thing economically afloat, they would've undermined themselves. If they had annihilated black people during Jim Crow, who was going to do the labor? And if they had annihilated black people in the 1960s? We're in too many crucial places. So, you see, there is a war-like dimension, but there are these other dimensions that those, from Clausewitz to Foucault, that invoke these kinds of metaphors might easily downplay. Now, I do believe that in the end we are on a battlefield, but the battlefield is not one in which you're at that point of contention primarily or exclusively. You've got a life to live, labor to render, songs to sing, people to love, and that's as important and as much a part of our talk about living a life in which white supremacy, male supremacy, and others are coming at us. So it's like Lefebvre, my dear brother, I don't want everyday life to be slighted by these metaphors of war, though in the end there is certainly a warlike quality to what we're dealing with.

EM: If we include all the people in the prison system and those under the control of the penitentiary and correctional institutions, which is almost 4 million people, and we know that one of the largest industries in the United States is the prison-industrial complex—California's largest industry, for instance—don't you think we have become a carceral society, a nation of prisons?

CW: Well, look at your question here in terms of industry. The biggest industry in California is the entertainment industry. I think that's bigger than the prison industry.

EM: Okay.

CW: See what I mean? Aerospace is major industry. That is to say that we'd have to examine the scope and scale and breadth and depth, so that the carceral industry, which has been expanding exponentially, every five years it seems, but it is not as central as the entertainment industry. Now of course the irony is that many of the top performers in the entertainment industry are the same color as those in the carceral industry, you know what I mean? But one's international, it's global. Hip-hop is one slice and that's billions and billions of dollars, right? We're not even talking about music as a whole, or TV and sports. My God, this country couldn't survive without Negroes and sports. They'd go crazy—wouldn't know what to do on the weekends. So you get the black presence in all these different instances, but back to your question: the carceral industry certainly is an industry. It's a growing industry, but it's primarily one that tries to target the working poor and very poor, given the fact that the society finds it difficult to find spaces for them, some significant value and use for them. And of course many make bad choices and decisions in the context in which they find themselves. And I think for me, again, the issue of linking struggles in everyday life to the various kinds of industries, structures, institutions, and the economy, especially, looms large here. There is a backlash right now. I mentioned Angela Davis. You can talk about the anti-death penalty movement.

EM: In fact, that is where my next question was going. In light of the Rehn-quist Court, which is against the equal application of rights, what should we do about the death penalty, this mechanism for legalized lynching?

CW: We have got to reshape public opinion, and I give a lot of fellow citizens credit for that. They've helped reshape the climate of public opinion. Hugo Bedau, who is my dear friend and a philosophy professor down at Tufts for many years. He has been struggling against the death penalty for almost thirty years. We would have gatherings twenty years ago, and there would be seven people. We'd have gatherings ten years ago, and we'd have seventy. Now we have a gathering and there are four hundred. He is the same person, same view, and part of the same movement, but it's expanding. He is one among many, and I give a lot of credit for that.

EM: What do you think of the new abolitionist movement?

CW: You know, I listen carefully and I learn much. I don't think I have fundamentally reached their conclusions yet. I'd love to see more education, rehabilitation, and what I call *paideia*. I've taught in prisons now for nineteen years, and some of my best examples of paideia—that kind of formation of attention on crucial issues, cultivation of the self, self-criticism, and maturation of the soul that really comes to terms with reality and history and mortality—I've seen in prisons, and that's part of the rehabilitation that ought to take place. Whether in fact you end up abolishing is something that I've yet to be fully persuaded on.

EM: Now shifting to the question of religion. You have been particularly preoccupied with the problem of evil. In fact, you think that prophetic pragmatism is distinctively concerned with questions of evil and the tragic. Do you think that the events of 9/11 should be talked about in terms of evil?

CW: Oh, sure, because evil for me is unjustified suffering. It's unwarranted misery, and that's certainly what it was. Now, of course, that also means you have to talk about what's going on in Colombia and Guatemala and El Salvador and Iraq also in terms of unjustified suffering and unnecessary social misery as evil. The question then becomes: What is our response to it? How do we understand where and why it emerges? How do we try to wrestle with it and overcome it? And that's a very complicated process. That has to do with both structures of institutions as well as the choices and decisions that agents make, that particular people make. There's a dialectical interplay between structure and agency here that we must never lose sight of. But to be preoccupied with evil is really, to me, just the attempt to be a decent and compassionate person who is concerned about other people's suffering and also trying to find some joy in the world. In some ways that is the best of a humanist tradition that goes from Amos to Socrates to W.E.B. Du Bois, and yet we also know that the same tradition can hide and conceal certain forms of unjustified suffering. There is evil shot through all of our traditions.

EM: Following up on this question, I know that you have been teaching a freshman seminar called "The Tragic, the Comic and the Political." Now let me ask you, the word evil *doesn't form part of the title there, but what is the linkage that you're trying to make between evil and the tragic? If we think of evil in the Augustinian sense, it's about human will—it is the human will that is the cause of evil in the world. Whereas the tragic is about the forces beyond the human will, so you're bringing together two philosophemes, which seem to be anathematic to each other.*

CW: That's a very good question. Now, I do believe, following Dewey, that we are acculturated organisms in transaction with our environment, and there are natural forces that can be stronger. When the cancer hit me, linked to a genetic inheritance that goes all the way back to whatever, I had to respond to it. There is no way that I can completely extricate it. I might get lucky and control it for a while, but there are forces that are far beyond human will. When a comet clashes with this planet sooner or later, there's not a whole lot human beings can do about that. You know what I mean? When you talk about human suffering being caused by something greater than human beings, we got natural evil. The Lisbon earthquake that Voltaire and Kant and others were so shaken by. That's very real, but on the other hand there are things we can do a hell of a lot about—like trying to understand the comet when it's coming, or trying to get some sense of when the earthquake's coming, given that we can't control it and so on. We've done a better job now than we were able to do in Lisbon, no doubt, and you've lived in California, so you understand that better than most people. But there are some other forms of suffering that we can do a hell of a lot about: suffering that has to do with corporate power, that has to do with narrow interests among elites in the nation-states, that has to do with xenophobic citizens attacking other citizens, especially our gay brothers and lesbian sisters these days. Those we can do a lot about. So that you're actually right, the comic tries to understand what it is that we acculturated organisms that transact with our environment can bring to minimize and alleviate the suffering, knowing that we will never have full control over it.

The comic allows us to look at those limitations and all the incongruities and hypocrisies of who we are, what our society is, and still smile through the darkness. The tragic fights all it can and then it runs up against the limits, the constraints, and goes down gloriously, but also recognizing a certain hubris, a certain kind of defective self-knowledge that may have been in part responsible for running up against that limit, the Oedipus, but there are different forms of the tragic and different forms of the comic and as somebody like Chekhov, who other than Shakespeare, I think, has the most profound conception of the tragic-comic. And it's interesting because there is no real philosopher that constitutes an analogue to Chekhov. I think the greatest comic philosopher was David Hume, who was preoccupied with the incongruities and limitations of not just human reason but human beings and yet still trying to get us to proceed in post-skeptical space, as it were.

But his sense of the tragic, I think, was in part underdeveloped. The tragic-comic go hand in hand—some of the deep passion, the willingness to be moved by the difficulty of walking that tightrope. You know, when Hume goes back to play backgammon, you get the sense that he is really suppressing all of this anxiety, which he is, since he is neoclassical figure in that sense: It's about stoic self-mastery and so on. Whereas Chekhov is a bit more—he is so moved by the heartbreak and the heartache of human-kind that he can't be restrained like Hume in a neoclassical way. He is the grandson of a slave. Yet he knows he needs to have some self-control as the medical doctor that he was and the great liberator figure that he was, reading philosophy all the time but also concerned about science—and agnostic, like Hume. Hume was probably agnostic too. So there is no easy religious solution for Chekhov. For me, you see, that's the real challenge: How do you keep the Socratic, critical energy flowing and the prophetic witness linked to compassion and the tragic-comic hope all intertwined for radical democracy?

EM: This is what you're discussing in Democracy Matters . . .

CW: Yes, in my book, *Democracy Matters,* I lay all this out.

EM: What do you make of President Bush's apocalyptic and messianic rhetoric?

CW: There is a long tradition of such rhetoric in American history, and Bush is just an instant in that tradition. He does view America in a Man-ichean way, as this pure city on the hill. It's an "us against them" stance. He finds it very difficult to ever be critical of America, not just publicly, but I think also in his own private space. He is part of this sense of Amer-ica as being this land of Adamic innocence, which has very deep roots in the country. There are other roots in the country that are more mature and more critically engaging of the complex reality of America's past and present, but he is part of the Manichean impulse in the tradition of innocence.

EM: And this messianic role of carrying the banner of democracy even if requires the use of military violence, torture, and repression?

CW: Of Christianity and democracy in the vulgar sense of both. Abso-lutely, but he is the exemplar of Constantinian Christianity and imperial America. Constantinian Christianity has deep roots in America and so does imperialism. There is also a prophetic Christianity and a deep demo-cratic tradition in America that cut against both of these, but they have always been in some ways weaker even though they made a difference in the making of the country.

EM: Now I don't want to give any credence to Samuel Huntington's idea that we are facing a clash of civilizations, but one could say that there are conflicts today, conflicts of religions. Against this background, what would you say about the role of religious talk today? Does it complicate, or does it help when we talk about a confrontation of religions?

CW: Well, I think that any time you have religious conflict you also have something else going on in addition to the clash of religion. There's always a social dimension, an economic dimension, and a personal dimension going on. I think right now we're experiencing a profound crisis of Christian identity in the country. There has always been a strong fundamentalist evangelical presence in the country that was highly suspicious of modern modes of skepticism, secularism, and criticism. Ironically, since Martin Luther King Jr., the Christian right began to learn lessons in terms of political organization and using their clout to bring power and pressure to bear because they saw the Civil Rights movement doing it on the other side of the ideological line. So they actually learned from brother Martin, the Jerry Farwells and others, and then [they] received, of course, unbelievable economic support from many corporate elites. And it became clear that if there was going to be a realignment of American politics—a kind of Southernization of American politics using racially loaded terms, from busing to crime to welfare to prisons and so forth, to realign the American public—then the Christian Right could be a major organized pillar for this. They were, in fact, brought in, in a significant way, to do that and not simply because the elites themselves were Christians. Sometimes it was outright manipulation because you've got Machiavellian calculations going on at the highest levels of certain deeply conservative circles.

So you end up with not just Constantinian Christianity, but the Christian Right being a fundamental pillar for imperial America. Look at the relation of the Christian Right and conservative Jews in America. This is what is intriguing about the Mel Gibson film, you see, because you get the erosion of that. People know that anti-Semitism has always been part and parcel of the Christian Right's perspective, and all of a sudden you get an alliance with conservative Jews defending Israel, based almost on blind faith, and now they discover, my god, our allies are anti-Semites! You don't say. I could have told you that a long time ago. Pat Robertson has publicly said things far more anti-Semitic than most. How is he going to be your ally? Well, because he supports Israel! Well, I thought that coalitions had something more substantive to them than merely a stance. The same is true with cutting back on domestic policy when it comes to social services, health care, jobs, education and so on. No, it's pro-defense, no it's pro-imperial expansion. The Christian Right, right now, is both powerful and dangerous and yet we know—and this is something we don't like talking about in the academy—that if 72 percent of Americans view themselves as not just Christians, but believe in Jesus Christ son of God, then the fight for democracy in America is partly a fight for democratic possibilities in the American Christian tradition. If you lose the latter, you can forget the former. You can come up with the most sophisticated theories of democracy in the world, but if you're not affecting the climate on the ground in such a way that certain Christians can think dem-o-cra-tic-ly and proceed politically under a radical democratic vision, then we're not going to get anywhere. In fact, you end up just giving more and more over to the Christian Right and Christian centrists.

EM: Many liberal intellectuals have argued that the war on terrorism is a just war—and this relates to the other question because just war theory emerges from Christianity, Augustine, Aquinas—liberals like Jean Bethke Elshtain, Paul Berman, and to a certain extent Michael Walzer. Do you think these wars against Iraq and, of course, Afghanistan were just wars?

CW: No, not at all. They were illegal, unjustified, and I think unnecessary. I think there are ways of trying to gain access, to hunt down gangsters and terrorists, without invading countries. This plundering of the livelihoods of thousands and thousands and thousands of innocent people, with very little regard for their welfare and well-being, has symbolic purposes—getting back to issue of the lust for revenge—letting the country know we're not going to take this; to let the country know we're macho and we're tough and so on. And the result is what? More instability and more insecurity, because that's what that kind of posing and posturing of a macho identity does. It just reinforces the whole cycle of anxiety and insecurity that is tied to all the bigotry and hatred and revenge and resentment that fan and fuel the worst of who we are as human beings. I think on the international front you've got to deal with multilateral institutions and international law: I don't think international law can justify it.

Then there is a deeper, moral question in terms of what kinds of costs there are and who is bearing them. When you have an invasion and you're unwilling to even count the number of innocent civilians you kill—I don't understand how any of these people can conclude that this is a just war. I mean, the Catholic tradition and others always talk about their caution and their preoccupation with not just minimizing, but keeping track of what the costs are, so you can argue ex post facto what happened. They don't even want to show the bodies of the American soldiers; that's a cost too on the American side. So it pains me to see a lot of fellow philosophers, social theorists, and what have you, caught within the legitimation machine of the larger imperial project. They may not share all of the imperial ambitions, but they can be easily used and deployed by those who are running that machine. That gross kind of seduction, I think, is highly unfortunate. I've seen some very decent and brilliant people who were easily used in that way.

EM: So do you think terrorism is the largest threat the United States faces in the 21st century or . . .

CW: No, the largest thing America faces in the twenty-first century is internal decay and decline, with us turning on each other unable to generate the web of trust requisite to keep the democratic experiment alive. Very much like the communists in the 1940s and 50s, who constituted a kind of external foe to hold America together, I think the Bush people are trying to constitute Islamic terrorists as an external foe to hold us together. But America has always had high levels of violence: from cars, to everyday violence, to domestic violence, to violence against workers, to violence against black people, brown people, and so on. And we're not even talking about genocidal attacks on indigenous people. As important as it is for the United States to do all that it can, in terms of not being attacked externally by gangsters from wherever, we've got so many everyday attacks that are taking place in this country that . . .

EM: Forms of state terrorism, economic terrorism . . .

CW: Well it's hard to even come up with a category, because there are so many different forms. Just look at the healthcare system. We spend more money than any other country, any other developed country, and yet we've got thousands and thousands of people who die because they don't have access. That's a kind of killing that is taking place. You've got workers who don't have access to safety who die. There's no talk about them, but that's a kind of killing. That can be avoided just like we would have liked to avoid 9/11. You've got young kids in poor communities whose souls are murdered, who don't have access to any quality education, no sense of significant safety, and so forth. They're dying all the time. Those are deaths too, and a lot of that stuff can be avoided. So that when I look at the obsession with this particular attack, which was vicious, I see the downplaying of all these other deaths that are taking place. I say something's wrong. I take the tears of George Bush seriously when he cries for the victims of 9/11, as I take my own tears seriously, but then I wonder why he does not cry for Louimo, when he is shot down by police as an innocent civilian? And I say to myself, if you cannot connect the tears for Louimo with the victims of 9/11, then you're missing something. I cried for both.

Bush only cried for one. Guiliani cried for one—you know what I mean? Something is wrong. Something is missing there. And then I began to wonder: Well, wait a minute, are these tears highly circumscribed? Are they forced? And again the Socratic, prophetic tells me if I can't be morally consistent, I need to check myself. I think that's the kind of challenge we need as thinkers, philosophers, citizens, and human beings put forth to each other.

EM: I have one last question and it's a question that I think we should always be asking. I ask myself this question as a Latino. It's been 101 years since W.E.B. Du Bois said that the problem of the 20th century would be the problem of the color line. By 2050, about 25 percent of U.S. citizens will be Latino. We're talking about the browning of United States: What will happen to the problem of the color line in the 21st century?

CW: That's a good question. That's a very good question.

EM: It worries me that the so-called "browning" of America might submerge the question of the African American, the black . . .

CW: You know, I think that because we deal with the legacy of white supremacy that affects brown and black and yellow and red and, in the end, it actually affects whites—they're all race concepts—as long as we keep the focus on the institutional and personal manifestations of that particular evil, then I'm not so sure that the numbers will make as big a difference. I think when Du Bois talked about the color line, he was really taking about this legacy of white supremacy. He goes on to say the way in which it affects Asian and Latin Americans and so forth. You can have a legacy of white supremacy at work with no white people around—just between blacks and browns. If we draw each other through that white supremacy's lens, then that legacy is still very much alive and we can't relate to each other's humanity. So it's not going be so much a matter of numbers, I think. It's going to be how we respond to that legacy in such a way that we can begin to dismantle some of the stereotypes, some of the prejudices, some of the institutional discriminations, some of the xenophobic perceptions, and so forth.

I think in the end, though, the major battle of the next 100 years is going be the battle between the deepening of democracy and the dismantling of empire. The degree to which blacks and browns decide to go, as a large majority, one way as opposed to another—those coalitions will probably be more important than simply how we divide up a particular pie within the domestic context, you see. And I think the brown brothers and sisters bring a depth and wisdom and experience of what it's really like to be colonized—in Texas and California and what is now New Mexico.

That history is something that is very rich and that is different than black folk. Black folk being enslaved and Jim Crowed is different than being colonized, having your border moved by soldiers by force, and so on. Coming from Mexico, coming from El Salvador, coming from another country and seeing America from the outside, gives one a cosmopolitan view—for Puerto Ricans the same way as for Dominicans. That gives a cosmopolitan view that a lot of black Americans don't have. From Alabama? Well, that's part of the country . . . well, most of the time. From Mississippi? Georgia? California? Yes, that's still within continental imperial U.S.A. You look at America from Mexico, from El Salvador, from Puerto Rico—it's like C.R.L. James and Stokey Carmichael, who are supposed to come from the Caribbean: they've got very different views of this country, and a lot of black people in America miss that.

EM: It's another form of double vision.

CW: Yes! Absolutely, but linked to this battle between the deepening of democracy and the dismantling of empire.

BIBLIOGRAPHY

Aboulafia, Mitchell. *The Cosmopolitan Self: Mead and Continental Philosophy.* Urbana and Chicago: University of Illinois Press, 2001.

——. *The Mediating Self: Mead, Sartre, and Self-Determination.* New Haven, Conn.: Yale University Press, 1986.

——, ed. *Philosophy, Social Theory, and the Thought of George Herbert Mead.* Albany: State University of New York Press, 1991.

Anderson, Fred, and Andrew Cayton. *The Dominion of War: Empire and Liberty in North America.* New York: Viking, 2005.

Anderson, Pamela Sue, and Beverley Clack, eds. *Feminist Philosophy of Religion: Critical Readings.* New York: Routledge, 2004.

Anscombe, Elizabeth. "Aristotle and the Sea Battle." *Mind* 65 (1956): 1–17.

Anscombe, G. E. M. *Intention.* Cambridge, Mass.: Harvard University Press, 2000 [1957].

Arendt, Hannah. "Crisis in Culture." In *Between Past and Future: Eight Exercises in Political Thought.* New York: Viking Press, 1968.

——. *The Human Condition.* Chicago: University of Chicago Press, 1958.

——. *Lectures on Kant's Political Philosophy.* Edited by Ronald Beiner. Chicago: University of Chicago Press, 1982.

Aristotle. *Nichomachean Ethics.* Translated by Terence Irwin. Indianapolis: Hackett, 1985.

——. *Poetics.* Translated by Richard Janko. Indianapolis: Hackett, 1985.

Asante, Molefi Kete. *The Afrocentric Idea.* Philadelphia: Temple University Press, 1998.

Baraka, Amiri (LeRoi Jones). *Blues People: Negro Music in White America.* New York: William Morrow and Company, 1963.

Barnouw, Dagmar. *The War in the Empty Air: Victims, Perpetrators, and Postwar Germans.* Bloomington: Indiana University Press, 2005.

Benhabib, Seyla. *The Claims of Culture: Equality and Diversity in the Global Era.* Princeton, N.J.: Princeton University Press, 2002.

Berlin, Isaiah. "Two Concepts of Liberty." In Berlin, *Four Essays on Liberty.* Oxford: Oxford University Press, 1969.

Blum, William. *Rogue State: A Guide to the World's Only Superpower.* New updated edition. London and New York: Zed Books, 2002.

Bohman, James. "Critics, Observers, and Participants." In *Pluralism and the Pragmatic Turn,* ed. J. Bohman and W. Rehg, 87–114. Cambridge, Mass.: MIT Press, 2001.

——. *Public Deliberation: Pluralism, Complexity and Democracy.* Cambridge, Mass.: MIT Press, 1996.

Bonilla-Silva, Eduardo. *Racism without Racists: Color-blind Racism and the Persistence of Racial Inequality in the United States.* Lanham, Md.: Rowman and Littlefield, 2003.

Boorstin, Daniel J. "Introduction to the Vintage Classics Edition." In Alexis de Tocqueville, *Democracy in America.* New York: Random House, 1990.

Bourne, Randolph S. *The Radical Will: Randolph Bourne Selected Writings, 1911–1918.* Edited by Olaf Hansen. New York: Urizen Press, 1977.

——. "Twilight of Idols." In *Radical Will,* 336–47.

——. "A War Diary." In *Radical Will,* 319–30.

——. *War and the Intellectuals: Collected Essays 1915–1919.* Edited by Carl Resek. Indianapolis/Cambridge: Hackett, 1999.

——. "The Collapse of American Strategy," in *War and the Intellectuals,* 22–35.

Boxill, Bernard R. *Blacks and Social Justice,* rev. ed.. Lanham, Md.: Rowman and Littlefield, 1992.

Brandom, Robert B. *Articulating Reasons: An Introduction to Inferentialism.* Cambridge, Mass.: Harvard University Press, 2000.

——. *Making It Explicit.* Cambridge, Mass.: Harvard University Press, 1994.

——, ed. *Rorty and His Critics.* Malden, Mass.: Blackwell, 2000.

Brent, Joseph. *Charles Sanders Peirce: A Life.* Revised and enlarged edition. Bloomington: Indiana University Press, 1998.

Burnett, Christine D., and Burke Marshall, eds. *Foreign in a Domestic Sense: Puerto Rico, American Expansion, and the Constitution.* Durham, N.C.: Duke University Press, 2001.

——. "Between the Foreign and the Domestic: The Doctrine of Territorial Incorporation, Invented and Reinvented." In *Foreign in a Domestic Sense,* 1–36.

Clendenning, John. *The Life and Thought of Josiah Royce.* Madison: University of Wisconsin Press, 1985.

Collins, Patricia Hill. *Black Feminist Thought.* New York: Routledge, 1991.

——. *Fighting Words: Black Women and the Search for Justice.* Minneapolis: University of Minnesota Press, 1998.

Cormier, Harvey, *The Truth Is What Works: William James, Pragmatism, and the Seed of Death.* Lanham, Md.: Rowman and Littlefield, 2000.

Cosmides, Leda, and Tooby, John. "Evolutionary Psychology: A Primer." 1997. University of California, Santa Barbara, available at www.psych.ucsb.edu/research/cep/primer.html.

Cox, Oliver C. *Caste, Class, and Race: A Study in Social Dynamics.* New York: Monthly Review, 1959.

Cruse, Harold. *The Crisis of the Negro Intellectual.* New York: William Morrow and Company, 1967.

Danto, Arthur. *The Analytical Philosophy of History.* New York: Columbia University Press, 1988.

Darwall, Stephen. "Fichte and the Second-Personal Standpoint." *International Yearbook for German Idealism* 3 (2005): 91–113.

Dewey, John. *The Early Works of John Dewey: 1882–1898.* 5 volumes. Edited by Jo Ann Boydston. Carbondale and Edwardsville: Southern Illinois University Press, 1972; hereafter *EW.*

——. *Impressions of Soviet Russia and the Revolutionary World.* New York: New Republic, Inc., 1929.

——. *The Middle Works of John Dewey: 1899–1924,* 15 volumes. Edited by Jo Ann Boydston. Carbondale and Edwardsville: Southern Illinois University Press, 1978; hereafter *MW.*

——. "Does Reality Possess Practical Character?" In *MW* 3: 125–42.

——. "Interpretation of Savage Mind." In *MW* 2: 39–52.

——. "Nationalizing Education." In *MW* 10: 202–10.

——. "Philosophy and Democracy." In *MW* 11: 41–53.

——. "Public Opinion in Japan." In *MW* 13: 255–61.

——. "Racial Prejudice and Friction." In *MW* 13: 242–54.

——. *Reconstruction in Philosophy.* In *MW* 12: 77–203.

——. *The Later Works of John Dewey, 1925–1953,* 17 volumes. Edited by Jo Ann Boydston. Carbondale and Edwardsville: Southern Illinois University Press, 1985; hereafter *LW.*

——. "A Critique of American Civilization." In *LW* 3: 133–44.

——. "Context and Thought." In *LW* 6: 3–21.

——. "Creative Democracy—The Task Before Us." In *LW* 14: 224–230.

——. *Ethics.* In *LW* 7.

——. "From Absolutism to Experimentalism." In *LW* 5:147–60.

—— "Imperialism Is Easy." In *LW* 3: 158–62.

——. *Logic: The Theory of Inquiry.* In *LW* 12:1–527.

——. "Message to the Chinese People." In *LW* 15: 369–70.

——. "No Matter What Happens—Stay Out" In *LW* 14: 364.

——. "The Pragmatic Acquiescence." In *LW* 3:145–51.

——. "Renascent Liberalism." In *LW* 11: 41–65.

Dewey, John, and James Tufts. *Ethics* (1908). *MW* 5.

Diamond, Jared. *Guns, Germs, and Steel: The Fates of Human Societies.* New York: W. W. Norton and Company, 1997.

Dirlik, Arif. *The Postcolonial Aura: Third World Criticism in the Age of Global Capitalism.* Boulder, Colo.: Westview Press, 1997.

——, ed. *What Is in a Rim? Critical Perspectives on the Pacific Region Idea.* Boulder, Colo.: Westview Press, 1993.

Doak, Mary. "Pragmatism, Postmodernism, and Politics." In *Pragmatism, Neo-Pragmatism, and Religion: Conversations with Richard Rorty,* ed. Charley D. Hardwick and Donald A. Crosby, 149–62. New York: Peter Lang, 1997.

Dower, John. *War without Mercy: Race and Power in the Pacific War.* New York: Pantheon Books, 1986.

Drinnon, Richard. *Facing West: The Metaphysics of Indian-Hating and Empire Building.* New York: Schocken Books, 1990.

Du Bois, W.E.B. *The Souls of Black Folk.* Edited with an Introduction by David W. Blight and Robert Gooding-Williams. Boston: Bedford Books, 1997.

Dudziak, Mary. *Cold War Civil Rights: Race and the Image of Democracy.* Princeton, N.J.: Princeton University Press, 2000.

Dussel, Enrique. *The Underside of Modernity: Apel, Ricoeur, Rorty, and Taylor and the Philosophy of Liberation.* Translated by Eduardo Mendieta. Atlantic Highlands, N.J.: Humanities Press, 1996.

Eldridge, Michael. "Dewey on Race and Social Change." In *Pragmatism and the Problem of Race,* ed. Bill E. Lawson and Donald F. Koch, 11–21. Bloomington: Indiana University Press, 2004.

——. *Transforming Experience: John Dewey's Cultural Instrumentalism.* Nashville, Tenn.: Vanderbilt University Press, 1998.

Ellis, Joseph J. *Founding Brothers: The Revolutionary Generation.* New York: Alfred A. Knopf, 2001.

Ellison, Ralph. "An Extravagance of Laughter." In Ellison, *Going to the Territory.* New York: Vintage, 1986, 145–97.

——. "What America Would Be Like Without Blacks." In *The Collected Essays of Ralph Ellison,* ed. John F. Callahan, 577–84. New York: Modern Library, 1995.

Evison, Harry C. *The Long Dispute: Maori Land Rights and European Colonization.* Christchurch: Canterbury University Press, 1997.

Emanuel Eze, ed. *Race and the Enlightenment.* Oxford: Blackwell, 1997.

Ferguson, Niall. *Empire: The Rise and Demise of the British World Order and the Lessons for Global Power.* New York: Basic Books, 2004.

Fisher, N. R. E. *Hybris: A Study in the Values of Honour and Shame in Ancient Greece.* Warminster, England: Aris and Philips, 1992.

Flaherty, James. "Rorty, Religious Beliefs, and Pragmatism." *International Philosophical Quarterly* 45:2 (2005): 175–85.

Frazier, E. Franklin. *The Negro Church in America* / C. Eric Lincoln, *The Black Church Since Frazier.* New York: Schocken Books, 1974.

Friedman, Thomas. "Peking Duct Tape." *New York Times OP-ED,* 16 February 2003, 11.

——. "From Supercharged Financial Markets to Osama bin Laden, the Emerging Global Order Demands an Enforcer: That's American's New Burden." *New York Times Magazine*, 28 March 1999, 6.

Frye, Marilyn. *The Politics of Reality.* Freedom, Calif.: Crossing Press, 1983.

Frye, Northrop. *Anatomy of Criticism.* Princeton, N.J.: Princeton University Press, 1957.

Gadamer, Hans-Georg. *Truth and Method.* New York: Seabury Press, 1992.

Gates, Henry Louis, Jr. *Loose Canons: Notes on the Culture Wars.* Oxford: Oxford University Press, 1992.

——. *The Signifying Monkey: A Theory of African-American Literary Criticism.* Oxford: Oxford University Press, 1998.

Gates, Henry Louis, Jr., and Cornel West. *The Future of the Race.* New York: Vintage, 1996.

Geertz, Clifford. "The Uses of Diversity." *Michigan Quarterly Review* 25:1 (1986): 105–23.

——. *The Interpretation of Cultures.* New York: Basic Books, 1973.

Gerstle, Gary. *The American Crucible: Race and Nation in the Twentieth Century.* Princeton, N.J.: Princeton University Press, 2001.

Gilroy, Paul. *Against Race: Imagining Political Culture Beyond the Color Line.* Cambridge, Mass.: Harvard University Press, 2000.

——. *The Black Atlantic: Modernity and Double Consciousness.* Cambridge, Mass.: Harvard University Press, 1993.

Giovanni, Nikki. *Racism 101.* New York: Quill, 1994.

Gitlin, Todd. *The Twilight of Common Dreams: Why America Is Wracked by Culture Wars.* New York: Owlet Press, 1996.

Glaude, Eddie, Jr. *Exodus! Religion, Race, and Nation in Early Nineteenth Century Black America.* Chicago: University of Chicago Press, 2000.

Gooding-Williams, Robert. "Race, Multiculturalism and Democracy." *Constellations* 5:1 (1998): 18–41.

Grant, Verne. *The Origin of Adaptations.* New York: Columbia University Press, 1963.

Gunn, Giles. *Beyond Solidarity: Pragmatism and Difference in a Globalized World.* Chicago: University of Chicago Press, 2001.

Habermas, Jürgen. *The New Conservatism: Cultural Criticism and the Historians' Debate.* Cambridge, Mass.: MIT Press, 1989.

——. "Popular Sovereignty as Procedure." In Habermas, *Between Facts and Norms: Contributions to a Discourse Theory of Law and Democracy.* Cambridge, Mass.: MIT Press, 1996, 463–90.

——. *Theory of Communicative Action,* Volume 1: *Reason and the Rationalization of Society.* Translated by Thomas McCarthy. Boston: Beacon Press, 1984.

Hall, Stuart. "What Is This 'Black' in Black Popular Culture." In *Black Popular Culture,* ed. Gina Dent, 21–33. New York: New Press, 1998.

Hegel, G. W. F. *Elements of the Philosophy of Right.* Edited by Allen W. Wood and translated by H. B. Nisbet. Cambridge: Cambridge University Press, 1991.

——. *Lectures on the Philosophy of World History: Introduction, Reason in History.*

Translated by H. B. Nisbet. Cambridge: Cambridge University Press, 1822–30 [rpt. 2002].

Held, David, Anthony McGrew, David Goldblatt, and Jonathan Perraton. *Global Transformations*. Stanford, Calif.: Stanford University Press, 1999.

Hickman, Larry, ed. *Reading Dewey: Interpretations for a Postmodern Generation*. Bloomington: Indiana University Press, 1998.

Higginbotham, Evelyn Brooks. "Rethinking Vernacular Culture: Black Religion and Race Records in the 1920s and 1930s." In *The House That Race Built*, ed. Wahneema Lubiano, 157–77. New York: Vintage, 1998.

Hochschild, Jennifer L. *The New American Dilemma: Liberal Democracy and School Desegregation*. New Haven, Conn.: Yale University Press, 1984.

Hollinger, David A. *Postethnic America: Beyond Multiculturalism*. Revised and updated edition. New York: Basic Books, 2000.

Holmes, Oliver Wendell, Jr. "A Soldier's Faith." Available at www.globalfuture .com/memorial-holmes1895.htm.

hooks, bell. *Feminist Theory: From Margin to Center*. Boston, Mass.: South End Press, 1984.

Horsman, Reginald. *Race and Manifest Destiny: The Origins of American Racial Anglo-Saxionism*. Cambridge, Mass.: Harvard University Press, 1981.

Huntington, Samuel P. "The Clash of Civilizations?" *Foreign Affairs* 72:3 (Summer 1993): 22–49.

Ignatieff, Michael. "The Burden." *New York Times Magazine*, 5 January 2003, 22ff.

———. *Empire Lite: Nation Building in Bosnia, Kosovo and Afghanistan*. London: Vintage, 2003.

———. "Human Rights as Idolatry." In *Human Rights as Politics and Idolatry*, ed. Amy Gutmann et al., 53–98. Princeton, N.J.: Princeton University Press, 2001.

———. "Human Rights as Politics." In *Human Rights as Politics and Idolatry*, ed. Amy Gutmann et al., 3–52. Princeton, N.J.: Princeton University Press, 2001.

———. "Why Are We in Iraq? (And Liberia? And Afghanistan?)" *New York Times Magazine*, 7 September 2003, Sec. 6, 85.

James, William. *Essays in Radical Empiricism*. Edited by F. Bowers, F. Burkhardt, and I. Skrupskelis. Cambridge, Mass.: Harvard University Press, 1912 [rpt. 1976].

———. *Essays in Religion and Morality*. Cambridge, Mass.: Harvard University Press, 1982.

———. "Robert Gould Shaw: Oration by Professor William James." In *Essays in Religion and Morality*, 64–74.

———. *The Letters of William James, vol. I*. Edited by Henry James. Boston: Atlantic Monthly Press, 1920.

———. *The Principles of Psychology*. Cambridge, Mass.: Harvard University Press, 1890 [rpt. 1981].

———. *The Will to Believe and Other Essays in Popular Philosophy*. New York: Dover, 1880 [rpt. 1956].

———. "Great Men and their Environment." In *The Will to Believe*, 216–54.

———. "The Moral Philosopher and the Moral Life." In *The Will to Believe*, 184–215.

———. *Writings 1902–1910.* New York: Library of America, 1987.

———. "The Moral Equivalent of War." In *Writings 1902–1910,* 1281–93.

Joas, Hans. *G. H. Mead: A Contemporary Re-Examination of His Thought.* Cambridge, Mass.: MIT Press, 1997 [1985].

Kant, Immanuel. *Critique of Judgment.* Translated by Werner S. Pluhar. Indianapolis: Hackettt, 1987.

———. *Practical Philosophy.* Edited and translated by M. Gregor. Cambridge: Cambridge University Press, 1996.

Karenga, Maulana. "Society, Culture, and the Problem of Self-Consciousness: A Kawaida Analysis." In *Philosophy Born of Struggle: Anthology of Afro-American Philosophy from 1917,* ed. Leonard Harris, 212–28. Dubuque, Iowa: Kendall/Hunt, 1983.

Kim, David. "Empire's Entrails and the Imperial Geography of 'Amerasia.'" *City: Analysis of Urban Trends, Culture, Theory, Policy, Action* 8:1 (April 2004): 57–88.

Kitcher, Philip. "Race, Ethnicity, Biology, Culture." In *In Mendel's Mirror: Philosophical Reflections on Biology,* 230–57. Oxford: Oxford University Press, 2003.

Klinger, Cornelia. "The Subject of Politics—The Politics of the Subject." In *Democracy Unrealized,* ed. Okwui Enwezor et al., 285–302. Ostfildern-Ruit, Germany: Hatje Cantz Publishers, 2002.

Korsgaard, Christine. *Creating the Kingdom of Ends.* Cambridge: Cambridge University Press, 1995.

Kukathas, Chandran. "Are There Any Cultural Rights?" *Political Theory* 20 (1992): 105–39.

LaFeber, Walter. *The Clash: U.S.-Japanese Relations Throughout History.* New York: W.W. Norton, 1997.

Lawson, Bill E., and Donald F. Koch, eds. *Pragmatism and the Problem of Race.* Bloomington: Indiana University Press, 2004.

Levine, Lawrence W. *Black Culture and Black Consciousness: Afro-American Folk Thought from Slavery to Freedom.* Oxford: Oxford University Press, 1977.

Lewontin, R. C. "The Apportionment of Human Diversity." *Evolutionary Biology* 6 (1972): 381–98.

Locke, Alain. "The New Negro." In *The New Negro,* ed. Alain Locke. New York: Atheneum, 1969.

Lorde, Audre. *Sister Outsider.* Freedom, Calif.: Crossing Press, 1984.

Lowe, Lisa. *Immigrant Acts: On Asian American Cultural Politics.* Durham, N.C.: Duke University Press, 1996.

Luban, David. "Eight Fallacies about Liberty and Security." In *Human Rights in the "War on Terror,"* ed. Richard Ashby Wilson, 242–57. Cambridge: Cambridge University Press, 2005.

Lusane, Clarence. *Race in the Global Era: African Americans at the Millennium.* Boston: South End Press, 1997.

Lye, Colleen. *America's Asia: Racial Form and American Literature, 1893–1945.* Princeton, N.J.: Princeton University Press, 2005.

MacKinnon, Catharine. *Are Women Human? And Other International Dialogues.* Cambridge, Mass.: Harvard University Press, 2006.

———. *Feminism Unmodified: Discourses on Life and Law.* Cambridge, Mass.: Harvard University Press, 1987.

Madhubuti, Haki R. *From Plan to Planet: Life-Studies: The Need for African Minds and Institutions.* Chicago: Third World Press, 1973.

Mahan, Alfred T. *The Problem of Asia and Its Effects upon International Politics.* Port Washington, N.Y.: Kennikat Press, 1900.

Mansfield, Harvey C. *Manliness.* Cambridge, Mass.: Harvard University Press, 2006.

Mayr, Ernst. *Populations, Species, and Evolution; An Abridgment of Animal Species and Evolution.* Cambridge, Mass.: Harvard University Press, 1970.

McCumber, John. *Time in the Ditch: American Philosophy and the McCarthy Era.* Evanston, Ill.: Northwestern University Press, 2001.

Mead, George Herbert. *Mind, Self and Society.* Chicago: University of Chicago Press, 1934.

———. *Movements of Thought in the Nineteenth Century.* Edited with an introduction by Merritt H. Moore. Chicago: University of Chicago Press, 1936.

———. *Selected Writings: George Herbert Mead.* Edited by Andrew J. Reck. Chicago: University of Chicago Press, 1964.

———. "National-Mindedness and International-Mindedness." In *Selected Writings,* 355–70.

———. "Philanthropy from the Point of View of Ethics." In *Selected Writings,* 392–407.

———. "The Psychology of Punitive Justice." In *Selected Writings,* 212–39.

———. "The Social Self." In *Selected Writings,* 142–49.

———. *The Philosophy of the Present.* Edited by Arthur E. Murphy. Chicago and London: University of Chicago Press, 1980.

Menand, Louis. *The Metaphysical Club: A Story of Ideas in America.* New York: Farrar, Straus, and Giroux, 2001.

Mendieta, Eduardo. "Imperial Religions, 'Clash of Civilizations,' and the People's Church." Presented as the 10th Annual Hispanic Lecture in Religion and Theology, Drew University, April 20, 2005.

———. "The Literature of Urbicide: Friedrich, Nossack, Sebald, and Vonnegut." *Theory & Event,* 10:2 (2007), available at http://muse.jhu.edu.libproxy.cc .stonybrook.edu/journals/theory_and_event/v010/10.2mendieta.html.

———. "Surviving American Culture: On Chuck Palahniuk." *Philosophy and Literature* 29 (2005): 394–408.

Michaels, Walter Benn. *Our America: Nativism, Modernism, and Pluralism.* Durham, N.C.: Duke University Press, 1995.

Mills, Charles. *Blackness Visible: Essays on Philosophy and Race.* Ithaca, N.Y.: Cornell University Press, 1997.

———. *The Racial Contract.* Ithaca, N.Y.: Cornell University Press, 1997.

Mintz, Sidney W., and Richard Price. *The Birth of African-American Culture: An Anthropological Perspective.* Boston: Beacon, 1976.

Misak, Cheryl. *Truth, Politics, Morality: Pragmatism and Deliberation.* London: Routledge, 2000.

Morrison, Toni. *Beloved.* New York: Alfred A. Knopf, 1987.

——. "Home." In *The House that Race Built,* ed. Wahneema Lubiana, 3–12. New York: Random House, 1998.

——. "Rootedness: The Ancestor as Foundation." In *Black Women Writers, 1950–1980: A Critical Evaluation,* ed. Mari Evans, 229–45. New York: Anchor Press, 1984.

——. "Unspeakable Things Unspoken: The Afro-American Presence in American Literature." In *The Black Feminist Reader,* ed. Joy James and Tracy Denean Sharpley-Whiting, 24–56. Malden, Mass.: Blackwell, 1984.

Moses, Wilson Jeremiah. *Black Messiahs and Uncle Toms: Social and Literary Manipulations of a Religious Myth,* rev. ed. University Park: Pennsylvania State University Press, 1992.

Mueller, John. *Overblown: How Politicians and the Terrorism Industry Inflate National Security Threats, and Why We Believe Them.* New York: Free Press, 2006.

Nietzsche, Friedrich. *The Birth of Tragedy and The Genealogy of Morals.* Translated by Francis Golffing. New York: Random House, 1956.

——. "Homer's Contest." In *The Portable Nietzsche,* ed. and trans. Walter Kaufmann, 32–38. New York: Viking Press, 1974.

Nussbaum, Martha. *The Fragility of Goodness.* New York: Cambridge University Press, 2001.

——. *Sex and Social Justice.* Oxford: Oxford University Press, 1999.

——. *Upheavals of Thought: The Intelligence of the Emotions.* Cambridge: Cambridge University Press, 2001.

Okihiro, Gary. *Margins and Mainstreams: Asians in American History.* Seattle: University of Washington Press, 1994.

Palumbo-Lui, David. *Asian/American: Historical Crossings of a Racial Frontier.* Stanford, Calif.: Stanford University Press, 1999.

Pappas, George. "Dewey's Philosophical Approach to Racial Prejudice." In *Philosophers on Race,* ed. Tommy Lott and Julie Ward, 285–97. Malden, Mass.: Blackwell, 2002.

Perlman, Joel. "'Race or People': Federal Race Classifications for Europeans in America, 1898–1913." Washington University in St. Louis, Economics Working Paper Archive, 2001. Available at http://econwpa.wustl.edu:8089/eps/mac/papers/0012/0012007.pdf.

Pinker, Steven. *The Language Instinct.* New York: William Morrow and Company, 1994.

Posner, Richard. "'How to Skip the Constitution': An Exchange." *New York Review of Books,* 11 January 2007.

——. *Not a Suicide Pact: The Constitution in a Time of National Emergency.* New York: Oxford University Press, 2006.

——. *The Problematics of Moral and Legal Theory.* Cambridge, Mass.: Harvard University Press, 1999.

Pratt, Scott. *Native Pragmatism: Rethinking the Roots of American Philosophy.* Bloomington: Indiana University Press, 2002.

Putnam, Hilary. *Renewing Philosophy.* Cambridge, Mass.: Harvard University Press, 1992.

Quine, W. V. "Two Dogmas of Empiricism." In *From a Logical Point of View,* 20–46. New York: Harper and Row, 1963.

Radway, Janice. "What's in a Name?" *American Quarterly* 51:3 (1999): 1–32.

Rawls, John. *Justice as Fairness: A Restatement.* Cambridge, Mass.: Harvard University Press, 2001.

Rockefeller, Steve C. *John Dewey: Religious Faith and Democratic Humanism.* New York: Columbia University Press, 1991.

Rorty, Richard. *Achieving Our Country: Leftist Thought in Twentieth-Century America.* Cambridge, Mass.: Harvard University Press, 1999.

——. *The Consequences of Pragmatism.* Minneapolis: University of Minnesota Press, 1982.

——. *Contingency, Irony, and Solidarity.* New York: Cambridge University Press, 1989.

——. "Feminism and Pragmatism." In *Truth and Progress: Philosophical Papers, Volume 3,* 202–27. New York: Cambridge University Press, 1998.

——. "Feminism, Ideology, and Deconstruction: A Pragmatist View." *Hypatia* 8:2 (1993): 96–103.

——. "Fighting Terrorism with Democracy," *The Nation,* October 21, 2002, available at www.thenation.com/doc/20021021/rorty

——*Philosophy as Cultural Politics, Philosophical Papers, Volume 4.* Cambridge: Cambridge University Press, 2007.

——. "Justice as a Larger Loyalty." In *Philosophy as Cultural Politics,* 42–55.

——. "Pragmatism and Romanticism." In *Philosophy as Cultural Politics,* 105–19.

——. *Philosophy and the Mirror of Nature.* Princeton, N.J.: Princeton University Press, 1979.

——. "Post-Democracy: Richard Rorty on Anti-terrorism and the National Security State." *London Review of Books,* 1 April 2004, 10.

——. "Pragmatism as Romantic Polytheism." In *The Revival of Pragmatism: New Essays on Social Thought, Law, and Culture,* ed. Morris Dickstein, 21–36. Durham, N.C.: Duke University Press, 1998.

——. "The Professor and the Prophet." *Transition* 52 (1991): 70–78.

——. "Religion in the Public Square: A Reconsideration." *Journal of Religious Ethics* 31:1 (2003): 141–49.

——. *Take Care of Freedom and Truth Will Take Care of Itself: Interviews with Richard Rorty.* Edited by Eduardo Mendieta. Stanford, Calif.: Stanford University Press, 2006.

——. *Truth and Progress: Philosophical Papers, Volume 3.* New York: Cambridge University Press, 1998.

——. "Universality and Truth." In *Rorty and His Critics,* edited by Robert B. Brandom, 1–30. Malden, Mass.: Blackwell, 2000.

Rose, Tricia. *Black Noise: Rap Music and Black Culture in Contemporary America.* Hanover, N.H.: Wesleyan University Press, 1994.

Rosenbaum, Stuart E., ed. *Pragmatism and Religion: Classical Sources and Original Essays.* Urbana: University of Illinois Press, 2003.

Royce, Josiah. *The Philosophy of Loyalty.* New York: Macmillan, 1915 [1908].

——. *War and Insurance: An Address.* New York: Macmillan, 1914.

Ryan, Alan. "The Legal Theory of No Legal Theory." *New York Times Book Review,* September 14, 2003.

Schauer, Frederick. "Amending the Presuppositions of a Constitution." In *Responding to Imperfection,* ed. S. Levinson, 145–62. Princeton, N.J.: Princeton University Press, 1995.

Schleifer, James T. *The Making of Tocqueville's* Democracy in America, 2nd edition. Indianapolis: Liberty Fund, 2000.

Schlesinger, Arthur M., Jr. *The Disuniting of America: Reflections of a Multicultural Society,* rev. ed. New York: Norton, 1998.

Seigfried, Charlene. "John Dewey's Pragmatist Feminism." In *Reading Dewey: Interpretations for a Postmodern Generation,* ed. Larry Hickman, 187–216. Bloomington: Indiana University Press, 1998.

——. *Pragmatism and Feminism: Reweaving the Social Fabric.* Chicago: University of Chicago Press, 1996.

Sellars, Wilfrid. *Empiricism and the Philosophy of Mind.* Cambridge, Mass.: Harvard University Press, 1997.

Shalin, Dimitri N. "G. H. Mead, Socialism, and the Progressive Agenda." In *Philosophy, Social Theory, and the Thought of George Herbert Mead,* ed. M. Aboulafia, 21–56. Albany: State University of New York Press, 1991.

Shaw, Angel Velasco, and Francia, Luis, eds. *Vestiges of War: The Philippine-American War and the Aftermath of an Imperial Dream, 1899–1999.* New York: New York University Press, 2002.

Simmons, Rachel. *Odd Girl Out: The Hidden Culture of Aggression in Girls.* New York: Harcourt, 2002.

Singh, Nikhil. *Black Is a Country: Race and the Unfinished Struggle for Democracy.* Cambridge, Mass.: Harvard University Press, 2004.

——. "Culture/Wars: Recoding Empire in an Age of Democracy." *American Quarterly* 50:3 (1998): 471–527.

Slotkin, Richard. *Regeneration through Violence: The Mythology of the American Frontier, 1600–1860.* Middletown, Conn.: Wesleyan University Press, 1973.

Smith, Rogers, M. "Beyond Tocqueville, Myrdal, and Hartz: The Multiple Traditions in America." *American Political Science Review* 87:3 (September 1993): 549–66.

Sophocles. *The Oedipus Cycle: Oedipus Rex, Oedipus at Colonus, Antigone.* Translated by Dudley Fitts and Robert Fitzgerald. New York: Harcourt, Brace and World/Harvest Book, 1977.

Spencer, Herbert. *The Study of Sociology.* Ann Arbor: University of Michigan Press, 1874 [rpt. 1961].

——. *The Principles of Ethics, Volume I.* Indianapolis: Liberty Classics, 1897 [rpt. 1978].

Steinmetz, Sebald Rudolf. *Die Philosophie des Krieges.* Leipzig: Verlag von Johann Ambrosius Barth, 1907.

Stuckey, Sterling. *Slave Culture: Nationalist Theory and the Foundations of Black America.* Oxford: Oxford University Press, 1987.

Stuhr, John J., ed. *Philosophy and the Reconstruction of Culture: Pragmatic Essays after Dewey.* Albany: State University of New York Press, 1993.

Sullivan, Shannon. "From the Foreign to the Familiar: Confronting Dewey Confronting Racial Prejudice." *Journal of Speculative Philosophy* 18:3 (2004): 193–202.

——. *Revealing Whiteness: The Unconscious Habits of White Privilege.* Bloomington: Indiana University Press, 2006.

Thomas, Brook. "A Constitution Led by the Flag: The *Insular Cases* and the Metaphor of Incorporation." In *Foreign in a Domestic Sense*, ed. Christine D. Burnett and Burke Marshall, 82–103. Durham, N.C.: Duke University Press, 2001.

Tocqueville, Alexis de. *Democracy in America.* New York: Random House, 1990.

Tully, James. "The Struggles of Indigenous Peoples for and of Freedom." In *Political Theory and the Rights of Indigenous Peoples*, ed. D. Ivison, P. Patton, and W. Sanders, 36–60. Cambridge: Cambridge University Press, 2000.

Van Deburg, William L. *New Day in Babylon: The Black Power Movement and American Culture, 1965–1975.* Chicago: University of Chicago Press, 1992.

Wallace, Alfred Russel. *The Malay Archipelago: The Land of the Orang-utan and the Bird of Paradise: A Narrative of Travel, with Studies of Man and Nature.* London: Macmillan, 1883.

Waters, Mary C. *Black Identities: West Indian Immigrant Dreams and American Realities.* Cambridge, Mass.: Harvard University Press, 2001.

Weber, Max. *Economy and Society: An Outline of Interpretive Sociology.* Edited by Guenther Roth and Claus Wittich. Berkeley: University of California Press, 1978.

——. *The Methodology of the Social Sciences.* Edited and translated by Edward A. Shils and Henry A. Finch. New York: Free Press, 1949.

Weiler, J. H. "A Constitution for Europe? Some Hard Choices." *Journal of Common Market Studies* 40 (2002): 563–80.

West, Cornel. *The American Evasion of Philosophy: A Genealogy of Pragmatism.* Madison: University of Wisconsin Press, 1989.

——. *The Cornel West Reader.* New York: Basic *Civitas* Books, 1999.

——. "The Crisis in Contemporary American Religion." In *The Cornel West Reader*, 357–59.

——. "The Historicist Turn in Philosophy of Religion." In *The Cornel West Reader*, 360–71.

——. "Prophetic Christian as Organic Intellectual: Martin Luther King, Jr." In *The Cornel West Reader*, 425–34.

——. "Religion and the Left." In *The Cornel West Reader*, 472–79.

——. "Subversive Joy and Revolutionary Patience in Black Christianity." In *The Cornel West Reader,* 435–39.

——. *Prophesy Deliverance! An Afro-American Revolutionary Christianity.* Philadelphia: Westminster Press, 1982.

Westbrook, Robert B. "Bourne Over Baghdad." *Raritan* 27 (2007): 104–17.

——. *Democratic Hope: Pragmatism and the Politics of Truth.* Ithaca, N.Y.: Cornell University Press, 2005.

——. *John Dewey and American Democracy.* Ithaca, N.Y.: Cornell University Press, 1991.

Williams, William Appleman. *Empire as a Way of Life: An Essay on the Causes and Character of America's Present Predicament, along with a Few Thoughts about an Alternative.* New York: Oxford University Press, 1980.

Wilson, Catherine. "How Did the Dinosaurs Die Out? How Did the Poets Survive?" *Radical Philosophy* 62 (1992): 20–26.

Wise, Gene. "'Paradigm Dramas' in American Studies." *American Quarterly* 31:3 (1979): 293–337.

Wolterstorff, Nicholas. "An Engagement with Rorty." *Journal of Religious Ethics* 31:1 (2003): 129–39.

Yoo, John. *War by Other Means: An Insider's Account of the War on Terror.* Chicago: University of Chicago Press, 2006.

——. *Powers of War and Peace: The Constitution and Foreign Affairs after 9/11.* Chicago: University of Chicago Press, 2005.

Young, Marilyn B. "The Age of Global Power." In *Rethinking American History in a Global Age,* ed. Thomas Bender, 274–94. Berkeley: University of California Press, 2002.

CONTRIBUTORS

Mitchell Aboulafia is Professor of Liberal Arts and Philosophy and Director of Liberal Arts at The Julliard School. He is author of *The Cosmopolitan Self: George Herbert Mead and Continental Philosophy; The Mediating Self: Mead, Sartre, and Self-Determination; The Self-Winding Circle: A Study of Hegel's System; Philosophy, Social Theory, and the Thought of George Herbert Mead;* and co-editor of *Habermas and Pragmatism.* He is the author of articles in social theory, American philosophy, and nineteenth- and twentieth-century European thought, and co-editor of the journal *Contemporary Pragmatism.*

James Bohman is the Danforth I Professor in the Humanities at Saint Louis University. He is author of *Democracy Across Borders: From Demos to Demoi; Public Deliberation: Pluralism, Complexity, and Democracy; New Philosophy of Social Science: Problems of Indeterminacy;* as well as *Decentered Democracy: From Pluralism to Cosmopolitanism* (forthcoming). He has co-edited *Pluralism and the Pragmatic Turn; Deliberative Democracy: Essays on Reason and Politics;* and *Perpetual Peace: Essays on Kant's Cosmopolitan Ideal.*

Robert Brandom is Distinguished Service Professor of Philosophy at the University of Pittsburg, a fellow of the Center for the Philosophy of Science, and a fellow of the American Academy of Arts and Sciences. He is author of *Making It Explicit: Reasoning, Representing, and Discursive Commitment; Articulating Reasons: An Introduction to Inferentialism; Tales of the Mighty Dead: Historical Essays in the Metaphysics of Intentionality;* and has edited Wilfrid Sellars' *Empiricism and the Philosophy of Mind* and *Rorty and His Critics.*

Harvey Cormier is Associate Professor of Philosophy at Stony Brook University. He is author of *The Truth Is What Works* and of essays on William James's pragmatism, Nietzsche's view of freedom, Henry James's realism, William James's pragmatic view of race, and Josiah Royce's view of logic, among other topics. He is currently putting together an anthology of papers on Stanley Cavell.

Chad Kautzer is Assistant Professor of Philosophy at the University of Colorado Denver. He is author most recently of "*Topographia Dominium:* Property, Divided Sovereignty, and the Spaces of Rule," in Gary Backhaus, ed. *Colonial and Global Interfacings.* He was guest editor of a special issue of the journal *Peace Review* (2004) on the topic of law and war, and is currently co-editing a volume on property and modern moral philosophy and an anthology on Hegelian critical theories of race, gender, and post-colonialism.

David H. Kim is Associate Professor of Philosophy and Chair of the Philosophy Department at the University of San Francisco. He has served as Chair of the American Philosophical Association Committee on the Status of Asian and Asian American Philosophers and Philosophies, and he has been a resident fellow at Harvard's W.E.B. Du Bois Institute for African and African American Research. His research and teaching interests include ethics, political philosophy, philosophical psychology, and non-Western or hybrid philosophies (e.g. African American philosophy, modern Asian philosophy, and Asian American philosophy). He is editor of *Passions of the Color Line* (forthcoming) and editor (with Ronald Sundstrom) of a forthcoming special edition of *Philosophy Today* on Asian America and American philosophy. His current work focuses on black and Asian conceptions of race and imperialism.

Eduardo Mendieta is Professor of Philosophy at Stony Brook University, where he is also the director of the Center for Latin American and Caribbean Studies. He is author of *The Adventures of Transcendental Philosophy* and *Global Fragments: Globalizations, Latinamericanisms, and Critical Theory.* He is presently at work on another book entitled *Philosophy's War: Logos, Polemos, Topos.* His most recent book publications are a collection of interviews with Angela Y. Davis, entitled *Abolition Democracy: Beyond Empire, Torture and War,* and an edited volume of interviews with Richard Rorty, entitled *Take Care of Freedom, and Truth Will take Care of itself.*

Lucius T. Outlaw Jr. is Professor of Philosophy and Associate Provost for Undergraduate Education at Vanderbilt University. He is author of *Critical Social Theory in the Interests of Black Folks; On Race and Philosophy;*

and more than fifty articles in journals such as *Philosophical Forum, Journal of Social Philosophy, Man and World, Graduate Faculty Philosophy Journal, Journal of Ethics,* and a number of anthologies.

Max Pensky is Professor of Philosophy at Binghamton University. He is author of *The Ends of Solidarity: Discourse Theory in Ethics and Politics; Melancholy Dialectics: Walter Benjamin and the Play of Mourning;* and editor of *Globalizing Critical Theory; Old Europe, New Europe, Core Europe: Transatlantic Relations in the Wake of the Iraq War* with John Torpey and Daniel Levy; *Jürgen Habermas, Time of Transitions: Political Essays; The Actuality of Adorno: Critical Essays on Adorno and the Postmodern; Jürgen Habermas, The Postnational Constellation;* and *Jürgen Habermas, The Past as Future.*

Richard Rorty (1931–2007) was Professor of Comparative Literature at Stanford University, Stuart Professor of Philosophy at Princeton University, and Emeritus Professor of Humanities at the University of Virginia. His works include *Philosophy and the Mirror of Nature; Contingency, Irony and Solidarity; Achieving Our Country; Philosophy and Social Hope;* and four volumes of *Philosophical Essays.*

Tommie Shelby is Professor of African and African American Studies and of Philosophy at Harvard University. His is author of *We Who Are Dark: The Philosophical Foundations of Black Solidarity* and coeditor (with Derrick Darby) of *Hip Hop and Philosophy: Rhyme 2 Reason.* Other recent publications include "Justice, Deviance, and the Dark Ghetto," *Philosophy & Public Affairs* (2007); "Race and Social Justice: Rawlsian Considerations," *Fordham Law Review* (2004); "Blackness and Blood: Interpreting African American Identity," with Lionel K. McPherson, *Philosophy & Public Affairs* (2004); and "Ideology, Racism, and Critical Social Theory," *The Philosophical Forum* (2003).

Shannon Sullivan is Professor of Philosophy, Women's Studies, and African and African American Studies at Pennsylvania State University, where she is currently Head of the Philosophy Department. She is author of *Revealing Whiteness: The Unconscious Habits of Racial Privilege* (Indiana University Press, 2006); *Living Across and Through Skins: Transactional Bodies, Pragmatism, and Feminism* (Indiana University Press, 2001), and co-editor (with Nancy Tuana) of *Race and Epistemologies of Ignorance.*

Cornel West is Professor of Religion and African American Studies at Princeton University. He is author of *Democracy Matters; The Future of American Progressivism,* with Roberto Unger; *The Future of the Race,* with Henry Louis Gates Jr.; *Keeping Faith: Philosophy and Race in America;*

Beyond Eurocentrism and Multiculturalism; Race Matters; and *The American Evasion of Philosophy: A Genealogy of Pragmatism.*

Robert Westbrook is Professor of History at the University of Rochester. He has published widely on the history of pragmatism, and his books impinging on the subject include *John Dewey and American Democracy; Democratic Hope: Pragmatism and the Politics of Truth;* and *In Face of the Facts: Moral Inquiry in American Scholarship,* co-edited with Richard Fox.

Cynthia Willett is Professor of Philosophy at Emory University. She is author of *Irony in the Age of Empire: Comic Perspectives on Democracy and Freedom* (Indiana University Press, 2008); *The Soul of Justice;* and *Maternal Ethics and Other Slave Moralities;* and editor of *Theorizing Multiculturalism.*

INDEX

Milton Keynes UK
Ingram Content Group UK Ltd.
UKHW020842310524
443451UK00007B/459